Our Proud Mountain Roots and Heritage:

A Supplement

By

**George Andrew Triplett, Robert Charles Triplett,
Sofia Frances Triplett & Alexandra Lee Triplett**

Edited by: George R. Triplett

Table of Contents

Dedication

We dedicate this book to our grandmother, Frances Rossi Triplett. Before she left us way too soon, in 2006, we spent much time with her. Since her passing, we have developed a better understanding of her illness and how she fought it so that she could spend more time with us. Family meant everything to her. This collaborative effort would not have been possible without her commitment to this family.

November 24, 1934 – May 27, 2006

Frances Michaeline Rossi Triplett

About the Author

George R. Triplett and his four grandchildren – George, Robert, Sofia and Alexandra – completed this book together.

George R. Triplett is 87-years old. He grew up in both Randolph and Pocahontas Counties. At an early age, he developed a love for the outdoors and strong passion for hunting and fishing. He married Frances M. Rossi in 1956, and they had three sons – George, Jr., Charley and Jeff. He married Norma Rector in 2007. He earned his law degree from West Virginia University in 1962, and he still practices law in Elkins, West Virginia. He and Norma reside in Elkins.

George A. Triplett is 23 years old. He graduated from Princeton University in 2022 with a degree in environmental policy, and he is currently in his second year as a graduate business student at Portland State University.

Robert C. Triplett is 21 years old. He is a senior at Wake Forest University, where he is studying economics and mathematics.

Sofia F. Triplett is 21 years old. She is a senior at Georgetown University, where she is studying human science.

Alexandra L. Triplett is 18 years old. She is a sophomore at West Virginia University, where she is studying exercise physiology.

Acknowledgement

We want to thank a few key individuals for their significant contributions to this project.

First and foremost, we recognize the late Dan Vest, who selflessly gave a tremendous amount of his time to this project on behalf of the Randolph County Historical Society. Mr. Vest passed away on July 16, 2021. He will be greatly missed.

Second, our grandfather, George R. Triplett, had the idea of capturing the history of our family and community. He spent dozens of hours with Mr. Vest discussing the research, compiling and organizing the data, and starting the text to get us well on our way to completing this project.

Third, we recognize Penny Vandevander for her contributions in research, organization and assembly of the beginning stages of the text. Without the contributions of these three individuals, this project would not be complete.

Next, we would like to extend special thanks to Geraldine Arbogast Watts, Nancy Harris Booth, Wendy Morgan, Brooke Binns, Mark DeMotto, Roger and Judy Ware, Charles Sheets, Clarence "Dump" Arbogast, Minta Lothes, Donald "Donnie" Cromer, Norma Townsend Rector Triplett and Ginger Fox for their efforts.

Also, we would like to extend thanks to the many others who contributed.

Oh, mountains,
You are where I go when the world is too loud,
Yes, when I get lonely in my crowd.

You humble me;
Lost in you, I am but a pebble.
And though I do what I can,
I cannot do all,
So, I thank you for reminding me of this,
And of how beauty makes sadness turn to the opportunism of freedom.

This is the human struggle,
To scratch memories, to acquire, to be satisfied with these,
But even mountains turn to dust.
These words came to me
In the trusting quietness, you teach by beauty and scope
Which say to me that time will give me what I want if I continue.
What else is there to fill the moments between our busies?
Much that I usually wish would be quiet.

Your people tell their stories,
And your breezes whisper simplicity's wisdom.
So, though stories fade, there is always time.

by Robert Charles Triplett
July 2021

No literary merit is claimed in the presentation of this book for an informal, incomplete introduction to life in Randolph and Pocahontas Counties. The purpose of the writers is to present facts and, if any event of historical value will be saved for future generations, the authors will feel compensation for their labors. An undertaking embodied within this book involves labor, research and lifestyle understood by the average individual. Encouragement and assistance have been received from many sources not practical to enumerate, but nonetheless cherished and appreciated.

Tennyson in his great poem, "Ulysses" writes "I am a part of all that I have met." I believe that line to the fullest. I believe that every experience, every acquaintance, every friend, every teacher and even those we observe around us become important parts of our nature and personality.

I believe that the environment in which we live blends its essence into our being and we become kindred with the immediate world about us. The effect of lofty mountain beauty or of pure rushing streams leaves an imprint on our nature and makes for itself a permanent place in a corner of the heart.

I cannot remember when I was too young to be impressed by the beauty of a mountain sunset or to be awed by black thunder clouds rolling down from the top of Cheat Mountain.

Neither can I recall when the town in which I live did not offer experiences to whet my curiosity, please my fancy or arouse the kind of amusement that gives laughs for years to come.

"I only pray my four grandchildren, George Andrew Triplett, Robert Charles Triplett, Sofia Frances Triplett, and Alexandra Lee Triplett, are instilled, taught, and ingrained by their parents with the same positive mental attitude, work ethics, hope, faith, and love handed down from all the Upper Cheat River Basin families. That they, if ever down, will climb to the top of Cheat Mountain, and look down at the beautiful valley and Cheat River flowing below, and that will help them find peace of mind." - George R. Triplett

UNIT 1: Our Mountain Families' Military History

"Old men start the wars - young men fight them."

The earliest historical records we could find list an Arbogast as a Pagan Frank Master to the Militia of the Roman Emperor, Valentinian II. Arbogast assumed imperial authority in Gaul after Valentinian II was murdered in 392 A.D. and began a long line of French Kingsmakers, placing Eugenis on the throne of the Western Empire. Both individuals were defeated in 394 A.D. Eugenis was slain, and Arbogast's death was listed as a suicide.

In December of 1944, the 101st Airborne Division, under the command of General Anthony McAuliffe of Logan, West Virginia, quartered at Mourmelon-le-Grand, Camp Chalone, where Caesar the Roman Emperor was said to have quartered two divisions of infantry and several squadrons of the light horse here during the latter stages of his Gallie campaign, just 30 miles from Bastogne, Belgium where General McAuliffe refused to surrender to the German Army.

Colonel Robert Wolverton of Elkins, West Virginia, commanded the 506th Parachute Infantry Regiment and was killed June 6, 1944, D-Day, in Europe. Michael Arbogast took part in the Battle of Point Pleasant on October 10, 1774, and served under General Andrew Lewis during the French and Indian war.

Adam, John, and David, sons of Michael Arbogast, served in the unit commanded by Captain Peter Hull during the Revolutionary War.

Francis Triplett of Fauquier County, Virginia, met Daniel Morgan in the spring of 1754. Triplett fought in the French-Indian War under General George Washington as part of the Virginia Militia. Triplett later fought for Commander Daniel Morgan in the Revolutionary War and was in a battle on September 28, 1778, at Saratoga, New York, to Monmouth, New Jersey. On January 17, 1781, Triplett was part of the Battle of Cowpens in South Carolina, which lasted about 35 minutes. Colonel Francis Triplett commanded about 160 sharpshooter riflemen who were accurate at 200 yards and known as the "Flying Army" under the command of General Horatio Gates, General Lafayette, and General Daniel Morgan. General Cornwallis' Colonel, Benjamin Tarleton, was in command of 1,200 "crack" British soldiers, who had killed and wounded 400 and captured 701 prisoners, with 200 remaining in the custody of the cruel, vicious killer of women and children, Colonel Ben Tarleton. It has been stated that "the battle marked a turning point in American Democracy. The road through the American position led symbolically, if not quite literally, to Yorktown and British surrender on 19 October 1781." Daniel Morgan stated: "I was desirous of having a stroke at Tarleton...& I have Given him a devil of a whipping [sic]." January 26, 1781. "Frank" Triplett's battalion, three rifle companies, were long service companies from Augusta (West of Blue Ridge) Fauquier and Rock Bridge Counties, Virginia. "The Battle of Cowpens" inspired the production of the movie *The Patriot*, starring Mel Gibson.

Triplett's men could reload their "long tom rifles" in 20 seconds. They fired when they saw "the whites of the British eyes." Triplett won distinction in the battle of Monmouth, New Jersey, and Cowpens. Congress presented him with a sword for his service at Cowpens.

General Daniel Morgan commanded Major (Colonel) Francis Triplett, who was 54 years old, at the Battle of Cowpens. General Morgan was believed to be born on January 17, 1736, near Draperstown Cross of Calleneseree County Derry, Ireland; he was 45 years old on January 17, 1781, at the Battle of Cowpens.

Jacob Argabrite (Argabright, Arabigast, or Arbogast), of Rockingham County, Virginia, volunteered for service against the Indians in May of 1778 under Captain Robert Craven. He was stationed at Westfall's and Hutton's Forts in the Tygart Valley (now Randolph County, West Virginia).

John Harris was the youngest son of James Harris and Anne Boleyn. Thomas Harris and George Harris are believed to be born in Essex, New Jersey and to have served as part of the Seventh Regiment of the State Troops, Continental Army and New Jersey Minutemen. It is also believed that other Harris family members participated in the Battles of Monmouth, Cowpens, and Yorktown.

Major William Harris served under Col. Hayes and Col. Pickens at the Battle of Cowpens on the same battlefield line as Triplett's Flying Army of 160 accurate long tom riflemen.

John Triplett, son of Colonel Francis Triplett, settled on Kelly Mountain around 1790 and was a member of the Virginia Militia's Maurice Company and settled on a land grant from the Revolutionary War on the Shaver's Fork of Cheat Mountain, which is now located in Randolph County, West Virginia.

Note: Portrait is wrongly titled "S. N. Luckett." The portrait is of John Richards Triplett. His gravestone, shown on the right, was also wrongly titled with incorrect dates. John R. Triplett lived from 1785 to 1843.

John Chenoweth, the father of Lemuel Chenoweth, served in the Revolutionary War. Many of those in our family's lineage is listed as pensioners of the Revolutionary War and patriots at Cowpens. Lemuel Chenoweth designed and constructed covered bridges throughout his life. He was born on June 25, 1811.

Many ancestors from local families, including, but not limited to, the Arbogast, Chenoweth, Harris, Triplett and Kittle families, served and fought for independence from the beginning of 1776 until the surrender at Yorktown.

CIVIL WAR

"The Civil War came to Tygart Valley on June 3, 1861, in Philippi, in Barbour County." This was the first land battle of the Civil War. Confederate colonials retreated to Huttonsville, Randolph County. The next battle that occurred in Randolph County was at Rich Mountain in Beverly. General Robert E. Lee's first battle was fought at the campaign headquarters in Elkwater, in the upper part of the Tygart Valley. This battle started in July 1861 and lasted until September 12-13, when Lee was defeated at Fort Milroy, near Cheat Bridge in Shaver's Fork. General Lee remained here until October 1861, when he withdrew because the Cheat Mountain Campaign had failed. Lee had not won a foot of Northwest Virginia from the Federals.

On September 12, 1861, at the Battle of Elkwater, Cheat Summit, Cheat Bridge, a member of Eighth Tennessee got his first look at General Robert E. Lee advancing towards him. He said, *"he looked like a hero. As he sat on his large white horse, half hid in the bushes, the man's greatness could be easily distinguished, even by the casual observer, and alike by the common soldier... Grand and dignified, he sat there, the soldier and the Christian, a hero, and a statesman, seeming to grasp the situation and to hold it in the hollow of his hand."*

The following is a list of individuals from Randolph County who fought for the Confederate Army. George W. Printz compiled it for "Maxwell's History of Randolph County". The list includes:

James Anthony

Joseph H. Anthony was killed at Fort Steadman

Jackson Apperson

Jefferson Arbogast, who was killed at the "Bloody Angle" Spottsylvania Court House

Moses Bennett

John W. Bosworth

Lieutenant S. N. Bosworth

Sergeant Joseph Chenoweth Major, who was killed at the Port Republic

Z. T. Chenoweth

Eli Currence

Emmett Crawford

Burns Crawford died of wounds in 1863

Jacob Currence Captain

N.S. Channell

Cyrus Crouch, who was killed at Fredericksburg

Milton Crouch, who was killed at Cold Harbor

Garland Cox, who died in prison

Peter Cowger

Henson Douglass, who was killed at the "Bloody Angle" at Spottsylvania Court House

William Daft

Edward Daft

Adam Folks corporal

John Folks, who was killed in the Wilderness Campaign

George Gainor

Eugene Hutton, was killed at Bunker Hill, Virginia

George E. Hogan

Levi Hevener

Adam Hevener, who was killed at Spottsylvania

Andrew Hevener, was a scout for Lee and killed at Elkwater;

J. F. Harding Captain, after Major of Cavalry

Marion Harding, killed at Elkwater, Oct. 1862

George Harding, who died in a camp

Thomas Herron

Edward Kittle, who was killed at "Bloody Angle," Spottsylvania Court House

Marshall Kittle, was killed at Beverly at the Hill Raid 1864;

Asa Kelly, died of wounds at the Battle of McDowell

Charles Kelley

John Logan

G. W. Louk

John Louk

Claude Louk

Dudley Long, Third Lieutenant, was killed at Petersburg

Corporal J. H. Long, was killed at Port Republic

Thomas Long, died in a hospital

O. H. P. Lewis

Lieutenant Walter Lewis, died in a hospital

Thomas Lewis, killed at Cedar Mountain

John Lewis, Sr.

William Lemon, died of wounds

Jacob Lemon, died in a hospital

James W. Lemon

John D. Moore, died in a hospital

Andrew C. Mace

Elisha McCloud

John B. Pritt

Newton Potts

John Quick, died from wounds

Claude Rader

George W. Rowan

Corporal Jacob Riggleman

Washington Riggleman

Joshua Ramsay

Branch Robinson

George Salsbury, Lieutenant

Hiram Smith

Chesley Simmons

David Simmons

Joseph Simmons

Franklin Stalnaker, died in a hospital

Absalom Shifflett

D. H. Summers

John C. Swecker

John M. Swecker

Thomas Shelton

David Shelton

Joseph Stipes, killed at "Bloody Angle"

William Stipe

Joseph Vandevander

Adam Vandevander

William H. Wilson

Corporal James W. Wilson

W. H. Wamsley

Enoch Wamsley

L.D. Westfall

John M. Wood

Joseph Wood

Randolph Wise, who lost an arm in Chantilly

Many families were divided during the Civil War, seeing brothers, fathers, and relatives fighting for the Union Army and other family members fighting for the Confederate Army. Jasper Wilmoth Triplett and Oliver Triplett were the sons of Job Triplett. Job and his brother Frank were the sons of John Triplett (Bosworth 156, 157).

At the Sinks of Gandy on March 20, 1864, Oliver was killed, Jasper was wounded (Charles Emedio Triplett currently has a mini ball from grave), and Frank escaped. Note: George, Joseph, and Lemuel Arbogast were members of the Home Guards, commanded by Capt. Sampson Snyder shot Jasper Wilmoth Triplett and killed Oliver Triplett (Bosworth 375, 376).

Eighteenth Virginia Cavalry: J. D. Adams, John Bennett, Jacob Chenoweth, Judson Godden, Sergeant, Charles Myers, L.G. Potts, William Powers, George Powers, Thomas Powers (killed), Adam C. Stalnaker, Eli Taylor, Judson Taylor, Haymond Taylor (killed at Winchester I, 1864), Elam Taylor, Lieutenant, H. H. Taylor, F. M. Taylor, Perry Taylor, J.W. Triplett, Oliver Triplett (killed at the Sinks), Frank Triplett, James D. Wilson, George Ward, Perry Weese, Duncan Weese, Haymond Weese, and Lafayette Ward.

On the night of March 20, 1864, a squad of Confederate scouts consisting of Adam C. Stalnaker, Jasper Triplett, Oliver Triplett, Anthony Triplett, Taylor Chenoweth, James D. Wilson, Jacob Wilmoth, Luther Parsons, Lafe Ward, and Dow Adams was fired upon by 33 home guards, known as Swamps, while they were sleeping at the Sinks of Gandy. The Sinks of Gandy is located at the head of Dry Fork River. Oliver Triplett was killed instantly. Jasper Triplett and Adams were severely wounded and were thought to be dead at the time. However, after removing their boots, they showed signs of life, were clubbed with muskets, and were left for dead. Later, they regained consciousness, and Adams, in a dazed condition, fell into the fire and was severely burned. Mr. Teter, who lived nearby, found the wounded men the next day and cared for them in his home. Eighteen missiles had hit Adams, yet both he and Triplett recovered. Those escaping injury fled to the adjacent woods. Messrs. James D. Wilson and Adam Stalnaker, having departed the camp without their shoes, wrapped their feet in the capes of their coats, tied them on with their handkerchiefs, and waded through the snow several feet deep to Hightown, eight miles distant. Messrs. Perry Weese, John Taylor and Eli Taylor were with the Confederate scouts, but Mr. Weese stopped for the night with Mr. Teter, who lived nearby. He was surprised and captured before the soldiers at the camp were fired upon but were helpless to warn his comrades. Messrs. John Taylor and Eli Taylor, fearing a night attack, did not remain with the main body of the scouts but were passing the night about a half mile distant when the discharge of muskets warned them of their danger. They made their escape and Mr. Weese was turned over to the Federal Authorities and sent to Camp Chase, where he remained until the close of the war. These Confederates were returning from a visit to their homes. They also designed to surprise and capture the Federal wagon train of supplies on its way from Webster Station to Beverly. Preparation was made for the attack a few miles below Beverly, but when the train appeared, the guard was too strong for their small force, and their objective was abandoned.

George Arbogast and Joseph Arbogast were members of Samp Snyders' Home Guard Indignant Scouts and Swamp Dragons. Jefferson Arbogast, a confederate soldier, was killed at the "Bloody Angle," Spotsylvania Courthouse. All three were descendants of the families of Hans and Michael Arbogast. Sampson Snyder sponsored Jasper Wilmoth Triplett's reinstatement of citizenship in 1867 after the Civil War. Jerome Barnabas Harris is an enigma to his descendants in many areas of his life; he was approximately 25 years old when the Civil War began. When his name came up to be drafted into the Union Army, his parents paid to prevent him from having to serve. The second time he became eligible for the draft, they bought a team of horses and hired a man to take Jerome to California and keep him until the war was over. It was said that he was a Southern sympathizer, which was why he did not join the Union Army. His daughter, Mary Harris Wamsley, was the wife of David Wamsley. David came from a family that supported the Confederacy. David's father had been captured and imprisoned near the end of the war.

French Harding fully discloses his time from May 1861 through May 1865 as a captain for the Confederate States of America. Harding served as part of Virginia's 31st Infantry and 20th Cavalry until he fired the last shot of the Civil War on April 18, 1865, at Knapps Creek in Pocahontas County. Harding surrendered on May 24, 1865, to Captain Beckel at Beverly, approximately four years after Harding originally left for the Army.

Harding started across Cheat Mountain on the Staunton-Parkersburg Turnpike through Shaver's Run and Slavins' and Dent's Cabin on the Greenbrier River. On his second night, he stayed with Mr. Martin VanBuren Arbogast on the eastern fork of the Greenbrier River - some distance north of Camp Bartow. He was the grandfather of Col. Ned "Chick" Harding of Beverly, a graduate of West Point and a commander for a squadron of B-17 bombers during WWII.

An incredible incident occurred during the Civil War in Arbovale, named after Adam Arbogast, when Arbogast's brother, Reverend Henry Arbogast, was dragged from his home and shot near Frost. Adam was also marked for death and, through the quick action of his ten-year-old niece, was able to escape after hearing a conversation at the village store saying, "we got Henry last night, and we will get Adam tonight." Adam and his wife, Margaret, packed the saddle bags on a horse after explaining to the children that Adam must immediately flee for safety. Adam relocated to Upshur County while Margaret kept vigil all night downstairs, reading her Bible in the front room by lamplight. Margaret, with one arm, carried the weight of the family and farm for at least two years. Margaret was known for being strong in every way, especially in her faith in God.

SPANISH AMERICAN WAR

Little history is known about our family's service and participation in the Spanish American War since the war's duration was just 109 days. Company E's Second Battalion's first West Virginia Volunteer Infantry of Elkins, under the command of Captain Jan F. Collett, answered the president's call for volunteer units at the outbreak of the Spanish American War, and they rendezvoused with other units at Camp Lee near Charleston on April 26, 1898. Captain Collett remained in the Army and served in the Philippines for almost 20 years, later returning to Randolph County, where he became a Sheriff.

WORLD WAR I

Dr. H. W. Daniels, M.D., of Elkins, was killed during WWI, and Elkins' American Legion Post is named after him.

These young men were among the dozens of service men from Randolph County who made the supreme sacrifice for their county in World War II. (PM)

Our entire family, all descendants of Europe, answered President Franklin D. Roosevelt's call to arms on December 7, 1941, after the bombing of Pearl Harbor, until the German Army surrendered at 0230 hours on May 7, 1945. Germany surrendered to General Dwight D. Eisenhower in a temporary headquarters located in a schoolhouse at Reems, Germany. The war in Europe was over.

Captain Hodie W. Daniels, 2nd from left, entered the U.S. Army Medical Corps in 1917, after serving for many years as a doctor in the City of Elkins and Randolph County. He was killed in France while serving with the American forces in 1918. American Legion Post No. 29 in Elkins was named in his honor. (DLR)

Captain Frank C. Wimer and thirty-nine members of the original Company G, 201st Infantry, West Virginia Army National Guard, pictured July, 1937. The company was organized on January 9, 1937. (ERCL)

General Richard Sutherland, an alumnus of Davis and Elkins College and a graduate of Yale University, served as an aide to General Douglas McArthur during World War II. General Sutherland, the son of U.S. Senator Howard Sutherland of Elkins, accompanied General McArthur when he returned to the Philippines and was aboard the battleship Missouri when Japan surrendered in 1945. (PM)

The largest group of Randolph County men to leave for examination and induction into military service during World War II departed Elkins on May 12, 1942. After examination at Clarksburg, many of them entrained for Fort Hayes, Columbus, Ohio that evening, and were soon assigned to many military posts to train for duty for the duration of the war. (PM)

The first group of draftees from Randolph County selected to enter the service prior to the opening of World War II is here assembled in front of the Forestry Building waiting to depart for examinations on April 22, 1941. Included in the group are Bus Leake, Clair Metheny, Raymond Satterfield, Ron Shreve, and many other young men from the county. (PM)

These volunteer soldiers assembled beside the Coal and Coke Building on Third Street near the Elkins train station in preparation for their departure for the Spanish-American War in 1898. Captain Zan F. Collett was the commanding officer of this Elkins unit. (CM)

Ralph "Doc" Harris, Augie Varchetto, and Louis Antolini (top right) were among those drafted in WWII 1942 draft (largest from Randolph County).

On September 2, 1945, the conflict in World War II's Pacific theatre ended when Japan surrendered to General Douglas MacArthur aboard the Battleship Missouri with his aid General Richard Sutherland, an alumnus of Davis and Elkins College, a graduate of Yale University and the son of U.S. Senator Howard Sutherland of Elkins, West Virginia. General Sutherland accompanied General MacArthur when he returned to the Philippines. General Sutherland was a youngster present at Beverly when the courthouse was relocated to Elkins for Randolph County, the county seat in the Fall of 1889.

The Appalachian Mountain families certainly, since the French and Indian War, have paid and sacrificed their lives for democracy and freedom, particularly the families of Pocahontas and Randolph Counties, part of the West Augusta region where George Washington made his 1770's statement: "Rally Around me men of West Augusta and we shall raise this Bleeding Nation From the sand." The Mountain men and women responded. The Randolph County Honor Roll was a high billboard erected on the County Courthouse lawn in Elkins to identify the young men from the county who entered military services during World War II. Hundreds of names were placed on the Honor Roll from 1942-1945. Hundreds of young men from these mountain counties made the supreme sacrifice for their Country in World War II. The wartime working women who labored in the WWI I factories were known as "Rosie the Riveters." President Franklin D. Roosevelt stated, "if I wanted a man to do an honest day's work for an honest day's pay, I would go to the mountains of West Virginia."

Colonel James Wolverton of Elkins, West Virginia, was born on October 5, 1914, and was universally loved by his men because he put them first. A graduate of West Point, he was commander of the Third Battalion's 506 Parachute Infantry Regiment 101st Airborne "Screaming Eagles." From Tacoma, Georgia, to Normandy on D-Day, Wolverton was known for his participation in "Operation Overlord" on June 6, 1944, which was the name given to the invasion of Normandy. Ben Hiner, a native of Durbin, West Virginia, served as a mail clerk for Company E, also known as "Easy Company." The Easy Company was highlighted in the television series "Band of Brothers."

On June 5, 1944, around 2000 hours, Colonel Wolverton gathered the regiment on the parade grounds and began a special prayer, saying, "*God Almighty! In a few short hours, we will be in battle with the enemy. We do not join battle afraid. We do not ask favors or indulgence but ask that, if you will, use us as your instrument for the right and an aid in returning peace to the world. We do not know or seek what our fate will be. We only ask this that if die, we must, that we die as men would die, without complaining, without pleading and safe in the feeling that we have done our best for what we believed was right. Oh, Lord! Protect our loved ones and be near us in the fire ahead, and with us now as we each pray to you.*"

Ralph Bennett was moved by what he heard and responded, "Col. Wolverton talked to us just like he was one of the guys and seemed genuinely concerned at the prospect of us not all getting back alive. No one spoke during the whole thing, and you could have heard a pin drop. Afterward, he dismissed us, and we returned to our own tents. I picked up my Thompson and all my gear and marched the squad out to join the battalion for the first parade. Then, loaded down like pack mules with all our equipment, we made our way out to the plane" (Gardner, Day).

Within 30 seconds of leaving the aircraft, Colonel Wolverton was killed. His parachute had become entangled in a tree, and he was shot hanging in his harness. Wolverton never reached French soil - near St Côme-du-

Mont. A few days later, Ben Hiner and others rescued Wolverton's body from the apple tree. Hiner later became wounded in his abdomen. The 82nd, 101st Airborne, and many others fought their way to Germany's surrender. On Wednesday, June 5, 1946, around 50 survivors from the 506th traveled to Kansas City to honor Wolverton's last wishes at the Muhlbach Hotel. His widow, Kay Wolverton, helped to arrange the reunion on behalf of her late husband and the 200 men, from the 3rd battalion who had lost their lives since that fateful night. Edward Shames expressed, "there are just two things I am most proud of about my service in the 506 Parachute Infantry Regiment, 101st Airborne Division, my battlefield commission, and the fact that the 3rd Platoon brought more men home from the war than any other of the 500 Platoons in the division."

A locally known WWII veteran and airman was Dabney "Lloyd" Kisner, Jr., who died at 100 years of age in 2020. Kisner, a native of Durbin, flew more than 50 missions over Germany while serving as a bombardier/navigator of a B-26.

It is believed that Kisner was deterred from bombing a primary target and then dumped all of the squadron's bomb loads on Hitler's hidden missile base that was located on a cleared mountaintop in Germany. The colonel met Kisner when landing and congratulated him instead of "chewing him out." Kisner was quoted in the 2019 *Unsung Hero* series published by The Inter-Mountain Newspaper, saying, "When we got to the target, we flew a circle and saw those two old targets down below us had been fixed up. When I was looking at them, I saw a markup on the mountain. I thought I was going to hit the other one (on the mountain), and I did, which is a no-no. … When it went off, it went off big. … We went on home to return to England, someone said, 'Kid, I hope you're right,' and I said, 'If I'm wrong, I'm wrong,'" he said. "When we landed, here came the colonel out to meet me. … When I got out of the airplane, I figured I was going to get chewed, and he said, 'Kid, you tore it up.' It kind of surprised me, because I was expecting to get chewed out for firing on the wrong target, but it worked out real good. I think I did get some chewing, but they still gave me credit for it."

Kisner served with an air crew on "Lady Liberty" as part of the U.S. Army Air Corps. Kisner appears back row far right wearing cap and goggles.

Listed here are the individuals from, or with connections to, Randolph County who were killed in action (K.I.A.) during World War I:

Daniels, Hoddie Wilbur	Fidler, Paul LeAvoy	Heckenberry, Cecil C.
Steward, James D.	Cutright, Amon	Huffman, Kenny
Kerns, Done	Mylius, William M.	Tusing, Kay
Lambert, Albert	Triplett, Jacob B.	Weese, Wilbur

Listed here are the known individuals from, or with connections to, Randolph County who died of disease during World War I:

Franch, Nick	McDaniel, Claud E.	White, Dennis
Flint, Lorenzo Dow	Phillips, Brady D.	White, Jason
Horick, Eli	Waybright, Luther	

The following list includes known individuals from, or with connections to, Randolph County who died from wounds sustained during World War I:

Ketterman, Randall G.

Louk, William F.

Phares, Hubert M.

Stewart, William Howard

Wamsley, Charles D.

The following list includes individuals from, or with ties to, Randolph County who were killed in action (K.I.A.) during World War II:

Albert, Charles E. Jr.	Bodkins, Curtis L.	Champ, Arthur D.
Arbogast, Junior B.	Briggs, Charles R.	Chenoweth, James E.
Armentrout, Forrest W.	Buchanan, James W.	Clingerman, Robert R.
Basil, Keiith	Carr, Samuel L.	Collett, Richard N.
Betler, Bernard O.	Carroll, James D.	Cole, William P.

Collins, Glen

Cooper, Isaac J.

Cosner, Walter W.

Cox, James H.

Crawford, John E.

Cutright, John B.

Daniels, Edward A.

Day, Homer J.

Defillippo, Guy

Deffibaugh, Junior

Digman, Junior F.

Edmond, Paul F.

Ervine, Leonard N.

Furby, Dale A.

Gainer, Harold N.

Gear, Austin L.

Gilmer, Guy N.

Grabowski, William J.

Haben, William C.

Hansford, Charles H.

Hardwick, Richard E.

Harper, Charles H.

Harris, Lawrence N.

Hice, Elmer L.

Hite, Doc N.

Hopkins, Bernard O.

Howell, Howard M.

Irwin, William J.

Kittle, James D.

Kittle, Ray D.

Kyle, Eldon L.

Lambert, Dennis J.

Lambert, Richard

Lee Masters, Paul F.

McCord, Doyle F.

McDonald, Glenvil R.

McEldonney, James H.

Merico, Don V.

Metheny, Russell L.

Mullenex. Kermit

Pennington, Mack D.

Phares, Jacob

Phares, Robert, E.

Phillips, Shirley J.

Porter, Warren J.

Riley, Joseph F.

Rinard, Cale R.

Sainato, Frank S.

Sainato, Victor C.

Scott, Paris L.

Simmons, Keith

Simons, Glen A.

Smith, Leslie R.

Stankus, Jack C.

Stankus, Lawrence C.

Stull, Raymond

Taylor, Cecil R.

Taylor, Francis T.

Taylor, Wilfred J.

Teter, Carl

Teter, Estin Jr.

Thomason, John B.

Vanscoy, Preston D.

Vanscoy, William L.

Wamsley, Carl D.

Watson, Clifford D.

Whetsell, Robert W.

White, Hubert L.

White, Junior N.

Williams, Phil M.

Winkler, Chelsey C.

Winkler, George H.

Wolverton, Robert L.

Zirkle, Doyle

General George Patton, U.S. 3rd Army Tank Commander, was the grandson of General George Patton of the Confederate States of America and was from Charleston, West Virginia, in the Civil War. General Patton's nickname was "Ole Blood and Guts." One non-commissioned infantryman said, "his guts, our blood."

The following is a list of individuals from, or with ties to, Randolph and Pocahontas Counties who served in WWII:

- Lt. Col. Robert Wolverton, Elkins, W.Va.; U.S. Army 506th Parachute Infantry Regiment, 101st Airborne K01 Division.

- Richard "Dick" Hiner, Durbin, W.Va.; U.S. Army. Dick Hiner also served in Korea. He was married to Patty Hoover Hiner.

- Ben Hiner, Durbin, W.Va.; U.S. Army 101st Airborne Division, 506th Parachute Infantry Regiment, marksmen.

- John Hiner, Durbin, W.Va.; U.S. Army.

- Steve "Bo" Hiner, Durbin, W.Va.; U.S. Army.

- Sgt. Herbert Coberly, Elkins, W.Va.; U.S. Army, 82nd Airborne, prisoner of war. Assigned to the First Platoon of Company "C" of the 509th Parachute-Infantry Battallion.

- Boggs Collins, Huttonsville, W.Va.; U.S. Army, 101st Airborne 1st Platoon of "C" Company of the 509th Parachute Infantry Battalion.

- John Russell, Mill Creek W.Va.; General U.S. Army.

- Ronald Lindsay, Valley Bend, W.Va.; U.S. Army.

- Colonel "Slim" Roberts, U.S. Air Force - an "ace" fighter pilot; trained at Davis and Elkins College, where he met and married Ruth Bennett. Roberts owned Peter Pan Cleaners, which is currently operated by his son, Jimmy Roberts, U.S. Army Special Forces, Vietnam War and Desert Storm Veteran.

- Jim Taylor, Bartow, W.Va.; U.S. Navy.

- Harry Jasper Triplett; Faulkner, W.Va.; U.S. Army, 716th Railroad Operating Sergeant, conductor and train master. H. Triplett served in several locations, including Belgium, France, and Germany, as part of the Operations Battalion.

- Archie Beck, Elkins, W.Va.; U.S. Army Air Corps, mechanic.

- Allen "Babe" Scott Harris, Beverly, W.Va.; U.S. Army Infantry, a machine gunner. Served at Guadalcanal through the Okinawa Invasion and survived with the same dog tags.

- Ralph Howard "Doc" Harris, Glady W.Va.; U.S. Army Signal Corps, Pacific Theater; was a member of Randolph County's largest draft induction in 1942.

- Jack Harris, Glady, W.Va.; U.S. Marine Air Force, tail gunner.

- James Harris, Glady, W.Va.; U.S. Army 24th Infantry Division, Combat Engineers; served in WWII, Korea and Vietnam (three tours).

- Eugene Lawton, U.S. Navy, Durbin, W.Va., married sister of Dabney Kisner. He is the father of Becky Benton.

- Lieutenant Lawrence Raines, Stalnaker Run, W.Va., U.S. Army P.O.W. at Batan March.

- Fielding Clinton Harris, Glady, W.Va.; U.S. Army, Post WWII.

- Robert Harris, Glady, W.Va.; U.S. Army.

- Leslie Bodkins, Bemis, W.Va.; U.S. Army, 745th Railroad Signal Operations Battalion.

- Wilbert "Web" Arbogast, Bowden, W.Va.; U.S. Army, Teamster.

- Adam "Bugs" Dahmer, Jr., Bemis. W.Va.: U.S. Navy, Dahmer attended Davis and Elkins College.

- Leonard Lantz, Bemis, W.Va.; U.S. Navy. Lantz attended Davis and Elkins College.

- Orvil Ray Shifflett, Bemis, W.Va.; U.S. Navy; served on U.S. aircraft carrier Yorktown.

- Maynard Shifflett, Bemis, W.VA.; U.S. Navy.

- Ronald Shifflet, Bemis, W.Va.; U.S. Navy.

- Eddie Simmons, Bemis, W.Va.; U.S. Army.

- Dewey "Hunter" Simmons, Bemis, W.Va., three-year prisoner of war (P.O.W.), U.S. Army.

- Keith Simmons, Bemis, W.Va.; U.S. Army; killed in action (K.I.A.) in France on July 11, 1944.

- George "Jack" Triplett, Bemis, WV; U.S. Army, a locomotive engineer for the 719th Railroad Operations Battalion; found dead in Flint W.Va., on August 13, 1963.

- Ralph Triplett, Bemis, W.Va.; U.S. Army.

- Claude White, Bemis, W.Va..; U.S. Army.

- Donald White, Bemis, W.Va.; U.S. Army.

- Woodrow White, Bemis, W.Va.; U.S. Army.

- Demsey Arbogast, Glady, W.Va.; U.S. Army

- Jessie Arbogast, Glady, W.Va.; U.S. Army

- Weldon Arbogast, Glady, W.Va.; U.S. Army.

- Harry Armentrout, Glady, W.Va.; U.S. Army.

- William Armentrout, Glady, W.Va.; U.S. Army.

- Earl Bonnell, Glady, W.Va.; U.S. Army.

- Louis "Pap" Bowers, Glady, W.Va., U.S. Army.

- Lenzie Jennifer Hedrick, Glady, W.Va.; U.S. Navy.

- Patrick Phares, Glady, W.Va.; U.S. Navy.

- Arthur Rhoades, Glady, W.Va.; U.S. Army.

- Robert "Red" Rhodes, Glady, W.Va.; U.S. Army; Member of the Davis and Elkins College football team.

- Cecil Strawder, Glady, W. Va; U.S. Army.

- Ora Strawder, Jr., Glady, W.Va., U.S. Army.

- Marvin Taylor, Glady, W.Va.; U.S. Army; Taylor became president of White Pass and Yukon Railroad in Canada after WWII.

- Bert Thompson, of Beverly, W.Va.; U.S. Army

- Frank Thompson, of Beverly, W.Va.; U.S. Navy

- Tracy York, of Elkins, W.Va.; U.S. Army.

- Bert Langford, of Jimtown, W.Va.; U.S. Marines.

- J. Herman Isner, of Kerens, W.Va.; U.S. Army.

- Donald Mole, of Elkins, W.Va.; U.S. Navy

- Augie Varchetto, of Elkins, W.Va.; U.S. Army, Davis and Elkins College football player, member of 1942 draft (largest draft from Randolph County).

- Joe Mams, of Elkins, W.Va.; U.S. Navy. Mams attended Davis and Elkins College, where he was a football team member, and married Pollie Kisner, sister of Dabney Kisner.

- Warren Teter, of Glady, W.Va.; U.S. Army.

- Herbert Thompson, of Glady, W.Va.; U.S. Army.

- Emory Thompson, Jr., of Glady, W.Va.; U.S. Army.

- Stratton Ogden, of Alpena, W.Va.; U.S. Navy.

- Hugh Thompson, of Sulley, W.Va.; U.S. Army.

- Seymour Thompson, of Sulley, W.Va.; U.S. Army.

- Jack Kane, of Cass, W.Va.; U.S. Navy.

- Red Kane, of Durbin, W.Va.; U.S. Merchant Marines.

- Earl Vance, of Durbin, W.Va.; U.S. Army.

- Alan Stewart, of Bartow, W.Va.; U.S. Marine Corps. Stewart was wounded in action in the Pacific Theater. Stewart was a member of the faculty at Greenbank High School.

- John Townsend, of Durbin, W.Va.; Army Air Corps. Townsend taught at Greenbank High School, graduated from West Virginia Wesleyan College, and earned a master's degree from Boston University.

- Robert S, Williams, of Durbin, W.Va.; U.S. Army Air Corps. Williams was captured by the Japanese in Corregidor, survived the infamous "Death March," and survived 42 months as a prisoner to the end of WW II.

- John Hunter Williams, of Durbin, W.Va.; U.S. Navy pilot.

- Ivan Clarkson, of Cass, W.Va.; U.S. Army.

- Roy Clarkson, of Cass, W.Va.; U.S. Army. Clarkson was a teacher at Greenbank High School and attended Davis and Elkins College and West Virginia University. He retired as a professor of biology and was a published author. Clarkson lived in Morgantown, when he passed away in 2022.

- Lt. Col. Meade Lancer Waugh, of Marlinton, W.Va.; U.S. Army.

- Capt. Thomas Edgar, of Hillsboro, W.Va., U.S. Army 101st Airborne. Edgar had both legs amputated in Dec. 1944 at Bastogne. He served in the West Virginia House of Delegates after WWII. Executive Officer to General McAuliffe at Bastogne.

- General Anthony "Nuts" McAuliffe, of Logan W.Va.; U.S. Army. The German Army surrounded McAuliffe, and when a German General demanded surrender, McAuliffe responded, "nuts". He commanded the 101st Airborne "Screaming Eagles."

- Aaron Sterling "Swarts" Hill, of Durbin, W.Va.; U.S. Army. Hill served 21 years as principal at Durbin, a science teacher at Greenbank High School, and earned a B.S. Degree from William and Mary and a master's at W.V.U.

- Basil Sharp, of Marlinton, W.Va.; U.S. Army. Sharp played football and graduated from Davis & Elkins College in 1939. He was wounded and died near Niederschlettenbach, Germany, with the 180th Infantry and 45th Division of the Seventh Army. He was killed in action. Dr. John Sharp never got to see his dad, Basil Sharp. He married Jane Price Sharp; they were both graduates of Davis & Elkins College.

- Robert Rector, M.D., of Elkins, W.Va.; U.S. Army. Rector graduated from Davis and Elkins College in 1942 and the University of Virginia Medical School in Richmond in 1946. Rector was a practicing surgeon at Davis Memorial Hospital.

- Donald Roberts, M.D., of Elkins, W.Va.; U.S. Army. Roberts was the treating physician of General George Patton and a graduate of the Medical College of Virginia, located in Richmond, Virginia. Dr. Roberts was a treating physician at Davis Memorial Hospital.

- Cyrus Kump, of Elkins, W.Va., U.S. Army, Colonel. Kump was a graduate of the Virginia Military Institute.

- Harold Mosser, of Davis, W.Va., U.S. Marines; Served as football and basketball coach for Green Bank High School. Was in the U.S Marine Corps and played basketball for Cam Henderson at Marshall University, along with Mervin Gutshall and Charlie Slack. That team won a national championship in the late 1940's.

- Hugh Arthur, of Frank, W.Va.; U.S. Army, pilot.

- Dr. Frank Widney, of Frank, W.Va.; U.S. Navy. Widney later became a dentist and married Margaret Kisner, sister of Dabney Kisner.

- John Bosely, Sr., of Frank, W.Va.; U.S. Navy. Bosely was the father of Bruce Bosely - retired #77 West Virginia University All-American and San Francisco 49er's football player - John Bosley, Jr., member of the W.V.U. football team and went on to be drafted by the Pittsburgh Steelers.

- William "Bill" Kisner, of Frank, W.Va.; U.S. Navy. Bill is the brother of Dabney Kisner.

- August LeMasters, of Durbin, W.Va.; U.S. Army. LeMasters was the father of Ronnie Lemasters of Huttonsville, W.Va.

- William "Bill" Channell, of Elkins, W.Va.; U.S. Army. Post-WWII field artillery. Bill married Wanda Currence, Mabie, W.Va.

- Melvin "Jack Hammer" Johnson, of Durbin, W.Va.; U.S. Navy.

- Arnold Swick, of Ellamore, W.Va.; U.S. Navy.

- Robert E. Maxwell, of Elkins, W.Va.; U.S. Army. Maxwell served as U.S. District Court Judge for the Northern District of West Virginia. Judge Maxwell was a graduate of Davis & Elkins College.

- Delbert Phillips, of Elkins, W.Va.; U.S. Army, Purple Heart recipient.

- Lee Sharp, of Spruce, W.Va.; U.S. Army. Sharp hunted in Africa to feed his fellow infantry soldiers.

- Clare Metheny, of Elkins, W.Va.; U.S. Army.

- Carney Dugger, of Cheat Bridge, W.Va.; U.S. Army.

- Charles E. Albert, Jr., of Elkins, W.Va.; Naval Air Corps, K.I.A. Albert was a 1940 graduate of D&E College.

- Owen "Ebbie" Bosworth, of Beverly, W.Va.; U.S. Army. Bosworth married Margaret Wamsley.

- William Wilson, of Beverly, W.Va.; U.S. Army. Wilson married Elizabeth Wamsley.

- Dale White, of Elkins, W.Va.; U.S. Marine Corps. White attended Davis & Elkins College. White was born in Spruce.

- Frank Wimer, of Elkins, W.Va.; U.S. Army. Wimer served in W.W.I and W.W.II. He earned the rank of Major and served as Commander of the Elkins National Guard. Wimer was the head football and basketball coach for Elkins High School for many years.

- Robert "Bob" Irwin, of Elkins, W.Va.; U.S. Marines. He was awarded the Purple Heart. Irwin played football and graduated from Davis and Elkins College in 1948. He went on to become the football coach for Elkins High School.

- Robert "Bob" Phillips, of Elkins, W.Va.; U.S. Army. Phillips was a member of the Davis and Elkins College football team and became an assistant football coach for the college. Phillips was a 1939 graduate of Elkins High School.

- Grady F. Guye, of Elkins, W.Va.; U.S. Army. Guye served as treasurer of the Davis and Elkins College Veterans Club in 1948. Guye married Judy Guye, former mayor of Elkins.

- Frank Pezzula, of Hopkins Mine, near Shaver's Fork, W.Va.; U.S. Army. Pezzula graduated from Davis and Elkins College and later became an administrator at Walter E. Reed Hospital in Bethesda, Maryland.

- Anthony "Tony" Pezzula, of Hopkins Mine, near Shaver's Fork, W.Va.; U.S. Army, Durbin. A. Pezzula graduated from Davis and Elkins College and practiced podiatry.

- Lawrence "Sarg" Raines, of Elkins, W.Va.; U.S. Army. Raines was a P.O.W. held by the Japanese for several years and survived the Bataan Death March. After Raines was rescued and recovered, he believed he made money from poker to start his own automotive business in Charleston, W.Va.

- Harvey Fansler, of Elkins, W.Va.; U.S. Army.

- Gail Swecker, of Huttonsville, W.Va.; U.S. Army. Swecker married Elizabeth Rosencrance Swecker.

- John Belan, of Mabie, W.Va.; U.S. Navy. Belan married Ila Ross Belan.

- Stanley Grabouski, of Mabie, W.Va.; U.S. Army.

- Peter Pezzaferatto, of Norton, W.Va.; U.S. Army Air Corps, pilot.

- Roger Bertolini, of Norton, W.Va.; U.S. Army.

- Peter Dominic Antolini, Norton, W.Va.; U.S. Army infantry, twice-wounded in WWII Battle of the Bulge. Co-captain of the W.V.U. football team. Married to Alice Harris of Glady, W.Va. Peter was a co-captain of the 1941 WVU football team.

- John Rossi, Coalton, W.Va.; U.S. Navy.

- Carmen Rossi, Coalton, W.Va.; U.S. Army.

- Vincent "Bugs" DiBacco, of Thomas W.Va.; U.S. Army, medic.

- Tony DeMotto, of Coalton, W.Va.; U.S. Army.

- Dee Fansler, of Elkins, W.Va.; U.S. Marines.

- Ted Williams, of Cassity, W.Va.; U.S. Marines.

- Lawrence Rossi, Coalton, W.Va.; U.S. Army.

- John Chenoweth, of Beverly, W.Va.; U.S. Army. Chenoweth was elected Sheriff of Randolph County in the 1940s.

- Urban Poe, of Elkins, W.Va.; U.S. Army, Purple Heart recipient (amputated arm).

- Louis Antolini, of Norton, W.Va.; U.S. Army.

- Patrick Antolini, of Norton, W.Va.; U.S. Army.

- William Grabowski, of Mabie, W.Va. U.S. Army, KIA.

- Tom Sparrow, of Elkins, W.Va.; U.S. Army, K.I.A.

- Glenn Hinzman, of Elkins, W.Va.; U.S. Army. He was awarded the Purple Heart.

- Chester Phillips, of Jimtown, W.Va.; U.S. Navy, Jimtown W.V. Phillips served as the West Virginia American Legion Commander after WW II.

- Bonn Brown, of Elkins, W.Va.; U.S. Marine, bomber pilot. After the service, Mr. Brown practiced law in Elkins.

- Henry Tharp, Beverly, W.Va.; U.S. Army, Purple Heart recipient.

- Guido Rossi, Coalton, W.Va.; U.S. Army, General George Patton's tank battalion.

Guido Rossi (right), with General Patton's tank battalion in Italy, during World War II

On this mission, Guido met his first cousin, Dominic Rossi, a former member of the surrendered Italian army.

- Robert "Bob" Queen, of Upshur County, W.Va.; U.S. Army. Queen was wounded and later became a coal operator in Barbour and Upshur Counties. Queen was the father of Robin Queen Triplett and grandfather of Robert Charles Triplett.

Numerous young men from the mountains who served and made the supreme sacrifice for our country are not listed in the preceding pages of this section. These individuals are unknown to the co-authors, who have diligently tried not to exclude anyone's efforts. Further, we know a few veterans from Korea, Vietnam, and Desert Storm who have ties to our family. These veterans may be disclosed in a future publication.

Members of the Arbogast, Harris, Triplett, Chenoweth, and Kittle families from Randolph Country were killed in WWI and WWII.

Boggs Collins, a native of Huttonsville, who was previously included in the list of fallen soldiers, served in the U.S. Army during WWII from 1942 until 1945 as part of the 1st platoon of "C" Company of the 509th Parachute Infantry Battalion. In Italy, France, and Belgium, Collins was wounded in action three times. Military campaigns in which Collins was involved included action in Tunisia, Naples-Foggia, Anzio, Rome-Arno, Southern France, Ardennes-Alsace, and Rhineland, according to information provided by www.509thgeronimo.org. Further, Collins achieved a number of accolades, including the Distinguished

Pictured – Sergeant Boggs C. Collins,
recipient of the Distinguished Service Cross

Service Cross, the Purple Heart Medal with two oak leaf clusters, the Parachutist Badge with two combat jump stars, the Combat Infantryman Badge, the Good Conduct Medal, the EAME Campaign Medal with Presidential Unit Citation with two oak leaf clusters, and five overseas service bars.

"On December 29, 1944, at about 0900 hours, during an assault on prepared enemy positions south of Sadzot, Belgium, heavy machine gun and rifle fire were received on the company's right flank. Sgt. Collins, leading the squad on that flank, turned his squad over to his assistant and doubled back, came upon the enemy machine gun position flank and wiped out the enemy positions with his Thompson sub-machine gun. Sgt. Collins then rejoined his squad and led them through the rest of the battle. Sgt. Collins is credited with killing (22) enemies during the company's actions on 28 and 29 December 1944. His conduct in action truly inspired his men to their best efforts," reads the 509th Battalion's website in reference to Collins being recommended for the Silver Star Medal.

POCAHONTAS COUNTY MILITARY HISTORY

Residents from Pocahontas County proudly served our country in all wars and conflicts dating back to the Civil War. This section discusses some of the contributions of Pocahontas County residents and also identifies members of that community who were killed in action in both World Wars and the Vietnam War.

WORLD WAR I

The following list includes individuals from Pocahontas County who were killed in action (K.I.A.) during World War I:

- Cook, James D.

WORLD WAR II

The following list includes individuals from Pocahontas County who were killed in action (K.I.A.) during World War II:

Adkinson, Robert L.	Cloonan, Clarence B.	Hannah, III, Samuel B.
Alderman, John M.	Curry, Everett M.	Hefner, Andy E.
Bennett, Othel B.	Dean, Harlan E.	Jeffries, William M.
Brock, Carl D.	Fertig, Cay S.	King, Letcher L.
Burns, George C.	Friel, Paul C.	McCarty. Letch
Burris, Frank E.	Gillispie, Owen K.	McNeill, James M.
Bussard, Eugene T.	Griffin, Ralph G.	McLaughlin, H. W.
Buzzard, Elmer W.	Grogg, Emil L.	McLaughlin, Decima E.

McLaughlin, Floyd E.

Meeks, Eugene B.

Mullenax, Raymond R.

Ray, George W.

Reed, Andrew O.

Reed, Harold L.

Rife, Jr., Henry

Sharp, Basil C.

Shiffler, George E.

Shinaberry, M.C. Van

Reenen, Cecil C.

Walker, James C.

Watts, William D.

Williamson, Clyde J.

**Thursday,
May 11, 1944**

PRAYER ON INVASION DAY

Both the Methodist and Presbyterian Churches of Hillsboro, invite and urge you to join with us in earnest prayer on the day when the Allied Forces shall begin the invasion of Western Europe. The call to prayer will be made by the tolling of the church bells. The church doors will be open all day, so that you can enter the sanctuary for silent prayer. On every hour during the day the bells will ring, and that will be the signal for those who will, to pause where they are, and offer a prayer. At 8:00 p.m., the congregations will assemble in their respective churches for a period of public prayer.

In our private and public observance of these arrangements, let us humbly confess our sins and those of our nation before God, interceding for the men who would face agony and death in the great invasion, praying not only that our forces might be victorious, "but even more earnestly that we might be a people whom a righteous God can trust with victory and power."

Our Army and Navy Boys

Mr. and Mrs. Guy Dean, of Lobelia, have been noti-fied of the death of their son, P. F. C. Harlan Dean, who was killed in action in Italy March 30, 1944.

- - -

Headquarters, European Theatre of Operations — When word was passed officially that airborne troops were in the theatre in strength, West Virginia had more than a passing interest, for hundreds of her sons were among the parachute and glider men ready for the assault on Hitler's roofless Europe. A leader of one of the rugged parachute infantry battalions is Col. Robert L. Wolverton, of Elkins. All American airborne troops – ground forces, who use gliders and troop carrier planes – have been attained at Fort Benning, Georgia, or at Mackall, North Carolina. They maneuvered in Tennessee.

Colonel Wolverton's outfit set a record by marching 110 miles in three days after 13 weeks basic training. Pocahontas County soldiers in the airborne troops ready for the invasion are –

Pfc. Gerald R. McNeill, Marlinton, radio operator. Pfc. Howard E. Bowers, Huntersville, ammunition bearer. Pfc. Carl C. Van-Reenan, Marlinton, mortar gunner. Pfc. Daniel G. Stone, Bartow, gunner. Corp. Jay B. Graham. Buckeye, fireman, now cook.

Mr. and Mrs. Elihu Moor have received word that the son, Ralph, has arrive safely "somewhere in England."

- - -

Staff Sergeant Oran L McLaughlin has been cited for a good conduct medal He is the son of Mr. Mary J McLaughlin, of Dunmore.

- - -

Pfc. Loran S. Jordon, of Greenbank, has arrived at a port "somewhere in India." He is one of a contingent of veterans from the North Africa and Italian fighting.

- - -

Miss Peggy Smith, who is in training for a Red Cross worker, foreign service, is home from Washington, D. C. for a few days with her parents, Mr. and Mrs. Zed S. Smith, Jr. Her brother, Major Z. S. Smith, III, is expected home from the South Pacific next Monday.

GOLDEN HORSESHOE

The West Virginia Club Golden Horseshoe Test, for Pocahontas County was held at Marlinton and at Greenbank May 5. The winners for the county are: Fred Mouser, Jr., Marlinton; Faye Morrison, Marlinton; Samuel Callison, Marlinton; Virginia McChesney, Brownsburg.

FIELD NOTES

While some have caught nice trout and enough of them, the bigger and better trout waters have been in poor shape for fishing. It has been raining too much and too often. I got mine alright

see 75 pg 12

*This is an article a couple of weeks before D-Day – Normandy Invasion.
It appeared in the Pocahontas County Times, May 11, 1944.*

Preserving Pocahontas

B. J. Gudmundsson, Preservation Officer

Lt. Col. John H. Mathews – KIA 1944 'Lest We Forget'

"Time will not dim the glory of their deeds."
~ General John J. Pershing

John Hubert Mathews was born in 1907 in Cass, W.Va., the son of Jasper S. and Lucy Ann Gillespie Mathews. He graduated from West Point in 1931, married Marie Delores Coffey, and they had one daughter, Barbara Jean. Before his departure for service in World War II he was stationed at Fort Devens, Texas, where he resided with his family. Lieutenant Colonel Mathews, U.S. Army, 16th Infantry Regiment, 1st Infantry Division, was Killed in Action at Omaha Beach, Normandy, France on June 6, 1944.

An excerpt from page 166 of the book "Omaha Beach, D-Day," by Joseph Balkoski, published by Stackpole Books reads:

"An advance party from the 16th Infantry's headquarters led by Lt. Col. John Mathews, the regiment's second-in-command, approached the Colleville draw in an LCM around 7:25 a.m. The team's job was to set up a command post and organize the 16th Infantry's beachhead. As the LCM scraped bottom and its crew prepared to drop the ramp, Mathews shouted, "This is it; good luck!"

see Preserving pg 10

Preserving, from page 1

HQ Company, 16th Infantry, Morning Report for June 6, 1944

"The Advance CP group in the LCM moved toward the beach in a rough sea, and upon nearing the beach encountered a considerable volume of artillery and machine gun fire. The tide was at low ebb, and to reach the beach it was necessary to traverse a wide stretch of water, making way through various lines of beach obstacles fitted with mines.... As the men hit the water approximately waist-deep, machine gun fire swept the section, and a bullet tearing through Master Sergeant Carpino's gas mask struck Lt. Col. Mathews in the head. Not knowing he was dead, Sgt Carpino, with much difficulty, got his body to shore only to learn that he had been killed instantly."

Lt. Col. John Hubert Mathews is buried at Plot H Row 19 Grave 8, Normandy American Cemetery, Colleville-sur-Mer, France. He was awarded the Distinguished Service Cross, Silver Star, and Purple Heart, and listed on the World War II Honor Roll by the American Battle Monuments Commission. He is remembered with a marker at the Arbovale Cemetery in Pocahontas County, West Virginia. (ID: PHP001072)

Access the "Preserving Pocahontas" Digital Library at www.pocahontaspreservation.org or www.preservingpocahontas.org

If you have historical records or photographs to be scanned for the county Historical Archive contact Preservation Officer B. J. Gudmundsson at 304-799-3989 or email info@pocahontaspreservation.org

Prints of photographs are available.

Pictured is an excerpt from Preserving Pocahontas about John Matthews, published on May 27, 2021.

KOREAN WAR

The following list includes soldiers from Pocahontas and Randolph Counties who died in the Korean War:

POCAHONTAS COUNTY:

		Born	Died
Carr, Bernard E.	Army Pvt	1932	9/1/1950
Collins, Franklin	US Navy	1933	killed in submarine
1951 Green Bank High School Graduate			
James, Davis Eugene	Army Cpl	1924	5/18/1951
Moore, Oren Richard	Marin PFC	3/29/1930	10/6/1952

RANDOLPH COUNTY:

		Born	Died
Armentrout, James S.	Army Cpl	8/24/1930	5/18/1951
Blosser, Jackey Dale	Army Cpl	1929	12/2/1950
Booth, Gilbert H.	Army Cpl	1932	5/28/1951
Bostick, Charles	Army Pfc	1932	5/28/1951
Chandler, James O.	Army Pfc	1933	6/13/1953
Clark, Jr., Boyers Morgan	Navy ITJG	4/18/1924	2/2/1951
Coffman, Ronal W.	Army Pvt	1932	7/23/1923
Ginger, Robert L.	Army Pvt	1930	10/4/1951
Gum. William K.	Army Pvt	1934	7/7/1953
Hedrick, Howard E.	Army Pvt	1934	6/7/1953
Long, Warren G.	Army Cpl	1927	8/3/1950
Lunsford, Jr., James E.	Army Pvt	1932	7/25/1951
Mace, Buhl Jennings	Army Pvt	1932	2/15/1951
Marco, Charles Eugene	Army Pfc	1/3/1931	8/2/1950
Marstiller, Francis Julian	Air Force TSGT	8/14/1927	12/22/1952
Stuckey, Donald L.	Army Pfc	1931	11/27/1950
Webster, William E.	Army Pfc	1929	11/27/1950
Wood, Charles Edgar	Army Pfc	12/7/1931	10/17/1951

<u>**VIETNAM WAR**</u>

Forty-eight years ago, President Richard Nixon signed the Paris Peace Accords, ending all United States involvement in the Vietnam War. West Virginia did not go untouched by this war, as 36,578 soldiers from the Mountain State served during the campaign. According to the West Virginia Encyclopedia, 1,182 soldiers from West Virginia were killed, a higher per capita death rate than any other state in the nation. Pocahontas County lost more of its sons, per capita, to the Vietnam War than any other county in the nation.

The following list includes soldiers from Pocahontas County who died in the Vietnam War:

- PFC Luster Clark Friel, Marlinton, April 15, 1966
- SP4 Lewis Dixon Wilmoth, Frank, July 25, 1967
- SSG Jake Harold VanMeter, Jr. Slaty Fork, October 7, 1967
- Sgt. Samuel Dewey Rider, Jr., Marlinton, March 3, 1968
- Sgt. Watson Underwood, Jr., Huntersville, April 2, 1968
- Sgt. Douglas Wayne McCarty, Frost, April 11, 1968
- Cpl. Leroy David Sprouse, Dunmore, June 25, 1968
- Sgt. John Ray "Chipper" Williams, Marlinton, November 29, 1968
- SP4 Jack Lee Rexrode, Bartow, March 19, 1969
- C.P.L. Lee Roy David Sprouse, May 25, 1968

Source: Vietnam Veterans of America, Chapter 1100, Marlinton and virtualwall.org.

The following list includes soldiers from Randolph County who died in the Vietnam War:

- James Antolini
- Randall Arbogast
- Dennis Baxter
- Gary Burgess
- Tex Patrick
- Roger Griffith
- Thomas Hess
- Bernard Jones
- Fred Kerns

- Cecil Kittle Jr.

- Steven Mollohan

- Garry Shannon

- David Shiflett

- Roger Simmons

- Samuel Summerfield

- Russell Taylor

- Robert Thompson

Robert Triplett, the contributor to this book and grandson of George Triplett, wrote the following short passage about the selfless role that a soldier plays, when serving in the military:

"The military is a unique pursuit in that it requires more commitment than most other activities. No matter the reason or reasons that someone joins the military, that person still risks paying the ultimate price, which is their life. Soldiers receive no reward for this other than honor, medals, or applause, none of which heal wounds, and money that they could find elsewhere without putting themselves at risk. The team's success in any other establishment creates favorable outcomes for those involved, but this is not the case for military victories. Success of the team in the military requires a great, admirable capacity for foresight, an appreciation of the importance for oneself to act in the support for the common good, however that is defined. These people appreciate why their actions and sacrifices are necessary, that that appreciation is a rarity, and that the fact that it is a rarity means that they should do it because someone has to do it. I am trying to put words to selflessness itself.

The best military leaders, then, inspire this selflessness in their followers. I imagine that convincing oneself to fight for the United States is easier than fighting for a Communist country, where freedom and the benefit of all are not the status quo to preserve."

<u>**References**</u>

Babits, Lawrence E. *A Devil of a Whipping: The Battle of Cowpens*. The University of North Carolina Press, 1998.

Blackhurst, W.E. *Of Men and a Mighty Mountain*. McClain Printing Company, 1965.

Bodkins, Steve. *Bemis & Glady West Virginia: A History of Two Mountain Towns*. McClain Printing Company, 2006.

Bosworth, Dr. A. S. *History of Randolph County, West Virginia*. Southern Historical Press Inc., 1916.

Chapman, Odie Velta Nestor. *They Rest Quietly: Cemetery Records of Randolph County, West Virginia*. McClain Printing Company, 1996.

Gardner, Ian. *Airborne: The Combat Story of Ed Shames of Easy Company*. Osprey Publishing, 2015.

Gardner, Ian, and Roger Day. *Tonight We Die As Men: The Untold Story of Third Battalion 506 Parachute Infantry Regiment From Toccoa to D-Day*. Osprey Publishing, 2009.

Doyle, Charles H. & Stewart, Terrell, *Stand In The Door! The Wartime History of the Elite 509th Parachute Infantry Battalion.* Phillips Publications, 1988.

Gundmendson, B. J. *Pocahontas County Times*. 2021, p. 6.

Harris, Joseph M. *1620 - Chart for George Triplett*. June 16, 1999.

Keifer, Sarah J. *American Genesis: Genealogical and Biographical Sketches of the New Jersey Branch of the Harris Family in the United States*. 1888, p. 29.

Maxwell, Hugh. *History of Randolph County*. Acme Publishing Company, 1898.

Moss, Bobby Gilmer. *The Patriots at the Cowpens*. A Press, 1985.

Pocahontas County Historical Society. *History of Pocahontas County, West Virginia 1981: Birthplace of Rivers*. May 1981, p. 536.

Price, Calvin W. "Pocahontas County Times: Seventy-Five Years Ago, 'Our Army and Navy Boys.'" *Pocahontas County Times*, December 26, 1946.

Rice, Don. *Randolph 200: A Bicentennial History of Randolph County, West Virginia- 1787-1987*. Walsworth Publishing Co., Inc., 1987.

Roy, Carrie Harman. *Captain Snyder and His Twelve of West Virginia*. Carlton Press Inc., 1977.

Russell, T. Triplett, and John K. Gott. *Fauquier County: In the Revolution*. Heritage Books Inc., 2007.

Sharp, Curtis. *An American Family: History and Descendants of Michael Arbogast and Mary Elizabeth Samuels. Volume One: Their History. Immediate Family and Descendants of Odessus Adam, Their First Child*. CreateSpace, 2017.

Thacker, Victor L. *French Harding: Civil War Memoirs*. 4th ed., McClain Printing Company, 2000.

The West Virginia Encyclopedia. Edited by Ken Sullivan. West Virginia Humanities Council, 2006.

Vietnam Veterans of America, Chapter 1100, Marlinton, Pocahontas County, West Virginia.

Virtualwall.org.

Ware, Chad. *Elkins High School: A Football History - A Collection of Tiger Teams, Coaches, Players and Statistics Through the Years and Much More. 1915-2019*. McClain Printing Company, 2020.

Ware, Roger. Military Historian. Elkins, WV.

Ware, Judith. Elkins, WV.

Zambone, Albert Louis. *Daniel Morgan: A Revolutionary Life*. Westholme Publishing, L.L.C., 2018.

UNIT 2: The Greatest Asset to Mountain Students is Higher Education

Davis and Elkins College Front Lawn, ca. 2017

The City of Elkins and Davis & Elkins College share a common heritage. Both were established through the efforts of Senators Henry G. Davis and Stephen B. Elkins. Founded under the auspices and control of the Presbyterian denomination in 1904, the college began with a faculty of four – that included the president, who taught courses and coached football. The student body was made up of nine people. The campus itself was made up of one all-purpose building on a 25-acre area overlooking the river in southern Elkins. Tuition to the institution was $50 per annum, the board was $110, and room rental was $36 per year. In 1926, after Mrs. Elkins had given Halliehurst Hall and the adjacent farm to the Board of Trustees, the college was moved to its present location.

Although the central purpose and focus of the College is a liberal education for those seeking baccalaureate degrees, D&E has also long had outstanding departments for Business Administration, Education, and Health and Physical Education. In recent years, departments of Nursing and Recreation Management and Tourism have been organized, several two-year associate degree and adult education programs have been developed, and the nationally known Augusta Heritage Center for Appalachian Arts and Crafts. From the beginning and through the years, an outstanding faculty committed to teaching and concern for students, rather than research, has been characteristic of the College. Likewise, the encouragement of student activities in drama, music, publications, clubs, student governments, and athletics has been notable. Successful participation in inter-collegiate athletics became a tradition early in the history of the College. The Famous Scarlet Hurricane football and basketball teams of the 1920s and '30s continued the tradition of D&E teams winning state championships (established in 1917 when the basketball team first won such distinction), and, in later years, D&E soccer teams won not only state and regional, but also national championships. Women's field hockey and basketball teams also participated successfully in state, regional and national competitions.

Fully accredited in 1946, the College began to grow in the post-World War II era and has become not only one of the region's important educational and cultural institutions but also a major financial significance to Elkins and Randolph County, annually pouring millions of dollars into the economy. By the mid-1980s, some 900 students enrolled each year, and there were some 60 faculty members and College Officers as well as a support staff numbering approximately 100. The 170-acre campus, with more than twenty buildings, as well as athletic fields, tennis courts, and other recreational facilities, is noted for its beauty. Undoubtedly, Davis & Elkins College is the most significant legacy of Senators Davis and Elkins now extant in the city they established 100 years ago.

Dr. Thomas R. Ross said, "Every student brings his character to assist in the development of this character by the presence of good, and the absence of evil influences is the college policy. Four faculty members reside in the college dormitory and dine at the students' dining tables. The absence of personal contact with the professor is the ground of the change now made at Princeton (I have referenced the tutorial system), and in the near future, other colleges and universities will doubtless follow Princeton's example. The wholesome results of personal contact between teacher and pupil cannot be overestimated." (Randolph County Historical Society 22).

Others who have less direct contact with the various "publics" of the college but whose services were essential to include such men as Warren ("Tom") Daniels, superintendent of maintenance for years, and his successor, Ralph Forinash. Some of their staff have served longer than any administrator and longer than all but the most senior faculty members. Notable among them are Willard Chenoweth, Richard Byrd, Junior Stevenson, Lawrence and Ricky Plum, Howard and Thomas Shockey, Larry Caywood, and the 'night patrol' consisting of Shirley Ervin, Lester Arbogast, and Bill Collins. (Ross 298)

Almost everyone has known Gerald Morrison, the friendly 'Campus Postmaster.' For fifteen years, he cheerfully carried out the responsibilities of distributing vast streams of mail and campus messages. Once "The Senator" devoted an editorial to him as one who exemplified Christianity in his daily life and work. A "Senatus" was later dedicated to him, and most recently, the student government president, Andrew McCorkle, presented 'Jerry' a red jeep on behalf of the students and the college.

D&E Campus mail carrier – Gerald "Jerry" Morrison

There are others, of course, such as Roger Dague, Wayne Harkins and their staff in the food service at the dining hall, Dr. Samuel Kump Roberts and nurse Frances P. Paden in charge of health service, W. Earl Bennet,

Jr. and Martin Baechtel in the Institutional Research Office, and Thomas Vogel and Anne Stottlemeyer in the Development Office. Some, like Bonnie Phares, Irene Crawford, Margaret Gutshall, Ruth Chabut, Virginia Harshbarger, Louise Girard, Rita Kyle, Jocelyn Teter Riggleman, Barbara Skinner, Lois Frantz, Dixie Singleton, Shelby Gordon, Sandra Vannoy, Patricia McDonald, Sharon Skinner, Shirley Sharp, Wilfred Lothes, Bill Arbogast, barber, Elizabeth 'Beth' Guy Kittle, Mabel Phares, Margaret Isner Meadows, Natalie Barb, who all served in various roles over the years, left long ago. Many others cannot be mentioned because of limitations of space, but they know that their lives, too, have been a part of the rich history of Davis and Elkins College (Ross 298).

Thomas Richard Ross, born in Missouri, earned M.A. and Ph.D. degrees from Harvard. A veteran of World War II, he served in combat intelligence with the Fifth Air Force unit in the Far East. Since 1949, Dr. Ross has been a member of the faculty at D&E until the 1980s.

"Throughout its history, D&E has not so much reinvented itself as adjusted to changing times. All the while, it has stayed on course, even if it was required to zig and zag from time to time. D&E has remained true to its mission." With these words, David R. Turner introduces his centennial history of Davis & Elkins College. Turner, who is the recipient of the Thomas Richard Ross Professor of History and the Humanities accolade, builds upon Ross's 75-year history of the college in a series of essays and photographs intended to place the college in perspective rather than supplying a chronicle of events. Readers will enjoy scenes showing the natural beauty of the campus and its historical buildings, and alumni, especially, will appreciate Turner's overview of student activities, athletic endeavors, and the contributions of devoted faculty and staff members.

In contemplating D&E's future, Turner quoted former college president Thomas Mann, who said it was a complicated task to "embrace the new while tapping the wisdom of the past." Turner wrote, "Davis & Elkins proudly enters its second century committed to improvement, but also never forgetting the unpretentious style of the past. It remembers well the humanity of everyone who works and strives on its campus."

"We would be well to remember William Faulkner's address to the Nobel Committee, in which he said that the individual is immortal, not because he alone, among creatures, has an inexhaustible voice but because he has a soul, a spirit capable of compassion, sacrifice, and endurance. The poet, the writer, must write about these things. It is his privilege to help man endure by lifting his heart, by reminding him of the courage, honor, hope, pride, compassion, pity, and sacrifice that have been the glory of his past. The poet's voice needs not merely be the record of man; it can be one of the props or the pillars to help him endure and prevail. Let us hope that Davis & Elkins holds to Faulkner's advice in the future and continues to shape its mission." (Turner 103).

"Football, however, waned in popularity at D&E. The years passed, and the glory of the 1920's and 30's faded. On the NCAA's recommendation, the schedule was trimmed to local and regional teams, the money ran out, and the Buccaneer recruiting style of Henderson was eliminated. In 1961, after one disastrous season after the other, D&E terminated football. Although Henderson's gridiron glory had come at a price, it still remains the most exciting era in D&E athletic history, many would say. However, D&E was not the only school that suffered a comedown from the twenties - glory many a power – Fordham and Columbia come to mind, as these schools also experienced similar declines." (Turner 28).

David Werner, a lineman from Elkins, West Virginia, weighed about 250 pounds and previously played for West Virginia University and Tulsa, Oklahoma. He transferred to D&E for the 1955 football season. Werner chewed tobacco and, before the first offensive play, would pick up a handful of dirt, spit tobacco juice in that dirt, and rub it in the face of the opposing lineman on the first play. This led to several brawls, suspensions and penalties.

The 1948 Davis and Elkins College Football Team

Davis & Elkins College and Randolph County were represented in the 1946 National Football League championship game, played between the Chicago Bears and Washington Redskins in Municipal Stadium in Baltimore. The game included Ace Federovich (D&E, played for the Bears), Herman Ball (D&E, Redskins assistant coach), Al Baisi (WVU, played for the Bears) and Joe Stadyhar (WVU, played for the Bears).

The 1955 Davis and Elkins College Football Team

In addition to being named as the recipient of the Thomas Richard Ross Professor of History and the Humanities accolade, Dr. David Turner, Ph.D., is the author of many publications and received the Lois Lathan Teaching Excellence award in 1993. Some of the following photos are courtesy of Dr. David R. Turner, author of *D&E 100 Years of History.*

John "Ace" Federovitch was holding up his end of the bargain, Basil Sharp, late 1930s. Basil Sharp was killed during WWII in Germany. Federovitch played and coached at D&E with Red Brown and Press Marovich.

Athletic Director Jennings Randolph, *left*, and Coach Cam Henderson
with the 1932-33 basketball team

Davis and Elkins Men's Basketball team - 1948

The 1949-50 basketball team went to the National Intercollegiate Basketball Tournament in Kansas City, Missouri. The team ultimately lost to the University of Tampa in the semifinals. The five starters for D&E were known as the Fabulous Five that season.

The D&E men's soccer team won the National Association of Intercollegiate Athletics National Championship in 1970.

In 1956, there was a fire in one of the buildings at Davis and Elkins College, now known as Science Hall. This fire was the only reason that George Triplett, book contributor, passed calculus. Alexa, the youngest of George Triplett's grandchildren and contributor to this book, also studied pre-calculus on the second floor of this building many years later, in 2022. Gerald Lawrence, former football player, worked as a laborer cleaning the bricks to rebuild Science Hall while attending Davis and Elkins College.

DAVIS & ELKINS COLLEGE STUDENTS

A list of known students of Davis & Elkins College is provided in Appendix A.

References

Board of Trade of Elkins, West Virginia. *Elkins West Virginia: November, Nineteen Six- The Coming Metropolis of the State*. Acme Publishing Company, 1906.

Davis & Elkins College. *Davis & Elkins College: Alumni Today 2015*. Davis & Elkins College, 2015.

---. *D&E Senatus: 1940 Davis & Elkins Yearbook*. 1940th ed., 1940.

---. *D&E Senatus: 1948 Davis & Elkins Yearbook*. 1948th ed., 1948.

---. *D&E Senatus 1956: 1956 Davis & Elkins Yearbook*. 1956.

National Football League, Official Program. Chicago Bears v. Washington Redskins. 1946.

Rice, Don. *Randolph 200: A Bicentennial History of Randolph County, West Virginia- 1787-1987*. Walsworth Publishing Co., Inc., 1987

Turner, David R. *Davis & Elkins College: One Hundred Years Honoring our Traditions, Celebrating our Future*. WDG Publishing, 2004.

UNIT 3: Davis Memorial Hospital School of Nursing

Senator H.G. Davis and Mrs. Davis built Davis Memorial Hospital as a memorial to their eldest son, Henry G. Davis, Jr., who was lost at sea. The construction of the institution began in the winter of 1902. Although Mrs. Davis did not live to see the completion of the hospital, special memorial services were held for her in the building. On November 23, 1903, an agreement to form a corporation known as the Davis Memorial Hospital was recorded in the Randolph County Courthouse. These incorporators later received a deed from H.G. Davis, which transferred the title to the hospital's board of trustees. Presently, Davis Memorial Hospital is located at 812 Gorman Avenue in Elkins (DMH Bulletin 2).

Once the land for the site of the hospital was purchased, the main building was constructed and equipped by Senator H.G. Davis. The hospital was given to the board of trustees to serve the people of the local community.

The hospital was constructed of stone and brick and roofed with red slate. The original octagon-shaped hospital had a capacity of 40 beds. In 1910, its size was more than doubled by adding two large stone and brick wings. In 1942, another wing was added, which was composed of two floors. The first floor of the addition housed the x-ray and deep therapy department. The second floor included private rooms and the pediatrics department. The bed capacity of the hospital was increased to 104. The hospital served as a general non-profit institution. It was approved by the Joint Commission on Accreditation of Hospitals and is a member of the American Hospital Association and the Hospital Association of West Virginia (DMH Bulletin 3).

The original incorporators of the hospital were: H.G. Davis, Hallie D. Elkins, Grace Davis Lee, John T. Davis, Bessie A. Davis, Katherine Elkins, C.M. Hendley, Fannie Kerens, C.W. Dailey, and Howard Sutherland.

Former presidents of the hospital board include the following individuals: H.G. Davis, John T. Davis, Thaddeus Pritt, Hallie D. Elkins, Katherine Elkins Hitt, Bruce Lee Kennedy, and Thomas Davis Lee.

Sen. Henry Gassaway Davis (Ross 1)

THE NIGHTINGALE PLEDGE

I solemnly pledge myself before God and in the presence of this assembly, to pass my life in purity and to practice my profession faithfully.

I will abstain from whatever is deleterious and mischievous, and will not take or knowingly administer any harmful drug.

I will do all in my power to maintain and elevate the standard of my profession, and will hold in confidence all personal matters committed to my keeping and all family affairs coming to my knowledge in the practice of my calling.

With loyalty will I endeavor to aid the physician in his work, and devote myself to the welfare of those committed to my care.

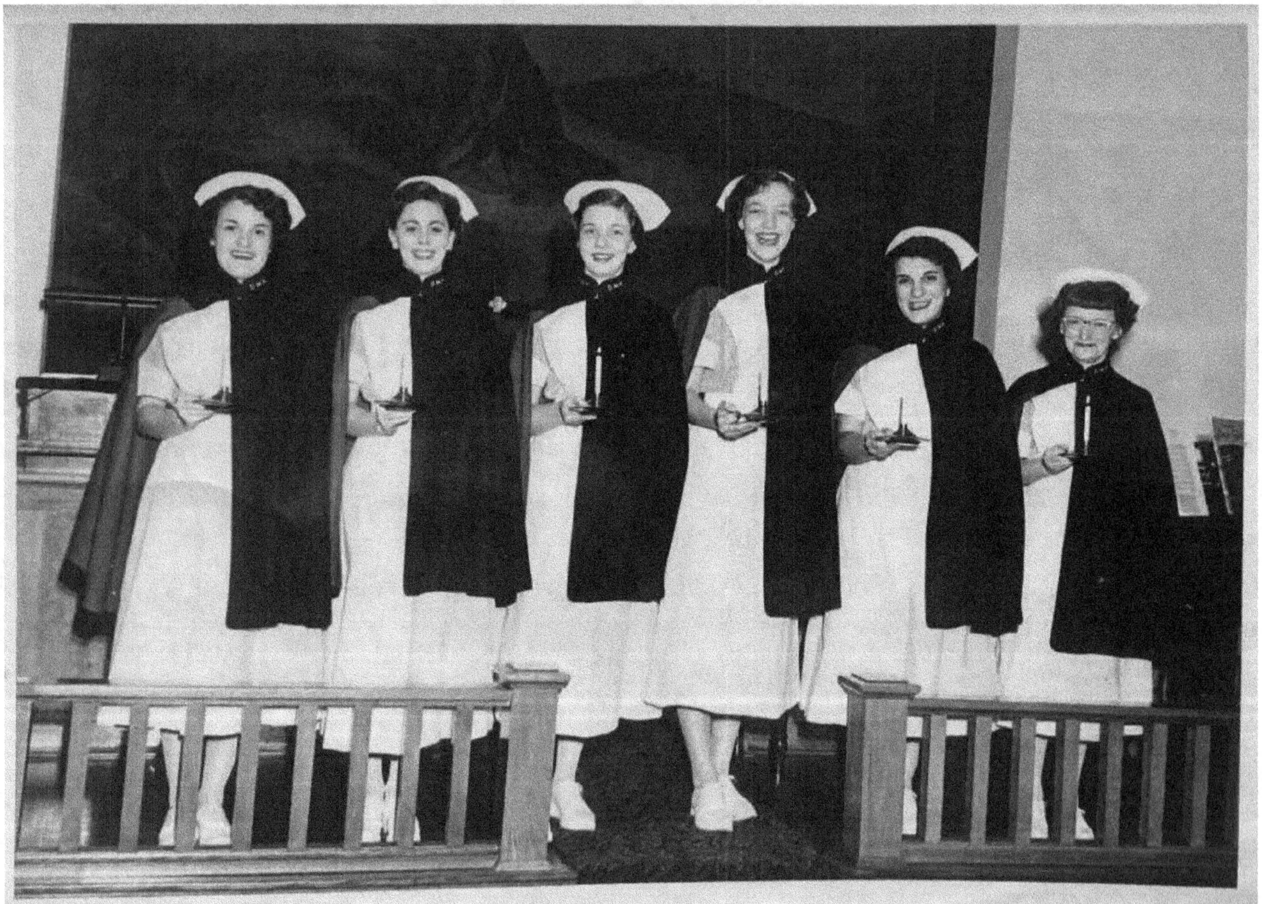

Nursing students are pictured here during their graduation ceremony. Left to right: Norma Jean Townsend, Patty Brown, Gail Swick, Betty Karikoff, Joan Rossi and Glenna Mae Coberly

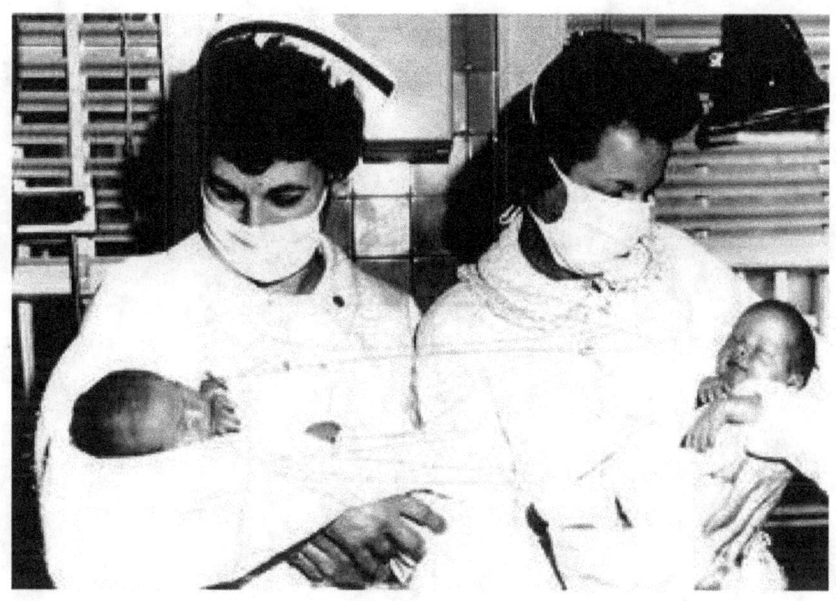

Frances Triplett left, and another nursing student is pictured holding newborn twins born at Davis Memorial Hospital

"The Davis Memorial Hospital School of Nursing was opened in 1903. The school offers a three-year basic professional program leading to a diploma in nursing and eligibility for licensure in professional nursing as a registered nurse. The school has graduated nearly 250 nurses who have served in various fields of nursing in this and other communities and in the Armed Services during World War I, World War II and the Korean Conflict. Until 1937, the student nurses had their living quarters on the hospital's third floor. The new student nurses' residence, the Katherine Elkins Hitt Memorial Hall, was built and equipped in 1937 by William F. Hitt and given to the hospital in memory of his wife, Katherine Elkins Hitt. Mr. Hitt was a member of the Board of Trustees from January 1937 until he resigned in June 1945 because of pressing business. The West Virginia Board of Examiners fully accredits the School of Nursing for Registered Nurses" (DMH Bulletin 3).

Photo of Patricia Currence Whetsel, 1954 graduate with Betty Karickoff Smith, 1956 graduate.

PHILOSOPHY OF THE INSTITUTION: The patient's mental and physical well-being requires nursing care of the highest type. Nursing is a profession in which an inspired person applies art, science, skill, and kindness toward the welfare of the patient. Public health and disease prevention are important integral parts. Competent teachers should provide education in adequately equipped and pleasant surroundings where the student can absorb knowledge and develop into well-rounded individuals. The School of Nursing shall make available to the student the knowledge and techniques necessary for her to become a successful professional nurse and a cheerful, useful citizen.

<u>AIM OF THE SCHOOL</u>: The aim of the Davis Memorial Hospital School of Nursing is to provide a sound

The first annual commencement exercises of the Elkins City Hospital Training School were held Thursday evening, October 10, 1907, in the Elkins Opera House, when a class of four young women received their diplomas. They were, L. to R., Edna Gay Mason, Mary Margaret Scallon, Pearl May Baumgartner, and Helen Justine Foster. The diplomas were presented by Dr. A.M. Fredlock, following the completion of a three-year training program, of which only one year was completed at the City Hospital. (RCHS)

educational program for well-qualified students to prepare them for first-level positions in the basic areas of professional nursing and ultimately to prepare them for total, safe, effective nursing care of the patients in hospitals and homes. The various aspects of the educational program are further planned to allow each student to develop her potential as a well-adjusted individual in a democratic society and to develop an appreciation of civic and social responsibilities to her profession and community.

<u>OBJECTIVES</u>:

1. To provide opportunities for learning to care for the sick with skill and understanding based on scientific knowledge, giving due consideration to nursing care of the whole patient, including the physical, social, and psychological factors involved.
2. To develop positive health attitudes and to provide opportunities for participation in health teaching and health conservation to individuals and families.
3. To promote good interpersonal relationship skills through cooperation with allied health professionals.
4. To foster the development of a well-integrated personality.
5. To encourage and provide an opportunity for participation in student government and social and civic affairs of the school and the community so that the individual student may become an active participant as a citizen in a democratic society and a progressive member of the Nursing Profession.

Instructors from the school included the following: Ralph Booth, B.S., M.S., chemistry; William W. Wood, B.S., M.A., psychology; S. Benton Talbot, B.S., Sc. D., Donald R. Vosburgh, B.S. A.M., sociology; Red Cross, emergency and First Aid American Red Cross, Mary Tillson; residence director, Mabel Phares, A.B. registrar and secretary.

DMH NURSING SCHOOL GRADUATION --

"A poor man served by thee shall make thee rich;

A sick man helped by thee shall make thee strong;

Thou shalt be served thyself by every sense of service

Which thou renderest."

- E.B. Browning

<u>**REFERENCES**</u>

Bosworth, Dr. A. S. *History of Randolph County, West Virginia*. Southern Historical Press Inc., 1916.

Davis & Elkins College. *Davis & Elkins College: Alumni Today 2015*. Davis & Elkins College, 2015.

---. *Davis & Elkins College: Elkins, West Virginia, Alumni Directory 1998*. Bernard C. Harris Publishing Company, Inc., 1998.

---. *D&E Senatus: 1940 Davis & Elkins Yearbook*. 1940th ed., 1940.

---. *D&E Senatus: 1948 Davis & Elkins Yearbook*. 1948th ed., 1948.

---. *The Senatus 1956: 1956 Davis & Elkins Yearbook*. 1956.

Rice, Don. *Randolph 200: A Bicentennial History of Randolph County, West Virginia- 1787-1987*. Walsworth Publishing Co., Inc., 1987.

Special thanks to Mark DeMotto and Minta Lothes for contributing to this section.

UNIT 4: Cheat Mountain History

Our grandfather always said, "We didn't have much on Cheat Mountain, but we sure did have a lot."

Landowner and author John Frischkorn wrote about Cheat Mountain and the Cheat Mountain Club in his 2007 book. The following is an excerpt:

"Since the Indians first chased buffalo and elk across the Cheat Mountain, it was recognized as a most formidable and unusually high mountain ecosystem. Cheat Mountain is a grand ridge in scale and height; it extends 70 miles southwest to northeast from Snowshoe to a point located east of Elkins. Many of the highest points in West Virginia, ranging from 4,200 feet to 4,800 feet, call Cheat Mountain home. Several of these high points include the following: Bald Knob at 4,860 feet; Mace Knob at 4,687 feet; Beech Flat Knob at 4,682 feet; Ward Knob at 4,545 feet; Snyder Knob at 4,700 feet; Crouch Knob at 4,529 feet; Baron Knob at 4,454 feet; Hutton Knob at 4,246 feet; and Gaudineer Knob at 4,309 feet. The highest point in West Virginia, Spruce Knob, reaches 4,468 feet in elevation and can be found just a few miles east of the northern terminus, Cheat Mountain. Spruce Knob is only eight feet higher than Bald Knob, the destination of the Cass Scenic Railroad. Bald Knob is located near the southern end of Cheat, on the higher end of the mountain.

In the early days, the wilderness of Cheat was vast, the weather forlorn, and the lack of human settlement obvious. Winters brought great snowfall, sometimes over 200 inches every season. It was home for the snowshoe hare, fox, coyote, bear, deer, elk, otters, beaver, mink, muskrats, osprey, eagles, hawks, over 100 varieties of warblers, hatches, brook trout, the rare Cheat Mountain Salamander and Big-Eared Bat, as well as numerous rare species of plants.

In the summer and winter, the height of the mountain front stalls the prevailing southwesterly winds, causing more rain and snow to drop on Cheat than on any surrounding area. To the east, the rain shadow caused by the height of the mountain causes dry land trees, such as oak and pine, to predominate on the Allegheny Front. On Cheat, abundant rainfall and acidic soils welcome trees and plants such as Red Spruce, Beech, Birch and Maple. The largest stand of Red Spruce trees south of New York was on Cheat Mountain. In fact, the amount of virgin timber on Cheat was so abundant that early travelers wrote of huge, covered vistas and dark forests that blocked out so much sunlight that no scrub could grow underneath. This land is where greenbriers, poison ivy, mosquitoes, and ticks find no home. On the other hand, thickets of Rhododendron and Laurel were tumbled and twisted in many areas, leaving Civil War soldiers and early explorers tangled up, turned around, and sometimes lost for days.

According to historian W.F. Horn, Cheat Mountain was named for a French-Canadian fur trapper named Jacques Cheathe, born in Quebec in 1685. Cheathe worked with Jean DuPratz in the Shawnee Indian settlement on 'Le Belle Waters' (the Ohio River). In 1723 Cheathe was given rights to hunt, fish, and trade with the Cherokee Indians in northern Virginia. He named the beautiful waters of his private hunting preserve Cheathes River. Some think that instead of hunting and trapping, his primary mission was to keep a lookout for English settlers encroaching west of the French-English boundaries. Jacque Cheathes died at a French outpost near the mouth of the Cheat River in June 1734. Over time, the name of the river and mountain evolved from "Cheathes River" into "Cheat River" and "Cheat Mountain." Another theory suggests that people have adopted the name Cheat because of the raging waters and harsh conditions that "cheated" Indians or early settlers of their lives.

Meanwhile, other people argue this theory is unlikely because, during this time in history, Indians likely did not understand the concept of " cheating "; this concept was likely learned from white men. Finally, a third theory suggests that the name "Cheat" came from a story of a mountain at the southern end of the Seneca Trail in north Alabama called Cheat Knob. This knob was named for a Cherokee tribe who traveled as far north as the Shavers Fork River by way of the Greenbrier Valley.

It was not until the Civil War that people realized the potential wealth of timber on Cheat Mountain. In early 1861, the Union Army, under the command of General George B. McClellan, built a sawmill and established a fort at White Top, the gap in the middle of Cheat Mountain - located just west of Shaver's Fork on the Staunton to Parkersburg Turnpike. This fort became known as Cheat Summit and was higher in elevation than any other Union-occupied Civil War Fort.

For reference, there were actually three forts located on Cheat Mountain - Cheat Mountain Pass, Cheat Summit - also called White Top or Fort Milroy - and Back Allegheny. Cheat Mountain Pass was located to the west of Cheat Summit and down in the valley at the head of Riffle Creek. Riffle Creek is the stream one crosses when traveling east toward Cheat from Huttonsville. The middle and highest fort was called Cheat Summit - also known as White Top or Fort Milroy. The third fort was known as the 'first top' or Back Allegheny. This fort was situated at the crest of Back Allegheny Mountain and east of Cheat Summit, above what is now the town of Durbin.

These forts were built in an attempt to stop illegal trade among the Staunton to Parkersburg Turnpike. The purpose of the forts was to impede rebel efforts, obtain supplies, and keep the Confederates out of Western Virginia. Cheat Summit, the largest encampment and central fort, was occupied by up to 5,000 men, primarily from the 14th Indiana regiment under the leadership of Union general J.J. Reynolds, a West Point graduate, who commanded the Cheat Mountain, Huttonsville, and Elkwater area.

Countless tales of life at Cheat Summit were penned, including this one from Augustus Van Dyke, a member of the Indiana Fourteenth who wrote in his diary in 1861: "Here was the forest primeval, its murmuring pines and its hemlocks, deep dark, almost impenetrable, as inhospitable as the caverns that concealed themselves under the moss that shrouded its boulders, where the rain it raineth every day, and it snows in August... To the one who loves the wildly picturesque nature... this region could not fail to awe, please, or fascinate. The great granite boulders lie scattered in inextricable confusion as if they had fallen from the hands of giants in the battle against each other, and over them, there creep the staggering, trailing tendrils of what is vulgarity called 'sheep laurel.' Bursting out of the side of the mountain here and there are torrents of living water that go brawling down the side of the mountain to fall asleep in the placid ... pools of Cheat River, in whose depth and on whose laughing ripples play the mottled mountain trout... the sound of the axe and the thunder of the falling giant of the forest reverberated among the hills, and then began the building of an immense fort ... The walls were fourteen feet high, eight feet through at the base, and narrowing to four feet at the top. These walls were built of pine or hemlock, spruce, crib form, and the space filled with earth and stone." (Frischkorn, Carl F., *The Cheat Mountain Club: A Historical Recollection.* 2007).

Although no major battle took place at Cheat Summit, a number of skirmishes occurred, and one major Confederate campaign was mounted. On September 11, 1861, a freshly minted General, Robert E. Lee, aided by Generals W. W. Loring and H.R. Jackson, attempted to take the summit. A five-day campaign ensued, with Loring approaching the fort from Bartow on the east and Jackson coming in from Huntersville, the west, and General Lee's company. No Confederate troops made it to Cheat Summit Fort; hundreds from both sides gave their lives in the attempt. Gen. Robert E. Lee, who had been appointed coordinator of the Cheat Mountain Campaign of 1861 by the governor of Virginia, was leading his first major campaign in this assault on Cheat. His defeat was not highly publicized, although accounts of his leadership at Cheat have caused many scholars of the Civil War to question his fitness for his subsequent appointment as commander of the Confederate Army.

Many of the casualties of Cheat were the result of bushwhackers, named for their technique of hiding in the bush and engaging in surprise attacks. While General H.R. Jackson conducted the practice of bushwhacking and the use of "irregulars," Robert E. Lee had a strong distaste for guerrilla warfare. Lee was known to be a refined and well-educated Virginia gentleman of high moral standards. At this time in his career, he was not considered to be a hardened military man; the atrocities of war had not shattered his ideals. In the end, the Confederates called off the attack on Cheat Summit, and Lee soon returned to Virginia to be given command of the entire Confederate Army. The Cheat skirmishes could be won only by bushwhacking and ambushing, as there were no fields or towns to storm with lines of regulars. 'Hand-to-hand' and 'shoot-on-sight' tactics were employed in prosecuting this battle.

With only three Union forts and unfriendly natural conditions, Confederate soldiers and mule trail suppliers decided to take the long way south around Cheat Mountain through Huntersville rather than face unseasonably wet weather and horribly rutted roads. Records show that a major snowstorm hit Cheat Summit Fort (later called Fort Milroy) on August 13, 1861, causing many soldiers and horses to perish. All of the casualties sustained within the confines of Cheat Summit were caused by exposure to the elements and disease. Peculiar to this ecosystem is the fact that even during the dry season, water bubbles up from ground springs on top of Cheat Mountain, making it almost impossible for soldiers and animals to stay dry. In 1862 the fort was abandoned to the delight and celebration of the soldiers who had experienced too much of Cheat Mountain's inhospitable climate. The soldiers did not so fondly refer to Cheat Mountain as 'the country that God forgot.' A cemetery stands in testimony to the harsh times men had to endure at Cheat Summit Fort.

Industrial business development created a vibrancy in the Shavers Fork area of the Cheat River between the 1890s and 1950s. The growing railroad, timber, and coal mining activity in the area created a strong work ethic that became instilled in young people. Furthermore, mountain life exposed us to a plethora of natural surroundings, which ingrained a life-long love for outdoor activities and a love for family.

The term hillbilly can be associated with mountain people and their dedication to family and hard work. Jim Comstock, a nationally recognized writer and publisher from West Virginia, said a hillbilly is someone whose heritage, independence, and stubbornness can be linked to their deep mountain roots.

Comstock is credited with this quote, "A hillbilly is someone who can't look out his window without seeing the big hills and feeling small and big at the same time because of them. He's somebody with a heritage of independence his hill-folk family gave him because - cut off from other people by the mountains - they had to make it by themselves. Someone stubborn and tenacious because he's learned that while faith can move a mountain, it might take a little time. … He's friendly because mountains teach that there are more important things to fight than people - and that if your closest friends are both sides of a mountain distant, they're better held onto than fought with. And he's industrious. Even living lazily in mountain country can work a man pretty hard. He's somebody who knows that only God can make a tree - and figures that if He troubled to make a whole state of forested mountains, that state must be especially blessed. A West Virginia hillbilly is a man with wealth underfoot, wealth towering over his head, and only the beauty all around him coming easy. He has his troubles, but he has plenty of toughness and faith to stick it out, sometimes looking poorer than he feels. … Why not give that stubborn, tenacious, independent hillbilly - the real backbone of all of us - credit for what he laid the foundation of? Let's hope we have the guts to live up to him, facing the wonderful, favorable odds his grit preserved for us. Take away his name, and you take away the credit from him. Somebody asked George Washington what he'd do if it looked as if he were losing the war. He said, 'Give me but a banner to plant upon the mountains of West Augusta' - this name for this area in Washington's day - 'and I will gather around me the men who will lift our bleeding country from the dust and set her free.'"

Originally from British Columbia, Harvey Cromer served as a surveyor for the West Virginia Pulp and Paper Company. Cromer surveyed more than 70,000 acres of Cheat Mountain while living in a Swiss chalet and raising 14 children under a wood shingle roof. Cromer resided near the Cheat Bridge for more than 75 years until the coal mining operations in Cheat Mountain expanded in the 1970s.

In 1927, the Western Mountain Railroad was granted permission to purchase the Greenbrier, Cheat, and Elk Railroad for $1,585,000. The 75 miles of railroad and its rights of way were kept in business into the early 1990s because they could haul coal from the upper Cheat River and the Elk River coal mines to Baltimore, Maryland (Bodkins, 397, 402, 403). By June 1928, they had assigned 60-75 men to the section between Cheat Junction and Spruce to get the line in shape to handle the heavier traffic, which consisted mostly of locomotives, that was expected to travel over the section. Their crews began laying new ties, ballasting the low areas, raising the track to grade, and generally upgrading the lines.

Charlie Triplett, called "Triplett," was promoted to foreman of the new section and given full responsibility for upgrading and maintaining the newly acquired line. The railroad foreman's main responsibility was to ensure that the railroad track was maintained and in good condition to allow rail traffic's continuous, safe passage. The foreman and his crew were continuously checking gauges, raising tracks, tightening bolts, cutting brush, cleaning culverts, sweeping snow from switches, and changing rails and ties to keep the rail line in the best possible state of repair.

The foreman had to be an organized and dedicated individual who closely followed the strict rules and regulations set forth by the railroad company. The foreman's first duty every day was to call the dispatch office to receive orders about train traffic so the crew's work routine could be planned around that day's schedule. In addition, the foreman had to ensure that no track was taken out of service unless prompt notice was given and the proper authorities were contacted. The foreman was on continuous emergency call status and was frequently required to report to work in the middle of the night to remove a rock, tree, or another obstacle that had fallen onto the tracks. Elmer Davis was one of these track walkers and covered the section from below the High Falls to one mile below Bemis.

*The Cheat Mountain Club was built in 1912. It is located approximately two miles south of the intersection of
Cheat Bridge Road and U.S. Route 250.*

Evidence of a successful day of brook trout fishing on the Shavers Fork in the early 1900s

Fishing at Cheat Bridge
with George Triplett

Laura Dean Bennett
Staff Writer

These days, modern anglers often bring a plethora of tactics and equipment to the meandering streams of the Appalachian Mountains, where our trout can give even the most skilled fishermen a run for their money.

And many share the stories of the excitement of catching their first big fish.

Such is the case with George Triplett, Sr.

It's from the most humble beginnings that his love affair with the sport of fishing evolved.

Triplett has had a storied career as an attorney, Assistant United States Attorney and Circuit Judge.

He's still practicing law in Elkins with his son, Jefferson Triplett.

Triplett is the author of *Our Proud Mountain Roots and Heritage*, a well-known compilation of life on the Shavers Fork of the Cheat River during the heyday of the logging industry.

Born in 1935, Triplett grew up at Cheat Bridge, on the formidable mountain called Cheat – which some say was so named because so many men had been cheated of their lives there.

The logging town of Cheat Bridge was named for the nearby bridge that was built before the Civil War to serve the Staunton-Parkersburg Turnpike.

The current 1934 steel-truss bridge – a half mile north of Cheat Bridge – brings drivers across Shavers Fork on U.S. Route 250 as they enter the magnificent wilderness of the Monongahela National Forest.

Triplett's growing up years in the 30s and 40s were typical of that time and place – hard times, liberally dosed with irreplaceable outdoor adventures.

He loved to hunt on the mountain and fish in the river – from which have come some of his fondest memories.

"I had a million dollar childhood, growing up as I did on the Upper Cheat Basin," Triplett said.

"I grew up catching trout – both legally and illegally," he added, with a chuckle.

There were several dignitaries who came quite frequently to Shavers Fork of Cheat River for fishing vacations, and they stayed in tents.

As it turns out, many of them were government officials and one was a lawyer who made quite an impression on the young Triplett.

He would never be forgotten.

"One time when I was just a little guy, I ran into some of those gentlemen who came to Cheat Bridge," Triplett remembered. "They were big fishermen.

"That day a man by the name of Bill Thompson from Montgomery, West Virginia, came along.

"He saw the birch cut fishing pole I was using. He asked me what kind of pole I'd like to have. And I told him I wanted a rod so I could to fish the river and the creeks, and a line that didn't tangle.

"And he told me he thought that was a very intelligent answer.

"Well, he bought me that rod," Triplett continued. "It was a real nice telescoping rod, line and reel.

"Really something."

That act of generosity and kindness established the trajectory of Triplett's career.

"I've always had a high opinion of lawyers," Triplett said. "That's why I decided that that's what I wanted to be when I grew up."

A few days later that fine fishing rod proved itself.

"On the first day of trout season – back then that was the last day of April – I took that rod out, threw out with a worm at the big hole, and all of a sudden, I'd caught my first nine-inch native brook trout.

"I'll never forget it. It was 1940. I was five years old."

The Department of Natural Resources stocked brown trout on the Upper Shavers Fork, and Triplett liked to fish for them about 10 miles above Cheat Bridge at Big Run Bridge.

"There was a big old crabapple tree growing on the right hand side, just below the bridge.

"It grew over the section of riffles where I used to catch nice trout. There was a large brown trout I hooked several times but it always either broke my line or got off the hook."

Another big fish Triplett tried for, but could never catch, hung out at a nice fishing hole below the Cabin Fork railroad river bridge – about four and a half miles above Cheat Bridge.

"I used to always see this big old rainbow trout there. He was more than two feet long, and he was always there at that big hole. I tried everything, but he never would take any bait or hit anything. I could never catch him.

"He was just too smart to be caught.

"One time, about 1949, some adult friends of mine and I were fishing on the first day of trout season," Triplett related.

"We were fishing, and I was having good luck. I filled one of my drunken friend's creels with fifteen trout I had caught while he was sitting on the railroad track.

"I was beside this monstrous rock below the railroad track, and fishing a heavy riffle and any trout that was less than six inches in length was stuffed in my hip boots, and there were quite a few.

"All of a sudden, I heard voices calling out from above: 'How are you doing?'

"I turned to look and saw two bright silver badges, glinting in the sunlight. There were two game wardens standing about fifteen feet above me on the railroad grade. I crouched down on my knees at the rock, covering my hip boots with my heavy duck-back coat and answered them:

"'Doin' okay. Come take a look.'

"I started showing them the ten or so trout in my straw fish basket," Triplett said.

"They told me they hadn't seen such a fine catch. They had crossed the mountain searching for violators from Valley Head down Beaver Creek.

"After admiring the trout they just went on. Fortunately, I don't think they had any idea what I was doing," he chuckled.

George Triplett, Sr. proudly poses in front of Cheat Bridge photographs hanging on the wall in the law office of Triplett & Triplett in Elkins. Visitors to the office are often treated to entertaining anecdotes about his "million dollar childhood," growing-up on the Cheat River.

See *FISHING*, page 14

Triplett remembers another anecdote that might not strictly qualify as a fishing story, but it was certainly an adventure.

"I was about ten years old," he began. "We were living in Elkins then. I got permission to travel to Cheat Bridge to stay a few days with the family of a man who worked for my daddy on the railroad section.

"I rode the bus from Elkins to Cheat Bridge. I remember it cost 90 cents.

"I had my same telescope rod and reel with me, and I promised my parents to stay with Brooks Davis and his family at Cheat Bridge.

"Well, I met up with three guys – a doctor, a dentist and a well-known old mountain man. I went with them to their cabin about eight miles above Cheat Bridge at the remnants of an old Mower Lumber Company camp.

"We rode in a motorcar from Cheat Bridge to Beaver Creek.

"That night, due to the influence of some intoxicating liquors, the three older men kind of passed out. They had a hot fire, and I was sharing a bunkbed with the brother of the doctor, who was also "skidded" and sleeping on the lower bunk underneath me."

Things took an unfortunate turn when the dentist got sick.

"They got even worse when a deer snorted outside the cabin, and somebody roused up and shot at the deer," Triplett continued. "Shortly thereafter, I decided to vacate the camp. It was dark, but I managed to find my way to another camp.

"My parents didn't hear of the violation of my promise until many years later, thank goodness."

Although all of these fishing anecdotes seem to have taken place on the first day of fishing season, Triplett assured me that he did fish on lots of other days during the season.

In fact, he probably fished on most days during most fishing seasons.

Pocahontas County native and noted West Virginia author Tweard Blackhurst was teaching conservation at Green Bank High School when Triplett was a student there, and Cal Price was the famous editor of *The Pocahontas Times*, known for his interest in history and his editorials about local outdoor lore.

That's when Blackhurst gave Triplett the moniker, Cal Price, Jr.

"I was fifteen or sixteen years old, and I went bear hunting a lot, and I had to feed my bear dogs and it got expensive," Triplett recalled.

"So I'd take people bear hunting, and they'd pay me ten or twenty dollars, or sometimes more, to go bear hunting.

"And each time, I'd miss two or three days of school.

"I'd sit around and tell these stories about what I'd see while I was out in the woods, like watching two flocks of turkeys coming together or big bucks fighting in the moonlight or catching big fish.

"I guess my stories would remind Tweard of Cal Price and his panther stories. He called me Cal Price, Jr.," Triplett remembered fondly.

One of Triplett's sons, Dr. George Triplett, Jr., a retired anesthesiologist, remembers many adventures up on Cheat Mountain with his father.

"From the time I was young, especially when my grandparents were still alive, we took lots of fishing, hunting and camping trips up there." Dr. Triplett said.

"One time, when I was six years old, we were up there at Cheat Bridge. I remember this time because it was the time I met a beaver.

"It was a Saturday in April, around 1961 – the first day of trout season. There were no roads back up in there at that time, so everything was a long walk.

"We walked about five miles to a stream called Cabin Fork," he recalled.

"We started fishing. Dad was standing down in the stream, and I was up on the bank.

"All of a sudden, I looked up and about three feet away from me was a beaver – and I guess I was

See FISHING, page 15

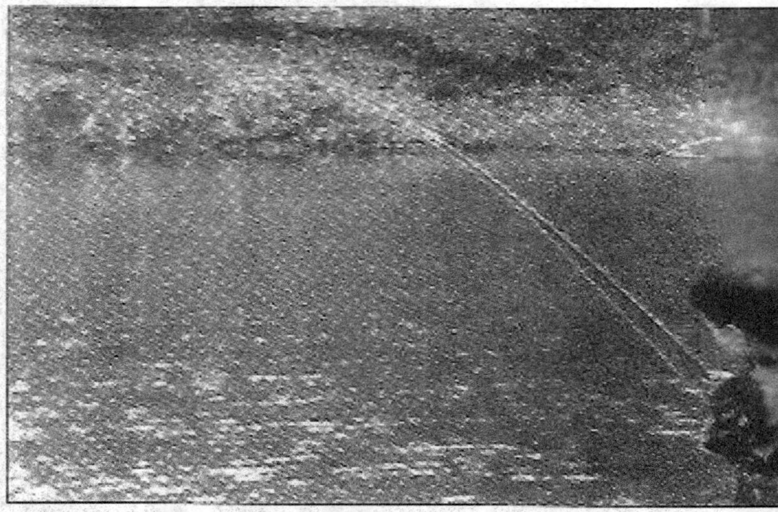

Taking after his grandfather, George Triplett, Sr., George Andrew Triplett, above, stepped up to carry on the family tradition of fishing on the Cheat River. In 2003, the then three-year-old youngster caught his first trout during a fishing trip there.

between it and the water.

"It stood up on its hind legs and looked hard at me.

"I hollered at Dad and about that time that beaver ran right between my legs and into the water.

"That's one fishing trip I'll never forget," he said.

"And we caught plenty of fish, too," his dad added.

The water flows on, fish come and go, but childhood memories, family ties and fish tales last a lifetime.

This article, "Fishing at Cheat Bridge with George Triplett", along with the following two prints was published in a supplement to The Pocohantas Times, Spring 2021. The article focuses on George Triplett and his deep-rooted connection to the area of Cheat Bridge.

Photos courtesy of George Triplett

George Triplett was an outdoorsman from an early age. When three year old George was setting off from the family home at Cheat Bridge — armed with a pop gun and his faithful dog Fido — his mother asked where he was going and he replied, "Coon huntin'!"

George Triplett wrote about his formative years growing up in Pocahontas County and the rich history of his family and the northern towns of the county, in his book, "Our Proud Mountain Roots and Heritage," at right.

As Don Rice wrote in his summation of the book for the cover, "[George]... grew to manhood on the waters of Shaver's Fork of Cheat River, where he experienced the waning years of the industrial vibrancy of the region, which had influenced the welfare of his family and friends for more than a half-century."

The book is available for check-out at McClintic Library in Marlinton.

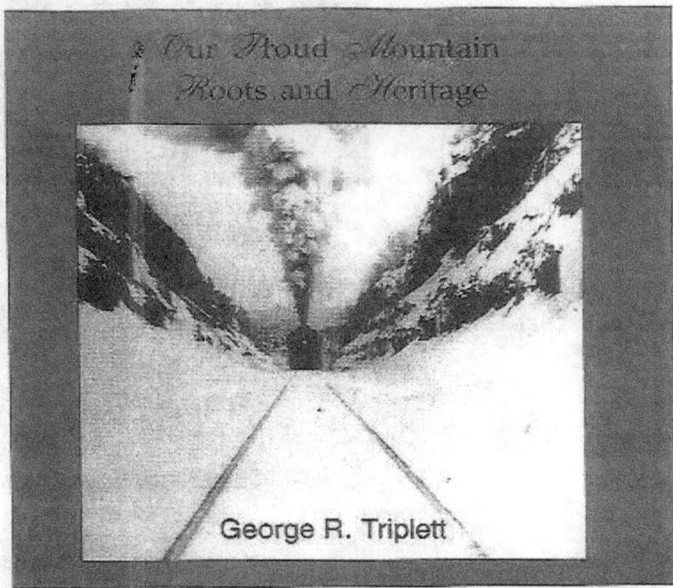

Bill Thompson, attorney from Montgomery, West Virginia.

A painting of the late Bill Thompson, an attorney from Montgomery, West Virginia. As described in the above article, Mr. Thompson was an inspiration to a five-year-old mountain boy in 1940.

Pictured above is a corner post set by Charlie R. Triplett (left) and George R. Triplett seated near the building site of his childhood home at Cheat Bridge, W.Va. (right), photos taken by Sofia Triplett, co-author, January 2022.

Pictured above (left) is a part of an old stovetop from the childhood home of George R. Triplett. Photo taken by Sofia Triplett, co-author, January 2022.

Slim - George's bear dog and loyal friend before his wife, Frances.

Pictured above, in all three photos, are the same rocks that were situated outside the childhood home of George R. Triplett in Cheat Bridge. The photos were taken nearly 85 years apart, in 1937 and in 2022.
The top left photo pictures a young George R. Triplett.

Cheat Bridge Was Town With Bridge

CHEAT BRIDGE exists in name only now. It is located approximately 1/2 mile South of U.S. 250 and W. Va. 92. Located on the old Staunton and Parkersburg Turnpike, between Huttonsville and Durbin, West Virginia. Built by Colonel Claude Crozet, a French engineer, who had fought with Napolean Bonaparte after the Revolutionary War.

Cheat Bridge was a booming town in the 1890's and up until the 1920's. The main industry was cutting timber, logging, getting the lumber to sawmills, then to market everywhere.

The road through Cheat Bridge was used by both the North and South during the Civil War 1861-1865. Railroads were built through Cheat Bridge, Spruce, Cass, Durbin and Elk River, West Virginia. The stagecoach was also running between Staunton, Virginia, and Beverly, West Virginia. Mail was carried by horseback.

The 100 ft. span bridge shown in the picture was built by Francis O'Neale, contractor, in 1841, and demolished in 1910, for $3,160.00. The above picture was made in 1890.

Post Office Was In A Home

The Cheat Mountain post office was located in Alfred Hutton's home from February 21, 1870, to February 2, 1881. The building which housed Uncle Sam's mail business was built in 1840, and burned to the ground one February day in 1881, but not before it got its picture struck. Pictured here are: Caroline Hutton (with son, Napolean B. Hutton); Charles S. Hutton (boy on fence); Mosella Hutton Woodford (in front of post, left of porch); Elihu Moore (in front of gate); Alfred Hutton (Postmaster)-(right of tree); 5th from right – man unknown; Eugene E. Hutton (on banister behind 5th man from right); 4th from right – unknown; Henry Wills (3rd from right); John Atkan (2nd from right); Huck McDonald (extreme right). All others unknown. Cheat Mountain's first postmaster was Alfred Hutton.

Cheat Bridge.

Clockwise from top left: (1) (l to r): Patty Payne, George Triplett, Nancy Harris; (2) George Triplett, Charles E. Triplett, George R. Triplett, Jr.; (3) Charlie Robert Triplett; (4) George Triplett & Nancy Harris (Glady); (5) George Triplett & Nancy Harris; (6) Geneva Harris Triplett.

UNIT 5: Pocahontas County Schools

Green Bank High School 1917-1918

BIG FILL SCHOOL

Big Fill School was located five miles from Durbin, Cheat Mountain, and Cheat Bridge. Grades one through eight were taught at Big Fill School. The school was closed in 1938, and students then attended school in Pocahontas County.

Approximately five miles northwest of Durbin on Route 250 on a slight embankment stood the little one-room school known as Big Fill School. As one entered the school room, one would first notice the pot-belly wood stove in the center of the room. Then, your eyes traveled to the homemade wooden desk of the students with no place to keep their books. Next, one may notice the pegs on the wall to hang their wraps, a rude table in the back of the building with one water bucket, and one metal dipper to be used by the children for drinking water. The teacher's desk was also a homemade item. The small, one-room school still stands today and is used as a hunting cabin.

Some of the students who attended Big Fill School include the following: George Gragg, Price Gragg, Virginia Gragg, Arthur Cromer, Beatrice Cromer; Alpha Cromer, Franklin Cromer, Ellen Cromer, Homer Lockridge, Reece Lockridge, Florence Lockridge, Hellen Lillian and Crystal Lockridge, Bill Gregory, Ted Gregory, Troy Gregory, Dennis Gregory, Naomi Arbogast, Delbert Ryder, Sam Ryder, Virginia Ryder, Dorothy Ryder, and Lola Belle Ryder, Glen Wilcox, Opal Wilcox (wife of Governor W. W. Barron), Leon Wilcox, Juanita Simmons, Mary Simmons, Daisy Arbogast, Ash Arbogast, Ralph Arbogast, Steward Arbogast, Edward Arbogast, Kyle Arbogast, Homer Arbogast, Parker Arbogast, Joe Arbogast, Paul Arbogast, Lucy Arbogast, Icy Arbogast, Wilson, Foster, Henry, Earl, Brady, Grace, Myra, Ruth and Bernetta Kelly.

Some of the teachers who taught at Big Fill School include the following: Mr. Brady, Mr. Stats, Price Gragg, Virginia Gragg, Asa Wright, Ross Wood, Mrs. Maude Laudermilk, Minnie Cromer, Berdie Greathouse, Violet Nottingham, Virginia Poscover, Marie Parg, Glenn Tracy, and Minnie Parg.

<u>**Durbin Schools**</u>

In 1921, the Durbin and Frank schools consolidated, and an eight-room brick building was constructed. The new school was built approximately seven miles from Cheat Bridge, Randolph County. This building was torn down around 2000. George Triplett started first grade in 1941, during the outbreak of WWII.

Durbin Elementary School staff in the 1940s included the following: Mr. Poscover, principal; Mrs. Violet Hoover Arthur, 1st grade; Miss Margaret Wilson, 2nd grade; Mrs. Frona Williams, 3rd grade; Mrs. Hope Hull Mallow, 4th grade; Miss Marie Parg, 5th grade; Ms. Jack, 6th grade; Miss Kramer, 7th grade; and Mr. K.B. Wilmoth, 8th grade.

The first school in Durbin was upstairs in a granary located on the west end of town, commonly called "Pig's Ear." The first teacher was the late Judge Summers Sharp, who taught a three-month term at Thornwood and then went to Durbin for three months. Eight students were enrolled in this school.

Early in the 1900s, a two-room schoolhouse was built on the property now owned by Jake Thompson. C. Forest Hull was the principal and taught the upper grades, and Miss McKeever taught the lower grades. This building was used until 1921.

In 1921, the Durbin and Frank grade schools were consolidated when a new brick building with eight classrooms was constructed. As the enrollment increased several years later, three additional classrooms, an auditorium, and a lunchroom were built. Around 1950, all the one-room schools in the upper part of Green Bank District were consolidated into Durbin School.

C.E. Flynn was the first principal of Durbin School. Other school principals include the following: L.S. Shires, C.E. Batson, Ralph Hedrick, Jack Richardson, Claude A. McMillion, Max Poscover, A.S. Hill (21 years) and Allen D. Stewart (five years). Margaret Wilson taught second grade for 42 years; Hope Hull Mallow and Marie Parg each taught for 39 years. Other members of the faculty prior to 1972, who had ten or more years of service, include the following individuals: Jeanne H. Gragg, Willa Whanger, Bonnie N. Hill, Faye Truss, Ruth B. Jennings, Frona F. Williams, Violet Hoover Arthur, Miss Kramer, K.B. Wilmoth, and Marguerite Kisner Widney.

For many years, the Durbin School was used as a community center for nearly all social functions, athletic events and public meetings. It was with deep sorrow that the citizens of Durbin and its vicinity heard the school was to be moved to Green Bank in 1977. Citizens felt as though something was taken from their community that could never be replaced.

The Durbin grade school had 144 steps, leading up the hill from U.S. Route 250. These concrete steps remain, long after the school was demolished, although they were covered over by brush, as of 2022.

<u>Green Bank High School</u>

In 1915, the District's board of education voted to give authority to float bonds to construct a high school. A dispute over the proposed site arose between Cass and Green Bank communities. J. W. Goodsell, president of the board, voted in favor of Green Bank because it was nearer to the center of the school's population. The citizens of Cass became determined to defeat the bond issue and elect a new board. Others were against the bond because it would increase their taxes, and some did not think a high school was needed.

Green Bank High School, around 1917

In 1931, a one-room schoolhouse from Arbovale was moved to the campus by S.H. Elliott. The structure was set on concrete pillars for a fee of $250. The vocational agriculture department would use the building. Over the years, this structure has been expanded with the addition of five unused former school buildings. The main building eventually grew to include a hot lunchroom, cookroom, one classroom, shop, and restroom. In 1935, a hedge of white pines separating the playground into two sections was set out by Harvey Warwick and a WPA crew under the supervision of C.E. Flynn, the county superintendent. Also, in 1935, the hot lunch program was started. A.S. Killingsworth built the second addition to the main building in 1936 at the price of $11,332. It consisted of two classrooms, a boys bathroom, and a library - all overtop the gymnasium. The building was later torn down, and a brick bus garage was built to store six school buses.

In 1939, F.F.A. was organized; this program is now one of the oldest in the state. In 1946, an addition was made to the Vo-Ag building to include freezers in the kitchen. This enabled the Vo-Ag students to assist in butchering meat in the lunchroom. In 1944, the band was organized under the direction of Anna Margaret Johnson. Soon after, in 1946, a new floor was laid in the gym, and a new heating system was added. Over the years, the courses added to the curriculum were economics, sociology, physics, solid geometry, boy's home education, girl's farm shop, dramatics, Spanish, second-year algebra, and conservation, emphasizing forest conservation. One annual project of the senior class was the planting of seedlings. This project first began in 1949, and one can observe these trees on the Old Pike. Another addition to the educational institution was the issuance of a "Merit Diploma." To earn this diploma, a student was required to maintain a high academic record, show and practice good citizenship and leadership, participate in many extracurricular activities, and show leadership in the community.

A school levy was passed in early 1915, and doors were opened to Green Bank High School on September 24, 1917. The school was closed in 1970 when Green Bank consolidated with Pocahontas County High School. When Green Bank High School closed in 1970, it was academically approved by the West Virginia

Department of Education and the North Central Association of Secondary Schools. More than 2,000 students graduated from this educational institution between 1919 and 1970.

As printed in the school's 1970 yearbook, principal Virgil Harris said, "...We have tried to look into the future for a longtime plan. This plan will not be realized as long as we think 'we can't.'" When we direct our thoughts in the direction of their being a necessity, it will be realized. Some will say it can't be done. Our answer to that is 'it can be done when we West Virginians realize that our most important asset.'"

Principals of Green Bank High School included the following individuals: W. P. Haught, 1917-19; C.M. Koon, 1919-20; N. Phay Taylor, 1920-23; T. P. Harwood, 1923-32; John O. Roach, 1932-36; Claude A. McMillion, 1936-45; Mack Brooks, Mar.-June 1945; Virgil B. Harris, 1945-70.

Green Bank High School 1950's faculty included: Mr. June Riley, Mr. David Smith, Mr. Raymond Swadley, Miss Minnie Parg, Mr. Allen Stewart, Coach Kenneth Simms, Mr. Warren Blackhurst, Mr. John Michael, Virgil Harris, Principal, Harold Mosser, Dan Wickline.

George R. Triplett graduated as part of the class of 1953. Triplett participated in football from 1950-1952; he quit during the 1951 season after he injured his shoulder. Years later, he discovered that his shoulder had been fractured. Green Bank High School was located 23 miles from Cheat Bridge, Triplett's home.

Story by Don and Judy Cromer, Dan Wickline, Harold Mosser, John Townsend, and Marvin Whetzel: One of Green Bank High School's popular teachers was Mr. Warren E. Blackhurst. He taught English and public speaking, among other subjects. Blackhurst was an avid hunter, fisherman, taxidermist, and the best narrator for the Cass Scenic Railroad. He also habitually reviewed the absentee excuses that students would bring after missing school. He often said that his favorite one came from a Cheat Mountain boy. It seems that George Triplett had missed two days of school during deer hunting season. When Triplett returned to school the next day, Mr. Blackhurst wanted to see his absence excuse. The first excuse read: "Please excuse me from school on Monday so I can deer hunt." The second excuse for Tuesday read: "Please excuse me yesterday because I had to stay home to skin my deer." Skinning a deer probably took about half an hour, and Mr. Blackhurst flatly said the excuse for Tuesday was the best he had ever seen.

Students who were part of the final graduating class in 1970 included the following: Robert Beverage, Betty Brewster, Rebecca Chestnut, Cheryl Colaw, Dottie Colaw, Patrick Coleman, Leonard Collins, Karen Conn, Michael Crist, Clearance Ervine, Fredric Gardener, Linden Good, James Gragg, Barbara Greathouse, Steve Hamed, David Hawkins, Gary Hedrick, Arne Hungerbuhler, Michael Hickson, Sue Ann Kelly, Rosemary Lambert, Sharon Lowe, James McLaughlin, Marilynn McLaughlin, Sidney Moore, Cathay Moyers, Robert Oliver, Debra Poling, Glema Rexrode, Roger Ryder, Charlotte Shears, Larry Sheets, Henry Shinaberry, Wanda Smith, Linda Snyder, Edward Tallman, Linda Taylor, Victoria Taylor, Harold Tyson, William Waybright, and Rhonda Wenger.

Faculty in 1970 included the following: Virgil B. Harris, principal; Donna Hommema, secretary; Harold Brooks, Linda Cassell, Harold Crist, James Hingeley, Rosalind Hingeley, Clisby Kessinger, Minnie Parg, Donna Rountree, David Smith, Peggy Smith, Allen Stewart, Kenneth Vance, Sharon Vance, June Riley, Ernestine Grogg, Ruth Riley, Grace Arbogast, Lousie Butcher, Carole Young, Margaret Offutt, Leona Brown, Mary Brundage, Jo Ann Fromhart, Charles Young, Louis MacKenzie, and Dan Taylor.

Faculty at last graduation of GBHS. Back row: Grey Cassell, Supt. L-R Harold Crist, June Riley, Kenny Vance, James Hingely, Dave Smith. Front row: Virgil Harris, Principal, Rosalind Hingely, Minnie Parg, Donna Pennington, Sharon Vance, Peggy Smith, Harold Brooks.

Included in this photo are the members of Green Bank High School's Faculty.

THE GREEN BANK HIGH SCHOOL MOTTO:

"United we stand. Divided we fall."

First row: Harold Mosser (Coach), Bobby Bennett, Kenneth Shears, William Sutton, Paul Tenney, and Marlin Shears; second row: Donald Grogg, Donald Gum, Sam Falgord, Bruce Bosley, Grey Cassell, Ivan Sutton, Eugene Teter, (Manager); The Golden Eagles enjoyed one of their greatest seasons in basketball, winning 27 in a row before dropping a 42-40 game to Fairview for the state B championship. William Sutton and Bruce Bosley were placed on the all-state tournament team. The team traveled over 2,300 miles and visited in 15 state counties during the season.

First row: Danny Nicely, Ray Galford, Paul Tenney, Ivan Sutton, Grey Cassell, Marlin Shears, Kenneth Shears, Henry Dickenson; *second row*: Mr. Mosser, (Coach), Bruce Bosley, Lloyd Nicely, William Sutton, Harold Lambert, Kenneth Cassell, Charles Bryant, Junior Vandevender, Jerry Crist, Bobbie Bennett, Eugene Teter (Manager); *third row*: Ray Sage, Thomas Tenney, George Triplett, Sam Galford, Howard Slaven, Merlin White, Billy Gainer, Bobby Dill, John Harris, Kirk Kerr. The Golden Eagles enjoyed a successful football season by winning the Northern Greenbrier Valley Championship. They dropped the conference game to Alderson by a 19-18 score. When another season rolled around the familiar faces of Paul Tenney, Grey Cassell, Donald McLaughlin, William Sutton, Marlin Shears, John Hevener, Kenneth Cassell and Lloyd Nicely were missed.

A list of all students who graduated from Green Bank High School can be found on the following pages.

Graduates of
Green Bank High School

CLASS OF 1919

Grace Curry

CLASS OF 1920

Virginia Dare Moomau
Helen Beard
Bertie Beard
Lillian Beard
Lucille Oliver

CLASS OF 1921

Mary Hunter Moomau
Bruce Brown
Lyle McLaughlin
Vesta Sharp
Moro Beard
Thorne Kerr
Leone Oliver
Blanche Patterson
Hallie Bosworth
Rachel Sheets
Carl Friel
Kerth Nottingham
Valera Ervine
Lila Orndorff
Kermit Arbogast

CLASS OF 1922

Hunter Arbogast
Fannie Kerr
Lynne Kerr
Bruce Kerr
Delbert Gillispie
Warren McLaughlin
Dorsey Geiger
Ruth Sutton
Estes Crist
Hallie Arbogast
Delford Sheets

CLASS OF 1923

Linnie Thompson
Robert Eades
Genevieve Orndorff
Martha Phares
Freda Williams
Thelma Conrad
Edgar Shinaberry
Bonnie Beard
Eula Warwick
Violetta Nottingham
Edna Wilfong
Clyde Idleman
Margaret Wood

CLASS OF 1924

Martha Reitz
Beulah Brill
Sylvia Riley
Clyde Cassell
Sylvia Taylor
Colleen Siple
Ida Jackson
Edith Townsend
Flora Phillips
Joy Belle Arbogast
Mabel Arbogast
Wilma Slayton
Effie Moore
Thelma Collins
Sallie Warwick

Mary Phares
Mack Brooks
Verna Siple

CLASS OF 1925

Dolly Hiner
Leta McLaughlin
Marvin McLaughlin
Layke Oliver
Ruth Hamrick
Hazel Tracy
Clara Warwick
Gretchen Williams
Bill Reitz
Hazel Greathouse

CLASS OF 1926

Arnold Frazee
Elizabeth Blackhurst
Fame Shifflett
Kathleen Taylor
Hope Hull
Marie Parg
Minnie Parg
Glen Friel
Harper Cassell
Arnold Wilhide
Virginia Burner
Margaret Wilson
Oran McLaughlin
Wilson Robertson
Roxie Phillips
Violet Phillips
Ethel Burner
Pauline Hughes
Marguerite Imes
Lanty Ervine
Virgil Wenger
Audra Dill
Glen Tracy
Delma Watts
Rella Phillips

CLASS OF 1927

Ruth Wilfong
Eloise Burner
Zoe Kirkpatrick
Olen Hiner
Mary Ervine Gaudineer
Eleanor Kenealy
Mary Frances Clark
Clark Kenealy
Hallie Beard
Paul Burner
Margaret Moulton
Helen Kumm
Bedford Chestnut
Grace Arbogast
Gatrel Gibson
Grace Hamrick
Wallace Robertson
Lona Hiner
Leonard Hoover
Edyth Wooddell
James G. Wilhide
George Kerr
Clarence Gragg
Paul Sutton
William Johnston
Laura McLaughlin
Dora Sutton
Imogene Pritchard
Paul Gum
Mildred Pritchard

CLASS OF 1928

Mary Warwick
Virginia Williams
Warren Blackhurst
Everett Sheets
Mildred Nottingham
Virgil Spencer
Evelyn Kerr
Dallas Livesay
James Bailey
Doris Robertson
Virginia Hiner
Helen Friel
Hazel Hull
Nina Heltzel
Evangeline Sutton
Bessie Mae Frazier
Gary Beverage
Mary Stewart
Gus Riley
Erma Marshall
Pearl Tracy
Thelma Grogg
Aggie Gum
Lyle Shifflett
Lyle Friel

CLASS OF 1929

Harold Blackhurst
Delber Sheets
Earl Bailey
Granville Elliott
Joe Jackson
Annie Moulton
Estelle Crowley
Eleanor Wilson
Mary Wilson
Ann Wenger
Virginia Lambert
Jewell Hudson
Mabel Galford
Sam Clark
June Riley
Beatrice Phillips
Gladys Phillips
Julian Puffenbarger
Dorothy Holland
Martha Hiner
Layke Beard
Margaret Kramer
Beryl Sheets
Elizabeth Bailey

CLASS OF 1930

Bessie Ervine
Dan Friel
Paul Friel
Opal Gillispie
Laura Hannah
Clyde Hoover
Burke Hudson
Hudson Hull
Keith Jennings
Elizabeth Matheny
Margaret Lightner
Joe Kenealy
Merritt McLaughlin
Wilma Nottingham
Elizabeth Oliver
Reva Phillips
Charles Pritchard
Stella Sheets
Alma Siple
Roy Spencer

Leonard Tracy
Ruth Vint
Virgie Wilfong

CLASS OF 1931

Sylvia Arbogast
Woodford Aldridge
Helene Barkley
Homer Blackhurst
Ruby Blackhart
Mildred Clark
Ivan Clarkson
Evelyn Crowley
Alonza James Elliot
Bertha Elliot
Glenna Helmintoller
Mary Hiner
Wilma Hudson
Blanche Kelley
Ruby McNeer Kerr
Clark McCutcheon
Lena McLaughlin
Francis Mogle
Mary Elizabeth Mogle
Gaynelle Orndorff
Alvin Richards
Marie Shifflett
Oscar Slavin
Lowell Snyder
Hazel Spencer
Columbia Talercio
Gladys Taylor
Mildred Watts
Franklin Widney
Louise Wilmoth

CLASS OF 1932

Jesse Browne Beard
Wilma Alice Beard
Marian Agnes Blackhart
John Gordon Boggs
William Lacy Brown
Elmer Davis Burner
James Clarence Burner
Lincoln Charles Burner
Wayne Cassell
Odie George Clarkson
Alice Florence Cover
Katherine Virginia Cover
Anne Louise Greathouse
Alice Hevener Hannah
Roma Gertrude Hoover
Uriah Howard Hevener
Ethel Kathleen Hudson
Harriet Louise Hull
Frances Louise Kenealy
Clifford Monroe Kincaid
Roy Blanine Kirkpatrick
Charles Austin Lightner
Page Maneran Young
Virginia Marie Malcom
Gladys Virginia McLaughlin
Marshall Morgan Matheny
Eloise Virginia Moore
Jesse Howard Moore
Genevieve Moss
Bonnie Lorene Nicholas
Leona Pearle Nicholas
Quinn Link Oldaker
Nellie Frances Perry
Dortha Mae Phillips
Frances Moore Pritchard
Mary Elizabeth Ralston
William Perry Shaw
William Leroy Sheets
Margaret Jeanette Stewart

Thelma Viola Stretch
Hazel Lorena Sutton
Isabel Taylor
Harney Hull Warwick
Yancy Harry Waugh
Elizabeth Hope Wooddell

CLASS OF 1933

Ray W. Arbogast
Minerva Hilma Barkley
George Allen Belcher
Francis Clark Blackhurst
Stuart Carleton Boggs
Kathlyn Fay Brown
Mary Mildred Brown
Faye Eugenia Burner
William Roy Byrd
Sherron Virginia Calhoun
Earl Stuart Cassell
Victor J. Collins
Viola Delores Crowley
Ernestine Adeline Dill
Mary Ellen Eddy
Evelyn Marie Flynn
Georgia Goodsell Frazier
John C. Friel
Mildred Wilson Fuhrman
Layke S. Geiger
Hazel Arlene Gochenour
Marie Zelma Gochenour
Rella Marie Gum
Virginia Lee Guthrie
Richard E. Hamrick
Lanty Woodrow Herold
Doris Marie Hoover
Alice Gwendolyn Jennings
Hazel Maysell Lambert
Samuel Arthur Lancaster
Bruce Eugene Lawton
Lewis E. Lyle
Marjorie Constance McCutcheon
Arling McLaughlin
Georgia McLaughlin
Ernest Newton Moore, Jr.
Robert A. Nickell
Stephen Edward Pritchard
Sara Lee Ralston
Elizabeth Ann Reda
Ivan Lee Riley
Mary Irene Shafer
Ora Danies Sheets
Samuel Fred Spencer
James Hunter Stretch
Ray H. Stuart
Junius R. Summerson
Camille Kathern Talercio
Bettie Gilmor Taylor
Thelma Ruth Taylor
Joseph William Urbanick
Ruby May Waddell
James Hall Wilson, Jr.

CLASS OF 1934

Boyd Hull Beverage
Garnet Leone Beverage
Woodrow Wilson Burner
Letitia Pearl Buterbaugh
Willa Mary Colaw
James Phillip Cook
Nina Gertrude Corbett
George Alexander Duncan
Harry Earl Duncan
Mary Delia Ervine
Ethel Rae Eye
Marjorie Eloise Fuhrman
Helen Geraldine Galford
Obed Lee Gochenour
Evelyn Dice Herold
Richard Neil Hevener
Louise Elizabeth Jennings
Mabel Alexis Kincaid
Marguerite Virginia Kisner
Martha Sue Elizabeth Kramer
Raymond R. McNickel
Edward James Moore, Jr.
Marie Katy Mullenax
Audrey Myrl Nottingham
Ray W. Orndorff
Delbert Dale Phillips
Mildred Bessie Phillips
Richard Wayne Porter
Edna Louise Richards
Kenna Ford Rexrode
Mary Madeline Slavin

Ralph Vincent Snyder
Vergie Grace Spencer
Kenneth N. Taylor
Carl Winfred Wright
Stella Mae Yates
Ben McNeil Yeager

CLASS OF 1935

Molly Anderson
Isabel Auldridge
Ruth Beard
Dora Beard
Earl Foster Beverage
Woodrow Wilson Beverage
James M. Moyer
May Blackhurst
Albert Uhlan Burr
Cleo Cassell
Paul Hunter Collins
Virginia Campbell
Evelyn Dill
Grant Eddy
Edwin Lee Galford
Ruth Gray
Leonard James Goodsell
William Ray Gillispie
Wilbur Byron Gochenour
William H. Gillispie
Lena Gumm
Luther Whitman Hull
John Forest Hughes
Samuel Baldwin Hannah
George V. Hannah, Jr.
Elizabeth Hannah
Edna Hevener
Bertie Lee Huff
Violet Hoover
Crystal Houchin
John M. Hiner
Margaret Louise Ervine
Martha Judy
Maggie Lantz
Hildagarde Leader
Alma Mae Miller
Clifford Moss
Stella McFerrin
Dorothy McLaughlin
Lewis Michael
Chadwick H. Pritchard
William C. Plyler
Olive Ratliff
Merle Rexrode
Eleanor Rhea
Pearl Spencer
Thelma Swink
Emogene Swisher
Theodore W. Slavin
Wanita Sheets
Lena Stewart
Rudolph Urbanick
Harry Junior Widney
Katherine Wright
Eunice Wiley

CLASS OF 1936

Pershing Arbogast
Ward Ashford
Harry Banton
Earl Belcher
John Bosley
Phyllis Buterbaugh
Eldon Campbell
Lucille Cassell
Ralph Cassell
Glenna Clarkson
Alfred Collins
Dale Collins
Paul Collins
Paul Cobb
Beatrice Cromer
Virginia Cromer
Clyde Crowley
Audra Curry
Ruth Flynn
Doris Fuhrman
Ralph Gillispie
Jean Griffeth
Ruth Hannah
Sarah Hannah
Virginia Houchin
Paul Hudson
Nellie Judy
Wilbur Kenealy
Geraldine Kisner
Edna Lambert

Robert Nottingham
Eloise Orndorff
Woodsie Ratliff
Mary Ruth Richards
Joe Riley
Violet Ryder
Hildreth Sheets
Phillip Sheets
Chester Shrader
Allene Shumate
Evelyn Lee Slavin
Norman Smith
Bernice Sutton
Keith Thompson
William Viering
James Williams
Helen Wimer
Rachael Noel

CLASS OF 1937

Anna Mae Ashford
Dexter Auldridge
Elizabeth Beard
Ethel Mae Bennett
Wallace Beverage
Eva Bowling
Grace Brown
Eugene Burner
Elmer Cooke
Nellie Cover
Celia Cromer
Marvin Dill
Virginia Gragg
Clyde Hamrick
Dorothy Jean Herold
Tommy Herold
Milly Lee Hevener
Ethel Jennings
Ada Kramer
Neil Nottingham
Drexler Oldaker
Eugene Puffenbarger
Betty Ellen Pritchard
Earl Ralston
Victor Reda
Pearle Ryder
Nell Smith
Doris Snyder
Richard Sutton
Adam Talercio
Raymond Tracy
Wardell Wooddell
Delores Wright
Mary Wiley
James Wiley
Kathleen Young
Timie Young

CLASS OF 1938

Clara Jane Wooddell
Harry Lee Blackhurst
Pauline Gray Barkley
Kerth McCoy Friel
Edith Louise Collins
Harmon Wilson McLaughlin
Fannie Ruth Spencer
Howard R. Lewis
Naomi Virginia Slaven
Ernest Raleigh Smith
Catherine Blackhurst
Fred Lawrence
Mary Frances Beverage
Earl Kenton Slavin
Abbie Grace Ryder
William Hevener Hannah
Margaret Mae Gum
Ward William Crowley
Nadine Anna Edy
Robert S. Williams
Mary Ann McCutcheon
Nancy Virginia Wilson
William Adair Moyer
Jeanette Bible
Wallace Arlie Galford
Alma Ann Cromer
Jacob C. Sheets
Woodsie Ellen Eliott
Marion Gray Cramer
Nora Letha Collins
Louise Reda
Goldie Ruth Hevener
Neil Loraine Beard
Mary Ellen Bradley
Virginia Gray Gum
Dolly June Houchin

Rockford N. Hamed
Katherine Frances Talercio
Edward Brown Smith
Ruth Madeline Rexrode
Ben M. Hiner

CLASS OF 1939

Kathleen Cassell
Thurlene Cassell
Jean Conrad
Lucille Meeks
Iva Murphy
Jean McCutcheon
Bertina O'Brien
Kathleen Potter
Helen Puffenbarger
Frances Seiler
Maydelle Shinnaberry
Geraldine Taylor
David Auldridge
Frank Collins
Woodrow Corbett
Harry B. Hill
Harold Kessler
James Mack
Brooks Mullenax
Tim Pharr
Thurman Sheets
Albin Urbanick
Bobby Wooddell
Lacy Walton
Zula Barkley
Joyce Brown
Evelyn Hickman
Woodsie Elliot
Hazel Gillispie
Jewel Orndorff
Alma Phillips
Nola Propst
Mary Helen Riley
Emma Simmons
Ethel Taylor
Dorothy Wimer
Steryle Brown
Howard Cassell
Sammie Jennings
Albert Kirkpatrick
Arnold Porter
Orville Sheets
Paul Simmons
Edward Smith
Bill Steward
Lake Swink
Earl Wood

CLASS OF 1940

Mildred Lorranine Keyser
William Dane Irvine
Marie Lane Dill
William Jackson Fuhrman
Evelyn Irene Fox
Earl Lee Houchin
Harry Eris Wooddell
Frederick Carter Pritchard
Madge Jewell McPherson
John Howard McCutcheon
Helen Mae Slaven
Donald Eugene Slayton
Mable Gertrude Sheets
Harold Hannah Gum
Katherine Jane Rexrode
Jarrett Hunter Crowley
Gayle Marie Cassell
Maxwell Moomau Shinaberry
Mary Helen Riley
Delbert Fenton Lambert
Rosa Sinclair Hendley
Carl Theodore Rosburg
Martha Ethel Hendley
Lloyd E. Kisner, Jr.
Lois Dare Nottingham
Boyd Ray Cassell
Nellie Virginia Gabbert
Geneva Cloe Shiflett
Jack McCauley
James Junior Snyder
Beulah Galford
Roy Dale Cassell
Martha Mae Grogg
Norman Andrew Miller
Nellie Elizabeth Lewis
Russell Monroe Clarkson
Twila Marie Calhoun
Calvin Paul Spenser
Dessie Gertrude Stamper

Merle Muston McLaughlin
Helen Irene Nelson
Clarence Dale Stone
Irene Dare Crist
Harold Lee Nickell
Bessie Catherine Beverage
Leonard Collins
Opal Freeman
Edward L. Freeman, Jr.
Clarence Rockford Ervine
Samuel Jennings
Gay Cameron Sheets
Lake Swink
Donald Beard

CLASS OF 1941

Margaret Lee Arbogast
Beatrice Bessie Blackhurst
William Franklin Ashford
Jack Wilson Banton
Marvin McNeil Bennett
Harold Edward Byrd
Louise Brown
Mary Margaret Beard
Jessie Pearl Brown
Anna Elizabeth Burner
Juanita Pearl Carder
Bernard Lee Carder
Guy Reed Cassell
Janet Evon Cassell
Thelda Cassell
Francis Gray Conrad
Anna Mae Friel
Roscoe Dennis Fitzgerald
Marvin Lee Fowler
Bertha Louise Gum
Martha Grace Gum
Leonard Dendly Galford
A. C. Hill
Dewey J. Hiner
Samuel Frank Talercio
Russell P. Tallman
Anna Lee Tracy
Ella Victoria Vanosdale
Hazel Marie Warner
Howard Conwell Wilfong
Junior White
Dorothy Jane Harouff
Jack Hoover
Sylvia Lee Hudson
Moreau A. Keller
Lucille Marie Kincaid
Kathleen Virginia Kramer
Ruth Margaret Lawrence
Virgil Lambert
Wallace G. Lightner
Mary Florence Matheny
Jacob Kenneth Mauzy
Robert Monroe Myers
Charles Boyc Meek
Gladys Gertrude Mick
Leta Mae McLaughlin
Joan Isabel Pritchard
Clarence McLaughlin
Stella Agnes Rose
Raymond Hull Slaven
James Richard Snyder
Mary Virginia Spinoe
Everett Henry Shrader
Jamie Asbury Sheets
Jessy Warren Shiflett
John William Melbourne Shinaberry

CLASS OF 1942

Nellie Burner
Marilee Campbell
Thelma Pugh
Geneva Sheets
Ruth Vandevander
Alline Brown
Mary Hunter Lantz
Mary Frances Tallman
Betty Wooddell
Mary Emma Smith
John Townsend
Izetta McCauly
Mary Lee Davidson
Ruth Viola Wilfong
Ruby Lee Wood
Dallas Propst
Helen Louise Filuta
Mary Talercio
Bernice Ellen Hamed
Bertha Gregory
Albert Simmons

Sterl Lee Vandevander
Ruth Adell Simmons
Susan Sheets
Jack Kane
Odessa Lee Barkley
Robert Fox
Gene Keyser
Tom Houchin
Alice Cassell
Jerry Cassell
Mary Eunice Simmons
Emil Grogg
Audra Ruth Friel
Allen Stewart
Ernest Hamrick
Robert Gillispie
Mildred Potter
F. Clyde Simmons
Grace Wilfong
Edwin Rexrode
Mary Frances Swink
William Kisner
Mary Archer Hannah
Jim Taylor
Annie Sara Hannah
Jack Phillips
Alma Cassell
Ray Dahmer
Katherine Mary Fuhrman
Garland Smith
Jane Sheets
Edwin Burton Kincaid
Norma Viola Slaven
William Donald Watts
Jerry Gray
Mabel Dare Bostic
June Wilfong
Imogene Duskey
Robert Wooddell
Martha Dahmer

CLASS OF 1943

Alice Jane Ruth Arbogast
Mary Elizabeth Arbogast
Mabel Hull Banton
Ethel Marie Brown
William Delbert Cassell
Dorothy Dale Cooper
Kizel Willard Craddock
Harold Crist
Ruby Gray Deputy
Bernard Porterfield Galford
Gertrude Manda Galford
Harper Hudson Galford
Raymond Galford
Permilla Good
Anna Margaret Gum
Harold Gustafson
Lois Isabel Hiner
Ruby Susan Houchin
Sarah Belle Hughes
George Heltzel Hull
Mary Hunter Kane
Pauline Mae Kisner
Delford Brison Lambert
Fred William Lantz
Mary Virginia Leader
Braunda Lee Matheny
James May
James Michael
Carol Mullenax
Robert Daniel McCutcheon
Mary Hunter McLaughlin
Norma Hunter
Mary Pezzuli
Thomas Edward Pritchard
Ralph Rader
Lanty Dale Ryder
Henrietta Susan Sharp
Rowena Alice Sheets
Marshall Grey Shinaberry
Maxine Thelma Shinaberry
Lucille Blanche Simmons
William Robert Simmons
Kathleen Lucille Snyder
Stella Esther Sponaugle
Rhoda Lucretia Summerfield
Paul Archie Townsend
Ivan Grey Vandevander
Maggie Jane Wimer
Robert Newton Woods

CLASS OF 1944

Virginia Lee Hevener
Wanda Lee Robertson

Margaret Hughes
Bertha Hoover
Gertrude Moss
Crystal Gum
Allene Kesler
Meredith Lightner
Beatrice Cassell
Norma Swink
Myrtle Gillispie
Peggy Crist
Betty Lou Delung
Margaret Eary
Bessie Brown
Billie Arbogast
Ruth Talercio
Maxine Fisher
Ruth Blackhurst
Agnes Phillips
Mary Catherine Burner
Susan Porter
Hazel Rexrode
Audra Rexrode
Pauline Campbell
Neil Simmons
Charles Wimer
Roy Clarkson
Carroll Oldaker
Albert Vint
Eugene Leaders
Betty Elliott
Ruby Hill
Mary Louise Moore
Jessie Robertson
Anna Sue Fuhrman
Pauline White

CLASS OF 1945

Dallas Buterbaugh
Anna Plyer
Catherine Sheets
Annabelle Brown
Jewell Sutton
Berdeen Simmons
Mary Etta Nelson
Ruby Gum
Carol Conrad
Betty Conley
Evelyn Galford
Marilee Ryder
Alice Vandevander
Louise Gillispie
Gaynelle Rexrode
Lucille Stewart
Dorotha Grogg
Helen Moats
Roberta Jane Hiner
Betty Jo Riley
Twila Shinaberry
Thomas Moore
Ernest Sampson
Harold Ryder
Paul Wilmoth
Albert Wilfong
Lewis Keller
James Kramer
Charles McElwee
Carl Beverage
Dewey Hickman
Leonard Curry
Mary Hunter Gum
Maydell Turner
Maxine Foe
Ruth Vance
Norman Dickenson
Robert Fuhrman
Neil Hill
Roy Nickell
William Zopp
William Mullenax
Henry Cummins

CLASS OF 1946

Jimmy Pritchard
Stanley Shears
Gertrude Cales
Faye Swink
Emma Galford
Beulah Dahmer
Walter Lee Ralston, Jr.
Robert Brown
William Townsend
Pauline Dahmer
Harold Wooddell
Al Smith McCutcheon
Virginia Townsend

Mary Margarett Deputy
Julia Fisher
Ruth Margaret Beverage
Joel Hannah
Jolene McLaughlin
Ellen Taylor
Peggy Wanless
Iola Rexrode
Dorothy Lee Mick
Melvina Sheets
Elaine Wilfong
Ernestine VanDevander
Sadie Nelson
Franklin Noel
Amil Ervin
Peggy Wagner
Rebecca Moyers
Naomi Sutton
Norman Sheets
Ernestine Shinaberry
Thelma Vance
Ida Gaye Hiner
Ruth Nelson
Russell Gabbert, Jr.
Bertha Lee Dill
Henrietta Ralston
Charles Lindberg Houchin
Jeanne Cover Rader
Joanne Cover Kane
Helen Arbogast
Gertrude Crover McDannels
Marian Tracy

CLASS OF 1947

Alice Marie Sutton
George H. Harris
Blanche Evelyn Hamed
Donald Shears
Eula Mae Taylor
Earl Delung
Betty Galford Kennison
Julian Maxwell Gum
Norma Gragg
Robert McQuain
Audrea Katherine Sheets
Neil Gragg
Leah Estelle Duckworth
Arlie Ryder
Norma Lee Arbogast
Troy Steiner Moore
Mary Jo White
Edwin Doyle
Doris Elizabeth Simmons
L. E. Campbell
Betty Dare Brown
Bonnie Dell Pugh
Dorothy Louise Campbell
Goldie Mae Slavins
Pearl Lucinda Runkin
Russell Cassell
Monna Bell Vandevander
Robert Eades, Jr.
Jeanne Tenney
Hubert Hoover Rexrode
Cornelia Hart Bennett
Kenneth Duskey
Mary Gatha Gum
Samuel Robert Wagner
Cora Sue McElwee
Lewis Shinaberry

CLASS OF 1948

Helen Tracy
Julian Tracy
Junior Mahaffey
Mary Dare Hedrick
Mary Edna Wimer
Berlin Galford
Virgil B. Harris, Jr.
Louise Virginia Mullenax
Betty Ruth Conrad
John Edward Slaven
James Wooddell
Bonnie Louise Sheets
Joyce Mick
Richard Snyder
Robert Greathouse
Martha Jean Campbell
Freda Aretta Rexrode
Blake Breitenhart
Gene Crist
William Halterman
Louise Shears
Mary Alverta Taylor
Leon Ryder

Julian McLaughlin
Irene Miller
Lorene Shears
Reon Lambert
Archie Wilfong
Nellie Simmons
Geraldine Mae Gum
Evelyn Helen Taylor
George Jr. Cromer
Myra Maxine Cassell
Nelva Marie Simmons
Mary Louise Wilfong
Elouise Marie Lambert
Helen Pearl Mullenax
Roberta Jeanne Sheets

CLASS OF 1949

Patricia McPherson
Gertrude Blackhurst
Maxine Vandevander
Hubert Taylor
Jeanette Rankin
Jack Moore
Kathleen Ryder
Arnold Galford
Anita Buterbaugh
Paul Kessler
Delores Nottingham
Roy McLaughlin
Mary Miller
William Arbogast
Mildred Chapel
Allen Sheets
Dollie Galford
Robert Waugh
Betty Grimes
Laurence Taylor, Jr.
Peggy Taylor
Luster Simmons
Moni Tracy
Gay Wright
Betty Orndorff
James Nottingham
Mildred Michael
Arlie Rexrode
Amy Riley
Hubert Gillispie Conrad
Clara Mae Sutton
William Sutton
Mary Evelyn Campbell
John Ralston
Thelma Varner
Albert Law Tenney
Eleanor Shields
Robert Cumin
Shirley Simmons
Gale Shinnaberry
Joyce Hamrick
Leonard Meador
Zane Taylor
David Gragg
Mary Arleen Curry
James Plyler
James Shores
George Kane

CLASS OF 1950

Mary Alice Alderman
Sarah Jane Arbogast
Hazel Marie Brewster
William Wilson Brock
Neal Kenneth Cassell
Lawson Lee Cassell
Ruby Anderson Cornette
Clara Dahmer
Juanita Virginia Dahmer
Dorothy Mae Dickenson
Hanley Ward Ervin
Gloria Dean Eye
Ella Sabins Freeman
Franklin D. Hamrick
Nancy Jean Harris
Evelyn Sue Hertig
Estell E. Hickman
Edsel Lee Hiner
William Leo Judy
Jolene Dare Kerr
Sudie Frances Lambert
Dallas Louise May
Martha Ellen McCutcheon
Gerald Dale McLaughlin
Donald B. Meeks
Calvin Keith Meeks
Edward Lee Meeks
Anna Lee Miller

Edna Lee Miller
Ruby Vandevander Mullenax
George William Pyler
Carolyn Louise Ryder
Jerry Clark Shears
James Frederick Sheets
Alice Jessie Simmons
Robert Lee Simmons
Virginia Dare Snyder
Helen Pearl Snyder
Betty June Sutton
Helen Jane Taylor

CLASS OF 1951

John Brown
Grey Cassell
Kenneth Cassell
Virginia Shephard
Eleanor Snyder
Steve Barnasky
Ray Grogg
Robert Wilfong
Daisy Rexrode Wright
Barbara Howe
Betty Sheets
Katherine Simmons
Joe Wilfong
Audrey Kessler
Anna Lee Murphy
Peggy Lynn Shores
Lawrence Shifflett
Faye Turner Swink
Richard Nottingham
Lloyd Nicely
Frank Collins
Eugene Dilly
Lilly Belle Moore
Henry Dickenson
Evelyn Hevener Beverage
Velma Stanley
William Sutton
Marlin Shears
Betty Grogg
Wanda Tracy
Twila Wenger
Mary Wilfong
Patsy Elbon
Roxie Galford Moore
Dicel Hoover
Donald McLaughlin
Joanne Rose
Paul Tenny
Betty Lowe
Billy Waugh
Millie Ryder
Jo Betty Pritchard
Boyd Wright
Elaine Peck
Dorsey Mouts

CLASS OF 1952

Bobbie Bennett
Mary Barnasky
Bruce Bosley
Dixie Beard
Charles Collins
Shirley Brubaker
Marion Currence
Linda Cassell
Ray Galford
Mary Cassell
James Gragg
Mary Frances Chestnut
June Higgins
Fay Collins
Merle Moore
Barbara Conrad
Richard Meador
June Crist
Danny Nicely
Shirley Downey
Franklin Rankin
Mary Dare Doyle
Charles Rexrode
Wanda Gabbert
James Rexrode
Margaret Galford
Samuel Ryder
Alice Gillespie
Kenneth Shears
Yvonne Gilmore
Douglas Simmons
Gaynell Grimes
James Simmons
Jenny Harris

Zane Simmons
Helen Jackson
Billy Terry
Barbara Keys
Lester Waybright
Wilda May
Harold Wilfong
Anna Mae Moore
Merle Kerr
Bonnie Mullenax
Florene Nottingham
Sue Sawyers
Leota Shields
Margaret Shiflett
Louise Taylor
Eva Varner
Elizabeth Mace

CLASS OF 1953

Betty Bennett
Frances Brewster
Charlotte Cassell
Julia Curry
Janet Gainer
Thelma Hoover
Mildred Lambert
Shirley Murphy
Elva June Phillips
Bonnie Rankin
Gladie Sampson
Margaret Slaven
Imogene Snyder
Betty Lou Tacy
Jean Taylor
Naomi Wenger
Delorsie Wright
Charles Brock
Charles Bryant
Jerry Crist
Robert Dill
William Gainer
Calvin Galford
Julian Gillispie
Jack Gragg
Donald Grogg
Donald Gum
Donald Lambert
Lewis Mace
Eugene Nelson
Julian Nottingham
Charles D. Ryder
Jimmie Ryder
Ray Lewis Sage, Jr.
Edward Simmons
Howard Slaven
Ivan Clark Sutton
Lyle Taylor
George Triplett
Junior Vandevander
Robert Ware

CLASS OF 1954

Barbara Blackhurst
Donna Brubaker
Mary Ann Cassell
Phyllis Greathouse
Jean Gum
Patricia Hall
Nancy Judy
Jane McLaughlin
Rachel McCutcheon
Phyllis Myers
Nancy Nicholas
Patricia Nottingham
Barbara Nottingham
Shirley Peck
Wilma Riley
Jane Russell
Dorene Simmons
Betty Simmons
Delores Snyder
Doris Snyder
Barbara Taylor
Gladys Turner
Margaret Vint
Connie Wilfong
Eleanor Wymer
Betty Young
Joe Baylor
John Beard
Leonard Beverage
Billy Joe Chestnut
Howard Collins
James K. Dickenson

Alfred Ervin
Kent Galford, Jr.
William Galford
Ronald Gladden
Robert Vance
Forrest Grogg
Hunter Hamrick
John Harris
Paul Hiner
Kirk Kerr
Gary McPherson
George Moore
Robert Neighbors
Frank Nelson
William Orndorff
George Pritchard
Delbert Rexrode
Charles Sheets
Warren Slavens
Alfred Sutton
Elbert Whanger
Jennings Wright
Donald Yates

CLASS OF 1955

Joyce Arbogast
Carrie Arbogast
Jo Ann Bennett
Hope Bolton
Monota Carpenter
Colleen Dill
Nancy Gillispie
Mildred Greathouse
Barbara Gum
Doris Hamrick
Letha Harper
Ella Nora Hill
Alice Hively
Violet Hoover
Connie Johnson
Dorothy Lambert
Evelyn Mace
Doris McLaughlin
Katherine Mullenax
Georgia Puffenbarger
Betty Rexrode
Peggy Sheets
Mary Jean Simmons
Patty Simmons
Barbara Slaven
Louise Tallman
Lorene Thomas
Betty Thompson
Carma Wenger
Lois Wooddell
Carol Wright
Roy Carpenter
Johnny Cassell
Donald Cromer
Phillip Davis
Rodney Gainer
Calvin Galford
Thomas Wyatt
Ralph Geiger
Blair Gragg
Charles Gray
George Hoover
Gene Kesler
Brown Meeks
Edward Monk
Allen Moore
Marvin Moss
Donald Mullenax
Harold Neighbors
Allen Nottingham
Donald Nottingham
James Oliver
Virgil Summerfield
James Sutton
Lyndell Sutton
Benjamin Taylor
Jerry Taylor
Keith Tracy
Franklin Vandevander
Homer Varner

CLASS OF 1956

Emory Wyatt
Helen Brown
Ruth Collins
Georgia Curry
Charlotte Dahmer

Ruth Ann Grogg
Maxine Harman
Colleen Hughes
Nancy Jackson
Mona Kelley
Gladys Lambert
Jean Lambert
Shirley Lambert
Cora Lee McLaughlin
Sylvia Moore
Evyleen Murphy
Betty Nelson
Mary Ellen Nicely
Phyllis Purkey
Ruth Rankin
Joyce Rexrode
Anna Belle Sheets
Bessie Simmons
Mary Simmons
Caroline Tacy
Sue Ellen Taylor
Peggy Tharp
Betty Vance
Nancy Wenger
Nancy Wilfong
Lyndell Brooks
Bob Brubaker
Brown Cassell
Kyle Cassell
David Cromer
Ben Elbon
Richard Galford
Ronald Gray
George Jackson
William Jackson
William Jordan
Jerry Long
Ronald Monk
Dale Mullenax
Terry Sage
James Sheets
Wayne Sheets
Donald Starcher
George Tallman
Kenneth Tallman
David Tyson
William Vandevander

CLASS OF 1957

Patsy Burner
Carolyn Carpenter
Betty Cook
Elouise Curry
Sue Ervin
Carol Galford
Retha Galford
Mary Geiger
Sandra Hevener
Judy McLaughlin
Helen Mullenax
Bonnie Moore
Dolly Nelson
Elouise Nicholas
Frances Nicholas
Betty Oliver
Carol Oliver
Glenda Phillips
Georgia Rexrode
Jackie Rexrode
Mary Ryder
Lilly Sharp
Janet Tallman
Betty Lou Taylor
Thelma Vannoy
Jennie Weber
Mary Margaret Wooddell
Ronnie Arbogast
Martin Barkley
Russell Burris
Grover Craddock
Chester Cromer
John Gainer
Tom Gainer
John Gillispie
Ben Gragg
Philmore Kerr
David Nelson
Allen Mahaffey
Charles Peck
Carl Pennington
Thurman Sampson
James Simmons
Eddie Sheets
Samuel Tyson
Elmer Workman
Joyce Waybright

CLASS OF 1958

Beverly Arbogast
Louise Barkley
Gwendolyn Blackhurst
Mary Pat Brown
Jean Clarkson
Linda Dickenson
Robertine Gilmore
Linda Greathouse
Betty Gum
Connie Hamrick
Judy Hedrick
Patricia Hefner
Patty Hoover
Marsha Neighbors
Nancy Nottingham
Shirley Orndorff
Roberta Rankin
Helen Ray
Geraldine Rexrode
Jonette Sampson
Nancy Sampson
Alma Simmons
Nancy Simmons
Evelyn Tallman
Sarah Tyson
Earlene Wilfong
Autry Arbogast
John Bosley
Thomas Burner
Jack Cassell
Gary Davis
Donald Day
Carl Feather
Robert Jackson
Ernest McLaughlin
Kenneth McLaughlin
Boyd Myers
Kermit Nottingham
Gene Tallman
Donald Waybright
Earl Wayne Wenger
Julian Whanger

CLASS OF 1959

Arthea Bradley
Doris Brubaker
Chester Cassell
Delmer Cassell
Juanita Cassell
Thelma Collins
William Cox
Barbara Cromer
Gilbert Dahmer
Carolyn Davis
Eugene Davis
Rodney Doyle
William Elliott
William Ervin
Bertha Galford
Claude Gaujot
Sterle Gillispie
Carol Greathouse
Mulvie Grimes
Nancy Howdyshell
Connie Lambert
Doris Lambert
Lonnie Lambert
Lowell Lambert
Charles Matheny
Eddie McLaughlin
Alice Meeks
Charles Moore
Donald Moore
Lelia Moore
Ralph Moore
Wendell Monk
Freddie Moss
Barbara Myers
Helen Nelson
Ruby Nelson
Carolyn Nottingham
Carol Nottingham
Geraldine Nottingham
Clark Phillips, Jr.
Linda Purkey
Edward Riley
Molly Russell
Warren Shears
Charles Sheets
Rose Marie Sheets
Allen Shiflett
Barbara Simmons
Iona Starks
Marvin Tallman

Ralph Taylor
Daniel Tyson
Kenneth Vance
John Vandevander
Robert Vandevander
Clark Wooddell
Theodore Taylor

CLASS OF 1960

Nellie Arbogast
Bessie Campbell
Jewel Cosner
Shelva Galford
Betty Gragg
Linda Grimes
Marie Greathouse
Frances Helmick
Dallas Hill
Judy Howdyshell
Thelma Lambert
Joyce McLaughlin
Shirley McLaughlin
Ester Moore
Marcia Moore
Violet Murphy
Linda Mullenax
Jo Ann Nicholas
Phyllis Oliver
Kay Patterson
Maxine Rexrode
Carol Richmond
Jo Ann Rowe
Mary Seabolt
Mary F. Sheets
Lois Simmons
Shelia Slavens
Dollie Waybright
Julia Waybright
Patricia Wilfong
Mary F. Young
James Arbogast
Lyle Brooks
Walter Byrd
Thomas Carpenter
Franklin Curry
David Gainer
John Galford
Roger Galford
James Geiger
Gary Tallman
Buddy Gragg
Ivan Dale Greathouse
Richard Hedrick
Joseph Jackson
Delmas Mullenax
William Nelson
William Nottingham
James Rexrode
Wallace Shears
Larry Sutton
Earl Ware
Julian Ware
Dharl Wilfong
Norman Winans

CLASS OF 1961

Bonnie Arbogast
Bonnie Kaye Beard
Agnes Grey Beverage
Ruth Ann Burner
James William Carpenter
Danieth Ruth Coleman
Carol Dee Collins
George Franklin Collins
Linda Karen Collins
Rebecca Jean Collins
Jarrett Hunter Crowley
Terry Lee DeHaven
Amanda Lou Doyle
Charlotte Carole Elza
Juanita Grace Ervin
James Francis Findley
Gayle Maxine Galford
Ruth Emma Gaylor
Patricia Matthews Hevener
Dreama Elaine Lambert
Beulah May McLaughlin
Robert Elburn Moore
Steven Robert Moore
Howard Newton Mullenax
Isaac Lee Myers
Margaret Chloe Nelson
James Arthur Prater
Nina Lee Rankin
Martha Louise Sheets
William Lee Sheets
Eileen Dorothy Sutton
David Swecker
Barbara Ann Taylor
Wanda Jane Taylor
Cleveland Edward Tyson
Marilyn Davis Whanger
Danny James Wilfong
Edward Arnold Wyatt

CLASS OF 1962

James T. Arbogast
Charlotte Beverage
Rebecca Blackhurst
Chester L. Blanchard
Ray Allen Byrd
Arthur Collins
Edith Cosner
Janet Cox
Jane Davis
Pauline Dickenson
James Galford
Wayne Galford
Nadine Gillispie
Judith Gragg
Marvin Grogg
Jean Helmick
Timothy Hevener
Patricia Horner
Charles Jackson
John W. Moats
Douglas Monk
Arthur Mullenax
Franklin Murphy
Madeline Myers
John Henry Nelson
Carol Orndorff
Sandra Rowe
Willard Shears
Barbara Simmons
Norma Simmons
Loretta Swecker
Judith Tacy
Harlan R. Tallman
Doris Turner
Dallas Vannoy
Margaret White
Delores Wilfong
Mary Wilfong
Lamar Wooddell
Roy Workman, Jr.
Robert Young

CLASS OF 1963

Keith Brown
Gary Coleman
Neven Elza
Lloyd Foe
Judy Gainer
Carol Gardner
Wayne Gillispie
Larry Greathouse
Deborah Harker
Patty Howdyshell
Mary Johnson
Donna McCutcheon
Joan Monk
Helen Moore
David Mullenax
Karen Mullenax
Bonnie Peck
Sandra Rankin
Rebecca Sheets
John Simmons
Lyle Tallman
Robert Ware
Donald Wenger
Lewis Wilmoth
Judith Wyatt

CLASS OF 1964

Harry Russell Aldridge
Charles Edwin Brewster
George Forrest Brewster
Harold Wayne Brooks
Lucy Brown
David Joe Cain
Roger Cain
Peggy Campbell
Jane Carpenter
Shelby Cassell
Donald Darrell Crews
Sandra Curry

Ruth Ann Grogg
Maxine Harman
Colleen Hughes
Nancy Jackson
Mona Kelley
Gladys Lambert
Jean Lambert
Shirley Lambert
Cora Lee McLaughlin
Sylvia Moore
Evyleen Murphy
Betty Nelson
Mary Ellen Nicely
Phyllis Purkey
Ruth Rankin
Joyce Rexrode
Anna Belle Sheets
Bessie Simmons
Mary Simmons
Caroline Tacy
Sue Ellen Taylor
Peggy Tharp
Betty Vance
Nancy Wenger
Nancy Wilfong
Lyndell Brooks
Bob Brubaker
Brown Cassell
Kyle Cassell
David Cromer
Ben Elbon
Richard Galford
Ronald Gray
George Jackson
William Jackson
William Jordan
Jerry Long
Ronald Monk
Dale Mullenax
Terry Sagv
James Sheets
Wayne Sheets
Donald Starcher
George Tallman
Kenneth Tallman
David Tyson
William Vandevander

CLASS OF 1957

Patsy Burner
Carolyn Carpenter
Betty Cook
Elouise Curry
Sue Ervin
Carol Galford
Retha Galford
Mary Geiger
Sandra Hevener
Judy McLaughlin
Helen Mullenax
Bonnie Moore
Dolly Nelson
Elouise Nicholas
Frances Nicholas
Betty Oliver
Carol Oliver
Glenda Phillips
Georgia Rexrode
Jackie Rexrode
Mary Ryder
Lilly Sharp
Janet Tallman
Betty Lou Taylor
Thelma Vannoy
Jennie Weber
Mary Margaret Wooddell
Ronnie Arbogast
Martin Barkley
Russell Burris
Grover Craddock
Chester Cromer
John Gainer
Tom Gainer
John Gillispie
Ben Gragg
Philmore Kerr
David Nelson
Allen Mahaffey
Charles Peck
Carl Pennington
Thurman Sampson
James Simmons
Eddie Sheets
Samuel Tyson
Elmer Workman
Joyce Waybright

CLASS OF 1958

Beverly Arbogast
Louise Barkley
Gwendolyn Blackhurst
Mary Pat Brown
Jean Clarkson
Linda Dickenson
Robertine Gilmore
Linda Greathouse
Betty Gum
Connie Hamrick
Judy Hedrick
Patricia Hefner
Patty Hoover
Marsha Neighbors
Nancy Nottingham
Shirley Orndorff
Roberta Rankin
Helen Ray
Geraldine Rexrode
Jonette Sampson
Nancy Sampson
Alma Simmons
Nancy Simmons
Evelyn Tallman
Sarah Tyson
Earlene Wilfong
Autry Arbogast
John Bosley
Thomas Burner
Jack Cassell
Gary Davis
Donald Day
Carl Feather
Robert Jackson
Ernest McLaughlin
Kenneth McLaughlin
Boyd Myers
Kermit Nottingham
Gene Tallman
Donald Waybright
Earl Wayne Wenger
Julian Whanger

CLASS OF 1959

Arthea Bradley
Doris Brubaker
Chester Cassell
Delnor Cassell
Juanita Cassell
Thelma Collins
William Cox
Barbara Cromer
Gilbert Dahmer
Carolyn Davis
Eugene Davis
Rodney Doyle
William Elliott
William Ervin
Bertha Galford
Claude Gaujot
Sterle Gillispie
Carol Greathouse
Mulvie Grimes
Nancy Howdyshell
Connie Lambert
Doris Lambert
Lonnie Lambert
Lowell Lambert
Charles Matheny
Eddie McLaughlin
Alice Meeks
Charles Moore
Donald Moore
Lelia Moore
Ralph Moore
Wendell Monk
Freddie Moss
Barbara Myers
Helen Nelson
Ruby Nelson
Carolyn Nottingham
Carol Nottingham
Geraldine Nottingham
Clark Phillips, Jr.
Linda Purkey
Edward Riley
Molly Russell
Warren Shears
Charles Sheets
Rose Marie Sheets
Allen Shiflett
Barbara Simmons
Iona Starks
Marvin Tallman

Ralph Taylor
Daniel Tyson
Kenneth Vance
John Vandevander
Robert Vandevander
Clark Wooddell
Theodore Taylor .

CLASS OF 1960

Nellie Arbogast
Bessie Campbell
Jewel Cosner
Shelva Galford
Betty Gragg
Linda Grimes
Marie Greathouse
Frances Helmick
Dallas Hill
Judy Howdyshell
Thelma Lambert
Joyce McLaughlin
Shirley McLaughlin
Ester Moore
Marcia Moore
Violet Murphy
Linda Mullenax
Jo Ann Nicholas
Phyllis Oliver
Kay Patterson
Maxine Rexrode
Carol Richmond
Jo Ann Rose
Mary Seabolt
Mary F. Sheets
Lois Simmons
Shelia Slavens
Dollie Waybright
Julia Waybright
Patricia Wilfong
Mary F. Young
James Arbogast
Lyle Brooks
Walter Byrd
Thomas Carpenter
Franklin Curry
David Gainer
John Galford
Roger Galford
James Geiger
Gary Tallman
Buddy Gragg
Ivan Dale Greathouse
Richard Hedrick
Joseph Jackson
Delmas Mullenax
William Nelson
William Nottingham
James Rexrode
Wallace Shears
Larry Sutton
Earl Ware
Julian Ware
Dharl Wilfong
Norman Winans

CLASS OF 1961

Bonnie Arbogast
Bonnie Kaye Beard
Agnes Grey Beverage
Ruth Ann Burner
James William Carpenter
Danieth Ruth Coleman
Carol Dee Collins
George Franklin Collins
Linda Karen Collins
Rebecca Jean Collins
Jarrett Hunter Crowley
Terry Lee DeHaven
Amanda Lou Doyle
Charlotte Carole Elza
Juanita Grace Ervin
James Francis Findley
Gayle Maxine Galford
Ruth Emma Gaylor
Patricia Matthews Hevener
Dreama Elaine Lambert
Beulah May McLaughlin
Robert Elburn Moore
Steven Robert Moore
Howard Newton Mullenax
Isaac Lee Myers
Margaret Chloe Nelson
James Arthur Prater
Nina Lee Rankin
Martha Louise Sheets

William Lee Sheets
Eileen Dorothy Sutton
David Swecker
Barbara Ann Taylor
Wanda Jane Taylor
Cleveland Edward Tyson
Marilyn Davis Whanger
Danny James Wilfong
Edward Arnold Wyatt

CLASS OF 1962

James T. Arbogast
Charlotte Beverage
Rebecca Blackhurst
Chester L. Blanchard
Ray Allen Byrd
Arthur Collins
Edith Cosner
Janet Cox
Jane Davis
Pauline Dickenson
James Galford
Wayne Galford
Nadine Gillispie
Judith Gragg
Marvin Grogg
Jean Helmick
Timothy Hevener
Patricia Horner
Charles Jackson
John W. Moats
Douglas Monk
Arthur Mullenax
Franklin Murphy
Madeline Myers
John Henry Nelson
Carol Orndorff
Sandra Rose
Willard Shears
Barbara Simmons
Norma Simmons
Loretta Swecker
Judith Tacy
Harlan R. Tallman
Doris Turner
Dallas Vannoy
Margaret White
Delores Wilfong
Mary Wilfong
Lamar Wooddell
Roy Workman, Jr.
Robert Young

CLASS OF 1963

Keith Brown
Gary Coleman
Neven Elza
Lloyd Foe
Judy Gainer
Carol Gardner
Wayne Gillispie
Larry Greathouse
Deborah Harker
Patty Howdyshell
Mary Johnson
Donna McCutcheon
Joan Monk
Helen Moore
David Mullenax
Karen Mullenax
Bonnie Peck
Sandra Rankin
Rebecca Sheets
John Simmons
Lyle Tallman
Robert Ware
Donald Wenger
Lewis Wilmoth
Judith Wyatt

CLASS OF 1964

Harry Russell Aldridge
Charles Edwin Brewster
George Forrest Brewster
Harold Wayne Brooks
Lucy Brown
David Joe Cain
Roger Cain
Peggy Campbell
Jane Carpenter
Shelby Cassell
Donald Darrell Crews
Sandra Curry

Louise Davis
Sherry DeHaven
Ginger Dickenson
Larry Wayne Elza
Randall Wayne Hedrick
Robert Franklin Hickson
George Hipes, Jr.
Barbara Sara Hoover
Jean Horner
Carolyn Howell
Rose Mary Hunter
Karen Kane
Diane Kerr
Edward Glendi Lambert
Roy Henry Lambert
Woodford Hull Lantz
Norris Franklin Long
Deanna Lusk
Linda McCutcheon
Gloria Monk
Sara Moore
Danny Eugene Moss
Larry Taylor
Jesse Lee Nelson
Rowena Nicholas
Barbara Nottingham
Ruth O'Brien
John Patterson
Jackie Plyler
Stephen Luther Plyler
Ronald Leon Ray
Gene Leon Rexrode
Rebecca Rexrode
Gracie Rexrode
Donna Riley
George Bernard Shears
Kay Sheets
Samuel Markwood Sheets
Mary Smith
Charlotte Turner
Earl Louis Vance, Jr.
James David Whanger
Betty Wilfong
Beverly Wooddell

CLASS OF 1965

Barbara Jean Banton
Janie Bond
Phyllis Ann Burner
Madonna Ann Cover
Bonnie Dae Foe
Barbara Jean Galford
Shirley Jean Galford
Mary Ada Grimes
Sandra Kay Gum
Betty Jean Houchin
Georgia Grace Kelly
Martha Sue McCray
Donna Kay McQuain
Arlene Lee Mullenax
Charlene Lee Mullenax
William Vandevander
Vonda Marie Mullenax
Delores Jean Murphy
Patsy Eliza Myers
Mary Ella Neighbors
Patricia Ann Nottingham
Lille Katherine Oliver
Linda Marie Sharp
Connie Sue Taylor
Mary Alice Taylor
Juanita Jean Taylor
Alice Elaine Tyson
Elma Kathy White
Margaret Karen White
Mary Ellen White
Clifford Barkley
Samuel Beverage
David Doily
Roger Lee Ervin
Rodney Gardner
David Hamed
James Hill
Frederick Jacobs
Thomas Lightner
Thomas Long
Larry McLaughlin
Raymond Nicholas
Keith Plyler
Carl Rose
Robert Sheets
Douglas Stewart
Jerry Turner
Norman Vance
William Vandevander
Vincent White

Hunter Wilfong
Samuel Wilfong
Richard Wolfe

CLASS OF 1966

Mary Ann Aldridge
Marilyn Jean Baldwin
Kay Dare Bennett
Beverly Jean Brewster
Delores Jean Brewster
Barbara Jean Brown
Donna Kaye Burner
Barbara Jean Cassell
Paula Mae Clarkson
Dorothy J. Collins
Erma Lucille Collins
Millie E. Collins
Mary Ellen Cook
Carolyn S. Davis
Violet Davis
Linda Kay Elza
Linda Jean Foe
Beverly Anne Galford
Donna Jean Greathouse
Barbara Kay Hill
Minerva Jean Kerr
Mae Karen Lantz
Connie J. Mullenax
Mary Sue McLaughlin
Jane Ann Nottingham
Ruby Jane Kerr
Gloria Gail Riggsby
Henrietta M. Shinaberry
Sherry L. Smith
Beverly Ann Taylor
Gabriele Von Horner
Patricia L. Wasto
Nancy Kay Waybright
Jeunie Madge White
Candice Rae Widney
Charlotte G. Wilfong
Patsy Jean Wilfong
Nancy Sue Workman
James Edward Arbogast
Benjamin Brown Campbell
James Edward Cassell
William Ellis Curry
Dewey Hunter Ervine, Jr.
David Andy Geiger
Glen Paul Grandon
Daniel Wayne McQuain
Thomas Blair Oliver
Jesse Lynn Peck
Charles Eugene Rexrode
Danny Asbury Sheets
Donald Burr Sheets
William Howard Simmons
Donald Wayne Vannoy
Robert Dennis Wade

CLASS OF 1967

Daniel Lee Arbogast
Karen Sue Arbogast
Ronald E. Bowyer
Thomas Howard Brown
Judith Ann Cassell
Edwin Lowell Good
Rebecca Sue Colaw
Phyllis Elaine Daugherty
Dane Carroll Davidson
Agnes Doyle
Charles Edward Edgell
Mary Regina Elliott
Jerry Galford
William Henry Galford
Randolph Lee Gardner
Margaret Alice Geiger
Lewis Harold Good
George Grey Gragg
David Lynn Grimes
Diana Pearl Grogg
Anna Sheets Hayes
Connie Lee Hickson
Rosalie Donna Hill
Dewey Asbery Jackson
Melvin Kenneth Johnson
John Michael Kane III
Rosella Kuhlken
Nancy Jane Lightner
Ralph Grady Lowe II
Charlotte Anne Mullenax
Denver Clyde Offutt, Jr.
Roger Lee Orndorff
Beulah Rae Parker

Bernard David Pasternak
Brenda Mae Sheets
Catherine Faye Sheets
Robert Allen Sheets
Benjamin Blain Simmons
Lewis Clark Snyder
Neil Keith Snyder, Jr.
Daniel Richard Stone
Jerry Wayne Tallman
Judy Mae Vandevander
William Clark Vandevander
James Leslie Varner
Eugena Waybright
Carolyn Jean Weaver
Carolyn Sue Wenger
Margaret Karen White
Ricky Hull Wilfong
Lois Charlene Wooddell

CLASS OF 1968

Arnold Lee Bond
Delbert Russ Cosner
Robert Allen Crist
Richard Donald Ervine
Lewis Marshall Foe
Evelyn Kaye Caplinger
William Kermit Foe
Steven Phillip Lamp
Larry Evans Matheny
William Earl Moore
Harold A. Nottingham
James David Sheets
Howard E. Shinaberry
Raymond Wayne Taylor
David Lynn Vandevander
Ralph David Waybright
Burke A. Whitmire
David Lee Wilfong
David Lyle Wilfong
Larry Gene Wooddell
Ronald Lee Wooddell
Viola Burdette
Patricia Cassell
Diane Rose Ervine
Louise Galford
Shirley Gaylor
Donna Geiger
Susan Gillispie
Carolyn Good
Doris Henderson
Lois Ann Hill
Twila Hoover
Nancy Hunter
Kathy Kelly
Linda Kay Lewis
Judith Faye Lusk
Jane Ann McLaughlin
Sharon Rose Miller
Louise G. Mullenax
Corinda Price
Lennie Scott
Sandra Jean Sheets
Rebecca Taylor
Donna Curry Warner
Connie Marie White
Mary Ann Whitmire
Joyce A. Wilfong
Linda Diann Wimer

CLASS OF 1969

Garry Lee Arbogast
Roger Lee Barkley
James Roy Brown
David Harold Collins
Ernest Berl Collins
John Wesley Edgell
Terry Lee Grimes
Danny Richard Hedrick
William Howard Hevener
Charles Harry Hoover
Daniel Bruce Horne
Neil Horner, Jr.
Robert Steven Kuhlken
Jerry Allen Matheny
David Lynn McLaughlin
Kenneth Marshall McQuain
William Albert Means
Danny Lee Meeks
Larry B. Plyler
Randall Clark Shears
Wetzel Roy Sheets
William Boyd Wright
Roberta Gaile Baldwin
Margie Sue Barkley

Linda Sue Brown
Shirley Catherine Cain
Regina Lois Collins
Dianne Lynn Curry
Linda Kay Greathouse
Elsie Etta Herron
Diana Sue Lambert
Marilyn Dawnita Lambert
Deborah Ann McQuain
Clarice O'Neil Mace
Donna Lou Matheny
Nancy Sue Moore
Rosella Mary Orndorff
Judy Darlene Puffenbarger
Dawnita Fae Pugh
Donna Faye Sheets
Janet Sue Sheets
Avis Kathleen Simmons
Phyllis Jean Tracy
Wilma Lee Vannoy
Teresa Eileen Vinoski
Patricia Ann Workman

CLASS OF 1970

Robert Beverage
Patrick W. Coleman
Leonard D. Collins
Michael D. Crist
Clarence E. Ervine
Fredric P. Gardner
Linden R. Good
James A. Gragg
Steven M. Hamed
David Hawkins
Gary A. Hedrick
Arne E. Hungerbuhler
Michael D. Hickson
James D. McLaughlin
Sidney Brent Moore
Robert M. Oliver
Roger E. Ryder
Larry A. Sheets
Henry H. Shinaberry
Edward W. Tallman
Harold L. Tyson
William N. Waybright, Jr.
Betty Lou Brewster
Rebecca J. Chestnut
Cheryl L. Colaw
Dottie L. Colaw
Karen L. Conn
Barbara J. Greathouse
Sue Ann Kelley
Rosemary L. Lambert
Sharon Jean Lowe
Marilynn McLaughlin
Cathy D. Moyers
Wanda J. Smith
Debra L. Poling
Glema N. Rexrode
Charlotte M. Shears
Linda Snyder
Linda L. Taylor
Victoria L. Taylor
Rhonda C. Wenger

References

Bennett, Laura Dean. *Pocahontas County Times: Compass*. Spring 2021, p. 6.

Bodkins, Steve. *Bemis & Glady West Virginia: A History of Two Mountain Towns*. McClain Printing Company, 2006.

Bodkins, Steve. *Forgotten Towns: Pocahontas & Randolph Counties, WV*. McClain Printing Company, 2012.

Maxwell, Hugh. *History of Randolph County*. Acme Publishing Company, 1898.

Mountain Breeze. Greenbank High School Classes of 1924, 1945, 1946, 1951, 1953 and 1970.

Pocahontas County Historical Society. *History of Pocahontas County, West Virginia 1981: Birthplace of Rivers*. May 1981, p. 536.

Rice, Don. *Randolph 200: A Bicentennial History of Randolph County, West Virginia- 1787-1987*. Walsworth Publishing Co., Inc., 1987.

Sullivan, Ken and Deborah J. Sonis. *The West Virginia Encyclopedia*. West Virginia Humanities Council, 2006.

Thacker, Victor L. *French Harding: Civil War Memoirs*. 4th ed., McClain Printing Company, 2000.

Triplett, George R. *Our Proud Mountain Roots and Heritage*. McClain Printing Company, 2003.

Zinn, Jack. *R. E. Lee's Cheat Mountain Campaign*. McClain Printing Company, 1974.

UNIT 6: Early Rural Communities –

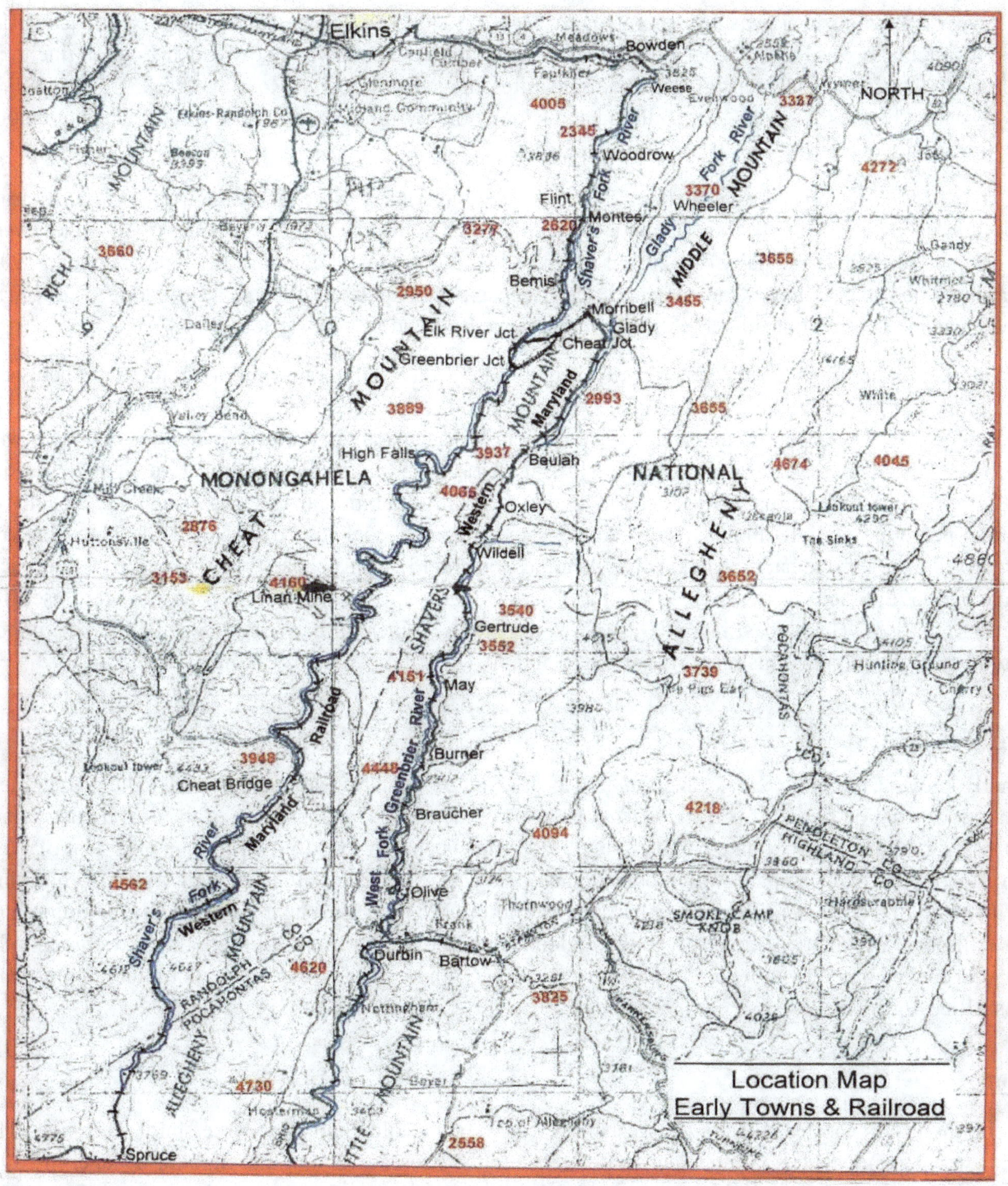

Randolph County, W.Va.

COALTON

The town of Womelsdorff was incorporated on May 8, 1895, and named after O.C. Womelsdorff, a Pennsylvanian who was the first coal operator in the community. The town is now called Coalton due to its location in a thriving coal center. It is located three miles above the mouth of Roaring Creek, Norton, W.Va. and was served by the Coal and Coke Railroad and later by the Baltimore and Ohio Railroad. The population in 1910 was 650, decreasing in 1930 to 373 (Rice 166).

The Davis Colliery Company owned about 25,000 acres of coal lands and coal mining rights in the Roaring Creek field in Randolph and Barbour Counties. Coalton had a major operation consisting of 200 coke ovens built during 1902-1904. The daily capacity of the mine was 2,000 tons of coal and 325 tons of coke in 1906. At Harding, the Davis Colliery Company had a daily capacity of 1,000 tons of coal and 150 tons of coke. The railroad became the Coalton Branch of the Coal and Coke Railroad in 1906. (Rice 99)

At Coalton, 15 miles from Elkins and on the Coal and Coke Railroad, the most important mine, probably the best equipped mine in the State, was situated. There were 200 coke ovens, and the coke manufactured was of very high quality. The coal used for mining coke barriers had a capacity of 1,800 tons and was equipped with a 90-foot belt, which conveyed the crushed coal to any part of the bin for distribution. Two eight-ton lorries were employed. A patent crusher was used in connection with the bin, and this had a crushing capacity of 150 tons per hour. A 4-12 picking band conveys the prepared coal to the crusher belt. Three electric locomotives were used to haul the coal from the mines, one of 13 ½ tons capacity and two of 6 ½ tons each. On average, 375 people were employed at the Coalton Plant, and 21 mules and 5 horses were used for gathering purposes. The highest rate of wages was paid to the miners at between $75 and $100 per month. The total cost of equipping this plant was around $500.00. (Board of Trade of Elkins 87)

NORTON

Formerly known as Roaring Creek Junction, it is located on the western side of the Tygart Valley River, near the mouth of Roaring Creek. It was founded in 1916 and experienced an expansion of the coal industry until 1920, when it had an approximate population of 1,000. It was named for R.F. Norton, the president of West Virginia Coal & Coke Company which owned and operated the mine. It is located eight miles from Elkins, near the main line of the CSX Railroad, the successor to the Western Maryland Railroad and Baltimore and Ohio Railroads, which at one time served the region. When the town was established, it was designed to be the model coal community with comfortable homes, a YMCA and other conveniences not found in most coal towns. (Rice 166).

MABIE

The community is located nine miles west of Beverly on the old Staunton Parkersburg Turnpike. The settlement was first called Roaring Creek in deference to the stream which ran through the village. In 1897, W.H. Mabie erected a band mill in the community, resulting in the town being named after him. (Rice 165)

<u>**MONTES**</u>

A lumber mill was established there by D.D. Brown and M.M. Brown in 1907, six miles south of Bowden on the Western Maryland Railroad. It was built on the east side of Shavers Fork River opposite the Western Maryland Railroad tracks and was connected to the railroad bridge and railroad spur. (Rice 166)

The Summerfield blacksmith shop at Montes provided shoeing for George Washington "Pud" Triplett's logging operations, located about 10 yards from this book's front cover photograph. The photograph on the book's cover shows the co-authors during the summer of 2019. The 13-acre property was owned by Clarence "Dump" Arbogast. Clarence was the son of Arley Arbogast. Arley's faher, James "Will" Arbogast, was married to Ruth Coberly (sister to Harl M. Coberly). Will and Ruth's children were John, Garnett, Wilbert "Webb," Sylvia, Goldie (married Ferguson), Opha, Howard (father of Geraldine Arbogast Watts), and Wilda Arbogast Young, of Cumberland, Maryland. Wilda is now 95 years old. Wilda's mother, Ruth, died when she was 18 months old; as of 2023, she is the sole living child of Will and Ruth Arbogast. Wilda continues to attend the annual family reunion held on the third Sunday of July in Bowden, W.Va.

The Brown and Hill, M.M. and D.D. Brown Lumber Companies operated at Montes. The Morribell Lumber Company operated Morribell and Montes Cumeto. Pictured above are George "Pud" Triplett and two workers of the Montes lumber camp in front of the Triplett-Summerfield blacksmith shop located about 20 feet from the front cover of book with Arm & Hammer Baking Soda on signs for acid reflux and one dollar coupon on a plug of tobacco. This photo was taken around 1905-1908.

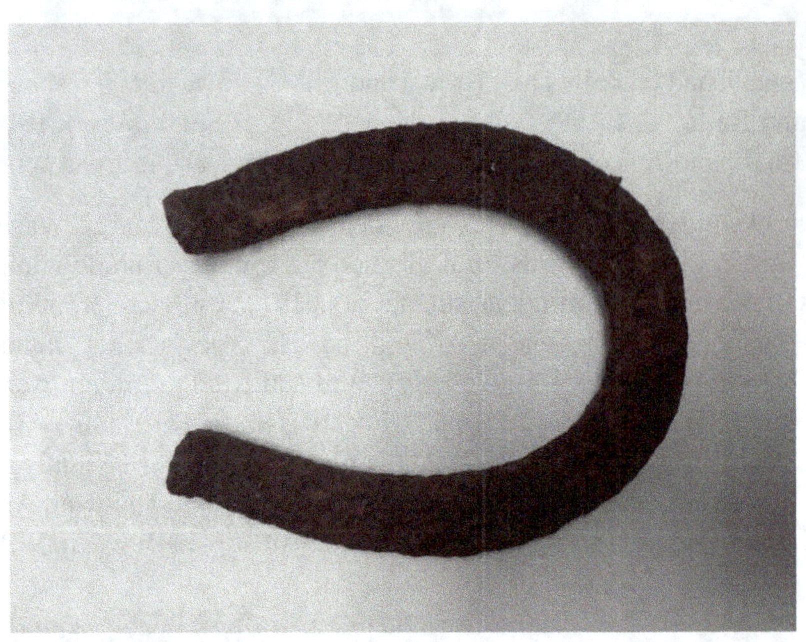

Horseshoe from Triplett-Summerfield blacksmith shop in Montes, W.Va. Made 1905-1908. Horseshoe provided by Clarence "Dump" Arbogast, to each co-author in August 2019

Pictured above (left to right): Alexandra L. Triplett, Robert C. Triplett, Charles E. Triplett (back), George A. Triplett and Sofia F. Triplett at the original site of the Triplett-Summerfield blacksmith shop (described above). This photo taken in August of 2019.

Pictured above (left to right): Clarence "Dump" Arbogast, Alexandra L. Triplett, Robert C. Triplett, George A. Triplett, Sofia F. Triplett, George R. Triplett and Jeff Triplett, at Montes in August 2019, at the site of the Triplett-Summerfield blacksmith shop.

Photo taken at Montes, circa 1905. (Rice 81)

When the Brown Lumber Company came to Elkins, they contracted the American Bridge Company to construct a bridge enabling the heaviest Western Maryland Railroad engines to serve the mill site. The mill site was located on a 2,000-acre tract approximately five miles above Bowden, on the east side of Shaver's Fork, opposite the railroad. In 1907, the mill cut an average clearing for the year - 52,000 feet in a ten-hour workday. The Montes tract produced 44,800,000 feet of extra fine timber, which was over 22,000 feet per acre. Morribell Lumber Company sold the mill in 1909, and another 1,800,000 feet of timber was cut, making a total of 46,800,000 feet of timber having been processed at Montes. The Montes mill was in operation until 1911, when the Browns purchased land in the Bickle Knob area, and a mill was relocated to South Elkins. The Section Foremen at Montes were Arthur Davis, Dick Champ, and Hub Bodkins.

Pictured here is the Oxley Log Store located between Glady and Morribell (Rice 96).

FLINT

Flint was located up the Shavers Fork River toward Bemis and the mouth of Pond Lick Run, on the opposite side of the Montes Railroad Bridge. (Rice 164)

FAULKNER

This railroad siding once served a rock quarry on the Western Maryland Railroad alongside Shavers Fork, seven miles east of Elkins (Rice 164). Job Triplett and John Triplett built the "Triplett Homeplace" around 1800 from the Triplett-Revolutionary War Land Grant. Job was the son of John Triplett, who came to Randolph County around the year 1790. In the early 1900s, surveyors began mapping out and purchasing the rights-of-way along the Shavers Fork of Cheat River, Glady and Greenbrier River Valley, where the railroad tracts would be built. All rights-of-way would be 100 feet and measure 50 feet from the center to each side. Several landholders include J. W. Goddin (14.75 acres), Elizabeth Ann Flint (984 acres), Jasper Triplett (5 acres), and Z.D. Weese (10 acres). Attorney and United States Senator Howard Sutherland was a land agent for the C&I Branch of the railroad, 46 miles long, and had tunnels #1 near Elkins and tunnel #2 at Glady. Sutherland was the father of General Richard Sutherland, who accompanied General McArthur when he returned to the Philippines and was aboard the Battleship Missouri when Japan surrendered in 1945. The Triplett Family were legal, licensed whiskey makers. Jasper Triplett's children were Wade Hampton, Delphia Triplett, Flint, and George Washington "Pud" Triplett, who all made their homes in Faulkner. The current U.S. 33 East (Corridor H) from Elkins to Strasburg, Virginia, crosses both Faulkner and Bowden at the Bowden Bridge, which crosses Shavers Fork. The bridge is named in honor of Samuel Reed Summerfield, a descendant of Etta Arbogast Summerfield and Minard Summerfield and son of John Summerfield of Bowden.

Jasper, Eliza and "Pud" Triplett at Triplett homeplace, Faulkner, WV, built about 1800.

George Washington "Pud" Triplett.

Lora Triplett.

<u>BOWDEN</u>

The railroad station and post office were named for Harry X. Bowden, a local merchant and postmaster, in 1908. It is located eight miles outside of Elkins on the Western Maryland Railroad line going up the Shavers Fork River. The station closed on May 31, 1967, as the last scheduled passenger train left from Elkins to Bowden and Durbin. Several of our family members worked at various sections of the Western Maryland Railroad. Charlie Triplett worked on the Triplett and Bowden section, Bob Cromer worked on the Bemis section, and Harry Triplett worked on the Spruce section. (Bodkins 417)

Pictured is the Tygart Flyer traveling through Bemis (Bodkins 416).

The Arbogast, Revelle, Phares, Howell, Knutte, Vance, Calain, Tingler, Kimble and Coberly families were early settlers in Bowden.

Family rumors indicate that the Faulkner, Taylor, and Wolfe Run area provide the best water and protection (i.e., under rock cliffs and in laurel thickets) for the manufacturer from whiskey and moonshine revenue officers. Moonshine was also known as "white lightning," "fire water," "tonic," "the recipe," or "Devil's Brew."

Section foremen at Bowden were Lonnie Bennett, Ori Bonnell, Ira Vance, Charlie Triplett, Ernie Kimble, and Pip Fansler.

The Cheat River Lumber Company operated in Bowden. The road construction was discussed before the Randolph County Commission during the early 1900s to extend to Bemis from Montes but was never completed. The Lemuel and Barbara Rexroad Cemetery is situated on the hill above the Shavers Fork Bridge on land owned by Arlie Arbogast. A reunion pavilion is located on a gated road that crosses a bridge above Shavers Fork and ends at Wolfe Run, Montes.

<u>**REFERENCES**</u>

Bodkins, Steve. *Bemis & Glady West Virginia: A History of Two Mountain Towns*. McClain Printing Company, 2006.

---. *Forgotten Towns: Pocahontas & Randolph Counties, WV*. McClain Printing Company, 2012.

Rice, Don. *Randolph 200: A Bicentennial History of Randolph County, West Virginia- 1787-1987*. Walsworth Publishing Co., Inc., 1987.

Rice, William H. *Elkins, West Virginia 1889: The Magic City of Wilderness*. McClain Printing Company, 2007.

UNIT 7: Families

Hart Family

The Hart family is of English descent and has been present in Randolph County since 1785, when two brothers, Daniel and Edward Hart, found residence in the present town of Beverly. Daniel settled about one mile above Beverly on Files Creek Road near the old Buckley Mill site. The two brothers came to Randolph County from New Jersey. John and Daniel Hart were soldiers in the Revolutionary War and were sons of John Hart, who signed the Declaration of Independence. Joseph Hart, a son of Edward Hart, was born and reared near Beverly. He became a prominent lawyer, having been admitted to the bar of Randolph County in 1837. Joseph was also prominent in public and political affairs; he twice represented his county in the state legislature and was president of the county court. He moved to the summit of Rich Mountain in 1855 for the benefit of his health but continued to practice law until the beginning of the Civil War. His farm on the mountain top became the site of the Battle of Rich Mountain, and his residence was between the lines of the contending forces. He died on April 4, 1881.

Squire Bosworth Hart, son of Joseph and Susan (Pickens) Hart, was born near Beverly in 1841. He enlisted in Battery E. of the First West Virginia Artillery Division and served in the valley of Virginia. After the close of the war, he taught in a school until 1867, when he was elected county superintendent of schools. He was re-elected in 1869. In 1849, a coal mine was opened a short distance west of the mountain's summit on the Hart farm. The mine supplied demand in Beverly and nearby there until a railroad was built in the valley.

In 1868, Mr. Hart married Maria L. Organ of Upshur County. They had one child, who became the wife of Hon. Clyde Johnson, a prominent attorney of St. Mary's, W.Va. William Camden Hart, son of Calvin C. Hart and Julia Hart, was born December 19, 1868. He married Marietta E. Logan, daughter of William Thomas Logan and Elizabeth F. Logan. The couple had six children, Shirley D. Hart, Logan D. Hart, Dorothy Julia Hart, Marion L. Hart, Sheffey B. Hart, and Calvin E. Hart. William Camden Hart served as constable twice and as justice of the peace of Beverly District. Eli Triplett, who was the son of John Triplett and either Nancy Kittle Triplett or Sallie Kittle Triplett, married Margaret Hart, daughter of James Hart, and moved to Missouri.

Rossi Family

Around 1902-1906, the four Rossi brothers - Tony, Salvator, Emedio, and Jessie - came to America from Pratola Peligna, in the province of L'Aquila, Italy. They were the sons of Concesis and Michelline Rossi. The brothers arrived through Ellis Island, New York, and were some of the first employees at the Coalton coal mines and coke ovens. Their children worked alongside them to survive and feed their large families. Salvator moved to Steubenville, Ohio, and worked in steel mills. Tony left Coalton for Galloway, W.V., and later returned to Italy with his son, Dominic, after WWII. Conces Jessie "Hoover" remained in Coalton and married Anne Antolini, daughter of Tony Antolini. The couple raised 14 of the most hardworking, intelligent, successful, and professional children, including the current mayor of Coalton, James "Jim" Rossi. Emedio "Medie" married Agatha Saccoccia, daughter of Gustino Saccoccia and Nunziato, of Gennantonia, Pratola Peligna, in the province of L'Aquila, Italy; they raised 10 children in Coalton. They formed a hard-working, successful, and close family. It is understood that they have always been self-supportive and "green-thumbed."

The hard-earned investments and leadership of the two sons of Jesse and Annie Rossi led to the celebration of Coalton Days, which takes place every July on the third Saturday of the month. The celebration is sponsored by Michael Ross, who married Joan Keller of Norton.

Jim Rossi, the current mayor, re-elected June 1, 2021, by a vote of 75-17, paved all streets, and received a $3.3 million grant for a completely new water system.

Note: All references to "Grandma" and "Grandpa" in the captions of the following photos refer to our grandparents, Emedio Rossi and Agatha Saccoccia.

After being called upon by Emidio, Agatha immigrated to the United States in 1913. Sponsored by her Aunt Francesca Gennantonio, she arrived at Ellis Island, NY on February 13 onboard the passenger ship ADRIATIC, along with 29 other Italian immigrants.

The passenger ship ADRIATIC, on which Grandma traveled to the United States from Liverpool, England. Built in 1907 in Northern Ireland; 726 feet long (2.5 football fields); max speed 20 mph; max capacity of 2,825 passengers; provided service from Liverpool to New York.

Left to right: Grandpa, Grandma, and Grandma's Aunt Francesca, circa 1913

Grandma and Grandpa – 1913.

Marriage certificate for Emedio Rossi and Agatha Saccoccia – April 28, 1913.

THE UNITED STATES OF AMERICA

TO BE GIVEN TO
THE PERSON NATURALIZED

No. 3593055

CERTIFICATE OF CITIZENSHIP

Petition No 164

Personal description of holder as of date of naturalization Age 45 years sex male color white complexion dark color of eyes brown color of hair brown height 5 feet 5 inches weight 131 pounds visible distinctive marks wart on right temple

Marital status married race Italian (South) former nationality Italy

I certify that the description above given is true, and that the photograph affixed hereto is a likeness of me

ORIGINAL

Emidio Rosso
(Complete and true signature of holder)

United States of America
Northern Dist. of W. Va. ss:

Be it known that Emiddio Rosso then residing at Coalton, Randolph County, West Virginia having petitioned to be admitted a citizen of the United States of America, and at a term of the U. S. District Court of Northern District of West Virginia held pursuant to law at Elkins, West Virginia on November 15 1932 the court having found that the petitioner intends to reside permanently in the United States, had in all respects complied with the Naturalization Laws of the United States in such case applicable and was entitled to be so admitted, the court thereupon ordered that the petitioner be admitted as a citizen of the United States of America.

In testimony whereof the seal of the court is hereunto affixed this 15th day of November in the year of our Lord nineteen hundred and thirty-two and of our Independence the one hundred and 157th.

Austin C. Merrill
Clerk of the U. S. District Court

By *John W. Rine*, Deputy Clerk.

Seal

DEPARTMENT OF LABOR

Emidio Rossi's Certification of U.S. Citizenship

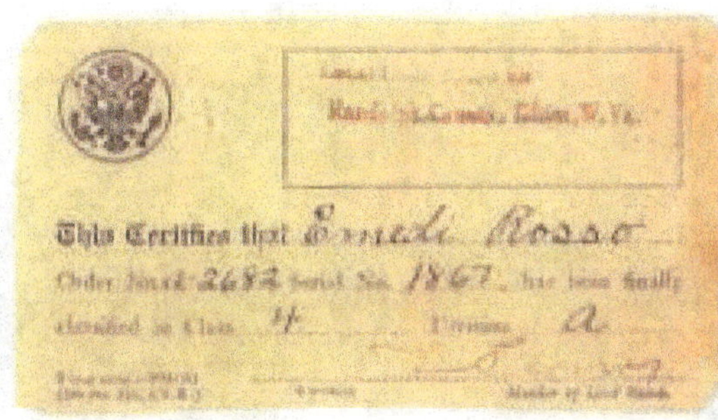

Grandpa's draft card

The family home in Coalton, by Irma Colabrese. Christmas 1998.

Grandma and Grandpa with (some of) their family.

Left to right: Mary, Guido, Julie, and Antionette

A recent article was written in the May 2, 2023 edition of The Inter-Mountain, announcing Michael DiBacco, being named one of the top graduating seniors at West Virginia University, receiving the "Order of Augusta", the most prestigious WVU award. The Order of Augusta represents the best and brightest of the graduating class. DiBacco will earn a master's degree in Science Journalism. Michael is the great-great grandson of Emedio and Agatha Saccoccia Rossi, great grandson of John and Mary Rossi DiBacco, grandson of Paul and Sandra DiBacco, and son of John and Erin DiBacco. His brother, Ryan DiBacco, is a sophomore at WVU. It is worth noting the Rossi Family achievements since the 1913 marriage in Thomas, West Virginia.

WEST AUGUSTA - AUGUSTA

Rampant land speculation and vaguely worded colonial charters resulted in conflicting claims to the territory surrounding the Monongahela Valley in the late colonial period. All the territory west of the Blue Ridge Mountains in 1773 was asserted by Lord Dunmore creating the District of West Augusta by proclamation, which is currently Northern West Virginia and Western Pennsylvania.

he ancient Italian region of Tuscany was settled in the third and fourth century B.C. by the Etruscans. It is from this historic and culturally important region that the surname Rossi emerges. The region became known as Tuscia or Toscana and incorporated the regions north of Viterbo and Bolsena.

Research into the surname Rossi has produced evidence of the early origins of the name in Florence, where it originated in Lombardic times (approximately the eighth century). The surname Rossi has such variations as Rosso, Rossa, Rossi, Del Rosso, De Rossi, De Russi, Lo Russo, Lorusso, La Russa, Larussa, Rosselli, Rossello, Rossellini, Ruggiu, Ruiu, Ruju, Rubiu, Rossillo, Rossetto, Rossit, Rossini, Rossitti, Rossitto, Rossotto, Russotti, Russello, Russetti, Russino, Russiani, Rossoni, Rossetti, Roussini, Rosselino, Rossato, Della Rossa, DeRossi, De Rubeis, Russo, and Russetto. Such variations were often the result of changes which occur in a language over the course of time and also because of differences in local dialects.

During the twelfth century, this family ruled over several castles in the regions around Siena and Volterra. The Rossi family branched out all over northern and central Italy, settling in the cites of Trento, Udine, Vicenza, Venice, Savigliano, Pisa, Ravenna, and Rome. Some of the family migrated as far south as Sicily. This southern branch of the family descended from Count Ugone Rosso of Sicily, whose ancestors were Normans.

Tuscany, the family's northern birthplace, became fragmented in the twelfth century as a result of the struggle between the papacy and the Holy Roman Empire. During this time of internal strife the Florentine Dante Alighieri emerged as the most prominent literary figures of Italy to date. One hundred years later Francesco Petrarca or Petrarch, whose sonnets have been compared to those of William Shakespeare, came on to the Italian literary scene. Giovanni Bocaccio, a literary contemporary of Petrarch wrote an eloquent description of the plague and its devastating force in Florence and Tuscany itself in his "Decameron", a collection of short stories written during the early fourteenth century. These influential figures in the literary tradition of Italy placed Florence and Tuscany at the forefront of Italian culture.

During the Middle Ages, the Rossi family gained prominence. There were three consuls in the area of Florence who acted as spokesmen for the government: Jacoppi Rossi in 1176, Gherardo Rossi in 1197 and Beringhieri Rossi in 1204. In 1325, Fidello del Rosso was prior at St. Piero; Giambattista Rossi was vicar of Ordine in 1564; Lorenzo Rossi was professor of philosophy at the University of Ferrara in the seventeenth century. The aristocratic Rossi family of Messina was prominent during the same century.

Florence was held by the Medici dynasty during the fifteenth and sixteenth centuries. Alessandro de' Medici became duke of Florence in 1530. Research into the surname Rossi indicates that members of the family were still associated with Florence. Andrea e Rosso, son of Antonio, became the most wealthy trade merchant in the city of Florence.

For nearly two hundred years Tuscany enjoyed political stability until 1735, when the current duke, Gian Gastone, was overthrown by the dynastic family of the Habsburgs. The husband of Maria Theresa of Austria, Francis of Lorraine, was given the ducal position to replace Lorraine which had been taken from him. His son, Leopold, proved to be one of the most successful leaders in Tuscan history. He made widespread governmental reforms and reorganized trade and taxation. He gave Tuscan landowners and squires more rights than they had previously enjoyed.

The French Revolution had a great impact upon the history of Tuscany. In 1799, French troops entered Florence and forced the duke to flee. The French quickly took hold of Tuscany. The Tuscans revolted against the French and managed to eradicate most of French influence, especially in the rural areas. With the help of the Austrians, the Italians regained Florence, but this victory was short-lived since the city fell into the hands of the French once again with the arrival of Napoleon.

While Italy was torn by foreign invasion and strife, one of the well known bearers of the surname, Dante Gabriel Rossetti, was born in 1783 in England. He was a noted painter and a poet. His father, Gabriel Rossetti, was born in Naples. Dante Gabriel was a member of the Pre-Raphaelite Brotherhood, a group of painters who were noted for their meticulous attention to detail in their paintings. Many of his paintings are on display today at the famous Tate Gallery in London. His sister, Christina Rossetti, was a poet and wrote for both children and adults. One of her most famous poems is entitled "Goblin Market."

Although settlement in the New World was discouraged until the unification of Italy at the end of the 19th century, a few Italians made the journey to the New World before the great migrations. During the late nineteenth century, and especially during the early twentieth century, more and more Italians came to the United States and Canada. Among these new settlers were: Armando Rossi, who sailed to New York in 1884; Catharine Rossi, who arrived in New York in 1844; and Theodore Rossi who arrived in New York in 1852. Others sailed to Pennsylvania, including Giovanni Rossi arrived in 1896; Raffaele Rossi arrived in 1897; and Romualdo Rossi who arrived in 1882.

Today, many Italians enrich the social, economic and cultural realms of North America and countries around the world. Among these are people such as one of the most recognized members of the Rossi family to date, the famous soccer player Paolo Rossi who led the Italian national team to World Cup victory in 1982. Also of note are: Florence Rossi of Tucson, Arizona, an author and editor who has written numerous poems, essays and articles; Lino Rossi, a pathologist at the Faculty of medicine at the University of Milan; Nick Rossi, an educator, writer, musician, and film producer who has written numerous books about music.

The earliest coat of arms of the family Rossi is:

A silver shield with a red lion.

SACCOCCIA FAMILY

Agatha Saccoccia, the mother of Frances M. Triplett, was born July 11, 1891, in Pratola Peligna, Aguila, Italy. Agatha was the daughter of Giustino Saccoccia and Nunigoto Gennantonia.

The train station in Grandma's and Grandpa's hometown in the province of L'Aquila in Italy

The Sanctuary of Maria ss della Libera -- Grandma's church in Pratola Peligna in the province of L'Aquila

Joe and Delesia Saccoccia with Grandma's sister Vincenza in Pratola Peligna in 1988.

OTHER ITALIAN FAMILIES MADE THEIR HOMES IN COALTON, NORTON, AND HARDING COMMUNITIES

Families in these areas include, but are not limited to, the following: DeMotto, Polce, Bertollini, Bertelli, Mastrogiuseppe, Pastine, Leombruno, Silvester, Putzulu, O'Kernick, Petrice, Travise, Marco, Amotto, Pezzaferatto, Baisi, Zangari, Altieri, Ceckum, Paski, Gennatonio, Benzini, Girard, Tarantelli, Butch, Tarentelli, Zambelli, DiBacco, Sainato, Ashe, Cruckshank, Portalese, DelSignore and Cirillo.

Martha Ellen Arbogast married Isaac Perry Vance; Ida Jane Arbogast married Perry Clark Arbogast; Christena Arbogast married Bernard Dellard Powers; Laura Susan Arbogast married George Triplett; James William Arbogast married Ruth May Coberly; Etta Arbogast married Minard Summerfield; Lemuel Earl Arbogast married Mary Margaret Howell; Anna M. Arbogast married John Peters; Jenny Florence Arbogast married William Fansler; Benjamin Harley Arbogast married Amanda E. Sacks; George Hobart Arbogast married Florence Smith.

According to referenced sources, "Arbogast" is derived from the Proto-Germanic roots "arb" (heritage) and "gist" or "gastric" (stranger or guest). In this case, "Arbogast" would mean "heritage guest." [8] "Arbogast" would be either a Frankish variant of the older name "Arbogast." The vast majority of Arbogast emigrating to America were from Germany.

The Arbogast name might be considered somewhat less common than names like Jones or Smith but is not a strange name. Yet its origin and use may pre-date many of the common names of today. "Arbogast" is an early <u>Germanic name</u> that was associated with the <u>tribe</u> of the <u>Salian Franks</u>. As early as 240 A.D., "Arbogast" was the name of a <u>clan</u> within that tribe. The name "Arogast" appears in the <u>Salic Law</u>, written in 507-511 A.D., which forms the basis of the Franks' legal system. The four Frankish authors of this law were Wisogast, Arogast, Sidogast, and Widogast. According to Zöllner and Heinzelmann a 4th-century Frankish general <u>Arbogast</u>, Flavius Arbogastes (the Latin variant of the older name "Arogast") served in the <u>Late Roman army</u> and in 394 he would have been considered second in command of the Western Roman empire. He died on September 8, 394, by his own hand (the only honorable thing to do) after losing a critical battle. A description of Flavius Arbogastes, offered by Christian accounts "Flavius Arbogaste was a first-class military commander with a fine record, very popular with the army and wholly loyal to the houses of Roman emperors Valentinian and Theodosius. Arbogast, the flame-like Frank, was no mere intriguer but a brave and well-trained soldier, probably the best General in the Roman Empire. A Franks by birth, exceedingly well-disposed to the Romans, completely immune to bribes, and outstanding as regards warfare in brain and brawn.

Other noteworthy Arbogast family members:

- o <u>Arbogast (Count of Trier)</u>, a 5th-century Frankish- Roman <u>comes</u> to <u>Trier</u>. He may have been the Arbogast who was Bishop of Chartres.

- o <u>Louis Francois Antoine Arbogast</u> (1759-1803) a French mathematician who published a well-known <u>calculus</u> <u>treatise</u> in 1800.

- o <u>Saint Arbogast</u> (c. 600s-700 A.D.), an <u>Irish missionary</u> who came to <u>Alsace</u>, France and became Bishop of <u>Strasbourg</u>. His given name "Arascach" was adated to the local name "Arbogast

- o <u>Todd Arbogast</u>, an American mathematician known for his work in subsurface modeling.

- o <u>Arbogast von Frankenstein</u>, a 10th-centry knight and sworn defender of the Frankenstein realm.

- o <u>Carl Arbogast</u>, compiler of the eponymous *Arbogast Method* used in <u>selection cutting</u> silviculture

The greatest number of Arbogast families is in 1st WV and 2nd PA, 3rd OH, and 4th IL. Thirty-seven states have Arbogast families.

On September 25, 1749, Michael and Hans Arbogast arrived in Philadelphia, Pennsylvania, on The Speedwell, a ship from Rottendam, Germany. The two men were listed as "Armgast." Michael first settled in Pennsylvania but left the P.A. German settlement in 1752 and came to Pendleton County, V.A. (now W.V.) to visit W.H. Arbogast, which may have been Hans. Michael swore "Oath of Allegiance" and settled in Highland County, Virginia, around 1760. Michael was naturalized in 1770 in Augusta County, Virginia. According to records, Michael was born and baptized on September 27, 1732, in Freiburg, Kehl Baden-

Wierttemberg, Germany, and was the son to Daniel and Christina Woodell Arbogast. His parents died in Cologne, Germany. He is considered to be one of the original pioneers of what is now Highland County, V.A. Michael had two daughters and seven sons. Some of his descendants are documented below in the Triplett Family lineage. (Sharp, 9-11)

HARRIS FAMILY

Mrs. Keifer, in her history of the Harris Family of New Jersey, wrote:

"Jerome B. Harris, son of Barnabas Tunis Harris and Rachel Marquis Harris, was born in 1836; married in 1871, name of wife not known; had six children: Lenora Harris, born April 3, 1872; Gailrod 'Gail' Harris, born April 21, 1874; Jerrold 'Buck' Harris, born January 21, 1876: Tunis 'Barney' Harris, born July 15, 1878; Mary Harris, born May 19, 1880; Raphael Harris, born March 1, 1882. Mr. Harris was a carpenter and builder by occupation. He resided at or near Beverly, Randolph County, Virginia, in 1883. Is a member of the Presbyterian Church and a man much respected in the community where he lives."

This information is incomplete and has several errors.

There are two histories of Randolph County, West Virginia. One was written by H.W. Maxwell in 1898 and republished in 1961 (McClain Printing, Parsons, WV). Both of these printings are identical in wording.

Another history of Randolph County, West Virginia, was written by A.S. Bosworth and published in 1975 (McClain Printing, Parsons, WV).

The Maxwell History provides that Jerome Harris, born in 1836, is the son of Tunis and married Mary Jane Crocket[t] (aka Croker). Children: Lenora, Gaylord ("Gail"), Gerrald ("Buck"), Tunis ("Barney"), Mary, Raphael ("Raph"), and William ("Poker Bill").

The other history of Randolph County, West Virginia, written by Dr. A.S. Bosworth and published in 1975 (McClain Printing, Parson, WV), states: "The Harris Family. Jerome B. Harris, son of Barnabas Tunis and Rachel Marquis Harris, was born in 1836. He married Mary Crocket. Six children were born unto them, Lenora, Gaylord, Jerrold, Tunis, Mary, and Raphael. This branch of the Harris family is descendant of James Harris, who was born in Bristol, England, in 1700—immigrated to New Jersey in 1725. He married Miss Boylen. A son, George Harris, was born in 1745. He married a Miss Tunis. A son, Barna[bas] Harris, was born at Pulaski, Lawrence County, Pennsylvania, in 1768. He Married Esther Miller. Of this marriage, Barna[bas] C. Harris was born in 1811. Barna[bas] C. Harris married Rachel Marquis, and unto them was Barna[bas] Tunis Harris, who married Rachel Marquis. Their son, Jerome B. Harris, was the ancestor of this branch of the Harris Family in Randolph."

Anyone can see Mr. Maxwell, Dr. Bosworth, and Mrs. Keifer had different versions of Harris ancestry. For a more detailed early life of the Harris Family, Mrs. Keifer's article, The Harris Family of New Jersey, states: "Barnabas Tunis Harris [and his wife] Rachel Marquis [Harris] had four children: Jerome B. Harris, born April 19, 1836; Merthyan Harris [a daughter], born September 20, 1837 [died June 30, 1848]; Marquis Harris, born February 1, 1839; Samuel Harris, born July 6, 1843; Mr. Harris was a farmer by occupation and resided at or near Pulask[i], Lawrence County, PA. He was a Presbyterian in religion. He died September 9, 1871, in his sixty-first year."

Jerome Harris' mother was Rachel Marquis. The Marquis Family is an interesting family. They were French Huguenots chased out of France after the Protestant Reformation. They first went to Scotland, where they were adopted into the McDonald clan, and from there to Letterkenny, Northern Ireland. One branch, ours, I believe, married into the Margaret Kidd family, a granddaughter of the infamous pirate Captain Kidd family who was hanged in Scotland in 1705 at the age of ninety-five. Another branch married into the Magruder family, and they trace their lineage back to Robert The Bruce. The progenitor of the Marquis family went to Switzerland, and that branch of the family was the attorney general for Switzerland in 1908. Also, the Switzerland family is reputed to be the owners of Nestle's Chocolate.

Mary Jane Crocket[t] (aka Crocker) was apparently quite a risk-taking lady, and her second marriage was to Jerome Barnabas Harris. Little is known of the Crocket[t] (aka Croker) ancestry, but the name is English, and the Crocket[t]s may have moved into Western Pennsylvania from one of the New England states. Shortly after the birth of Jerrold C. Harris, the family decided to leave Pennsylvania and go to West Virginia to open a hunting lodge in Rainelle. They packed their things and moved by ox cart into the wilderness of West Virginia. Their thinking was one hundred years too early for hunting lodges in that area.

Their dream hunting lodge must have died as we find them pushing slowly north again until they finally settle down in Beverly, West Virginia, for the rest of their lives. Their last two sons were born near or in Beverly: Raphael "Raph" Simeon Harris, born Mary 1, 1882; and William "Poker Bill" Crocket[t] (aka Crocker) Harris, born July 27, 1884.

Before the marriage of Mary Jane Crocket[t] (aka Crocker) Kissinger to Jerome Barnabas Harris, she was married to Mr. Kissinger. They had two children, a son, whose name was John, and a daughter named Nettie. While sailing down the Mississippi River, her husband came down with pneumonia and died. Then she and her two children came to live in New Castle, Pennsylvania.

Little is known of Mary Jane's first husband. Where they were going when they sailed down the Mississippi River, and why? Like most pioneers, they were probably trying to improve their life by seeking greener pastures somewhere else. Mary Jane Crocket[t] (aka Crocker) Kissinger Harris, by legend, is said to have been a relative of David Crockett.

After the death of her first husband, Mary Jane's parents offered her financial help, which she refused, saying, "made my bed, and I'll lie in it." The two Kissinger children were brought up with the seven children born to Mary Jane and Jerome. Mary Crocket[t] (aka Crocker) Harris was reputed to be a very strong-spirited mountain woman. Jerome Harris is buried on Reservoir Hill in East Dailey, Randolph County, West Virginia.

George Harris was born in Essex County, New Jersey about 1745 or 1746. He married Hannah Tunis (Tunisen) in about 1765, by whom he had eleven children. Mr. Harris was of the old Revolutionary stock; was in the war under General Washington; was sergeant of the Second Regiment of State Troops and Continental Army. Mr. Harris took part in the bloody battle of Monmouth, as did his brothers Thomas and John. During the Revolutionary War, he resided in the Colony of New Jersey. While in the army, his house was pillaged, and his stock was driven off. You will find that his descendants are found in nearly half of the states of the Union.

It has been a little over a century and a half since James left the shores of England as a single man. He was the progenitor of the Harris Family in the United States. Some of the oldest descendants served as soldiers in the Revolutionary War, some in the War of 1812, and some in the war between Mexico and the United States; and still later, some of the younger generations served as soldiers in the War of the Rebellion, which occurred from 1861 to 1865.

It is not known for a certainty that any royal blood has ever coursed through their veins; but the wife of James Harris was of English parentage and of the same name as the wife of Henry the Eighth, King of England. Let us look back to a little more than a hundred years ago and, step by step, along a savage wilderness, oppressed by foreign foes and assailed by murderous savages and ferocious wild beasts, suffering cold, hunger and disease, torn from kindred ties. For what purpose? To build up homes of peace and plenty for you and me. To open up a highway of light, liberty, and equal rights for us today; a country that abounds with free institutions of learning for all and a right to worship God after the dictates of our consciences. All this was purchased with a fortitude and suffering which we of today do not appreciate half enough; they bought all this with their best abilities and also with their heart's blood.

James Harris was born in the city of Bristol, Somersetshire. England, close to the border of Wales, about the commencement of 1700; and immigrated to America in 1725 (or about that time).

The Harris Family is among the forty-nine "best families" selected by the American Historical Genealogical Society for whom the society has published family histories during the past several years. The Harris Family has been prominent in the British Empire and the United States; its members have played important roles in war and peace. Family pride is a commendable trait and should be cultivated. All Harris' have just cause to be proud of their family history and traditions.

The legend persists that Miss Boleyn, who married James Harris, was a descendant of the Boleyn family that produced Anne Boleyn. There is a grain of truth in every legend, which becomes greatly exaggerated with each passing generation; Anne Boleyn was the second wife of Henry VIII and the mother of Queen Elizabeth I.

Boleyn is a place name, meaning one who came from Boulogne, France. Anne Boleyn's family immigrated from Boulogne to England. They were cloth merchants who became very rich and powerful in England. When the family became wealthy and married into the best families in England, they changed the spelling of the name to Boleyn. The family name can be found in old English records previous to that change as Bullen, Bullen, Bullan, Boullen, Boullan, de Boulans, Boullant, as well as many other spellings of the name. Regardless of how the name was spelled, it was always pronounced Bull-un.

The best evidence that Miss. Boleyn, who married James Harris, was collateral descendent of Anne Boleyn's family is, and the spelling of their surnames is the same. In the index to New Jersey Wills, 1689-1890, the names Bolan, Boland, Boll, Bollen, Bolles, Bollis, and Bolyan appear, but not Boleyn. The Boleyn Will was from Essex County, where James and his wife lived. Names, places, and dates have a tendency to change from generation to generation. Information is passed down from one generation to another by word of mouth, which can account for many variations. Even when information is written down, there can be errors in spelling. What is a fact in one generation can change at a later date; for instance, when James Harris came to Elizabeth-town, New Jersey, it was Essex County. Today it is Elizabeth and in Union County.

Some of the descendants pushed on to Iowa, Wisconsin, Michigan, Missouri, California, Nebraska, Kansas, Texas, Indiana, Colorado, Arizona, New York, Utah, Arkansas, Minnesota, Illinois, Kentucky, Washington Territory, Nevada territory, and the Dakota territory.

George Harris served in the Revolutionary War under General George Washington. He was a sergeant of the Seventh Regiment of State Troops and Continental Army, but most of the time served as a New Jersey Minuteman and fought in the Battle of Monmouth. George Harris' two brothers, Thomas and John, also took part in the Battle of Monmouth. George Harris lived in New Jersey during the Revolutionary Way. While he was in service, his house was pillaged, and his stock driven off.

Barnabas C. Harris married Ester Miller of Millersburg, Pennsylvania, on January 19, 1976. Their son Nehemiah married Anna McGuffey, a sister to William H. McGuffey, who wrote the McGuffey Readers and Speller. Professor McGuffey taught Moral and Mental Philosophy for many years at the University of Virginia.

Edwin Poe Harris entered the University of Virginia Medical School, graduated at the age of twenty-one, moved west, and practiced medicine among the Indians in Wyoming Territory and Missouri. At the Battle of Elk Horn, he was taken prisoner by the Confederates and forced into duty as a surgeon for the wounded Confederates. He was a captain in the Second Missouri Calvary at the time, and then he escaped from the Confederates in April 1862. Edwin Poe Harris's second wife was Ella May Wolf. She was one-fourth Cherokee, a daughter of Judge Thomas Wolf.

Dr. Harris took as his third wife, Lou Jannett Perry, in 1884. She was a Chickasaw who had been educated in the Eastern States. She possessed large farm properties, ferries, and cattle. They had no children. He gradually reduced his medical practice to special cases as an assistant surgeon for the Missouri Railroad.

Another descendent was John Harris, who amassed quite a fortune and owned 140 slaves, but the Civil War swept away almost everything he had. The legend shows that John Harris and David Crockett, who gave their lives at the Alamo during the United States – Mexican War, can be traced to the Harris lineage.

Samuel Gaillard Harris, also known as Gaylord, was the oldest son of Jerome Barnabas Harris and Mary Jane Crocket[t} (aka Croker) Kissinger Harris. He was born on April 11, 1874. He married Estella Nelson Harmon (Harman) in 1898 or 1899. She died on October 5, 1905. They had a son and a daughter. He married Ellen May Hutton on February 20, 1906, at Marlinton, Pocahontas County, West Virginia. They had six sons.

Many of the Harris descendants were farmers, carpenters, inn-keepers, cheesemakers, saloonkeepers, nurses, sheriffs, photographers, artists, newspaper editors, ministers, physicians, members of Congress, state legislators, soldiers (one West Point), sailors (on the Naval Academy at Annapolis), lawyers, civil engineers, dentists, wagonmakers, teachers, stagecoach drivers, manufacturers, oil businessmen and one a bishop of the Methodist-Episcopal Church.

Mrs. Keifer completed her history of the Harris family with these words, "to gather up, compile and write such a book as this; I think I would rather do ordinary household work when I think of the amount of time it has taken to gather up and arrange this book. I am amazed at my own perseverance."

"Gale" Gaylord an "Raph" Raphael Harris married the Nelson sisters from Beverly, sisters of Joe Nelson, as their first wives.

Raphael Simeon Harris looked like Dan Rather of *CBS News*; Raphael was the son of Jerome B. Harris and Mary Crockett Harris. Allen Harris was the oldest of six sons and five daughters. Allen was a highly-decorated WWII combat infantry survivor from Gaudal Canal to Okinawa Invasion in the South Pacific.

Raphael was first married to a Nelson, who died giving birth to Allen at Beverly, and his second marriage was to Lena Bowers, daughter of John Bowers. Raphael Simeon Harris and Lena Bowers Harris' children were Geneva Catherine Harris - born June 13, 1912, married Charlie Robert Triplett on September 12, 1929, and had one son, George Raphael Triplett, born Friday, September 13, 1935, Cheat Bridge; Mabel Harris Payne - married Harry Payne, their children were Thomas Harris Payne, Jack Payne, and Patty Ann Payne; Ralph Howard Harris - married Anna Mae Davis Harris, daughter of Elmer and Willa Davis, with no children born to the marriage; Greta Jane Harris - married Frank Miller, one daughter, Nancy Harris Booth; Robert Harris - married Ruth Freeberger and had seven children, Robert, Jr., Ruth Ellen, Sherry, Patty, Mary, Sandy, and Christopher Harris; Jeannette Harris - married Archie Beck, two sons, Fred and Daniel William Beck. Archie Beck was a Western Maryland locomotive repairman; Alice Mae Harris - married Peter Dominick Antolini and had three children, David Antolini, Joyce Antolini Hill, and Sheila Antolini Scott; Jack Harris – married to Marie Coontz, no children born to the marriage. Jack was a Western Maryland Railroad Conductor; James Jesse Harris - married Elizabeth Howard, four children, Kay, Lynn, Jeff, and Jay Harris; Fielding Clinton Harris - never married; Raphael Simeon Harris first married Ruth Nelson, mother of Allen Nelson Harris, who married Ruth Smith, and there were no children born.

DAN VEST

Charles Daniel "Dan" Vest's last written contribution to the George R. Triplett and Norma Townsend family ancestry was July 14, 2021, two days prior to his sudden, unexpected demise. Dan is a great-great-grandson of Ephraim Triplett. Ephraim was the first-born son of John Triplett and Sallie (Kittle) Triplett and the first of four children.

Dan was a leader in the Electrician's Union and Grand Master of the Grand Lodge of West Virginia Independent Order of Odd Fellows. He last resided in Elkins, Randolph County, West Virginia. He married Linda Lou Hardy, who is a descendant of Michael Arbogast and Mary Elizabeth Samuels. Linda's parents were Daniel Webster Hardy and Flossie Mable Bright Hardy. The three children born to Dan and Linda's marriage were Elizabeth Diane Vest, James Allen Vest, and Rebecca Dani Vest.

Dan was a most inspirational and dedicated researcher and contributor to the history and genealogy of families mentioned in this book. Without his research and help, this book would not have been published.

TRIPLETT FAMILY

ANCESTORS OF GEORGE RAPHAEL TRIPLETT

Parents: Thomas Triplett and Abigail Huse

Thomas was a descendant of Francis F. Triplett, born in 1602.

Thomas Triplett is the 14th generation great grandfather and biological descendant of authors George A. Triplett, Robert C. Triplett, Sofia F. Triplett, and Alexandra L. Triplett

FIRST GENERATION:

George Raphael Triplett, son of Charles Robert Triplett and Geneva Katherine Harris, was born on 13 Sep 1935 in Cheat Bridge, West Virginia.

George married Frances Mae Rossi, C.R.N.A., daughter of Emedio Rossi and Agatha Saccoccia, on 5 May 1956 in Coalton, Randolph County, West Virginia.

Children from this marriage were:

- o George Raphael Triplett, Jr., D.O., was born on 5 Nov 1956 in Farmville, Prince Edward County, Virginia.

- o Charles Emedio Triplett, CPA, was born on 22 Nov 1964 in Fairmont, Marion County, West Virginia.

o   Jefferson Lee Triplett, J.D., was born on 21 Jul 1970 in Elkins, Randolph County, West Virginia.

George next married Norma Jean Townsend, daughter of Norman William Townsend and Beatrice Ross, in January 2007.

Charleston Gazette, June 20, 1963, Photo Frances, JFK and Butch 6/20/1963

SECOND GENERATION (PARENTS):

Charles Robert Triplett, son of George Washington Triplett and Laura Susan "Lora" Arbogast, was born on 24 Apr 1905 in Cheat Shavers Fork, Faulkner, West Virginia, died on 17 Jan 1970 in Randolph County, West Virginia, at age 64, and was buried in Maplewood Cemetery, Elkins, Randolph County, West Virginia.

Charles married Geneva Katherine Harris on 12 Sep 1929 in Oakland, Garrett County, Maryland. The child from this marriage was George Raphael Triplett.

Geneva Katherine Harris, daughter of Raphael Semies "Ralph" Harris and Lena Bowers, was born on 13 Jun 1912 in Glady, Randolph County, West Virginia, died on 25 Jan 2002 in Elkins, Randolph County, West Virginia, at age 89, and was buried in Maplewood Cemetery, Elkins, Randolph County, West Virginia.

Geneva married Charles Robert Triplett on 12 Sep 1929 in Oakland, Garrett County, Maryland.

THIRD GENERATION (GRANDPARENTS):

George Washington Triplett, son of Jasper Wilmoth Triplett and Eliza Chenoweth, was born on 4 Sep 1874, died on 8 Jan 1928 at age 53, and was buried in Maplewood Cemetery, Elkins, Randolph County, West Virginia.

George married Laura Susan "Lora" Arbogast in 1907 in Randolph County, West Virginia. Children from this marriage were:

- o Charles Robert Triplett

Ira William Triplett was born on 10 Aug 1907 in Bowden, Randolph County, West Virginia, died in Feb 1978 at age 70, and was buried in Maplewood Cemetery, Elkins, Randolph County, West Virginia.

Harry Jasper Triplett was born on 8 Mar 1910 in Bowden, Randolph County, West Virginia, died on 24 Jan 1992 in Bowden, Randolph County, West Virginia, at age 81, and was buried in Elkins Memorial Gardens, Elkins, West Virginia.

Laura Susan "Lora" Arbogast, daughter of Lemuel Jefferson Arbogast and Barbara Ann Margaret Rexrode, was born on 12 Oct 1876 in Pendleton County, West Virginia, died on 28 Dec 1946 in Randolph County, West Virginia, at age 70, and was buried in Maplewood Cemetery, Elkins, Randolph County, West Virginia.

Laura married George Washington Triplett in 1907 in Randolph County, West Virginia.

Raphael Semies "Ralph" Harris, son of Jerome Barnabus Harris and Mary Jane Crocker "Crockett" [209], was born on 1 Mar 1882 in Beverly, Randolph County, West Virginia, died on 16 Apr 1950 in Glady, Randolph County, West Virginia at age 68, and was buried in Greenwood-Valley Bend Cemetery, East Dailey, Randolph County, West Virginia.

Raphael married Lena Bowers in Randolph County, West Virginia. Children from this marriage were:

- o Allen Scott Harris was born on 23 Jun 1908, died on 27 Jan 1975 at age 66, and was buried in Little Arlington Cemetery, Elkins, Randolph County, West Virginia.

- o Geneva Katherine Harris.

- o Mabel Margaret Harris was born on 8 Nov 1913 in Glady, Randolph County, West Virginia, died on 7 Aug 2006 in Parsons, Tucker County, West Virginia, at age 92, and was buried in Parsons Cemetery.

- o Ralph Howard Harris was born on 26 Apr 1915 in Beverly, Randolph County, West Virginia, died on 20 Jan 1966 in Valley Bend, Randolph County, West Virginia, at age 50, and was buried in Greenwood-Valley Bend Cemetery, East Dailey, Randolph County, West Virginia.

- o Greta Jane Harris was born on 10 Jul 1916 in Glady, Randolph County, West Virginia, died on 27 Jan 2011 in Elkins, Randolph County, West Virginia, at age 94, and was buried in Parsons Cemetery, Parsons, Tucker County, West Virginia.

- o Robert Harris was born on 24 Nov 1919 in Glady, Randolph County, West Virginia, died on 2 Aug 2009 in Minnehaha Springs, Pocahontas County, West Virginia, at age 89, and was buried in Crest Lawn Memorial Gardens, Marriottsville, Howard County, Maryland.

- Alice Mae Harris was born on 20 Mar 1920 in Glady, Randolph County, West Virginia, and died on 9 Apr 2012 in Elkins, Randolph County, West Virginia, at age 92.

- Janette Harris was born on 1 Jul 1921 in Glady, Randolph County, West Virginia, died on 30 Jan 2005 in Elkins, Randolph County, West Virginia, at age 83, and was buried in Elkins Memorial Gardens, Elkins, West Virginia.

- Jack Harris was born on 26 Dec 1925 in Glady, Randolph County, West Virginia, died on 27 Sep 1977 in Cumberland, Allegany County, Maryland, at age 51, and was buried in Greenwood-Valley Bend Cemetery, East Dailey, Randolph County, West Virginia.

- James Jerome Harris was born on 25 Jan 1927 in Glady, Randolph County, West Virginia, died on 14 Aug 1983 in Clarksville, Montgomery County, Tennessee at age 56, and was buried in Fort Donelson National Cemetery, Dover, Stewart County, Tennessee.

- Fielding Clinton Harris was born on 5 Apr 1929 in Beverly, Randolph County, West Virginia, died 12 Jul 1997 in Clarksburg, Harrison County, West Virginia at age 68, and was buried in Greenwood- Valley Bend Cemetery, East Dailey, Randolph County, West Virginia.

Lena Bowers, daughter of John O. Bowers and Margaret Catherine "Maggie" Whitecottton, was born on 15 Aug 1890 in Randolph County, West Virginia, died on 9 Feb 1967 in Elkins, Randolph County, West Virginia, at age 76, and was buried in Greenwood-Valley Bend Cemetery, East Dailey, Randolph County, West Virginia.

Lena married Raphael Semies "Ralph" Harris in Randolph County, West Virginia.

Fourth Generation (Great-Grandparents):

Jasper Wilmoth Triplett, son of Job Triplett and Sydney Wilmoth [26], was born on 29 Oct 1842 in Virginia, died on 29 Dec 1914 in Faulkner, Randolph County, West Virginia at age 72, and was buried in Maplewood Cemetery, Elkins, Randolph County West Virginia.

Jasper married Eliza Chenoweth in 1870. Children from this marriage were:

- Wade Hampton Triplett was born on 8 May 1873, died on 12 Feb 1961 at age 87, and was buried in Maplewood Cemetery, Elkins, Randolph County, West Virginia.

- George Washington Triplett.

- Delphia B. Triplett was born in 1877 in Randolph County, West Virginia, died on 10 Mar 1957 in Huntington, Cabell County, West Virginia, at age 80, and was buried in Elmwood Cemetery, Elmwood, Wayne County, West Virginia.

- Eliza Chenoweth, daughter of James C. Chenoweth and Mary Helmick, was born in Nov 1845 in Randolph County, Virginia, died on 29 Dec 1914 in Randolph County, West Virginia, at age 69, and was buried in Maplewood Cemetery, Randolph County, West Virginia.

Eliza married Jasper Wilmoth Triplett in 1870.

Lemuel Jefferson Arbogast, son of Elemuel Lemuel Arbogast and Susannah Bennett, was born in Jul 1851 in Circleville, Pendleton County, Virginia, died on 26 Oct 1935 in Randolph County, West Virginia, at age 84, and was buried in Taylor Cemetery, Bowden, Randolph County, West Virginia.

Lemuel married Barbara Ann Margaret Rexrode on 7 Nov 1870 in Pendleton County, West Virginia. Children from this marriage were:

- o Martha Ellen Arbogast was born on 16 May 1870 in Pendleton County, West Virginia, died on 11 Feb 1941 in Bedford County, Pennsylvania, at age 70, and was buried in Pinegrove Christian Church Cemetery.

- o Ida Jane Arbogast was born about 1872.

- o Jenny Florence Arbogast.

- o Christina Arbogast was born 15 Aug 1874-1875 in Circleville, Pendleton County, West Virginia, died on 25 Jan 1955 in Elkins, Randolph County, West Virginia, at age 80, and was buried in Maplewood Cemetery, Elkins, Randolph County, West Virginia.

- o Laura Susan "Lora" Arbogast

- o James William Arbogast was born in 1879.

- o Etta Elizabeth Arbogast was born on 28 Dec 1880 in Pendleton County, West Virginia, died on 30 Oct 1918 in Randolph County, West Virginia, at age 37, and was buried in Taylor Cemetery, Bowden, Randolph County, West Virginia.

- o Lemuel Earl Arbogast was born on 13 Jul 1884 in Onego, Pendleton County, West Virginia, and died on 16 Jan 1943 in Randolph County, West Virginia, at age 58.

- o Anna M. Arbogast was born about 1889.

- o Benjamin Harley Arbogast was born on 13 Mar 1894 in Pendleton County, West Virginia, died on 25 Mar 1962 in Randolph County, West Virginia, at age 68, and was buried in Mountain State Memorial Gardens, Elkins, Randolph County, West Virginia.

- o George W. Hobert Arbogast was born on 11 Sep 1897 in Pendleton County, West Virginia, died on 21 Apr 1986 in Stark County, Ohio, at age 88, and was buried in Mountain State Memorial Gardens, Elkins, Randolph County, West Virginia.

Barbara Ann Margaret Rexrode, daughter of George W. Rexrode and Eliza J. Hoover, was born on 23 Apr 1853 in Pendleton County, Virginia, and died on 15 Jul 1920 at age 67.

Barbara married Lemuel Jefferson Arbogast on 7 Nov 1870 in Pendleton County, West Virginia.

Jerome Barnabus Harris, son of Barnabus Tunis Harris and Rachel Marquis, was born on 19 Apr 1836 in Pulaski, Beaver County, Pennsylvania, died on 24 Apr 1900 at age 64 and was buried in Ward Cemetery, Randolph County, West Virginia.

Jerome married Mary Jane Crocker "Crockett". Children from this marriage were:

- o Lenorabell Ruth Harris was born in 1872 and died in 1952 in Pittsburg County, Oklahoma, at age 80.

- o Samuel Gaylord Harris was born on 11 Apr 1874 in Pulaski, Lawrence, Pennsylvania, and died on 10 Mar 1936 in Abingdon, Virginia, at age 61.

- o Jerald C. Harris was born in 1876 and died in 1960 in Valley Bend, West Virginia, at age 84.

- o Barney Yunis Harris was born in 1878 and died in 1940 in Glady, West Virginia, at age 62.

- o Mary H. Harris was born in 1880 and died in 1969 in Beverly, West Virginia, at age 89. Mary married David Wamsley.

- o Raphael Semies "Raph" Harris

- o William Crocker-Harris Harris was born in 1884 and died in 1971 in Beverly, West Virginia, at age 87.

Mary Jane Crocker "Crockett," daughter of William Henry Crocker and Alice E. Sprott, was born on 10 Dec 1844 in Slippery Rock, Butler County, Pennsylvania, died on 11 Jul 1929 in Valley Bend, Randolph County, West Virginia, at age 84, and was buried in Greenwood-Valley Bend Cemetery, East Dailey, Randolph County, West Virginia.

Mary married Jerome Barnabus Harris. Mary next married William Kissinger in about 1864. Children from this marriage were:

- o Nettie Alice Kissinger was born on 28 Feb 1865 in New Castle, Lawrence County, Pennsylvania, died on 18 May 1930 in Huttonsville, Randolph County, West Virginia, at age 65, and was buried in Old Brick Church Cemetery.

- o John Sylvia Kissinger was born in 1866 and died in 1937 at age 71.

- o John O. Bowers was born on 22 Feb 1849 in Virginia, died on 18 Jun 1931 in Glady, Randolph County, West Virginia, at age 82, and was buried in Glady Cemetery, Glady, Randolph County, West Virginia.

John married Margaret Catherine "Maggie" Whitecottton. Children from this marriage were:

- o Jacob Bowers was born on 25 Jul 1876 in Virginia, died on 16 Feb 1955 in Weston, Lewis County, West Virginia, at age 78, and was buried in Elkins Memorial Gardens, Elkins, West Virginia.

- o Texie Mary Bowers was born in 1887 in Pendleton County, West Virginia, died in 1912 in Elkins, Randolph County, West Virginia, at age 25, and was buried in Hazelwood Cemetery, Elkins, West Virginia.

- o Lena Bowers.

- o Sallie Bowers was born in 1880 and died in 1965 at age 85.

- o Lillie B. Bowers was born on 24 Oct 1890 in Randolph County, West Virginia, died on 29 May 1965 in Weston, Lewis County, West Virginia, at age 74, and was buried in Elkins Memorial Gardens, Elkins, Randolph County, West Virginia.

- o Bertha Bowers was born on 28 Feb 1892, died on 5 Mar 1985 at age 93, and was buried in Elkins Memorial Gardens, Elkins Randolph County, West Virginia.

Margaret Catherine "Maggie" Whitecottton, daughter of William Edward Whitecottton, Sr. and Mary Magdalen Mowrey, was born on 25 Jul 1853 in Highland County, Virginia, died on 10 Dec 1936 in Elkins, Randolph County, West Virginia, at age 83, and was buried in Glady Cemetery, Glady, Randolph County, West Virginia.

Margaret married John O. Bowers

FIFTH GENERATION (2ND GREAT-GRANDPARENTS):

Job Triplett, son of John Sullenger Triplett and Christina Sallie Kittle, was born in 1815 and died in 1865 in Randolph County, West Virginia, at age 50.

Job married Sydney Wilmoth on 13 Dec 1841 in Randolph County, Virginia. Children from this marriage were:

- o Jasper Wilmoth Triplett

- o Oliver R. Triplett was born in 1844, died in 1864 in Killed at Sinks of Gandy at age 20, and was buried in Co. An 18th Virginia Cavalry, CSA.

- o Lydia Ann Triplett was born in 1846, died in 1958 at age 112, and was buried in Elkins, Randolph County, West Virginia.

- o Martha J. Triplett was born on 22 Aug 1847, died on 6 Feb 1920 in Randolph County, West Virginia, at age 72, and was buried on 12 Feb 1920 in Kerens, Randolph County, West Virginia.

- o Lavinia C. Triplett was born in 1850 and died in 1865.

- o Benjamin Franklin Triplett was born in 1853 in Randolph County, Virginia, and died in 1900 at age 47.

- o William Owen Triplett was born on 23 Oct 1855, died on 10 Jun 1940 at age 84, and was buried in Elkins, Randolph County, West Virginia.

- o Granville Triplett was born in 1856 and died in 1966 at age 110.

- o Edmond Triplett was born in 1856 and died in 1856.

- o Nimrod Triplett was born in 1858 and died in 1968 at age 110.

o   Philadelphia May Triplett was born on 16 Oct 1862 in Bowden, Randolph County, Virginia, died on 2 Nov 1947 in Kerens, Randolph County, West Virginia at age 85, and was buried on 4 Nov 1947 in Israel Church Cemetery, Kerens, Randolph County, West Virginia.

o   Mary Cathrin Triplett was born in 1864 and died in 1944 at age 80.

Sydney Wilmoth, daughter of William Wilmoth and Mary Polly Taylor, was born in 1823 in Randolph County, Virginia, and died in 1865 in Randolph County, West Virginia, at age 42.

Sydney married Job Triplett on 13 Dec 1841 in Randolph County, Virginia.

James C. Chenoweth, son of Jehu Chenoweth and Eleanor Nellie Skidmore, was born on 21 Mar 1819 in Randolph County, Virginia, and died on 14 Sep 1889 in Randolph County, West Virginia, at age 70.

James married Mary Helmick circa 1840. Children from this marriage were:

o   Andrew Chenoweth was born on 27 Mar 1842 in Randolph County, Virginia, died on 20 Jan 1927 in Randolph County, West Virginia, at age 84, and was buried in Arnold Hill Cemetery, Elkins, Randolph County, West Virginia.

o   Eliza Chenoweth.

o   Jehu "Jerry" Chenoweth.

o   Perry Chenoweth.

o   George Washington Chenoweth was born in 1850 and died in 1907 at age 57.

Mary Helmick, daughter of George Helmick, was born in 1815 in Randolph County, Virginia, died in Beverly, Randolph County, West Virginia, and was buried in Chenoweth Cemetery.

Mary married James C. Chenoweth circa 1840.

Elemuel Lemuel Arbogast, son of Joseph E. Arbogast and Sarah Ketterman, was born Mar 1818-1820 in Pendleton County, Virginia, and died on 10 Jun 1903 in Cherry Grove, Pendleton County, West Virginia, at age 85.

Elemuel married Susannah Bennett on 2 Mar 1841 in Pendleton County, Virginia. Children from this marriage were:

o   Lucinda Arbogast was born on 1 May 1840 in Virginia, died on 31 May 1913 in Virginia at age 73, and was buried in Blue Grass Cemetery, Blue Grass, Highland County, Virginia.

o   Isaac Newton Arbogast was born on 15 Jul 1842 in Pendleton, Virginia, died on 20 Feb 1919 in Allegany, Maryland, at age 76, and was buried in Oak Hill Cemetery, Lonaconing, Allegany, Maryland.

o   Martin Van Buren Arbogast was born on 15 Jul 1844 in Circleville, Pendleton County, Virginia, died in Jun 1928 in Randolph County, West Virginia, at age 83, and was buried in Manzanola Cemetery, Crowley, Colorado.

- o Agnes Angeline Arbogast was born about 1846.

- o William J. Arbogast was born about 1848 in Pendleton County, Virginia, and died in 1938 about age 90.

- o Lemuel Jefferson Arbogast

- o George Wesley Arbogast was born about 1853.

- o James C. Arbogast was born about 1855.

- o Mary Susan Arbogast was born about 1858.

- o Jacob A. Arbogast was born about 1864.

- o Alfred T. Arbogast was born about 1869.

Susannah Bennett was born in 1824 in Virginia and died 1880-1885 in Circleville, Pendleton County, West Virginia, at age 56.

George W. Rexrode. George married Eliza J. Hoover on 15 Aug 1844 in Pendleton County, Virginia. Children from this marriage were:

- o Sarah C. Rexrode was born on 13 Jun 1845, died on 28 Sep 1905 at age 60, and was buried in Mill Creek Church of the Brethren Cemetery, Port Republic, Rockingham County, Virginia.

- o Mary E. Rexrode was born about 1847.

- o John A. Rexrode was born on 29 Nov 1848, died on 4 Apr 1915 at age 66, and was buried in Mouse Yokum Cemetery, Seneca Rocks, Pendleton County, West Virginia.

- o Benjamin C. Rexrode was born on 15 Dec 1850, died on 21 Apr 1922 at age 71, and was buried in Mill Creek Church of the Brethren Cemetery, Port Republic, Rockingham County, Virginia.

- o Barbara Ann Margaret Rexrode

Eliza J. Hoover. Eliza married George W. Rexrode on 15 Aug 1844 in Pendleton County, Virginia.

Barnabus Tunis Harris, son of Barnabus C. Harris and Esther Miller, was born on 21 May 1811 in Coitsville, Ohio, died on 9 Sep 1871 at age 60, and was buried in Pulaski Cemetery, Lawrence County, Pennsylvania.

Barnabus married Rachel Marquis in Sep 1835 in Pulaski, Beaver County, Pennsylvania. Children from this marriage were:

- o Jerome Barnabus Harris

- o Merthyan Harris was born on 29 Sep 1837 and died on 30 Jun 1848 at age 10.

- o Andrew Marquis Harris was born in 1839 and died in 1883 at age 44.

o   Samuel Findley Harris was born on 6 Jul 1843, died on 9 Jan 1914 at age 70, and was buried in Neshannock Presbyterian Cemetery, New Wilmington, Lawrence County, Pennsylvania.

Rachel Marquis, daughter of Andrew Marquis and Lydia Moorehead, was born on 2 Aug 1814 and died on 10 Apr 1870 at age 55.

Rachel married Barnabus Tunis Harris in Sep 1835 in Pulaski, Beaver County, Pennsylvania.

William Henry Crocker, son of Robert Marion Crocker and Elizabeth Warner, was born on 12 Mar 1817 in Lawerence, Pennsylvania, died on 23 Aug 1893 in Pennsylvania at age 76, and was buried in Slippery Rock Cemetery, Slippery Rock, Butler County, Pennsylvania.

William married Alice E. Sprott on 2 Dec 1840, in Lawerence, Pennsylvania. Children from this marriage were:

o   Elizabeth Crocker was born in 1841 and died in 1938 at age 97.

o   Edward Smith Crocker was born on 6 Feb 1843 in Slippery Rock, Butler, Pennsylvania, died on 23 Feb 1862 in Louisville, Jefferson County, Kentucky at age 19, and was buried in Cave Hill National Cemetery, Louisville, Jefferson County, Kentucky.

o   Mary Jane Crocker "Crockett"

George Hutchinson Crocker was born on 27 Sep 1846 and died on 12 Jan 1914 at age 67.

John Selbey Crocker was born on 26 Mar 1848 in Slippery Rock, Butler, Pennsylvania, and died on 17 Aug 1911 in Spokane, Washington, at age 63.

Charles S. Crocker was born in 1850 and died in 1873 at age 23.

Emaline Willhelmina Crocker was born on 15 May 1853 and died on 17 Oct 1938 in Deary, Latah, Idaho at age 85.

Luther Lee Crocker was born in 1855 and died on 11 Aug 1926 in Portland, Multnomah, Oregon, at age 71.

Margaret Priscilla Crocker was born on 22 Mar 1856 and died on 28 Feb 1936 at age 79.

Alice Virginia Crocker was born in 1857 and died in 1939 at age 82.

Catherine Watson Crocker was born about 1861 and died in 1901 about age 40.

Clara Louisa Crocker was born in 1864 and died in 1938 at age 74.

Edward Austin Crocker was born in 1866 and died in 1957 at age 91.

Caroline Olive Crocker was born on 20 Feb 1869 and died about 1916 about age 47.

Alice E. Sprott, daughter of David Sprott and Elizabeth Hutcheson, was born on 23 Aug 1823 in Saint Cuthberts, Edinburgh, Midlothian, Scotland, died on 1 Jul 1902 in Pennsylvania at age 78 and was buried in Slippery Rock Cemetery, Slippery Rock, Butler County, Pennsylvania.

Alice married William Henry Crocker on 2 Dec 1840, in Lawerence, Pennsylvania.

William Edward Whitecottton, Sr., son of James Whitecottton and Nancy Ann Raines, was born on 3 Jun 1829 in Pendleton County, Virginia, and died on 22 Jun 1911 in Cave City, Independence, Arkansas, at age 82.

William married Mary Magdalen Mowrey on 6 Jul 1851 in Highland County, Virginia. Children from this marriage were:

- o Solomon Whitecottton was born about 1852.

- o Margaret Catherine "Maggie" Whitecottton

- o Ann Eliza Whitecottton was born about 1855.

- o Mary Whitecottton was born in 1858.

- o William Edward Whitecottton, Jr. was born on 10 Mar 1858 in Circleville, Pendleton County, Virginia.

- o Sarah Eveline Whitecottton was born in 1861 and died in 1926 at age 65.

- o Gemima Whitecottton was born in 1863.

- o James Whitecottton was born in 1868 and died in 1934 at age 66.

Mary Magdalen Mowrey was born in 1827 and died in 1900 at age 73.

Mary married William Edward Whitecottton, Sr. on 6 Jul 1851 in Highland County, Virginia.

SIXTH GENERATION (3RD GREAT-GRANDPARENTS):

John Sullenger Triplett, son of Col. Francis B. Triplett and Benedicta Hedgman "Lucy" Sennett, was born on 28 Aug 1758, died on 1 Jun 1869 in Kelly Mountain, Randolph County, West Virginia at age 110, and was buried in Maplewood Cemetery.

John married Christina Sallie Kittle in 1800 in Randolph County, Virginia. Children from this marriage were:

- o Nancy Triplett was born on 11 Feb 1798 in Randolph County, Virginia.

- o Ephraim Triplett was born on 8 Apr 1802 in Randolph County, Virginia, and died on 8 Apr 1884 at age 82.

- o William B. Triplett was born in 1803.

- o Jacob Triplett was born on 26 Oct 1804 in Leadsville, Randolph County, Virginia, and died on 13 Mar 1862 in Beverly, Randolph County, Virginia, at age 57.

- o Elizabeth Triplett was born on 7 Jan 1806 in Randolph County, Virginia.

- o Loami Triplett was born on 11 Apr 1808 in Randolph County, Virginia.

- o Moses Triplett was born on 10 Oct 1809, died on 24 Jun 1849 at age 39, and was buried in Arnolds Hill Baptist Church Cemetery, Randolph County, West Virginia.

o Eunice Triplett was born in 1812 and died in 1900 at age 88.

o Anna Triplett was born in 1813 and died in 1840 at age 27.

o Job Triplett

o Ely Triplett was born in 1817 and died in 1879 at age 62.

o John J. Triplett was born in 1820 and died in 1904 at age 84.

o James Triplett was born on 7 Mar 1820 in Beverly, Randolph County, Virginia, died on 5 Aug 1904 in Eagleville, Harrison County, Missouri, at age 84, and was buried in Buntin Cemetery, Brooklyn, Harrison County, Missouri.

o Rachel Triplett was born in 1823.

o Mary Jane Triplett was born on 4 Sep 1824 in Montrose, Randolph County, Virginia, died on 13 Oct 1886 in Montrose, Randolph County, West Virginia, at age 62, and was buried in Primitive Baptist Cemetery, Montrose, West Virginia.

John next married Nancy A. Bennett, daughter of Jacob Bennett and Mary Persinger, in Apr 1829 in Randolph County, Virginia. Children from this marriage were:

o Martha Ellen Triplett was born in 1830 and died in 1908 at age 78.

o Catherine Rachel Triplett was born in 1832, died on 14 Aug 1917 at age 85, and was buried in Israel Church Cemetery, Kerens, Randolph County, West Virginia.

o Harriett Triplett was born in 1835.

o John J. Triplett was born on 8 Mar 1837 in Randolph County, Virginia, and died in 1887 in Randolph County, West Virginia, at age 50.

o Randolph Triplett was born on 28 Aug 1837 in Randolph County, Virginia, died on 15 Mar 1921 in Randolph County, West Virginia, at age 83, and was buried in Primitive Baptist Church Cemetery, Montrose, West Virginia.

o Hickman Triplett was born in 1840 and died in 1950 at age 110.

o Anthony Triplett was born on 18 Dec 1841 in Beverly, Randolph County, Virginia, and died in 1925 at age 84.

John next married Nancy A. Bennett, daughter of Jacob Bennett and Mary Persinger, in Apr 1829 in Randolph County, Virginia.

Christina Sallie Kittle, daughter of Jacob Kittle and Mary Ann Hendrickson, was born in 1783 and died in 1826 at age 43.

Christina married John Sullenger Triplett in 1800 in Randolph County, Virginia.

William Wilmoth, son of Nicholas J. Wilmoth and Sydney Ann Currence, was born on 23 Nov 1799 in Randolph County, Virginia, died on 11 Jun 1867 in Randolph County, West Virginia, at age 67, and was buried in Isner Wilmoth Cemetery.

William married Mary Polly Taylor on 26 Nov 1821 in Randolph County, Virginia. Children from this marriage were:

- o Sydney Wilmoth

- o Nicholas Wilmoth was born in 1824 and died in 1899 at age 75.

- o Elizabeth Eliza Wilmoth was born in 1825 and died in 1898 at age 73.

- o Sara Sally Wilmoth was born in 1828.

- o Benjamin Franklin Wilmoth was born in 1829 and died in 1906 at age 77.

- o Nimrod Wilmoth was born in 1832 and died in 1943 at age 111.

- o Jemima Jennie Wilmoth was born in 1834 and died in 1910 at age 76.

- o Isaac Wilmoth was born in 1837 and died in 1899 at age 62.

- o Lydia Ann Wilmoth was born in 1837 and died in 1890 at age 53.

- o Seymour Wilmoth was born in 1839.

- o Amanda Wilmoth was born in 1850 and died in 1959 at age 109.

- o Mary Bettie Wilmoth was born in 1851.

Mary Polly Taylor, daughter of Isaac Taylor and Elizabeth Hays [2078], was born on 5 Oct 1805 in Randolph County, Virginia, died on 11 Mar 1878 in Randolph County, West Virginia, at age 72, and was buried in Wilmoth-Isner Cemetery.

Mary married William Wilmoth on 26 Nov 1821 in Randolph County, Virginia.

Jehu Chenoweth, son of John Chenoweth and Mary Calvert. Jehu married Eleanor Nellie Skidmore. The child from this marriage was:

- o James C. Chenoweth.

Eleanor married Jehu Chenoweth.

George Helmick. George married someone. His child was Mary Helmick.

Joseph E. Arbogast, son of John C. Arbogast and Hannah Davis, was born on 17 Jan 1794 in Virginia and died on 8 Feb 1884 in Pendleton County, West Virginia, at age 90.

Joseph married Sarah Ketterman in 1820. Children from this marriage were:

- o Elemuel Lemuel Arbogast

- o Cain Arbogast was born in 1819 and died in 1900 at age 81.

- o Joseph Arbogast was born in 1826 and died in 1910 at age 84.

- o Sarah Ann Arbogast was born in 1835 and died in 1929 at age 94.

- o Sylvanus Arbogast was born in 1836 and died in 1902 at age 66.

- o Hannah Arbogast was born in 1836 and died in 1924 at age 88.

- o Jacob Arbogast was born in 1841 and died in 1931 at age 90.

Sarah Ketterman was born in about 1800.

Sarah married Joseph E. Arbogast in 1820.

Barnabus C. Harris, son of George Harris and Hannah Tunis, was born on 15 Aug 1768 in Essex County, New Jersey, died on 18 Dec 1849 in Mahoning County, Ohio, at age 81, and was buried in Hopewell Cemetery, New Bedford, Lawrence County, Pennsylvania.

Barnabus married Esther Miller on 19 Jan 1796 in Washington County, Pennsylvania. Children from this marriage were:

- o Col. Nehemiah Harris was born on 20 Jun 1801 in Pennsylvania, died on 11 Oct 1878 in Hardin County, Ohio, at age 77, and was buried in Grove Cemetery, Kenton, Hardin County, Ohio.

- o George Washington Harris was born on 21 Jun 1807, died on 13 Feb 1888 at age 80, and was buried in Hopewell Cemetery, New Bedford, Lawrence County, Pennsylvania.

- o Pamela Harris was buried in Grandview Cemetery, Carroll County, Carrollton, Ohio.

- o Hannah Tunis Harris was born on 5 May 1809, died on 9 Sep 1850 at age 41, and was buried in Lowellville Cemetery, Lowellville, Mahoning County, Ohio.

- o Barnabus Tunis Harris.

- o Phebe Harris.

- o Esther Harris.

- o John Harris.

- o Catharine Poe Harris.

- o Susannah Harris.

o   Sarah W. Harris was born on 25 Feb 1816 in Coitsville Center, Ohio, died in 1898 in New Bedford, Lawrence County, Pennsylvania, at age 82, and was buried in Hopewell Cemetery, New Bedford, Lawrence County, Pennsylvania.

Esther Miller was born in 1769, died on 2 Jul 1839 at age 70, and was buried in Hopewell Cemetery, New Bedford, Lawrence County, Pennsylvania.

Esther married Barnabus C. Harris on 19 Jan 1796 in Washington County, Pennsylvania.

Andrew Marquis was born in 1799.

Andrew married Lydia Moorehead. Children from this marriage were:

- Rachel Marquis.

- William Marquis.

- Sarah J. Marquis.

- John Marquis.

- James Marquis died in 1874.

- David Calhoun Marquis.

- Samuel Marquis.

- Elizabeth Marquis.

- Robert Marquis.

- Andrew Marquis.

Lydia Moorehead was born in 1792 and died in 1872 at age 80. Lydia married Andrew Marquis.

Robert Marion Crocker, son of Robert Crocker and Mary Polly Howe, was born in 1779 in Pennsylvania and died on 21 Dec 1863, in New Castle, Lawrence County, Pennsylvania, at age 84.

Robert married Elizabeth Warner in 1803. Children from this marriage were:

- Margaret Crocker was born in 1803 and died in 1887 at age 84.

- Thomas Crocker was born in 1804 and died in 1832 at age 28.

- Elizabeth Sarah Crocker was born in 1806 and died in 1877 at age 71.

- Rebecca Crocker was born in 1809 and died in 1879 at age 70.

- William Henry Crocker.

- Henry Crocker was born in 1820 and died in 1899 at age 79.

o   Robert Crocker was born in 1821 and died in 1893 at age 72.

Elizabeth Warner was born in 1784 and died in 1870 at age 86. Elizabeth married Robert Marion Crocker in 1803.

David Sprott was born in 1795.

David married Elizabeth Hutcheson. Children from this marriage were:

o   Jean Sprott was born in 1821.

o   Alice E. Sprott.

o   David Sprott was born in 1825.

o   James Sprott was born in 1827.

o   William Sprott was born in 1828.

Elizabeth Hutcheson was born in 1803. Elizabeth married David Sprott.

James Whitecottton, son of Harris Whitecottton and Margaret Shumate, was born in 1792 and died in 1855 at age 63.

James married Nancy Ann Raines. The child from this marriage was:

o   William Edward Whitecottton, Sr.

Nancy Ann Raines, daughter of James Robert Raines and Frances Thompson, was born in 1794 in Virginia and died in 1830 in Ringold County, Iowa, at age 36.

Nancy married James W. Whitecotton, son of Harris Whitecotton and Margaret Shumate, on 4 Apr 1815 in Loudoun County, Virginia. Children from this marriage were:

o   Jacob Whitecotton died in 1864.

o   James W. Whitecotton was born in 1827 and died in 1891 at age 64.

Nancy next married James Whitecottton.

SEVENTH GENERATION (4TH GREAT-GRANDPARENTS):

Col. Francis B. Triplett, son of Capt. William Triplett, Jr. and Elizabeth Hedgman were born in 1728 in Fauquier, Prince William County, Virginia, and died on 26 Jan 1795 in Culpepper, Fauquier County, Virginia, at age 67.

Francis married Benedicta Hedgman "Lucy" Sennett on 17 Mar 1758 in Prince William County, Virginia. Children from this marriage were:

o   Roger Triplett was born in 1750 and died in 1786 at age 36.

o William Triplett was born in 1754 and died in 1807 at age 53.

o Elizabeth Hedgman Triplett was born in 1757 and died in 1833 at age 76.

o Robert Triplett was born in 1758 and died in 1843 at age 85.

o John Sullenger Triplett.

o Hedgman Triplett was born in 1760 and died in 1837 at age 77.

o Benedicta Triplett was born in 1762 in Fairfax City, Virginia, and died in 1799 in Fleming, Kentucky, at age 37.

o Thomas Triplett was born in 1763 and died in 1833 at age 70.

o Francis Triplett was born in 1763 and died in 1833 at age 70.

o Francis Amelia Triplett was born in 1766 and died in 1795 at age 29.

o Maj. Robert Sennett Triplett was born on 22 Jun 1772 in Prince William, Virginia, and died on 25 Nov 1844 in Wood County, Virginia, at age 72.

o Ann Triplett was born in 1774 and died in 1866 at age 92.

o Mary Triplett.

o Hannah Triplett.

Benedicta Hedgman "Lucy" Sennett, daughter of Robert Sennett and Hannah Sennett, was born 1730-1738 in Charles, Maryland, and died 1794-1795 in Leeds, Fauquier, Virginia, at age 64. Benedicta married Col. Francis B. Triplett on 17 Mar 1758 in Prince William County, Virginia.

Jacob Kittle, son of Abraham Kittle and Christina Westfall, was born on 26 Jul 1757 in Sussex County, New Jersey, died on 4 Oct 1842 in Randolph County, Virginia, at age 85, and was buried in Arnold Hill Baptist Church Cemetery, Randolph County, Virginia.

Jacob married Mary Ann Hendrickson. Children from this marriage were:

o Elizabeth Kittle was born on 1 Sep 1776 in Orange County, New York, and died on 7 Jan 1843 in Barbour County, Virginia, at age 66.

o Gene Kittle was born on 10 Oct 1776 in Pennsylvania and died on 31 Mar 1845 in Randolph County, Virginia, at age 68.

o Sarah Kittle was born in 1782 and died in 1850 at age 68.

o Christina Sallie Kittle.

o Lydia Kittle was born in 1785 and died in 1852 at age 67.

- o Jemima Kittle was born on 15 Sep 1788, died on 25 Nov 1860 at age 72, and was buried in Arnolds Hill Baptist Church Cemetery, Elkins, Randolph County, West Virginia.

- o Moses Kittle was born in 1791 in Randolph County, Virginia, died in Mar 1825 in Randolph County, Virginia, at age 34, and was buried in Arnold Hill Baptist Church Cemetery, Randolph County, Virginia.

- o Mary Polly Kittle was born in 1793 and died in 1823 at age 30.

- o Benjamin Wilson Kittle was born in 1794 and died in 1870 at age 76.

- o George Kittle.

- o Anne Kittle.

- o Samuel Kittle.

- o Ione Kittle.

- o Margaret Kittle.

Jacob next married Mary Scott.

Mary Ann Hendrickson, daughter of John Hendrickson [340] and Lidia Kellder, was born on 3 Oct 1759 in Marbletown, Ulster County, New York, died on 9 Mar 1834 in Randolph County, Virginia, at age 74, and was buried in Arnold Hill Baptist Church Cemetery, Randolph County, Virginia. Mary married Jacob Kittle.

Nicholas J. Wilmoth, son of Thomas Wilmoth and Nancy Ann Agness Waite, was born on 24 Feb 1762 in Randolph County, Virginia, and died on 15 Jun 1829 in Randolph County, Virginia, at age 67. Nicholas married Sydney Ann Currence on 12 Aug 1789 in Randolph County, Virginia. Children from this marriage were:

- o John Wesley Wilmoth was born in 1790 and died in 1866 at age 76.

- o Thomas Wilmoth was born in 1792 and died in 1850 at age 58.

- o Susannah Wilmoth was born in 1793 and died in 1882 at age 89.

- o James Wilmoth was born in 1795 and died in 1822 at age 27.

- o Sarah Wilmoth was born on 26 Nov 1797 in Virginia, died on 19 May 1882 in Randolph County, West Virginia, at age 84, and was buried in Israel Church Cemetery, Kerens, Randolph County, West Virginia.

- o William Wilmoth.

- o Eli C. Wilmoth was born in 1801 and died in 1867 at age 66.

- o Samuel Wilmoth was born in 1804 and died in 1856 at age 52.

- o Currence Wilmoth was born in 1807 and died in 1857 at age 50.

- o Mary Wilmoth was born in 1810.

Sydney Ann Currence, daughter of Willian Currence and Lydia Steele, was born in 1765 and died in 1839 at age 74. Sydney married Nicholas J. Wilmoth on 12 Aug 1789 in Randolph County, Virginia.

Isaac Taylor. Isaac married Elizabeth Hays. The child from this marriage was Mary Polly Taylor

Elizabeth Hays. Elizabeth married Isaac Taylor.

John Chenoweth was born in 1652 in Isle of Wight.

John married Mary Calvert. Jehu Chenoweth & William Chenoweth (born in 1755) were children from this marriage.

Mary Calvert. Mary married John Chenoweth.

John C. Arbogast, son of Michael Arbogast, II and Mary Elizabeth Samuels, was born in 1762 in Virginia and died in 1821 in Circleville, Pendleton County, Virginia, at age 59.

John married Hannah Davis in 1786.

Children from this marriage were:

- o Jonathan Arbogast was born in 1789 and died in 1861 at age 72.

- o Rachel Arbogast was born in 1790 and died in 1879 at age 89.

- o Rebecca Arbogast was born in 1791 and died in 1878 at age 87.

- o Michael Arbogast was born in 1794 and died in 1830 at age 36.

- o Joseph E. Arbogast.

- o Moses Arbogast was born in 1799 and died on 26 Mar 1869 in Valley Head, Randolph County, West Virginia, at age 70.

- o Adam Arbogast was born in 1802 and died in 1860 at age 58.

- o John Arbogast was born in 1804 and died in 1880 at age 76.

- o Jesse Arbogast was born on 24 Sep 1810 in Augusta County, Virginia, died on 4 Mar 1887 in Dade County, Missouri, at age 76, and was buried in Pleasant Grove Cemetery, Greenfield, Dade County, Missouri.

Hannah Davis, daughter of John Davis, was born in 1761-1770 and died in 1830 at age 69. Hannah married John C. Arbogast in 1786.

George Harris was born in 1741 in Essex County, New Jersey, and died in 1822 in Washington County, Pennsylvania, at age 81.

George married Hannah Tunis in 1765. The child from this marriage was:

- o Barnabus C. Harris

Hannah Tunis. Hannah married George Harris in 1765.

Robert Crocker, son of Josiah Crocker and Deborah Davis, was born in 1759 and died in 1909 at age 150. Robert married Mary Polly Howe. The child from this marriage was:

- o Robert Marion Crocker

Mary Polly Howe was born in 1767 and died in 1810 at age 43. Mary married Robert Crocker.

Harris Whitecottton was born in 1768 and died in 1803 at age 35. Harris married Margaret Shumate. The child from this marriage was James Whitecottton.

Margaret Shumate was born in 1776 and died in 1819 at age 43. Margaret married Harris Whitecotton. The child from this marriage was:

- o James W. Whitecotton was born on 3 Mar 1792 in Pendleton County, Virginia, died on 19 Dec 1855 in Linden, Montgomery County, Indiana, at age 63, and was buried in Linden Cemetery.

Margaret next married Harris Whitecottton.

James Robert Raines was born in 1765 and died in 1858 at age 93.

James married Frances Thompson. Children from this marriage were:

- o George Washington Raines was born in 1794 and died in 1856 at age 62.

- o Nancy Ann Raines.

- o Barnett Raines was born on 17 Mar 1796 in Pendleton County, West Virginia, and died on 16 Dec 1888 in Pendleton County, West Virginia, at age 92, and was buried in Vance Family Cemetery, Onego, Pendleton County, West Virginia.

Frances Thompson was born in 1764 and died in 1853 at age 89. Frances married James Robert Raines.

EIGHTH GENERATION (5TH GREAT-GRANDPARENTS):

Capt. William Triplett, Jr., son of William Triplett, Sr. and Isabella Miller, was born in 1697 in Brunswick Parish, King George Virginia, and died on 10 May 1748 in Prince William County Virginia, at age 51.

William married Elizabeth Hedgman about 1723 in Culpepper, Virginia. Children from this marriage were:

- o Elizabeth Triplett was born in 1724 and died in 1789 in Fauquier County, Virginia, at age 65.

- o John Triplett was born in 1726 in Culpepper County, Virginia, and died in 1790 in Culpeper, Virginia, at age 64.

- o Thomas Triplett was born in 1727 and died in 1778 at age 51.

- o Col. Francis B. Triplett

- o Sarah Triplett was born in 1730 and died in 1774 at age 44.

- o James Triplett was born in 1733 and died in 1782 at age 49.

- o Nathaniel Triplett was born in 1740 and died in 1753 at age 13.

- o Anne Triplett Triplett was born in 1740.

- o Daniel Triplett was born in 1744 and died in 1771 at age 27.

- o William Triplett was born in 1748 and died in 1803 at age 55.

Elizabeth Hedgman, daughter of Nathaniel Hedgman and Catherine, was born in 1702 in Accokeek, Province of Virginia, and died in 1765 in Charles County, Province of Maryland, Colonial America, at age 63.

Elizabeth married Capt. William Triplett, Jr. about 1723 in Culpepper, Virginia.

Robert Sennett was born in 1700 and died in 1770 at age 70. Robert married Hannah Sennett. Children from this marriage were:

- o Benedicta Hedgman "Lucy" Sennett

- o Robert Sennett was born in 1745 and died in 1796 at age 51.

Hannah Sennett died in 1765.

Hannah married Robert Sennett.

Abraham Kittle, son of Richard Kittle and Rachel Van Etten, was born on 1 Jan 1730 in Wawarsing, Ulster County, New York, was christened on 6 Feb 1732 in Rochester Church, Kingston, Ulster County, New York, and died on 16 Sep 1816 in Randolph County, Virginia at age 86.

Noted events in his life were:

- o Abraham served in the military.

- o Abraham married Elizabeth Esters.

- o Abraham next married Christina Westfall on 30 Aug 1754 in Minisink, Orange County, New York. Children from this marriage were:

- Appolonia Prudence Kittle was born on 26 Jan 1755 in New York and died on 8 Jun 1815 in Randolph County, Virginia at age 60.

- Jacob Kittle.

- Herbert Richard Kittle was born on 20 Mar 1761 in New York and died on 14 Jan 1831 in Randolph County, Virginia, at age 69.

- Moses K. Kittle was born in 1763 and died in 1825 at age 62.

- Daniel C. Kittle was born in 1766 and died in 1823 at age 57.

- Ingra Kittle was born in 1768.

- Engeltie Kittle was born in 1769.

- Jurriaen Kittle was born in 1773 and died in 1813 at age 40.

- Julian Kittle was born in 1774.

- Maria Kittle was born in 1776 and died in 1841 at age 65.

- Sarah Elizabeth Kittle was born in 1834.

- John Kittle was born in 1864 and died in 1823 at age -41.

- Richard Kittle.

Abraham next married Mary Thixton Scott on 12 Sep 1805.

Christina Westfall was born in 1736 and died in 1801 at age 65. Christina married Abraham Kittle on 30 Aug 1754 in Minisink, Orange County, New York. Christina next married Abraham Kittle Sr. The child from this marriage was:

o Abraham Kittle Jr. was born in 1734 and died in 1814 at age 80.

John Hendrickson. John married Lidia Kellder. The child from this marriage was:

o Mary Ann Hendrickson.

Lidia Kellder. Lidia married John Hendrickson.

Thomas Wilmoth, son of Thomas Wilmoth and Margaret Ann, was born in 1734 and died on 24 Jan 1823 in Randolph County, Virginia, at age 89. Thomas married Nancy Ann Agness Waite about 1760 in Rockinham County, Virginia. Children from this marriage were:

o Nicholas J. Wilmoth.

o Thomas Wilmoth was born in 1766 and died in 1833 at age 67.

o Susannah Wilmoth was born in 1774 and died in 1854 at age 80.

- o   Jonathan Wilmoth was born in 1775.

- o   Phoebe Wilmoth was born in 1784.

- o   Deborah Wilmoth.

- o   Elizabeth Wilmoth.

- o   Mary Wilmoth.

- o   James Wilmoth was born in 1790.

Nancy Ann Agness Waite was born in 1738 and died in 1828 at age 90. Nancy married Thomas Wilmoth about 1760 in Rockingham County, Virginia.

Willian Currence was born in 1727 in Ulster, Ireland, and died on 7 Oct 1780 at age 53. Willian married Lydia Steele. The child from this marriage was:

- o   Sydney Ann Currence

Lydia Steele. Lydia married Willian Currence.

Michael Arbogast, II, son of Michael Arbogast and Catherina Konigin, was born 1732-1734 in Baden-Wurttenberg, Germany, died on 27 Aug 1812 in Pendleton County, Virginia, at age 80, and was buried in Blue Grass, Highland County, Virginia.

Michael married Mary Elizabeth Samuels 1758-1759 in Pendleton County, Virginia. Children from this marriage were:

- Adam Odesseus Arbogast was born on 25 Oct 1760 in Frederick County, Virginia, died on 9 Feb 1852 in Pocahontas County, Virginia, at age 91, and was buried in Arbogast-Yeager Cemetery, Travelers Repose, Pocahontas County, Virginia.

- John C. Arbogast.

- David Arbogast was born in 1765 and died in 1833 at age 68.

- Dorothy Arbogast was born in 1765 and died in 1839 at age 74.

- Mary Arbogast was born in 1765 and died in 1794 at age 29.

- Michael Arbogast was born in 1768 and died in 1813 at age 45.

- Peter Arbogast was born in 1770 and died in 1842 at age 72.

- Henry M. Arbogast was born in 1770 and died in 1844 at age 74.

- George Arbogast was born in 1777 and died in 1844 at age 67.

- Joseph Arbogast was born in 1778 and died in 1820 at age 42.

Mary Elizabeth Samuels was born in 1736 and died in 1772 at age 36. Mary married Michael Arbogast, II 1758-1759 in Pendleton County, Virginia.

John Davis. John married someone. His child was:

- Hannah Davis

Josiah Crocker, son of Cornelius Crocker and Lydia Jenkins, was born in 1759 in Barnstable, Massachusetts, and died on 13 Feb 1809 in Boston, Massachusetts, at age 50. Josiah married Deborah Davis. The child from this marriage was:

- Robert Crocker [1500]

Deborah Davis was born in 1746 and died in 1818 at age 72. Deborah married Josiah Crocker.

NINTH GENERATION (6TH GREAT-GRANDPARENTS):

William Triplett, Sr., son of Francis F. Triplett and Abigal Huse, was born in 1667 and died on 3 Dec 1738, in Virginia at age 71.

William married Isabella Miller in 1694 in Richmond County, Virginia. Children from this marriage were:

o   Isabella Triplett was born in 1695 and died in 1740 at age 45.

o   John Triplett was born in 1696 and died in 1773 at age 77.

o   Capt. William Triplett, Jr.

o   Daniel Triplett was born in 1698.

o   Francis Triplett was born in 1701 and died in 1767 at age 66.

o   Mary Triplett

o   Thomas Triplett was born in 1702 in Prince William County, Province of Virginia, and died in 1737 in Round Hill, Prince William County, Province of Virginia, at age 35.

o   James Triplett was born in 1704 in Prince William County, Province of Virginia, and died in 1764 in Virginia at age 60.

o   Elizabeth Triplett was born in 1760.

o   Margaret Triplett.

Isabella Miller, daughter of Capt. Symon Miller, was born in 1679 and died in 1760 at age 81. Isabella married William Triplett, Sr. in 1694 in Richmond County, Virginia.

Nathaniel Hedgman was born in 1682 and died in 1721 at age 39. Nathaniel married Catherine. The child from this marriage was:

o   Elizabeth Hedgman

Catherine was born in 1680 and died in 1708 at age 28. Catherine married Nathaniel Hedgman.

Richard Kittle, son of Jeremy Kittle and Elisabeth Classen Keator. Richard married Rachel Van Etten. Children from this marriage were:

o   Abraham Kittle

o   Susanna Nancy Kittle was born on 4 Jun 1738 and died in 1790 at age 52.

Rachel Van Etten, daughter of Jan Jacobsen Van Etten and Annetje Ariens Adriaens, was born on 20 Jun 1708 in Knightsfield, Ulster County, Province of New York, and died on 15 Dec 1754 in Ulster County, Province of New York at age 46. Rachel married Richard Kittle.

Thomas Wilmoth, son of Nicholas Wilmoth, was born in 1703 in Augusta, Hampshire County, Virginia, and died in 1778 in Staunton, Augusta County, Virginia at age 75. Thomas married Margaret Ann. The child from this marriage was:

o   Thomas Wilmoth

Margaret Ann. Margaret married Thomas Wilmoth.

Michael Arbogast was born on 27 Mar 1694 and died on 3 May 1743 in Kehl, Baden-Wurttemberg, Germany, at age 49. Michael married Catherina Konigin. The child from this marriage was:

- o   Michael Arbogast, II

Catherina Konigin was born in 1695. Catherina married Michael Arbogast, II.

Cornelius Crocker, son of Samuel Crocker and Sarah Parker, was born in 1704 in Barnstable, Massachusetts, and died in 1784 in Barnstable, Massachusetts, at age 80. Cornelius married Lydia Jenkins on 9 Nov 1727 in Barnstable, Massachusetts. The child from this marriage was:

- o   Josiah Crocker

Lydia Jenkins was born in 1705 and died in 1773 at age 68. Lydia married Cornelius Crocker on 9 Nov 1727 in Barnstable, Massachusetts.

TENTH GENERATION (7TH GREAT-GRANDPARENTS):

Francis F. Triplett, son of Thomas Triplett and Elizabeth Googe Martin, was born in 1635 and died in 1701 at age 66. Francis married Alice in 1655 in England. Children from this marriage were:

- o   Thomas Triplett was born in 1656 and died in 1725 at age 69.

- o   Elizabeth Triplett was born in 1658 and died in 1725 at age 67.

Francis next married Abigal Huse on 10 Oct 1664 in Richmond County, Virginia. Children from this marriage were:

- o   William Triplett, Sr.

- o   Thomas Triplett was born in 1669 and died in 1698 at age 29.

- o   Francis Triplett was born in 1672 and died in 1704 at age 32.

- o   Elizabeth Frances Triplett was born in 1673 in Richmond, Virginia, in Sittingburg Parish, and died on 10 Sep 1710 in Richmond, Colony of Virginia, British Colonial America, at age 37.

- o   Abigal Triplett was born in 1675.

- o   John Triplett was born in 1677 and died in 1700 at age 23.

- o   Daniel Triplett.

Abigal Huse was born in 1634 and died in 1708 at age 74. Abigal married Francis F. Triplett on 10 Oct 1664 in Richmond County, Virginia.

Capt. Symon Miller was born in 1642 and died in 1684 at age 42. Symon married someone. His child was:

- o   Isabella Miller.

Jeremy Kittle was born in 1643 and died in 1705 at age 62. Jeremy married Elisabeth Classen Keator. The child from this marriage was:

- o   Richard Kittle.

Elisabeth Classen Keator was born in 1678. Elisabeth married Jeremy Kittle.

Jan Jacobsen Van Etten was born on 3 Jan 1665 in Kingston, Province of New York, died on 22 Jun 1731 in Kingston, Ulster County, Province of New York at age 66, and was buried on 24 Jun 1731 in Kingston, Ulster, New York, British Colonial America. Jan married Annetje Ariens Adriaens. The child from this marriage was:

- o   Rachel Van Etten.

Annetje Ariens Adriaens was born on 29 Aug 1645 in Oude Kerk, Amsterdam, Holland, died in 1717 in Dutchess, New York, Rhinebeck, Dutchess County, New York at age 72, and was buried in Hurley Dutch Reformed Ch Cem, Hurley, Ulster, New York. Annetje married Jan Jacobsen Van Etten.

Nicholas Wilmoth was born about 1680 in Jamestown, Virginia. Nicholas married someone. His child was:

- o   Thomas Wilmoth.

Samuel Crocker was born in 1671 and died in 1759 at age 88. Samuel married Sarah Parker. The child from this marriage was:

- o   Cornelius Crocker.

Sarah Parker. Sarah married Samuel Crocker.

ELEVENTH GENERATION (8TH GREAT-GRANDPARENTS):

Thomas Triplett, son of Frances John Triplett and Joan Yeo, was born in 1602. Thomas married Elizabeth Googe Martin on 6 May 1622 in Waddesdon, Buckingham England. Children from this marriage were:

- o   Francis F. Triplett.

- o   Mary Triplett was born in 1637 and died in 1674 at age 37.

Elizabeth Googe Martin married Thomas Triplett on 6 May 1622 in Waddesdon, Buckingham England.

TWELFTH GENERATION (9TH GREAT-GRANDPARENTS):

Frances John Triplett was born on 25 Nov 1570 in Poundstone, Cornwall England and died in 1635 at age 65. Frances married Joan Yeo on 20 Sep 1599 in Cornwall, Devonshire England. Children from this marriage were:

- o   Thomas Triplett.

- o   Mary Felt Triplett was born 25 May 1625 in London, England and died about 1675-1676 in Rappahannock, Virginia about age 50.

Joan Yeo, daughter of William Yeo and Joanne Fulford, was born on 6 Jun 1584 in Barnstable, Devonshire England and died in 1626 at age 42. Joan married Frances John Triplett on 20 Sep 1599 in Cornwall, Devonshire England.

THIRTEENTH GENERATION (10TH GREAT-GRANDPARENTS):

William Yeo.

William married Joanne Fulford. The child from this marriage was:

> o   Joan Yeo.

Joanne Fulford married William Yeo.

An article published in the Washington Post by Maureen Joyce on June 2, 1982:

The Family Triplett: History and Legend of Old Fairfax

"A duel fought over one of the Triplett girls, a stone that could cure the bite of a mad dog, a mysterious will . . . ." They're all part of the lore of the Tripletts, friends, and neighbors of George Washington and one of Fairfax County's first families.

In the early 1700s, the Tripletts made their home in a grand estate along the King's Highway on land bordering Washington's Hayfield Farm.

The estate was known as Round Hill, named for the knoll rising 40 feet above the land on which the Tripletts built their home, according to Fairfax County historian Edith Sprouse.

The King's Highway is now Telegraph Road, the Kingman Complex has replaced Round Hill at Fort Belvoir, and all that remains of the Tripplett estate are three family gravestones: those of Lt. William Triplett of the Continental Army (1730-1803), William W. Triplett--believed to be his grandson--who died in 1858 at the age of 43, and Mary A. Triplett--who may or may not have been William W. Triplett's wife--who died in 1850 at the age of 40.

For the past several months, the U.S. Army Corps of Engineers has been clearing and restoring the site, six miles south of Alexandria. At 2 p.m. tomorrow, the Corps will celebrate the restoration in public ceremonies to be attended by a number of Triplett family members, many of whom will be seeing the site for the first time.

The restoration was spearheaded by William Murden, a civilian who is chief of the dredging division of the Corps Engineers' Water Resource Support Center. The Corps has agreed to maintain the property, which will be open to the public.

Although the Triplett name has not won the fame of other fellow Virginians', county historians say the family was among the most prominent in early Fairfax history. For one thing, the Tripletts were close friends of Washington and frequent guests at his Mount Vernon estate.

In fact, much of what is known about the early Tripletts comes from Washington's diaries.

Washington frequently visited the nearby Triplett estate, one entry states, to go riding with the "well-known horsemen, William and Thomas Triplett," sons of Thomas Triplett and his wife, the former Sarah Massey.

And Washington apparently was grateful to the Tripletts for taking visiting relatives off his hands--especially those who liked hunting, a sport Washington disliked.

Even the Tripletts did not escape the general's well-known thriftiness. In one entry, a disgruntled Washington noted that he bought pork from a friend of the Tripletts even though the man charged more for the hogs after he and Washington had agreed on a price.

The diaries also reveal that William Triplett was hired to build an addition to Mount Vernon and received 18 for the project, which involved raising the roof of the house and laying new foundations.

In a 1968 account of the Triplett family, Thomas Triplett Russell of Miami cites a handbill, dated 1803, offering the Triplett home for sale. It describes a one-story brick house, 18 by 54 feet, with a kitchen below and three rooms in the "attic storey above," a standard floor plan of the times.

Another story was added later, along with outbuildings and 170 acres of land. William Triplett's youngest son George lived there until his death in 1822.

According to the family account, the house was burned to the ground "on a bleak winter night" in 1836. It was rebuilt in a more "modern" style. Later, the house was abandoned, and by 1927 it had been demolished. The property remained in the Triplett family until 1941 when it became part of Fort Belvoir.

According to Sprouse's research, the Triplett family originally came from the London area and was descended from the Rev. Dr. Thomas Triplett, a sub-dean of Westminster Abbey. Three of his sons--one of them Thomas Triplett--came to America in 1666.

Sprouse says Lt. William Triplett was a vestryman of Truro Parish and also owned pews in the Pohick Church and Christ Church in Alexandria. He married Sarah Massey, had five children, and is credited with adding 350 acres to the Round Hill estate.

In 1802, when William Triplett, Sr. drew up his will, he specified that unless his children returned property previously given to them, "they would be excluded from any other part of the estate." He further specified that if they "cannot divide the estate peaceable nor do meet together with that love and affection which brother and sisters ought to do," that the trustees were to sell the whole estate.

"Apparently, the Triplett children were not 'peaceable,' " writes Sprouse, for the whole estate was sold, "everything from the coaches and harness to 100 pounds of old bacon."

And the Triplett family "madstone," a 19th-century "remedy for rabies," considered to be very valuable and good for a thousand uses, is now missing, although Sprouse suggests it might be at Mount Air, a Virginia plantation "just down Telegraph Road" from the Triplett home.

As for the other family legend, it seems that during the Victorian era, two of the suitors of Mary Triplett--described as "a great belle"--fought a duel over her. One of the men was killed and the other jailed, whereupon the object of their affection promptly married someone else."

BOWERS FAMILY

Our Bowers ancestor was John Bowers (1766-1797), who was married to Lucy, last name unknown, in Highland County, Virginia. According to history by Oren Morton, Bowers was referred to as a German Immigrant whose name was forgotten. He was the father of Joseph Bowers and the husband of Lucy Mick. We believe this is the Lucy Powers recorded in Pendleton Records as Lucy Powers, who married Mathias Mick, II in 1797 upon the early death of John. The early language was written as it was heard, and the German P and B sounds were indistinguishable by the mostly British record keepers.

A. John and Lucy had three children who were documented in county records.

    i.   John Bowers, II, who married Christina Ruleman. Jack descends from John Bowers, II and Christina Ruleman through their son John Laban, his son Henry p., his son H. Pinkney, and then Jack.
   ii.   Joseph Bowers, who married Barbara Vandevander. Joseph lived near Pendleton/Highland line near Blue Grass. George Triplett descends from Joseph Bowers and Barbara Vandevander.
  iii.   Christina Bowers, who married John Amick. Christina moved to Nicholas County with the extended Amick family.
   iv.   Unknown named son who may be the ancestor of Pocahontas County John Edward Bowers (1821-1898) and sister Lavina Bowers (1814-1880). This son may have been named Charlie because there are Pendleton sales transactions naming an unaccounted-for Charlie Bowers.

B. William Harrison Bowers (1818-1910) married Margaret S. Sponaugle.

C. John O. Bowers (1849-1931) married first Almira Peck, who died 1876. He then married Margaret Tabitha Whitecotton on May 9, 1876, in Highland County VA

D. Jacob Bowers' birthdate is disputed. Some say 1871, some 1875, some 1876. Death record says July 15, 1876, but his parents are recorded there as John Bowers and M. Peck (not Whitecotton) E. Burnice Blanche Bowers married W. Triplett.

Harvey Cromer, standing in front of Cromer Swiss A-frame home at Cheat Bridge.

Harvey Franklin Cromer, Sr. Born: 1856, married Frances Arbana Malcomb Cromer. Born: Headwaters, Virginia. Harvey F. Cromer, Sr. was a surveyor and timber cruiser. Someone asked Harvey, Sr. if he had ever been lost on Cheat Mountain. He said, "No, I've never been lost, but I have been confused and wandered for several days."

Harvey Franklin Cromer, Sr. children - (not in order):

1. Pearl H. Cromer, no children- self-employed timber and sawmill operator.

2. Joseph Cromer, children: George, Jim, and Geraldine.

3. George Cromer, coal-fired steam Shay Engineer at West Virginia Pulp and Paper Co.

4. Susie Cromer "Sue," no children- Cheat Bridge Postmistress. Sue Cromer was the postmistress at the Cheat Bridge post office for many years. She carried the mail to Durbin on horseback. The train (Western Maryland?) would pass the Cheat Bridge Post Office, and to keep from stopping, they would toss the canvas bag to Aunt Sue, who was waiting by the tracks. If she had outgoing mail, she would tie it to a long bamboo pole that had a big loop on one end so the conductor could merely hold his arm out and run it through the loop and retrieve the mail.

5. Minnie Cromer married Arthur Anderson - no children. Her husband built Dabney Kisner's cabin near Cheat Bridge. Minnie taught at Big Fill Mountain School.

6. Edna Cromer.

7. Mary Cromer, no children, retired from Alderson Federal Women's Prison in Administration.

8. Blanche Cromer married Peter Elbon and then married Patsy Elbon Nottingham and Ben Elbon. She drove Cheat Bridge students to Big Fill to catch the school bus.

9. Harvey F. Cromer, Jr. "Harv," married Anne Greathouse, with children Donald B. and David.

    A. Donald B. Cromer started Westwood Animal Hospital, in Staunton, Virginia, at his home in 1972. A hospital was built in 1975. There are now three generations of Cromer men in the practice: Donald B. Cromer. D. Michael Cromer, and Thomas B. Cromer. All Cromer's, including daughter Leslie, are also farmers.

    B. Major David Owen Cromer, USAF, married to Patty Kellum Cromer, (both David and Patty are deceased).

10. Robert "Bob" Cromer, married Grethel Blanchard with children: Anne, Bobby, Delores, Gertrude. A natural outdoorsman. Many times, I remember him catching a full-grown bear and keeping it chained in the yard.

11. Arthur "Ott" Cromer married Ellie, children: Arthur, Jr., Ellen, Forrest, Victor, and Franklin Winchester, whose nickname was "Shotgun". Ott was a coal-fired steam Shay Engineer with West Virginia Pulp and Paper Co.

12. Doctor "Doc" Cromer, wife: Lillian, children: Helen, Barbara Lee. He was a surveyor.

13. J. Reuben Cromer, wife: Bell LeMasters, children: Roderick, Leslie, Hunter, Hope, Charles, Cecelia. He was a surveyor.

14. Charlie Cromer, coal-fired steam Shay Engineer, West Virginia Pulp and Paper Co.

Story from Don Cromer: *My dad had a 38-40 Winchester rifle that had previously been owned by his dad Harvey F. Cromer Sr. In the 1930's whitetail deer were very scarce on Cheat Mountain. Some were later brought in from Michigan and turned loose.   The trusty 38-40 had killed three deer with one shot!*

Donald "Donnie" Cromer and wife, Judy Cromer

Story from Don & Judy Cromer. *"When visitors were staying at the Club House, these boys had a favorite prank they would do. There was a deep hole in the river nearby, and when there were enough spectators, they would, one at a time, jump into the water and swim underwater to a safe place at the bank where they would exit the water to an underground cache unseen from the visitors. Naturally, the guests would sound an alarm that all the boys had likely drowned. After a time, they would swim back underwater and climb back onto the bank."*

Our wonderful Norma Jean Townsend, daughter of Norman William Townsend and Beatrice Ross Townsend, was born June 7, 1935, in a log home in the middle of the present US Route 33 and Norton Road, Norton, West Virginia. Norma attended Norton Grade School, Coalton High School, and Buckhannon-Upshur High School. She graduated from Elkhorn High School in McDowell County, West Virginia. Her mother, Beatrice, and maternal grandmother Nettie Florence Herron Ross, rode the Reynolds Line Bus from Elkins to Bluefield, West Virginia, then to Elk Horn for Norma's 1953 Elk Horn High School graduation. Norma is appreciative of her grandmother, Nettie Ross, who would bring her hot dogs from Elkins when Norma was a little girl. She often stayed with her grandparents Ernest David Ross "Pap" and Nettie Florence Herron Ross in Norton. Norma's father was a coal miner in Norton, and her mother was employed at Memorial General Hospital in Elkins.

Norma has one deceased sister, Shirley Dean Townsend, born in 1937. Shirley and her parents are buried in the Talbott Cemetery in Kingsville, West Virginia.

Norma was an excellent student and took pride in the Norton Grade School Patrol Girl position. She donned her yellow raincoat, cap, white patrol belt, badge, and West Virginia State Police uniform full-size stop sign with which she maintained the middle and bottom of Coalton-Norton Road, stopping all loaded coal trucks headed for the Ross-Leeder Coal Tipple to unload in Harding.

In 1953, Norma Jean entered the Davis Memorial Hospital School of Nursing and completed the three-year program during the spring of 1956. She passed her state boards, became a registered nurse, and practiced at Davis Memorial Hospital in Elkins for many years. Norma worked with the gynecology/obstetrics department for many years with Esther Girard Silvester, Kaye Smith, Twila Basil, and others. The student nurses scrubbed floors, cleaned bathrooms, sterilized needles, gave patients back rubs and other hard labor to help pay for their nursing school expenses. The students worked under the able supervision of Jessie Robinson DeMotto, Frances Weese, Millie Cox, and Virginia Wolfe. Furthermore, the student nurses were intelligent, beautiful, highly selected, rural, small-town ladies who had an early evening curfew. Norma's special friends during her nursing training were Gail Swick Lothes, Frances Rossi Triplett, Joan Rossi, Patty Brown, Betty Karicoff Smith, Betty Barkley Umpenhour, Phyllis Scott Jackson, Leta Gregory, Lou Ann Wine, Macie Lewis, Marie Cunningham, Gladys "Bunny" Turner Vance, Eleanor Pingley Zizzi, among many others. Her classmates enjoyed getting together often and would make a special weekend trip every year.

After being a widow for several years, Norma married George Raphael Triplett. She is lovingly known as "Granny" to all of her grandchildren. Norma has great pride in herself and ownership of her residential property. She enjoys feeding the birds and caring for her flowers. She is a loving, caring, and devoted wife, friend, and grandmother. She has maintained a weekly Monday Bible study and prayer group for the last 50 years. Norma's Pocahontas ancestry dates back to Zachariah Bennett, born around 1799, and Eleanor Brown, born around 1802.

Pictured above is Norma's great-grandson, Myles Eubanks, son of Kevin and Jamie Eubanks, after he won the South Carolina Golf Association Junior Championship in June of 2022

ANCESTORS OF NORMA JEAN TOWNSEND:

PARENTS

Father - Norman William Townsend, son of Thomas Newton Townsend and Minnie Mary Morrison. He was born on October 5, 1903, and he died on August 7, 1961.

Mother - Beatrice Ross, daughter of Ernest David Ross and Nettie Florence Herron. Beatrice was born on September 9, 1906, in Virginia.

They married on September 11, 1933. Their children were:

- Norma Jean Townsend born on June 7, 1935. She first married Robert R. Rector, M.D., son of George H. Rector and Ella M. Moore. Her second marriage was to George Raphael Triplett, son of Charles Robert Triplett and Geneva Katherine Harris.

- Shirley Dean Townsend was born in 1937.

GRANDPARENTS

PATERNAL GRANDPARENTS

Grandfather - Thomas Newton Townsend, son of William T. Townsend and Hannah E. Barnett. He was born in about 1870 and died on February 28, 1940, in Randolph County, West Virginia.

Grandmother - Minnie Mary Morrison.

They were married, and their children were:

- Norman William Townsend

- Lucille Gladys Townsend

- Olive G. Townsend

- Mary Townsend

- Maude Ellen Townsend

- Gail Townsend

MATERNAL GRANDPARENTS

Grandfather - Ernest David Ross was born in about 1880 and died in about 1969.

Grandmother - Nettie Florence Herron. Daughter of Charles Herron and Mary Jane Howell. Born on December 3, 1888 and died on July 17, 1984.

They were married and their children were:

- Beatrice Ross

- Gladys Daisy Ross (Born on November 20, 1908 and died on February 9, 1974.

- Herman Hershall "Buck" Ross. Born on July 3, 1911 and died on April 11, 2006.

- Ella Ross. Born in about 1914.

- Sarah Ross.

- Charles Woodrow "Chap" Ross. Born on March 17, 1916 and died on April 29, 2003.

- Amos Clinton Ross. Born on May 24, 1920 and died on August 21, 2004.

- Edith Ross.

- Ila Rose Ross. Born on December 5, 1924 and died on August 5, 2015.

GREAT GRANDPARENTS

PATERNAL GREAT GRANDPARENTS

Great-grandfather - William T. Townsend.

Great-grandmother - Hannah E. Barnett was born in about 1839. Daughter of Zachariah Barnett and Eleanor Brown.

They married in 1864 in Pocahontas County. Children born to the marriage were:

- Perry Townsend. Born about 1864.

- Sallie E.F. Townsend. Born about 1865.

- James A.E. Townsend. Born about 1866.

- Thomas Newton Townsend.

- Jacob Stephan Townsend. Born on August 31, 1877 and died on March 23, 1931.

MATERNAL GREAT GRANDPARENTS

Great-grandfather - Charles Herron. Son of Jacob Herron and Lucy McDaniel. Born on October 18, 1847 and died on December 6, 1932.

Great-grandmother - Mary Jane Howell. Born in May 1854 and died in 1930.

The following children were born to their marriage.

- Minnie A. Herron. Born in December 1872.

- George Benson Herron. Born in 1882 and died in 1963.

- Martha Herron. Born in June 1886.

- Jesse Jones Herron. Born in November 1887 and died in 1968.

- Nettie Florence Herron.

- Jehu A. Herron. Born in November 1892.

- Charlotte Herron. Born in July 1895

GREAT-GREAT GRANDPARENTS

Zachariah Barnett (born in about 1799) married Eleanor Brown (born in 1802). Their children were:

- Josiah Barnett, born December 4, 1826, died May 11, 1899.

- Sarah Jane Barnett, born December 4, 1827.

- Thomas Barnett, born 1830.

- James B. Barnett, born 1833.

- Stephen H. Barnett, born 1836.

- Hannah E. Barnett, born 1839, married William T. Townsend.

- Martha A. Barnett, born 1841.

- Jasper N. Barnett, born 1846.

- John A. Barnett, born 1850.

Jacob Herron, married Lucy McDaniel. Their children were:

- John Herron, born 1837, died 1925.

- Jacob Herron, born 1840, died 1927.

- Absalom B. Herron, born 1844, died 1906.

- Charles Herron, born October 18, 1847, died December 6, 1932, married Mary Jan Howell.

- Martha A. Herron, born 1852.

- Francis Herron, born 1855, died 1936.

In 1961, Norma married Robert R. Rector, M.D., a widower. Both Dr. Rector and Norma Jean are graduates of Davis and Elkins College. Norma is the stepmother of:

A. Jane Rector Bennett, formerly married to David Riggleman. Their children are:

- Jamie Riggleman Eubanks. Her husband is Kevin, and their children are Dorian and Myles Eubanks.

- Robert Riggleman. His wife is Jessica, and their children are Gabriel and Alex Riggleman.

Jane was married to Calvin Bennett, who died May 12, 2023.

B. Sue Rector Young. Her husband is Rick Young.

C. Evelyn "Bun" Rector Banks. She is the widow of James Banks, III. Their children are:

- Rebecca Banks Ewing. Her husband is Greydon Ewing. Their children are Caedmon, Rhodes, Leland and Townsend.

- Rachel Banks Novasell. Her husband is Steffon Novasell. Their children are Silas, Forrest and Ada Novasell.

- Ian Banks.

- James Banks, IV.

BOYERO-GONZALEZ FAMILY

Silvia Boyero Triplett was born July 21, 1969, in Salamanca, Spain. She is a registered nurse practitioner. Silvia is the wife of Jefferson Lee Triplett and the mother of George, Sofia, and Alexa Triplett.

PARENTS

Mother – Esther Boyero of Salamanca, Spain.

Father – Jose Andres Bovero Gonzales.

Their children were:

- Silvia Boyero Triplett.
- Helga Boyero Boyero.
- Ester Maria Boyero Boyero.

MATERNAL GRANDPARENTS

Grandfather - Perfecto Boyero Vicente.

Grandmother - Maria Cruz Serrano Gomez.

Their children were:

- Esther Boyero Serrano.
- Benedicto Boyero Serrano.
- Perfecto Boyero Serrano.
- Daniel Boyero Serrano.
- Javier Boyero Serrano.
- Basilio Boyero Serrano.

PATERNAL GRANDPARENTS

Grandfather - Eugenio Boyero.

Grandmother - Esther Gonzalez.

Their children:

- Amador Boyero Gonzalez.
- Ana Maria Boyero Gonzalez.

- Amalia Boyero Gonzalez.

- Jose Andres Boyero Gonzalez.

- Maria Luz Boyero Gonzalez.

- Eugenio Boyero Gonzalez.

Jeff & Silvia Triplett with their children – Sofia, Alexandra, and George – July 2022

REFERENCES

Booth, Nancy Harris. The Harris Family.

Bosworth, Dr. A. S. *History of Randolph County, West Virginia*. Southern Historical Press Inc., 1916.

Chapman, Odie Velta Nestor. *They Rest Quietly: Cemetery Records of Randolph County, West Virginia*. McClain Printing Company, 1996.

Cromer, Donald "Donnie" & Judith. The Cromer Family.

Eades, Charles Joseph. *Descendants of Michael Arbogast: Some Allied Families*. 2021.

Fitzpatrick, John C. *The Diaries of George Washington 1748-1799*. Mount Vernon Ladies Association, of the Union, Houghton Mifflin Company.

Harris, Joseph M. *1620- Chart for George Triplett*. 16 June 1999.

Hord, A. H. *Geneaology of the Triplett Family*. William and Mary College, 1914.

Hord, Reverend Arnold Harris. *Colonial Francis Triplett of Fauquier County, Virginia*. Tyler's Historical and Genealogical Magazine, 1929.

In Loving Memory: Fourth Volume - Back Mountain Road- Durbin to Cass: Nottingham, Hosterman, Wanless, Cass, Deer Creek. West Fork: Wildell, Gertrude, May. 2019.

In Loving Memory: Tenth Volume - Edray Road - Cass to Poage Lane: Stony Bottom, Clover Lick, Poage Lane Community, Meeks Road, Linwood Road, Laurel Run Road, Beverage Road, Little Italy Road, Barnett Road (Old Poage Lane). 2022.

Joyce, Maureen. "The Family Triplett: History and Legend of Old Fairfax." *Washington Post*, 2 June 1982.

Maxwell, Hugh. *History of Randolph County*. Acme Publishing Company, 1898.

Phares, Elihue. *Family Tree Research*. 2012.

Pocahontas County Historical Society. *History of Pocahontas County, West Virginia 1981: Birthplace of Rivers*. May 1981, p. 536.

Sharp, Curtis. *An American Family: History and Descendants of Michael Arbogast and Mary Elizabeth Samuels. Volume One: Their History. Immediate Family and Descendants of Odessus Adam, Their First Child*. CreateSpace, 2017.

Sharp, Curits. *An American Family: History and Descendants of Michael Arbogast and Mary Elizabeth Samuels. Volume Three: Descendants of Children: Henry, Peter, John, George*. CreateSpace, 2017.

Sharp, Curtis. *An American Family: History and Descendants of Michael Arbogast and Mary Elizabeth Samuels. Volume Two: Descendants of Children: David, Mary Elizabeth, Michael, Dorothy*. 2nd ed., CreateSpace, 2017.

Triplett, George R. *Our Proud Mountain Roots and Heritage*. McClain Printing Company, 2003.

Triplett, Robert C. *The Talon - Makes Me Wonder*. Woodberry Forest School, Spring 2018.

Vest, Charles E. *Ancestors of George Raphael Triplett*. July 14, 2021.

Vest, Charles E. *Ancestors of Norma Jean Townsend*. July 14, 2021.

Watts, Geraldine. *The Arbogast Family*. 2021, p. 12.

<u>BIBLIOGRAPHY</u>

Babits, Lawrence E. *A Devil of a Whipping: The Battle of Cowpens*. The University of North Carolina Press, 1998.

Bennett, Laura Dean. *Pocahontas County Times: Compass*. Spring 2021, p. 6.

Binns, Brooke. *Kisner Flew More than 50 Missions During WWII*. The Inter-Mountain, Sept. 3, 2019.

Blackhurst, W. E. *Riders of the Food*. McClain Printing Company, 1954.

---. *Of Men and a Mighty Mountain*. McClain Printing Company, 1965.

Board of Trade of Elkins, West Virginia. *Elkins West Virginia: November, Nineteen Six- The Coming Metropolis of the State*. Acme Publishing Company, 1906.

Bodkins, Steve. *Bemis & Glady West Virginia: A History of Two Mountain Towns*. McClain Printing Company, 2006.

---. *Forgotten Towns: Pocahontas & Randolph Counties, WV*. McClain Printing Company, 2012.

Booth, Nancy Harris. The Harris Family.

Bosworth, Dr. A. S. *History of Randolph County West Virginia*. Southern Historical Press Inc., 1916.

Chapman, Odie Velta Nestor. *They Rest Quietly: Cemetery Records of Randolph County, West Virginia*. McClain Printing Company, 1996.

Clarkson, Roy B. *Tumult on the Mountains: Lumbering in West Virginia 1770-1920*. 10th ed., McClain Printing Company, 1964.

Cromer, Donald "Donnie" & Judith. The Cromer Family.

Davis & Elkins College. *Davis & Elkins College: Alumni Today 2015*. Davis & Elkins College, 2015.

---. *Davis & Elkins College: Elkins, West Virginia, Alumni DIrectory 1998*. Bernard C. Harris Publishing Company, Inc., 1998.

---. *D&E Senatus: 1940 Davis & Elkins Yearbook*. 1940th ed., 1940.

---. *D&E Senatus: 1948 Davis & Elkins Yearbook*. 1948th ed., 1948.

---. *The Senatus 1956: 1956 Davis & Elkins Yearbook*. 1956.

Doyle, Charles H. & Stewart, Terrell, *Stand In The Door! The Wartime History of the Elite 509th Parachute Infantry Battalion*. Phillips Publications, 1988.

Eades, Charles Joseph. *Descendants of Michael Arbogast: Some Allied Families*. 2021.

Fitzpatrick, John C. *The Diaries of George Washington 1748-1799*. Mount Vernon Ladies Association, of the Union, Houghton Mifflin Company.

Frischkorn, Carl F. *The Cheat Mountain Club: A Historical Recollection*. 2007.

Gardner, Ian. *Airborne: The Combat Story of Ed Shames of Easy Company*. Osprey Publishing, 2015.

Gardner, Ian, and Roger Day. *Tonight We Die As Men: The Untold Story of Third Battalion 506 Parachute Infantry Regiment From Toccoa to D-Day*. Osprey Publishing, 2009.

Gundmendson, B. J. *Pocahontas County Times*. 2021, p. 6.

Harris, Joseph M. *1620- Chart for George Triplett*. 16 June 1999.

Hord, A. H. *Geneaology of the Triplett Family*. William and Mary College, 1914.

Hord, Reverend Arnold Harris. *Colonial Francis Triplett of Fauquier County, Virginia*. Tyler's Historical and Genealogical Magazine, 1929.

In Loving Memory: Fourth Volume - Back Mountain Road- Durbin to Cass: Nottingham, Hosterman, Wanless, Cass, Deer Creek. West Fork: Wildell, Gertrude, May. 2019.

In Loving Memory: Tenth Volume - Edray Road - Cass to Poage Lane: Stony Bottom, Clover Lick, Poage Lane Community, Meeks Road, Linwood Road, Laurel Run Road, Beverage Road, Little Italy Road, Barnett Road (Old Poage Lane). 2022.

Joyce, Maureen. "The Family Triplett: History and Legend of Old Fairfax." *Washington Post*, 2 June 1982.

Keifer, Sarah J. *American Genesis: Genealogical and Biographical Sketches of the New Jersey Branch of the Harris Family in the United States*. 1888, p. 29.

Maurer, B. B. *Mountain Heritage*. 10th ed., McClain Printing Company, 1980.

Maxwell, Hugh. *History of Randolph County*. Acme Publishing Company, 1898.

Moss, Bobby Gilmer. *The Patriots at the Cowpens*. A Press, 1985.

Mountain Breeze. Greenbank High School Class of 1924, 1924.

---. Greenbank High School Class of 1945, 1945.

---. Greenbank High School Class of 1946, 1946.

---. Greenbank High School Class of 1951, 1951.

---. Greenbank High School Class of 1953, 1953.

---. Greenbank High School Class of 1970, 1970.

National Football League, Official Program. Chicago Bears v. Washington Redskins. 1946.

Noe, Kenneth W., *The Howling Storm: Weather, Climate, and the American Civil War*. Louisiana State University Press, 2020.

Phares, Elihue. *Family Tree Research*. 2012.

Pocahontas County Historical Society. *History of Pocahontas County, West Virginia 1981: Birthplace of Rivers*. May 1981, p. 536.

Price, Calvin W. "Pocahontas County Times: Seventy-Five Years Ago, 'Our Army and Navy Boys.'" *Pocahontas County Times*, Dec. 26, 1946.

Rice, Don. *Randolph 200: A Bicentennial History of Randolph County, West Virginia- 1787-1987*. Walsworth Publishing Co., Inc., 1987.

Rice, William H. *Elkins, West Virginia 1889: The Magic City of Wilderness*. McClain Printing Company, 2007.

Ross, Thomas Richard. *Davis & Elkins College: The Diamond Jubilee History*. McClain Printing Company, 1980.

Roy, Carrie Harman. *Captain Snyder and His Twelve of West Virginia*. Carlton Press Inc., 1977.

Russell, T. Triplett, and John K. Gott. *Fauquier County: In the Revolution*. Heritage Books Inc., 2007.

Sharp, Curtis. *An American Family: History and Descendants of Michael Arbogast and Mary Elizabeth Samuels. Volume One: Their History. Immediate Family and Descendants of Odessus Adam, Their First Child*. CreateSpace, 2017.

---. *An American Family: History and Descendants of Michael Arbogast and Mary Elizabeth Samuels. Volume Three: Descendants of Children: Henry, Peter, John, George*. CreateSpace, 2017.

---. *An American Family: History and Descendants of Michael Arbogast and Mary Elizabeth Samuels. Volume Two: Descendants of Children: David, Mary Elizabeth, Michael, Dorothy*. 2nd ed., CreateSpace, 2017.

Sullivan, Ken and Deborah J. Sonis. *The West Virginia Encyclopedia*. West Virginia Humanities Council, 2006.

Thacker, Victor L. *French Harding: Civil War Memoirs*. 4th ed., McClain Printing Company, 2000.

Triplett, George R. *Our Proud Mountain Roots and Heritage*. McClain Printing Company, 2003.

Triplett, Robert C. *The Talon - Makes Me Wonder*. Woodberry Forest School, Spring 2018.

Turner, David R. *Davis & Elkins College: One Hundred Years Honoring Our Traditions, Celebrating Our Future*. WDG Publishing, 2004.

Vest, Charles E. *Ancestors of George Raphael Triplett*. July 14, 2021.

---. *Ancestors of Norma Jean Townsend*. July 14, 2021.

Vietnam Veterans of America, Chapter 1100, Marlinton, Pocahontas County, West Virginia.

Virtualwall.org.

Ware, Chad. *Elkins High School: A Football History - A Collection of Tiger Teams, Coaches, Players and Statistics Through the Years and Much More. 1915-2019*. McClain Printing Company, 2020.

Ware, Roger & Ware, Judith. Military Historians. Elkins, WV.

Watts, Geraldine. *The Arbogast Family*. 2021, p. 12.

Zambone, Albert Louis. *Daniel Morgan: A Revolutionary Life*. Westholme Publishing, LLC, 2018.

Zinn, Jack. *R. E. Lee's Cheat Mountain Campaign*. McClain Printing Company, 1974.

Appendix A

Aab, Bailey Jordan
Aaronson, Robert Howard
Aarsand, Knut J.
Aasen, Conrad C.
Abbiati, Willamina Davies
Abbondanza, Nadia R. Crowly
Abbott, Patricia A. Tabram
Abbott, Amber Nicole
Abbott, Susan R. Hartman
Abdulfattah, Mohammed Abdulaziz
Abegaz, Wongel Markos Belihu
Abel, Beth A. Lawrence
Abel, Scott J.
Abell, Jeanette M.
Abernethy, Louise Lucas
Abramov, Peter
Abramovic, Marissa B.
Abrams, Kenneth
Abruzzino, William A.
Abzueta, Emma H.
Acker, Barry L.
Ackerman, Jeffrey D.
Ackerman, Paul E.
Ackerman, Jeanne
Ackermann, E. Lynn Aeschbach
Acord, Judith A. Gaffga
Acosta, Andres
Adams, Patricia A.
Adams, Beth Ann
Adams, Hugh B.
Adams, Homer B.
Adams, Dwayne E.
Adams, Charles E.
Adams, Charles Edward
Adams, William Hollen
Adams, Nancy J. Wilderotter
Adams, Terry Janel Isner
Adams, Donna M. Fisher
Adams, Susan Marie

Adams, William S.
Adams, Donald
Adams, K. Travis
Adams-DePew, Rebecca Lynn
Adamson, Rebecca A.
Adamson, Virginia D. Vance
Adamson, Teresa Diane Halewa
Adamson, Victoria J.
Adase, Laurie Sekerka
Addeo, John R.
Adderley, Linda Y. Johnson
Addison, Lewis Hyde
Addleman, Barbara A. Dohm
Adeyina, Ayomide Olatunji
Adkins, Brian L.
Adkins, Renick M.
Adkins, Darla R. Moyers
Adkins, Karen S.
Adkins, Ronda S.
Adkins, Glen S.
Adkisson, Ralph G.
Adkisson, Danielle Marie
Adle, Hormoz
Adsit, Harry B.
Afati-Tanzi, Jane R. Tanzi
Agbai, Victor Ude
Aghazadian, Vartan
Aglidian, Kimberly A.
Agnew, Christy Janelle
Agnew, Bryant L.
Agudelo, Gabriel
Ahern, Hallie J. Simmons
Ahlstrom, David H.
Ahmed, Mohammed E.
Ahmed, Farzaneh Ishaq
Aichroth, Jeffrey T.
Aikens, Rosanne Calanni
Airhart, Andria G. Knight
Aitcheson, Leslie R. Eckhof
Aitken, George J.
Aitken, Molly Kathryn

Akers, Susan E.
Akins, Nicholas Scott
Alabdulkarem, Turki Fahad Ali
Alamo-Santana, Victor M.
AlAnsari, Aziz
Alansari, Mohamed
Alaskar, Haya Emad
Alazwari, Faris Mosfer
Alba, Johanna P.
Albariqi, Ali Ibrahim Sultan
Albasi, Donald G.
Albaugh, Ronald C.
Albaugh, Melissa R. Burky
Albaugh, David R.
Albee, Brady Wilson
Albogami, Abdullah Masoud
Albury, Rita M.
Alcorn, Joseph N.
Al-Dahlawi, Abdalla S.
Alday, Martha N. Williams
Alden, Harry A.
Alderton, Ruth
Aldossary, Essa
Aldous, John
Aldusymani, Nawaf
Abdulltif Ali
Aleraidi, Mohamed J.
Alesio, Amy E.
Alessi, Thomas C.
Alexander, Brian D.
Alexander, David J.
Alexander, James M.
Alexander, Bret Michael
Alexander, Emily Morgan
Alexander, James Robert
Alexander, Carole Ruth Purvis
Alexander, Edward T.
Alexander, Glenn
Al-Fadhel, Yousef R.
Alfadli, Sabaa
Alfaheid, Waleed Thamir Mohammed

Alfehiad, Abdullah Selah
Alfred, Erika Richand
AlGhamdi, Saad A.
Al-Ghamdi, Abdullah
AlGhazali, Yusuf A.
Alghodayan, Abdulrahman Mohammed
Algire, Connie J. Burch
Algire, Charles W.
Algrim, Judy Marie Lamber
Alhajri, Abdullah Mohammad
Alharbi, Abdullah Saud
Alharthi, Abdulaziz Abdullah
Al-Humaid, Ahmad Khalid
Al-Humaid, Abdulrahman Khalid
Ali, Jassim A.
Ali, Mohammed R.
Alibakhshi, Debra C. Grime
AlIbraheem, Waleed
Aliveto, Linda Settle
Al-Jamali, Laith Talir
Alker, Natalie K.
Alkhayal, Mashail Abdulmajeed
Alkire, David Andrew
Alkire, Christopher D.
Alkire, Teresa Elaine
Alkire, Rosetta Mae McDonald
Allard, Hunt M.
Allbee, James A.
Allee, Jade Satsuki
Allen, Deborah A. Hutchins
Allen, Robert A.
Allen, Colton Alexander Lynn
Allen, Elizabeth Allen
Allen, Mary B. Rohrbough
Allen, Martin D.
Allen, James D.
Allen, Nickalus David

Adams, Charlotte McCammon
Adams, Emily Nicole
Adams, Jeffrey Paul
Allen, Delores F. Scott
Allen, Charles G.
Allen, J. Garrott
Allen, Corinne Geary
Allen, Thomas Hunter
Allen, Stanley J.
Allen, Kelly J.
Allen, Russell L.
Allen, Elsie M. Norton
Allen, Jeff M.
Allen, James O.
Allen, Charlotte P. Boggs
Allen, Robert R.
Allen, Thomas R.
Allen, Susan Skiff
Allen, Audrey W.
Allen, Thomas W.
Allen, Linda
Allen, Meeghan
Allen, Geoffrey
Allen, Charlee
Allender, Carrie Louise Wratchford
Allen-McNally, Elizabeth Susanna
Allerton, George N.
Alley, Kim T.
Allie, Stephen P.
Allman, James Andrew
Allsopp, Joanne K. Myers
Allsopp, Craig O.
Al-Majid, Shawki M.
Almarri, Abdulhadi
Almengor, Genito N.
Almond, Paula Joan Johnson
Almossa, Yazeed Abdullah
Al-Muall, Khalid A.
Almulla, Mohanned Ahmed
AlMusalam, Muhana S.
Almutlaq, Ibrahim Ali
Almutlaq, Mohammed Ali
Alonso-Gortari, Juan
Al-Otaibi, Muhsin Raddah
AlOufy, Salim
Alqadhabi, Abdullah
Al-Qahtani, Bader

Mauck
Aitken, Eric
Aizawa, Chigusa
Akers, Christine E. Judy
Alrasheed, Abdullah Saleh
Alrashidi, Mohammed
Alruwayti, Saleh Abdulaziz
Alsegayh, Wadha Abdullah
Alshahrani, Muaiad
Alshammari, Yousef Shilash
Alshammari, Ahmed
Alshehri, Mufareh S.
Alshwmar, Abdullah Nasser
Alston, Gloria
Alsubaie, Saad
Alt, Christopher Edward
Al-Tameemi, Badur
Altamimi, Ali Nasser
Altemose, Rosemarie L. Tichy
Altewairgy, Abdullah Faisal
Altieri, Ira J.
Altman, Nicholas Nai Zheng
Altobelli, Joseph Anthony
Alu, Stacey A.
Aluise, Richard A.
Alvarado, Brenda Marla
Alvarez, Walter John
Alvarez, MarySheyla Katherine
Alvarez, Paul Neil
Alyami, Nayef Abdurahman
Alzahrani, Abdulrahman Mohammed
Aman, Andrea N.
Amatruda, Andrew F.
Amazan, Michel
Amberg, Richard J.
Ambrose, Mary Sherwood Willis
Ameer, Alexander
Amen, Rene Lunn
Amen, Richard M.
Amendola, Michele J.
Amendola, Michael J.
Amercani, Khalid J.
Amercani, Tammy L. Claypool
Americani, Mohoud
Ameyaw, Abel Agyei
Amidzic, Goran

Alfahid, Abdulaziz Saleh
Alfehaid, Mohamed Fahaid
Alfehaid, Abdlrahman Fahaid Mohammed
Amorese, Rebecca A. Guire
Amorese, Carl E.
Amorese, Roger M.
Amoroso, Madelyn F.
Amos, William J.
Amos, George M.
Amtsberg, Douglas A.
Amtsberg, Geraldine Feldman
Amundson, Richard
Ancell, James F.
Ancell, Rhonda G.
Ancell, Cecelia Tarantelli
Anders, Lisa J. Moen
Andersen, Thomas A.
Andersen, David Colin Frey
Andersen, Leighton E.
Andersen, Kenneth J.
Andersen, Lesley Jean Whitehead
Anderson, Alexis A. Kinkaid
Anderson, Joyce A.
Anderson, Vanessa Ann
Anderson, Robert B.
Anderson, Tracy Cole Cremeans
Anderson, Ana Conde
Anderson, Craig D.
Anderson, Ruth Davidson
Anderson, Jessica Desiraye
Anderson, Marquita Elizabeth DeLorme
Anderson, James G.
Anderson, Kathleen Goodwin
Anderson, Jeannette Grier
Anderson, William J.
Anderson, Patricia K.
Anderson, Emery L.
Anderson, Janet L.
Anderson, Kevin L.
Anderson, James L.
Anderson, Brian Lee
Anderson, Qiana M.
Anderson, Danielle N.
Anderson, Michael Nelson
Anderson, David R.

Allen, Sherri Dawn
Allen, James E.
Allen, Robert E.
Allen, Carolyn E.
Anderson, Steven T.
Anderson, Marcia Villotti
Anderson, Charles Wesley
Anderson, Rosetta White
Anderson, Duncan
Anderson, Mark
Anderson, Samantha
Anderson, Jennifer
Anderton, Joseph
Andreasen, Steven P.
Andres, Barbara J. Hamilton
Andres, William W.
Andrews, Ward B.
Andrews, Rebekah Elise Lee
Andrews, William Graham
Andrews, Brian J.
Andrews, Megan Joella Bruce
Andrews, Alfred N.
Andrews, Madge Schoonover
Andrews, Susan T.
Andrews, Mary Zolar
Andrews, Fletcher
Angel, Katherine Shaver
Angell, Charles D.
Angell, Phillip E.
Angstadt, Lyndsay H.
Annable, Nancy
Anoshin, Dmitriy A.
Ansell, Sharan J. Herring
Anterock, Joshua Adam
Anthony, Cheryl Lynne
Anthony, Rekya-Cordelia Nouna
Anthony, Catharine VanAtta
Antolin, Jozef
Antoline, Jacob Michael
Antoline, Kylie Morgan
Antolini, Kimberly Gay Rast
Antolini, Heather Lee Jack
Antolini, David P.
Antolini, Carl
Antonsen, Donald
Antulov, Elliott Jane
Aponte-Kocela, Amber Lee
Appel, Dylan

Moshabbab
Alrajab, Mona Hassan
Thyab
Alraqtan, Ahmed
Appleyard, Crickitt
Gretchen-Faye Pollak
Aquilante, Mary J. Kuegle
Ara, Yukiko
Arabea, Lisa A. Kohl
Aramini, Josette A. Trunzo
Araujo, Vicente A.
Arbaugh, Kimberly
Catherine Eye
Arbaugh, Ashley Deann
Yokum
Arbaugh, Ronald E.
Arbaugh, Anne R. Chilton
Arbaugh, Sheldon W.
Arbogast, Justin Adam
Arbogast, Elizabeth Anne
Morgan
Arbogast, Cynthia C.
Putzulu
Arbogast, Elizabeth Carol
Arbogast, Joshua Daniel
Arbogast, Candace Dawn
Arbogast, Zachary E.
Arbogast, Sara Elizabeth
Arbogast, Maurice H.
Arbogast, Lola J. Perrin
Arbogast, Olivia Jo
Mackenzie Hudok
Arbogast, Owen John
Arbogast, Angela K. Moore
Arbogast, Mary Kyle
Arbogast, Gary L.
Arbogast, Diana L.
Arbogast, Edwina L.
Arbogast, Kristie L.
Arbogast, Brandon Lee
Arbogast, Allison Leigh
Howell
Arbogast, Jaime Lynette
Arbogast, Roxie M. Phillips
Arbogast, Lori Michelle
Arbogast, Sandra Miller
Arbogast, Brittany N.
Shrader
Arbogast, Kelsey Oleta
Arbogast, Delmas R.
Arbogast, Erica Rachel

Amiri, Khalida
Ammann, Charles B.
Amodio, Greg John
Amoral, Geoffrey J.
Archer, Maude Crissman
Archer, Stephen P.
Ardito, William J.
Arehart, Michael D.
Ariola, Raven Blake
Arisaka, Kanako
Arlow, Janine Humenik
Armbruster, Monika L.
Ellrich
Armentrout, Stacy B.
Armentrout, Brenda Borror
Parker
Armentrout, Madonna C.
Petrice
Armentrout, Harold D.
Armentrout, Timothy D.
Armentrout, Ronnie David
Armentrout, Deanna Dawn
Arbogast
Armentrout, Bradley Edwin
Armentrout, Elwood G.
Armentrout, William G.
Armentrout, Daniel J.
Armentrout, Alexander Jared
Armentrout, Edgar Keith
Armentrout, Charlotte L.
Armentrout, Lucile M. Right
Armentrout, Sue McCulley
Armentrout, Carol Rice
Armentrout, Max
Armstrong, Eric Allen
Armstrong, David C.
Armstrong, Nicole Elaine
Armstrong, Doris G.
Armstrong, Daniel J.
Armstrong, Sherry J.
Armstrong, Mary Juanita
Cross
Armstrong, Cacie Kristina
Armstrong, Jennifer Lynn
Armstrong, Reta M.
Armstrong, Lisa M.
Armstrong, Kelsey Mae
Armstrong, J. Mark
Armstrong, Nicole R.
Armstrong, Charles R.
Armstrong, J. Bruce

Anderson, Jeffrey R.
Anderson, Hope S.
D'Angelo
Anderson, James T.
Arnold, Cynthia A.
Gochenour
Arnold, Cheryl Fitzgerald
Arnold, William H.
Arnold, Sarif J. Hennen
Arnold, Billy J.
Arnold, Trudy L.
Arnold, Thomas P.
Arnott, Frank L.
Arrasmith, James C.
Arrasmith, Robert H.
Arrasmith, Edward P.
Arrell, Christian Eric
Arroyo, Christina
Arthur, Chester L.
Arthur, Violet T. Hoover
Arthur, Hugh T.
Artis, Cynthia Wildman
Asbury, Cynthia L.
Ash, Allison Mikayla
Ash, Kenneth R.
Ash, Elizabeth
Ashby, Howard
Asher, Nancy L. Floyd
Ashford, Drew Kanoelani
Ashley, Jessica Ann
Ashri, Hussam Basim
Ashwell, Lori Gallagher
Askew, Patricia J. Beal
Asousa, Theodore C.
Assam, Jason Ryan
Assemi, Fariba
Assoian, George
Atabaki, Nazanine
Atchison, Bruce L.
Atchison, Judith Rittle
Atencio, Mariela J.
Atheneos, Perry
Atherton, Donna E. Watson
Atkins, Cassie Dawn Cooper
Atkins, Leann K.
Atkinson, Marilyn L.
Atkinson, Lewis L.
Atkinson, Margaret
Stalnaker
Atmanoglu, Seda
Aufderheide, Thomas C.

Applebee, Nancy Jordan
Applebee, Edward W.
Appleby, Autumn Brooke
Applegate, A. Bryant
Auld, Douglas C.
Ault, William C.
Aumendo, Kimberly
Catherine Lisowsky
Aumendo, Carmen
Aussenhofer, Lynn
Austin, Jasmine D.
Austin, Susan M.
Auten, James J.
Auvil, George E.
Auvil, Dallas H.
Auvil, Tiffany Marie
Auvil, Carl S.
Auvil, Bruce
Avanzato, Timothy B.
Avent, Bradley Thomas
Avery, James E.
Avery, Marvella Graybill
Avila, Marissa
Avolio, David Joseph
Avondo, Robert
Awad, Paul Alain
Ayala, Juan C.
Ayala, Beatriz Maria Soto
Ayars, Virginia Masters
Ayers, Michelle A.
Ayers, Elizabeth D.
Ayers, Tamara Lynn
Helmick
Ayers, Carlise Nicole
Ayersman, Jessica Kay
Aylor, Kristi Danielle
Ayres, Jereomy Lawrence
Azar, Khalid
Babad, A. Thomas
Babcock, J. Starr
Baber, Samantha Dawn
Babik, Carol Ann Straw
Bacastow, Kathryn Joan
Adams
Bacca, Britne K.
Bacca, Kortne K.
Bachtel, Kelli Denise
Bachteler, Frank H.
Back, Robert D.
Back, Susan Gore
Back, Floyd Warren

Arbogast, Morgan S.
Arbogast, Jack
Arbogast, Lurty
Archbold, David P.
Baer, Marc B.
Baer, Gary L.
Baer, Robert L.
Baer, Erica M. Coburn
Baer, Billy
Baez-Alayon, Coqui
Baez-Rodriguez, Surelys
Bagley, Gordon T.
Bailey, Kathleen Boserman
Bailey, Carol E.
Bailey, Kathy Jo
Bailey, Sheri L.
Bailey, Walter L.
Bailey, Carey M.
Bailey, Alain Reynold
Bailey, Carl T.
Bailey, Thomas W.
Bain, Sharon E.
Bainbridge, Donald L.
Bainey, Heather M.
Bain-Kerr, Janice Claire
    White
Bair, Greg R.
Baird, Heather Dawn
Baird, David Frederick
Baird, William G.
Baird, Ann LaBresque
Baird, Hugh P.
Baird, Robert R.
Baisden, Helen Dumire
Baisden, Carrie E. Bentley
Baker, Marijane A. Corrick
Baker, Sheri A. Ford
Baker, Doris A. Hoffman
Baker, Scott A.
Baker, Susan A.
Baker, Ryan A.
Baker, Amanda Beth
    Chambers
Baker, Margaret C.
Baker, Charles E.
Baker, Margaret Earle
Baker, Euphama Ford
Baker, Robert G.
Baker, Robert Hall
Baker, Robert L.
Baker, Christopher L.

Arndt, Roger
Arndt-Maynard, Stephanie P.
Arner, Harold L.
Arnold, Rebekah D.
Baker, Sharmaine Monae
Baker, Lyndell O.
Baker, William P.
Baker, Dan R.
Baker, Brett R.
Baker, Stokes S.
Baker, Matthew Staats
Baker, George W.
Baker, Jack W.
Baker, David W.
Baker, Zachariah
Balash, Fred
Balcerzak, Kathleen M.
Bald, William F.
Baldwin, Wayne A.
Baldwin, Kathy G.
Baldwin, John K.
Baldwin, Gary M.
Baldwin, Tyler Scott
Baldwin, Donald W.
Baldwin, William
Baldwin Wright, Beverly A.
Baliff, Robert
Ball, Jeffrey A.
Ball, Clifford B.
Ball, Brian Dean
Ball, John E.
Ball, Pamela J.
Ball, Amanda R.
Ball, Herman
Ball, Clara
Ballay, Carolyn A.
    Kemmerle
Ballinger, William D.
Ballou, Barbara Mitchell
Balltezegar, Katheryn R.
    Higbee
Bamberger, Craig L.
Bampton, Alice Elizabeth
    Fisher
Bampton, Frank J.
Bancroft, Cheri J. Agnew
Bancroft, Robert
Band, Barry S.
Band, Carol Yost
Bandel, Richard A.
Banerjee, Doyel

Aufderheide, Mary Ellen
    Tice
Augsbach, Otto J.
Augustine, Megan Marie
Bannon, Casey Lynn
Banzhoff, Bradley Tyler
Baptista, Andrew Bennett
Baran, Edward S.
Baranski, Rafal
Barb, Deborah A.
Barb, Michelle Dawn Lantz
Barb, Riley H.
Barb, Jay M.
Barb, Jan M.
Barb, David R.
Barb, Natalie Tyre
Barbe, Beverly G.
Barber, Richard E.
Barber, Frank H.
Barber, Mark Stephen
Barclay, Shelly J. Rally
Barcus, Traci S.
Bard, Rollin A.
Barger, Beth A. Bennett
Barger, Donna Kittle
Barilla, Barbara A. Kulish
Barker, Edna K.
Barker, Kendra L. Snider
Barker, Rose M. Light
Barkley, Morgan Elizabeth
Barkley, Agnes Gueiros
    Thompson
Barkley, Kipton K.
Barkley, John L.
Barkley, Russell L.
Barkley, Jennifer Wimer
Barkley, Virginia
Barley, Steven Bryan
Barlow, Lyndsey Shae
Barlow, Richard W.
Barlow, Jamie W.
Barnaby, Leacroft
Barnard, Winnifred Gross
Barnard, William K.
Barnard, Alex Lee
Barnard, Maudaline
    Montgomery
Barnard, Winifred N. Dye
Barner, Jeffrey G.
Barnes, Marilyn Ann
Barnes, Joseph C.

Badger, Brenda
Badgett, Lessy Shields
Badgett, Boyd William
Badri, Burhan S.
Barnes, Rex
Barnes, Deborah
Barnes, Goldie
Barnett, Elizabeth Bealer
Barnett, Morgan Grace
Barnett, William H.
Barnett, Mark L.
Barnett, Kathryn Michelle
Barnett, Michelle R.
Barnhart, Scotty Neil
Barnishan, Rod M.
Barnum, Monica Marie
    Decker
Barnum, Alan Michael
Barnwell, Michael T.
Barosa, Barbara Anne
Barr, Barbara A.
Barr, Lillian Edmond
Barr, William H.
Barr, Matthew Patrick
Barrante, Thomas
Barreto, Jaime A.
Barrett, Stephen Graham
Barrett, Janet L.
Barrett, William W.
Barrett, Andrew W.
Barrick, Anita K. Bennett
Barrick, Winifred Marstiller
Barrick, Lucinda Mullennex
Barron, Fred
Barrow, Barbara A. Bowers
Barrow, John D.
Barrow, Guy J.
Barrow, William
Barry, Edwin C.
Barry, Emily
Barsy, Imre J.
Bart, Janine
Bartgis, Dorothy E.
Barth, Marsha Layton
Barth, Michael
Bartholomew, Robert S.
Bartholomew, David T.
Bartles, Jacqueline S. Adams
Bartles, John T.
Bartlett, Beulah Isch
Bartlett, Sherry L. Hartman

Baker, Rebecca Leah
Baker, Wendell M.
Baker, Gary Neal
Baker, Jessicca Necole
Bartley, Angela Melissa
Bartley, Christine S.
Bartley, Glenna
Bartocci, George C.
Bartollas, Clemens L.
Bartolo, John A.
Barton, Timothy A.
Barton, Helen Bazzle
Barton, Thomas H.
Barton, Cyrus J.
Barton, Cynthia Jane
  Edwards
Barton, Phillip Kent
Barton, Jo Anne Miller
Barton, Diana W.
Bartow, Gail F.
Basabakwinshi, Anemone
Bascome, Jeffrey O.
Basel, Scott Anthony
Basil, William B.
Basil, Eileen Cecelia
  Knapp
Basil, Sarah E. Peck
Basil, Lloyd M.
Basil, Dylan R
Basil, Dorothy Sanders
Basil, Robert W.
Basil, Jack
Basler, Stephen C.
Bass, Katherine
Bassett, Cecil A.
Bassett, Andrew G.
Bassett, Regina M.
Bassett, Edwin R.
Bassitt, John
Basso, Jude A.
Bastone, Jeffrey T.
Basye, Jeffrey N.
Bataille, Louis T.
Bataineh, Suzanne
  Kathryn Allen
Bataineh, Hasan Z.
Batalion, A. L.
Bates, Brandon A.
Bates, James R.
Bates, Raymond
Bates, George

Banes, Steven R.
Banghart, Carol S.
Banks, Tyree Danyelle
Banks, Harter
Batson, Deloras Jacqueline
  Schuetz
Batten, Frankie L.
Batten, Jessica M.
Batterman, Kevin M.
Battista, Gail Hemming
Baublis, John L.
Bauer, Charles C.
Bauer, Christopher C.
Bauer, Brenda L.
Bauer, Blair
Baugh, Edward J.
Bauld, Margaret G.
  Snedegar
Baum, Charles A.
Baum, Ernest W.
Bauman, Barbara Jean
  Fairclough
Bauman, Michael W.
Baumen, Deborah D. Dickey
Baumgardner, Rachael Jo
Baumgardner, J. Adam
Bava, Faithe L.
Bava, Daniel Scott
Baxa, Franklin Lewis
Bayer, Patrick W.
Baylor, Robert F.
Baynum, Grier
Bayuk, Harold Alan
Bayuk, Mildred Ann
  Costello
Bayuk, Harold M.
Bayuk, Julian M.
Bayuk, Verne Shane
Bazzell, Tracy L.
Bazzle, Hansel
Bazzle, Ernest
Beadle-Ryby, Michele Ann
Beal, Maryalice Kathleen
Beal, Megan M.
Beale, Wesley Owen
Beall, Harvey B.
Beall, Lisa R.
Bean, Edward A.
Bean, Charles H.
Bean, James P.
Beard, Carl G.

Barnes, Mark E.
Barnes, Chauncey P.
Barnes, Clark S.
Barnes, Melinda Sue
Bearden, Pam Kisling
Beardsley, Wayne A.
Beasley, Brittany Erin
  Schade
Beasley, Brantley
Beatty, Kenneth D.
Beatty, Pearle Headley
Beatty, William M.
Beatty, Olive W. Marshal
Beaty R.N., D. Mildred
Beauford, Diane E.
Beauregard, Dannah M.
  Lapin
Beaver, Daniel Clyde
Beaver, Larry D.
Beaver, Meredith S. Kump
Beaver, Theresa
Bebee, Alice S. Garrison
Becerra, Lilia
Becerra, Astrid
Bechtold, Karen A.
Bechtold, David H.
Bechtolt, David C.
Beck, Edith Crissman
Beck, Donna L. Goshorn
Beck, Leslie M.
Beck, Linda
Becker, Karl Christopher
Becker, Gerald H.
Becker, Kelly Wynn Morris
Beckman, Robert Carl
Beckman, Tonya Marie
  Livengood
Beckwith, Nancy
  Kimbrough
Beckwith, Robert N.
Bedford, Sharon Bartlett
Bedminister, Michele Marie
  Daniel
Bednar, Robyn D. Griffin
Bedrosian, Peter
Beecham, George D.
Beek, Don
Beeman, David L.
Beer, Erin Elaine
Beer, Helen M. Goley
Beer, Rex W.

Bartlett, Courtney Megan
Bartlett, Gary R.
Bartlett, Walter
Bartlett, A. Browne
Behrhorst, Ellen J.
  Zimmerman
Beins, Thomas E.
Beird, Mary E. Adams
Bekenstein, David M.
Bekenstein, Sara Pearl
Belaiba, Oussama
Belan, Corina D. DeMotto
Belcher, Alex A.
Belcher, Elizabeth
Belefski, Mark J.
Belefski, Cynthia Knight
Belig, William
Bell, Chad A.
Bell, Virginia C. Myles
Bell, William Clifford
Bell, Amanda Dawn
Bell, Kristin E.
Bell, Ray J.
Bell, Pamela J.
Bell, Frank K.
Bell, Kris Lynn Stubblefield
Bell, Adrienne Marie Dague
Bell, Nancy Moline
Bell, Robert S.
Bell, Paul Sandor
Bell, Matthew T.
Bell, Ota
Bellantoni, Joseph F.
Belldina, Juda D.
Bellevue, Rickenjee
  Christopher
Bello, Jeffrey D.
Belt, Ashley Nicole Shank
Belt, Tiffany
Belter, Douglas L.
Beltz, Randall C.
BenAri, Nancy Henderson
Bender, Sally A. Mollohan
Bender, Nichole Amber
  Webber
Bender, Laurada C. Keister
Bender, Edith Darlene
Bender, Robert G.
Bender, Herbert Loren
Bender, Laura Rae
Bender, Donald

Batezell, Fenton P.
Batigne, Michael D.
Batsenikos, Josette F.
  deCourten
Benfield, John M.
Benham, Derek M.
Benigni, Amanda M.
Benjamin, John S.
Bennett, Ann A.
Bennett, William A.
Bennett, Gae Adamson
Bennett, Emmel Alice
  Zickefoose
Bennett, Deidre Anne
Bennett, Richard B.
Bennett, Janice C. Wilmoth
Bennett, John C.
Bennett, Amanda Charlene
  Shaver
Bennett, Oran D.
Bennett, William D.
Bennett, Robert D.
Bennett, Richard D.
Bennett, Kristina D.
Bennett, Bradley Dale
Bennett, Allison Diane
  Creech
Bennett, Vivian E. Hobart
Bennett, Mildred E. Wolf
Bennett, Orville E.
Bennett, Janet Elaine Roy
Bennett, Barbara Ellen
  Weese
Bennett, Charlene J.
  Gilmore
Bennett, Sarah J.
Bennett, Beverly J.
Bennett, Beverly Jo
  Fortney
Bennett, Lacy Jo
Bennett, Tammie Joan
Bennett, Macey Kayleen
Bennett, Mildred L. Bava
Bennett, Diane L. Winans
Bennett, Oran L.
Bennett, Herman L.
Bennett, Betty L.
Bennett, Brenda L.
Bennett, Natalie L.
Bennett, Renee LaRue
  Parks

Beard, D. L.
Beard, Michael S.
Beard, Madeline V. Godwin
Beard, D. Lee
Bennett, Jamie Lynn
Bennett, Phyllis M.
Bennett, Kermit Michael
Bennett, Clinton Michael
Bennett, Lindsay Michelle
Bennett, Ezra O.
Bennett, Jane Rector
Bennett, Iris Serina
Bennett, Joshua Seth
Bennett, Caroline Suzann
Bennett, Martin V.
Bennett, Bernard W.
Bennett, Ashley W.
Bennett, Catherine
Bennett '19, Nathanial
  Logan
Benoit, Matthew Joseph
Benovy, Andrew J.
Bensenhaver, Charles B.
Benson, Michele D. Louk
Benson, Ray E.
Benson, Gary J.
Benson, Dorraine Louise
  Reeb
Bentley, Scott D.
Bentley, Robert G.
Benton, Alwilda Cochran
Benton, William M.
Benton, Michael
Beougher, Brenda
Berdine, Debra Ann Harper
Berg, Vera Cornell
Berg, Vernon E.
Berg, Robert F.
Bergdoll, William S.
BergenPape, Jorge
Berger, Ronald A.
Berger, Jacklin S.
Berger, Leonard
Berkey, Conner Wayne
Berkley, Kelly
Berman, Victor D.
Berman, Jay D.
Berman, Christopher David
Berman, Richard T.
Bernard, Robert B.
Bernard, Susan Elizabeth

Begg, David
Begley, Rhys Lawrence
Behrens, Samuel Alan

Berner, Craig M.
Bernhard, Wilhelm K.
Bernstein, Mitchel E.
Berquist, Allan
Berry, John H.
Berry, John H.
Berry, Sarah Jade Kaiser
Berry, Lydia Jenkins
Berry, Cathy Lee
Berry, David Scott
Berry, Pamela
Bertett, Leonard A.
Berzito, Mildred Knaggs
Bess, Tracy Ward
Best, Stoddard L.
Best, Charles W
Beswick, Paul C.
Bethany, J. Patricia
Betler, Edward
Betler, Mary
Betts, William C.
Bever, Ronald
Beverage, Patricia S.
Beverly, Raymond
  Henderson D.
Beyer, Katherine Hedrick
Beylouney, Barbara Dawn
  Rambeau
Beziat, Matthew Casey
Bezzini, Peter C.
Bhattarai, Rajiv
Bhirombhakdi, Santi
Bialek, James
Bianchi, Joseph E.
Bianchini, Dominic Jude
Bianco-Rieti, Andrea
Bible, Crystal Alanna
Bickel, Peggy Jane
Bickford, Karen Elizabeth
Biddle, Kimberly L. Steward
Bielecki, Brooke Tesia
Bielemeier, Kenneth W.
Bielicki, Thomas P.
Bienias, Oliver Artur
Biernbaum, Mary Anne
  Droppleman
Biernbaum, John M.

Bender, Rachelle
Bendy, Robert H.
Bendy, Ethel Joanne Person
Bendy, Richard W.
Biggs, Jetta L. Coleman
Biggs, Wendy L.
Biggs, Gary W.
Bigler, Pamela A.
Biglow, Don
Bigney, Robert Mark
Bigsby, Charles D.
Bihl, Edwin A.
Bikoulova, Kristina
Biller, Juanita A.
Biller, Randall G.
Biller, Wilma L.
Biller, Mark L.
Billings, Kelsey Michelle
Bills, Cori Alexandria
Bills, Craig J.
Bills, Edd L.
Billups, Paul H.
Bin Muqbil, Fahad
Binkley, Alexandra Ann
  Marie
Binns, Patrick Brendan
Bioletti, John J.
Biringanine, Narhana
Birkbeck, Diane C.
Biser, Christopher Eugene
Biser, Amanda Nicole
  Moore
Bishoff, Brian J.
Bishoff, Jessica Lynn
Bishop, James C.
Bishop, Ruth Cox
Bishop, Lucille J. Borgwald
Bishop, Nora Joyce Goodell
Bishop, Melissa M. Polzer
Bishop, David M.
Bishop, Susan Pink
Bishop, Richard S.
Bishop, Mark W.
Biskar, Neal M.
Bissett, Kim E.
Bizjak, Amy L. Chunkala
Bizzell, Karen Judith
Bizzell, Jordan Timothy
Bjornstad, Kara Lynn
  Dragan
Black, Andrew A.

Bennett, Rodney Lee
Bennett, Heather Lynn Daft
Bennett, Deborah Lynn
    Long
Black, Leo M.
Black, Jessee Marie
Black, Linda S.
Blacka, Barry E.
Blacka, Edwin H.
Blacka, Catherine Kincaid
Blacka, Emma Pritt
Blacka, Harold R.
Blacka, Jack R.
Blackburn, Barbara Allyn
Blackburn, Todd Matthew
Black-Johnston, Paula J.
Blackwell, Sharon Lee
    Richardson
Blackwell, Robbin M.
Blackwood, Ola G. Doerr
Blackwood, Rena Gainer
Blackwood, Josephine
    Keiss
Blair, Eden L.
Blair, Robert
Blaise, Alan R.
Blake, Grace Armstrong
Blake, Wilbourne G.
Blake, Kelsey June
Blake, Linda K.
Blake, Phillip M.
Blake, J. Ronald
Blake, Rose
Blakes, Carl
Blanco, Harold
Bland, Noah Allan
Bland, Billy D.
Bland, Rosie W. Nethken
Bland, Byron
Blankenmeyer, Gerard J.
Blankenship, Beane Beane
Blankenship, Susan D.
Blankenship, Mary J.
    Gebrosky
Blankenship, Hal R.
Blanks, Mary Mayo
Blann, Christina Maria
Blanton, Nicholas B.
Blanzy, Bobbi E.
Blasche, Leslie J.
Blassmann, Silva Strazds

Bernard, Fred J.
Bernard, Eleanore Loeffler
Bernard, Richard O.
Berner, Karen Harmeier
Bleau, Elizabeth C. Leahy
Bledsoe, Aubreigh Inez
Bleil, Russell A.
Blendermann, Frances M.
    Villee
Blendermann, E. Martin
Blight, Russell Bruce
Bliven, James S.
Blizzard, Samuel O.
Bloedel, Thomas M.
Bloom, Ruth T. Boorady
Bloomquist, Leslie A.
    Riggleman
Blough, Cynthia L.
Bluhm, William C.
Blum, Paula M. Ruple
Blum, Stanley
Blumenfeld-Mazzolini,
    Catherine A.
Blumenthal, Jay S.
Blystone, Brian Keith
Blythe, Grayson Hunter
Boatman, Leigh A. Hamilton
Boatwright, Joseph Weldon
Boccella, John S.
Boccella, Jennifer
    Weissenberger
Bock, Christopher N.
Bockstoce, Jerry L.
Bodkin, Delmer L.
Bodkin, Woodrow W.
Bodkins, Kimberly J.
Bodkins, Terry L. Bennett
Bodkins, Tommie L.
Bodkins, Emilee Renee
    Coberly
Bodle, Jennifer L.
Bodnar, Nancy Jo Compton
Bodnar, Denny L.
Boecking, William D.
Boelter, Leslie Ryn
Boening, Robert L.
Bogar, Alison K.
Bogarad, Catherine D. Frost
Boger, April D.
Boger, Roxanna S.
Boggess, William C.

Biggar, Shawn R.
Biggers, Frank A.
Biggs, Mary Anne Morgan
Biggs, Lona L. Tacy
Boggs, Larry J.
Boggs, Tex L.
Bognanni, Michael A.
Bogner, Alan W.
Bogue, John
Bohaker, Elizabeth G.
Bohan, Helen Humphreys
Bohensky, Charles P.
Bohince, William S.
Bohlke, William M.
Bohme, Lee S.
Bohn, Heather Elizabeth
    Clay
Bohner, Steven H.
Boho, Maryann D. Dixon
Bohon, James Patrick
Bohorquez, Jasmine
    Daniela
Boillotat, Jeff E.
Boin, Susan L.
Boladz, Joseph D.
Bolding-Colaw, Linda E.
Boles, Christopher G.
Bolig, Kathy Opdyke
Bolinder, Aileen Angela
Bolinger, Brittany Danika
Bolinger, Willetta J. Swartz
Bolling, Tracey
Bolmenäs, Ester Therése
    Karolina
Bolt, Elizabeth Ann Kitchen
Bolt, Jamie L.
Bolton, Caroline B.
Bolton, Dessie H.
Bolton, Sabrina L. Bishoff
Bolton, Shannon Nicole
    England
Bolton, Edythe
Bolyard, Derek M.
Bolyard, Michele R. Shaffer
Bolyard, Jennifer Marie
    Friend
Bolyard, Jocie Rae
Bolyard, Carl
Bolyard, Michalea
Bolyard-Shankle, Shelley
    Lee Ann

Black, Lisa Ann
Black, Scott E.
Black, Chris J.
Black, John Jay
Bone, Megan E.
Bone, James W.
Boni, Stephen J.
Bonifazio, Richard J.
Bonnell, Richard A.
Bonnell, Christina L. Fisch
Bonnell, Elizabeth M. Ben
Bonnell, Nathaniel
Bonner, Julie A.
Bonner, Elizabeth Ann
Bonner, Hobert B.
Bonner, Marion F.
Bonner, Leslie Gayle Benn
Bonner, Madonna K.
    Varchetto
Bonner, Sydney K.
Bonner, Delton R.
Bonner, Anna S. Losh
Bonner, Marcus S.
Bonner, Sherry Shifflett
Bonnett, Brian Allen
Bonnett, Katherine S.
Bonney, Patricia J.
Boone, Terry L.
Boone, Thomas Paul
Booth, Douglas F.
Booth, Ruby L. Dahmer
Booth, Barbara Lynn
Booth, Edith Mae Reid
Booth, Sarah Nicole
Booth, Ralph R.
Booth, David R.
Booth, Jeremy R.
Booth, Holly Vannoy
Booth, Mary
Bordas, Bonnie E.
Borden, Billy R.
Borders, Donna J.
Boren, Robin G. Mosser
Bork, Irene A. Quimby
Bork, Harold C.
Borkowski, Susan C.
Borofsky, Anna Danielle
Borowski, Carolyn Bae
    Cunningham
Borowski, Desirae N.
    Richardson

Blaszczak, David A.
Blattner, Curtis D.
Blazek, Mark W.
Blazier, Mark J.
Borsa, Abed
Borton, Mary J. Maloney
Bose-Mullick, Aparajita
Boserman, Minnie J.
  Rowan
Boserman, Angela Stanton
Bosley, Jennifer D.
Bosley, Mandy L.
Bostic, Cordel L.
Bostic, Makesi
Boswell, Blake Steven
Bosworth, Jean A.
Bosworth, Mary Bell
Bosworth, Bernard Brown
Bosworth, Margaret C.
  Laderach
Bosworth, Charles E.
Bosworth, Ebba Erlandson
Bosworth, Margaret J.
  Wamsley
Bosworth, Beverly L.
Bosworth, Julia Maria
Bosworth, John
Botkins, Terri E. Parsons
Bott, Terry A.
Bott, Craig S.
Bottcher, Robin L.
Bottoms, Lawrence W.
Botula, Catherine W.
  Young
Bouchard, Marc A.
Bouchard, Rebecca Lynn
  Boone
Boulier, Jaime Kristine
Bounds, Wallace M.
Bourgeois, Esther B.
  Wilkey
Bova, Ronald B.
Bova, Ronald P.
Bova, Barry
Bove, Harmony R. Patton
Boville, Angela J.
Boward, S. H.
Bowden, N. Katherine Kyle
Bowen, Kendra Brianna
Bowen, Steven C.
Bowen, Anna M.

Boggess, Johnathon Paul
Boggs, Patricia A. Boxell
Boggs, John A.
Boggs, Neil F.
Bowers, Phyllis Griffith
Bowers, Louise Harman
Bowers, Gregory K.
Bowers, Anita Louise
  Giambrone
Bowers, Tracie P. Rickards
Bowers, Donnell R. Lambert
Bowers, Margaret Reitz
Bowers, Emma Seitz
Bowers, Caitlin T.
  Clark-Braverman
Bowers, William
Bowie, Arthur G.
Bowles, Ashley Teneille
Bowley, Cathy A.
Bowley, Todd A.
Bowley, Mariah Lindsey
Bowley, Sheree N.
Bowley, Tara T.
Bowling, Logan Richard
Bowman, Melody Dawn
Bowman, Ann E.
Bowman, Paul I.
Bowman, Ida LaRose Mayle
Bowman, Ellen Lee Strobel
Bowman, Wendy Matthews
Bowman, Tammie Taylor
Bowman, Clark W.
Bowman-Rich, Virginia Ann
Bowser, Brett W.
Bowser, Letha
Bowton, Gloria L. Saltzman
Boxley, Stephanie L. West
Boyce, Donna M. Dolan
Boyd, Pamela J. Boyd
Boyd, Bradley James
Boyer, Karen Melissa
Boyer, Priscilla Wingfield
Boyle, Jennifer Lillian
Boyle, Holly McKittrick
Boyles, Courtney
Boyrer, Kathryn J. Akers
Bracco, Barbara Hymes
Bracken, Mark H.
Bracken, Peggie June
  Chandler
Bracken, Marian

Bonafield, Aileen Phares
Bond, Beth Ann Jones
Bond, William M.
Bondurant, Robert W.
Bradfield, Zachary William
Bradford, Charles C.
Bradley, Wesley A.
Bradley, Linda Jean Nolle
Bradley, Jason Lee
Bradley, Ivy R. Simmons
Bradley, Edna Sue Wright
Brady, Kimberly D.
Brady, Lori E. French
Brady, Paul H.
Brady, Betty L. Parrack
Brady, Borden T.
Brady, G. Marion
Bragg, Elizabeth Hawes
Braham, Mary Jane
Braham, Lisa M.
Braithwaite, Tara L.
Brake, Richard F.
Brake, Paschel J.
Brake, Timothy Mark
Brake, Page
Branard, Barbara A. Hughes
Brancato, Kimberly A. Gray
Branch, Elizabeth Reed
Brand, Leslie
Brandenburg, Leah Erin
  Fletcher
Brandenburg, Harold J.
Brandli, Quentin Michael
Brandstrom, Dawn Elizabeth
  Hughes
Brandt, Robert A.
Brandt, Dorothy G.
  Fazenbaker
Brannen, James S.
Brannon, Sonya Marie
Branwell, Alan J.
Braun, Grant Edward
Braun, Daniel K.
Braund, Robert W.
Braxton, Jonathan L.
Bray, John D.
Braymer, Kenneth D.
Brecht, George K.
Breitsman, Melissa A.
Brelsford, Robin Thrall
Brelsford, George William

Borowski, Jonathan P.
Borra, W. Ellen
Borror, Gayla J.

Brenwalt, Kimberly
  Hoffman
Bressler, Jessica A.
Brewer, Brenda T.
Brewster, Judy Lynn
  Beckham
Bricknell, Colin George
Bridge, Douglas B.
Bridgers, Harvey Clifton
Bridgers, Martha E.
Bridgers, Laura Jean Knerr
Brier, Evelyn A. Delauder
Briggs, Mark A.
Brigham, Darlene Anne
  Kuehn
Bright, Matthew A.
Bright, Grace B.
Bright, Ronald C.
Bright, Suzan McClelland
Bright, Kathryn Taylor
Bright, Jacqueline Thornhill
Brill, Sarah Jennifer
  MacCoy
Brill, Dustin Shane
Brimley, Jonathan J.
Brinegar, Joan Barlow
Brink, Darcy L. Robbins
Brinkerhoff, William J.
Brinkley, Martha Lou
  Caplinger
Briscoe, J. Walter
Britt, James Otto
Brittle, Lindsey Marie
Britton, Haydee B.
Britton, Anita G.
Britton, Carla L.
Britton, Deborah Leah Ball
Britton, Karl M.
Broad, Stephen H.
Broadmeadow, Herbert E.
Brochinsky, Myron R.
Brock, William F.
Brock, Arden L.
Brock, Santford S.
Brock, Beryl Stalnaker
Brock, Andrew
Brockman, Ernst

Brown, Martha L. Chase
Brown, Suzanne L. Clevenger
Brown, Martin L.
Burke, Robert L.
Burke, Janet Lynne Kempf
Burke, Elwyn R.
Burke, Cameron W.
Burky, Joyce A. Bonner
Burky, Howard F.
Burky, William (Billy) H.
Burky, Alvin J.
Burky, Herman J.
Burky, Ernest R.
Burky, Gwendaline Wilmoth
Burleigh, William E.
Burner, Martha A.
Burner, Lisa J. Hedrick
Burner-Propst, Brittany D.
Burnett, John A.
Burnett, Christina Kay Hewitt
Burnett, Margaret R. Campbell
Burnham, Gavin Morris
Burns, Robert Alan
Burns, Kristina D. Miller
Burns, Russell D.
Burns, Frankie Desiree Tulin
Burns, Lula H.
Burns, Jean Hickman
Burns, William J.
Burns, Lydia Jo
Burns, Carolyn L. Waltrip
Burns, Richard L.
Burns, Mercedes Leigh
Burns, Louise M.
Burns, Donna M.
Burns, Gladys Macomber
Burns, Margaret Reid
Burnside, Regina Anne
Burnside, Dakota Cheyenne
Burnz, Nicholas Sean
Burpee, Deborah J. Stetser
Burr, Monnie David
Burr, A. Paul
Burrows, Sherry Ann
Burset-Bjorseth, Ronald William

Bruch, Eric R.
Bruffey, Paula A.
Bruffey, Mildred Bullivant
Brumage, Connie M. Kester
Busch, Gail W.
Buschman, Albert J.
Buschman, George J.
Busdeker, Melissa A. Wamsley
Bush, Cora Ann
Bush, Carol F.
Bush, Alyce Fox
Bushey, Sharon L. Betz
Bushovisky, Jennifer E. Rexrode
Bushovisky, Charles E.
Bushyeager, James Otis
Busic, Tyler L.
Bussard, Melinda E. Nixon
Bussey, Phillip
Butcher, Margaret A.
Butcher, Vivian Bullivant
Butcher, Glen D.
Butcher, John F.
Butcher, Cynthia H.
Butcher, Kerri Windell
Butler, Kenneth H.
Butler, Margaret M. Taylor
Butler, Richard P.
Butler, C. Evelyn Prinzivalli
Butler, Sandra S.
Butler, Alexandra Smith
Butler, J. Robert
Butler, L. Norman
Butt, Charles H.
Buttram, Alyssa Mae Gail
Butts, Wallace L.
Buvalla, Cheryl D. Nestor
Buxbaum, Peter A.
Buxton, Deloris Gibson
Buxton, James M.
Buzzard, Jane H.
Byam, Beverly Joan Armstrong
Byam, Andrew W.
Bye, Suzanne Jackson
Bye, Dennis L.
Byrd, Jack A.
Byrd, Elizabeth A.
Byrd, Joshua Cain
Byrd, William R.

Buckley, June M.
Buckley, Julieanne Taylor
Bucknam, Ruth E. Barlow
Buckwalter, Jeff Lincoln
Caba, Robert S.
Caban, Mark E.
Cablk, Steven Richard
Cacace, Anthony T.
Cadmus, Thomas F.
Cadwallader, John G.
Cady, Jennifer K. Bopp
Cafferty, Patricia D. Fay
Caggiano, Heather L. Hanscom
Cahill, William F.
Cahill, Shirley J. Rice
Cahill, Elizabeth M. Ksiazek
Cahill, Karen S.
Cahill, Maryanne
Cahn, William M.
Cain, David Allen
Cain, Candance B.
Cain, Suzanne D. Hamrick
Cain, Lauren Denise
Cain, James F.
Cain, Ann Lockridge
Cain, Mark Luther
Cain, John
Cain, Cecilia
Cairns, Alyssa Marie
Calain, Cynthia A. Sheets
Calain, Ervin Baxter
Calain, Amy Beth
Calain, Dennis Emanuel
Calain, Dwight J.
Calain, Thomas L.
Calain, Jack L.
Calain, Anna T.
Caldara, Ronald L.
Calder, Douglas J.
Calder, Charles John
Calderon, Jose R.
Calderon, Maximo
Caldwell, Mark A.
Cale, Jacalyn R. Crawford
Calebaugh, Kenneth
Calello, Samuel C.
Cales, Dana Fuhrman
Calhoun, Walter C.
Calhoun, Gladys M. Warnke
Calisti, Albert A.

Burgoyne, William G.
Burk, Rhiannon L.
Burke, Joseph B.
Burke, Hazel L.
Callander, Juliet E. Hancock
Callander, Steve R.
Callis, Brianna Marie
Callison, Sarah E.
Calloway, Brenda L. Damus
Calvert, Jason B.
Calvert, Samuel John
Calvin, Donald R.
Camarote, James H.
Cambria, George
Camenisch, Bruce
Cameron, Alistair James Haig
Cameron, Joseph L.
Cameron, Lorna L.
Camilletti, D. P.
Camisa, Edward H.
Camoni, Louis A.
Camp, William D.
Camp, Deborah L. Snyder
Camp, Frank W.
Campbell, Robin A. Barker
Campbell, Sheri A. Phillips
Campbell, Susan A.
Campbell, Rosa Lee Arbogast
Campbell, Vicki D. Roy
Campbell, Christopher D.
Campbell, Randlyn Danielle
Campbell, Cora E. Reed
Campbell, Susanne E.
Campbell, Neil G.
Campbell, William H.
Campbell, Bruce I.
Campbell, Christoper John
Campbell, Brenda K. Holston
Campbell, Becca L. Sainato
Campbell, Bruce L.
Campbell, Richard Lee
Campbell, Denise Lynne Hudnall
Campbell, Alma M. Crosier
Campbell, John M.
Campbell, Amber Nichole
Campbell, Paul R.
Campbell, John

Burton, James W.
Burton, Nancy W.
Burwell, Cynthia
Busch, Richard T.
Camplese, Kay A.
   Rosencrance
Campolio, Myrtle L. Wanless
Canache, Hector J.
Canales, Christopher Jude
Cancglin, Lisa Marie
Candelaria, John R.
Canfield, Floyd B.
Canfield, Marjorie Irons
Canfield, Carla J.
Canfield, Firmen Michael
Cangley, Bethany S. Paugh
Cann, Sandra M.
Canny, Rickie Ann
   Wessinger
Cantaral, Ellen Kay
Canterbury, Florence A.
   Maroney
Canterbury, Nathanial G.
Canterbury, David W.
Canterbury, Rebecca
   Yvonne
Cantillo Simon, Josemaria
Cantley, Brenda Burr
Cantrell, Beverly Ann Klus
Cantwell, Malcolm C.
Canupp, Norma Jean Goff
Canupp, Boyce L.
Caparulo, Nancy S. Walker
Capetanos, Thomas G.
Caplinger, Mazie Ellen
   Lewis
Caplinger, Ruth Evonne
   Rinehart
Caplinger, Rosanne L.
   Willouer
Caplinger, Jeffrey L.
Caplinger, Robert M.
Caplinger, Paula S. Weese
Caplinger, John S.
Caplinger, Hope
Capone, Michael F.
Cappadony, Ada Wamsley
Cappadony, Paul
Cappazolli, Luciano
Cappeluti,   Sharon
   Schnebly

Byrne, Charles Allen
Byrne, Debra L. Malangone
Byrne, Mandaine Olson
Byrom, William H.
Carambia, Christina Kay
Cararini, Jeanne Entwisle
Carathers, Michelle R. Jones
Caravella, Augustine J.
Carchidi, James
Card, Raymond Joseph
Carder, Lottie C. Devine
Carder, Janice E. Corley
Carder, Kenneth E.
Carder, Ashton E.
Carder, Carolyn Tackett
Cardot, Martha Quick
Carl, Hannah Ansel
Carl, Jim C.
Carle, Robert G.
Carlsen, Nancy Lee
Carlson, Alexis A.
Carlson, Paul Allen
Carlson, Annalee Bullion
Carlson, John C.
Carlson, Christal D.
Carlson, Faith Earl
Carlson, Leif P.
Carlson, Suzanne R. Courter
Carman, Michael H.
Carmichael, Deborah Sean
   Herr
Carmon, Jerome Pierre
Carnemark, Johanna
Carnes, Stephanie L.
Carney, Jack D.
Carney, Sierra Elizabeth
Carney, Jeffrey H.
Carney, Catherine H.
Carney, Andrew Sheridan
Carney, Robert T.
Carney, Gary
CaroSoto, Edmundo
Carpenter, Brodon Chase
Carpenter, Beverly D.
Carpenter, Grace E. Herring
Carpenter, Norman E.
Carpenter, Richard G.
Carpenter, Betty J. Morris
Carpenter, Brandy Jane
Carpenter, Steven Lee
Carpenter, Diane Ramos

Callahan, Jonathan Daniel
Callahan, Ava Jolene Stacy
Callahan, Michelle L. Mace
Callahan, Patricia Noon
Carper, Karen G.
Carper, Jessica Haileigh
   Hartley
Carpricthai, Suathora
Carr, Lori Ann Casey
Carr, Justin Dallas
Carr, Matthew Edward
Carr, Karen Elaine Davis
Carr, Stella Flanagan
Carr, William G.
Carr, Donald H.
Carr, William H.
Carr, Chata Ingram
Carr, Dorothy J.
Carr, Brenda K.
Carr, Linda K.
Carr, Terry L.
Carr, Tiffany LeAnn
Carr, Cindy Lou
Carr, Candy M.
Carr, Donna R. Goss
Carr, Pamela R. Stalnaker
Carr, Nicholas Ray
Carr, Penny S. Harlan
Carr, H. Scott
Carr, Melissa Sue
Carr, Roy W.
Carr, Harry
Carrico, Mark C.
Carrie, Susan Jane Robinson
Carrigan, Karen J. Simmons
Carrington, Corinne Suzanne
Carroll, Bradley Buck
Carroll, Andrew Colin
Carroll, Joseph E.
Carroll, Kellie J.
Carroll, Donald L.
Carroll, Donald Robert
Carroll, Lillian
Carson, Richard W.
Carte, Mason
Carter, Sonnee D. Phares
Carter, Thomas H.
Carter, Kyro J.
Carter, Madoka Nara
Carter, Frederick P.
Carter, Christopher Patrick

Campbell, Mildred
Campbell, Colin
Campbell, David
Campbell-Miles, Kathleen
Carter, D'Arcy
Carter, Mike
Carton, Evan
Carvajal, Jorge
Carvelli, Victoria
Carver, Patti A.
Carver, Cayla Ann
Carver, Fannie J.
Carvlin, Richard J.
Carwithen, Mary E.
Casciato, Jane C. Thomas
Cascio, Carla Denise
   Shinaberry
Case, Beth C.
Casella, Carla J. Roy
Casey, Judith A. Gear
Casey, Thomas W.
Cashdollar, Margaret M.
Cashell, David O.
Casipit, Monica
Casner, John E.
Casola, Peter M.
Casper, John M.
Casseday, John F.
Cassell, Violet Roberta
   Phillips
Cassell, A. R.
Cassella, Matthew S.
Cassells, Mary E.
Cassiday, Gail Louise
Cassidy, Cynthia Anderson
Cassidy, John W.
Casteel, Stephanie Ann
Castellano, Patrick V.
Caster, James H.
Castle, Jennifer Dawn Lanha
Castle, Ronald W.
Casto, Jeffrey G.
Casto, Samuel Gregory
Casto, Rebecca Jane
Casto, Robin L. Thompson
Casto, Patsy L.
Casto, Matthew Mark
Casto, Aaron Ray
Casto, Reanna Renee Tinn
Casto, Jonathan W.
Casto, Kristie

Cappola, Louis P.
Caprara, Sharon K. Evans
Capriotti, Paula Sissel
Caracciolo, John L.
Catchings, Leigh Elizabeth
Cathie, Walter C.
Cathie, Donna L. Manzella
Cathie, Richard L.
Cathie, Dianne Sue Lapp
Catlett, Kyli Jo
Catlin, John A.
Catlin, Ellen Virginia
  Maclean
Catrin, Bastien
Cattano, Stephenie M.
  Yessen
Caudill, Nancy L.
Caudy, Connie M.
Caufield, John Patrick
Cauley, Eugenia Griffith
Caulfield, James H.
Caulkins, Gloria A. Walther
Caulkins, Elizabeth J.
  Wallace
Cavaliere, Kimberly J.
  Burkholder
Cavaliere, Theodore
Cavallo, Kirk M.
Cavanova, Joan A. Schaff
Cavazos, Ada G. Lilly
Cave, Dolores J.
Cave, Charles L.
Cavender, Iola M. Casto
Cawthon, Cody Scott
Cecil, Nicholas Dean
Cecil, Carolyn E.
Cecil, Vance E.
Cecil, Mary L. Mann
Cecil, Linda L. Stafford
Celio, Victor E.
Cellone, Michelle Ann
  Augostine
Ceravolo, Joseph Vincent
Cerrato, Walter Albert
Cerrato, Mary Rosalie
  Ambrose
Certo, Robert J.
Certo, John
Cerven, Jo Anne Vaccaro
Cervera, Lee M.
Chabut, Ruth Ashby

Carpenter, Nicholas Tyler
Carpenter, George W.
Carpenter, Donna
Carpenter, Luke
Chamberlain, Alfred R.
Chamberlain, Alan R.
Chamberlin, Todd D.
Chamberlin, David S.
Chambers, Roxine Rusmea
  Janique
Champ, Martha G.
Chams, Hormoz
Chancellor, Jewel Ann
Chandran, Radha
Channel, Bonn S.
Channel, Aleen W. Talbott
Channell, Deborah A. Findley
Channell, Lehman Aldridge
Channell, Edna Armstrong
Channell, Russell Hale
Channell, Kelly L. Calain
Channell, Gary Lee
Channell, Jeannie Lynn Varner
Channell, Chelsea Lynn
Channell, Adriana Marceline
  Moss
Channell, Norvel O.
Channell, Marguerite
Channels, Kenneth P.
Chapin, Ralph
Chapline, Rosemary Reynolds
Chapman, April D. Boyles
Chapman, Thomas D.
Chapman, Dorothy E. Isner
Chapman, Joanne H. Doyle
Chapman, Andrew K.
Chapman, Traci R.
Chapman, Charles
Chappel, Douglas K.
Chappell, Peggy A. Harsh
Chappuis, Celeste Primeau
Charles, Marlon C.
Charles, John J.
Chartier-Birgenheir,
  Dianne M.
Chase, Charles A.
Chase, Justin B.
Chase, Sara E. Phillips
Chase, Ruth Kate Thompson
Chase, William Orn
Chase, Gretchen von Limbach

Carter, Bradley Randall
Carter, William T.
Carter, Alan T.
Carter, LaMonte
Chauncey, Elizabeth K.
  Leary
Cheadle, Deborah K. Jensen
Checa, Monserrat
Cheesman, Cherisse R.
Chelf, Karen A.
Chen, Maureen Liu
Chen, Jiamin
Chenard, Robert J.
Cheney, R. Nelson
Cheney-Rosati, Leola
Chenoweth, Brian B.
Chenoweth, Anna Bernice
Chenoweth, Scarlett D. Owens
Chenoweth, Bernard D.
Chenoweth, Kevin D.
Chenoweth, April Dawn
  Moyer
Chenoweth, Lenore E.
  Riggleman
Chenoweth, Fannie E.
Chenoweth, Okey E.
Chenoweth, Stetson Holt
Chenoweth, William Joseph
Chenoweth, Suzanne
  Kimberly
Chenoweth, Tracy L. Bowers
Chenoweth, Eleanor Louise
  McQuain
Chenoweth, Marsha N.
Chenoweth, Robert N.
Chenoweth, Elthadora Pence
Chenoweth, Patricia R. Tacy
Chenoweth, Michelle Y.
Chensky, Dorothy R. Bennett
Chepes, Glorianne Lisko
Chesley, Audie G.
Chesser, Kevin S.
Cheuvront, Alexander
  Mackenzie
Chewning, Nicholas A.
Chewning, Evangeline Dawn
Chewning, Amy Elizabeth
Chewning, Ranae L.
  Sutherland
Chewning, Jeffrey W.
Chilbert, Dana C. Tighe

Catala, Joseph M.
Catalano, Charles
Catalfamo, Darbie Marie
Catarineau, Luis Alejandro
Childs, James C.
Childs, Lauren E.
Childs, Shirley Oorlog
Childs, Robert
Chillington, Elizabeth E.
Chinalai, Nisara
Chiochanyont, Karen
  Freshour
Chiochanyont, Chumporn
Chiorazzo, Joseph M.
Chipps, Steven R.
Chisolm, April D.
Chiya, Kazumasa
Chizmar, Theodore J.
Chlumsky, Jennifer Candy
Chlumsky, Lawrence J.
Chmielewski, Richard M.
Chmura, Michelle L. Blanarik
Cho, Linda Y.
Choi, Mikyu
Choice, Ida S.
Chosney, Joseph Stephen
Christ, Patrick Edward
Christ, William Frank
Christian, Charles C.
Christian, Michael C.
Christian, Warren D.
Christian, Edward Thomas
Christian, Helen
Christiansen, Norman
Christie, Erik D.
Christie, Karen L. Cumming
Christy, Janet E.
Christy, David F.
Chruma, Joseph E.
Chryssomitis, Nickolaos
Chua, Sara J.
Chuffo, Marla Liguori
Chukueke, Judith Okezie
Chung, Henry
Church, Geneva C. Marstiller
Church, Daniel C.
Church, Carolyn Teter
Ciancutti, J. David
Ciccantell, Betty Ann
  Chambers
Ciceron, Quentin W.

Clausen, Ruth Elaine
Clay, Deidre De Barr
Clayborne, Justin A.
Clayborne, Acie
Collins, George F.
Collins, Harriet Holtzworth
Collins, George I.
Collins, William I.
Collins, George I.
Collins, Robert J.
Collins, Deanne Louise
Collins, Wendy M.
Collins, Jessica Marie
  Schaefer
Collins, Ashley Marie
Collins, Russell R.
Collins, Joan Salisbury
Collins, Stephen William
Collins, R. Sanders
Colliton, Dean W.
Colombo, Harold L.
Coltrain, Hannah Marie
Colussy, Susan Eileen Hillick
Colussy, Alan R.
Colvin, John A.
Colvin, George L.
Comb, Joanne E. Bertolet
Combs, Shade Charles
Combs, Delbert J.
Comer, Gerald
Comis, Elio
Commins, John Thomas
Compton, Rebecca C. Myers
Compton, Olin C.
Compton, Ryan Matthew
Compton, J.B.
Conary, Douglas L.
Conaway, Shirley R.
Conaway, Katee Renae
Condit, Tracey G.
Condo, Daniel Logan
Condry, Frances A. Dearien
Conklin, Brian D.
Conklin, Sandra J.
Conklin, Hazel W. Landis
Conlan, John G.
Conley, Paul D.
Conly, Richard
Connaughton, Kenneth N.
Connelly, Colleen
Conner, Clarence H.

Coats, Logan Andrew
Cobb, Karen Alyssa
Cobb, Ruth Eakin
Cobb, John M.
Connerton, Daniel A.
Conover, George E.
Conrad, Herman A.
Conrad, Shelly Cropper
Conrad, Holly E. Jack
Conrad, Dorothy G.
Conrad, Deborah Kaye
Conrad, Debra L. Reed
Conrad, Victor Leon
Conrad, Melissa Renea Ours
Conrad, Delores
  VanDevender
Conroy, David E.
Conroy, Carol S.
Constable, Mary E.
Constantine, Laura Anne
Contee, Raymond E.
Contino, Linda S.
Conway, Christina Alise
Conway, Lewis H.
Conway, Andrew J.
Conway, Roy
Cook, Michael A.
Cook, Richard A.
Cook, Hettie B.
Cook, Jim D.
Cook, Lori E. Aronson
Cook, Nancy E.
Cook, Wendy Fasting
Cook, Hugh H.
Cook, James J.
Cook, Belle L. Morton
Cook, Pauline Lawrie
Cook, Samantha Marie
Cook, Johnathon Michael
Cook, Gary P.
Cook, James R.
Cook, Thomas Reginald
Cook, Robert Roger
Cook, Christie Rose
Cook, Victoria Vanosdale
Cook, Charles W.
Cook, Wayne
Cooke, Kevin A.
Cool, Brent A.
Cool, Roy E.
Cool, Betty R. Legg

Coffman, Harold
Coffman, Nikita
Cogar, George A.
Cogar, Paul N.
Coombs, Linda C. Schacht
Coombs, Laura Lyman Jansky
Coon, Rebecca Armour
Coontz, Mary K. Goodwin
Coontz, Warren L.
Coontz, Cynthia Lynn
  Giambrone
Cooper, Debra A. Michelson
Cooper, Mark A.
Cooper, Scott A.
Cooper, Fredrick B.
Cooper, Jennifer C.
  Moneypenny
Cooper, Harold D.
Cooper, Norma D.
Cooper, Roxanna E. Reed
Cooper, Jacqueline F.
Cooper, Donald G.
Cooper, Denice J. Harman
Cooper, Wilma Leary
Cooper, Heather Lipscomb
Cooper, Nicole Lyn Isenhart
Cooper, Saira M. Khan
Cooper, Denise M. Varner
Cooper, Dayna Marie
Cooper, Dennis N.
Cooper, Frank P.
Cooper, Neal P.
Cooper, Tina R. Vandevander
Cooper, John R.
Cooper, Ernest S.
Cooper, Donald T.
Cooper, Bessie V.
Cooper, Kenneth W.
Cooper, Estin
Cooper, Grace
Cooper, Wilmoth
Cooper, Rhonda
Cooper, Sandra
Cooper, Maxine
Copeland, Robert L.
Copley, Joshua Clay
Coppock, Chenell Latrese
Corbett, Julie Jones
Corbett, Jennifer Rose Morris
Corbett, Eugene T.
Corbin, Patricia Robin

Collins, Angela Dawn
Collins, Benji Epperson
Collins, Clarence F.
Collins, Cassia F.
Corday, Peter
Cordell, Mary B. Ingham
Corder, Tammy R. Dunford
Cordle, Mark Shawn
Cordua, Jessie L. Bender
Core, Iden K.
Corey, Yumiko Sato
Coriell, Frederick A.
Coriell, Denise Whitmann
Corley, Richard A.
Corley, Arnett B.
Corley, Steven Bryan
Corley, Paul D.
Corley, Sybil G.
Corley, Denver Gale
Corley, Charlotte Golden
Corley, Hobert H.
Corley, Irene Holbert
Corley, Kimberly J.
Corley, Irene L.
Corley, Felicia M. Rhodes
Corley, Lesa Michele
Corley, Clair
Corll, Heidi
Cormier, Christophe Serge
  Erich
Cormier, Tammy Sue
  Williams
Cornell, Judith D. Detemple
Cornell, Amanda D.
Cornell, Neil H.
Cornell, Anthony J.
Cornell, Karen L. Pratt
Cornman, Judith A. Snatchko
Corrao, Teri R. O'Shea
Corregan, Robert D.
Corrick, Ernest B.
Corrick, Harriette Perry
Corrick, James
Corrie, Russell S.
Corts, James C.
Corvino, Paul C.
Corzine, Lester H.
Cosans, Seth Alan
Coschigano, Robert R.
Cosgrove, Karl D.
Cosic, Minja ante

Conner, Margaret J. Robbins
Conner, Donald L.
Conner, Gregory L.
Conner, Ruth S.
Costa, Paula C.
Costa, Maria E.
Costa, Eric F.
Costa, Carlos O.
Costello, Marilyn L. Seanor
Cottle, Sandra L.
Cotton, Jennifer L. Denmead
Cotton, Lee
Cottrell, Melody Ann
Cottrell, Michelle D.
Cottrell, Mary E.
Cottrill, Franklin Dale
Cottrill, Carrie Gayle
  McCartney
Cottrill, Halen McKenzie
  Lockhead
Couch, Kyle W.
Couchenour, Cynthia L.
  Cobb
Couchman, William V.
Cougan, John S.
Cougan, Helenjane Weiner
Coughlin, Sibyl Hayes
Coulter, Denise Broeren
Court, Daniel Wade
Courten, Camcy F. Boggs
Courten, Robert P.
Courtney, April D.
Cousens, Christopher
Cousin, Frances M.
Cousin, Marie Sycafoose
Coussoule, George T.
Coussoule, Alexander V.
Coutts, Lyle Adam
Covel, Daniel D.
Cover, Don E.
Coverdale, Marqui
Cox, Howard D.
Cox, David J.
Cox, Therese L. Cochran
Cox, Edward Lloyd
Cox, William R.
Cox, John T.
Cox, Troy W.
Cox, Charles W.
Cox, Goff
Coy, Warren G.

Cooleen, Mary C. Shimbo
Cooley, Kaelu Tolley
Coombs, David A.
Coombs, James W.
Crabtree, Samantha Leigh
Craig, Zoe Abigail
Craig, Robert Andrew
Craig, Richard D.
Craig, Marcia J. Davies
Craig, Elizabeth J. Moxon
Craig, Robert S.
Craig, Mary Ellen Updike
Craig, W. F.
Craine, Kristen M.
Cramer, Shirley B. Pigott
Cramer, Richard Burton
Cramer, Miles C.
Cramer, Elizabeth Lynne
  Maurer
Cramer, Wendell M.
Cramer, Judith Meinen
Crane, Michael C.
Crane, James H.
Crane, Kenneth W.
Crane, Lawrence W.
Crane, Steven
Cranmer, Sarah
Craun-Selka, Sophia Rose
Crawford, Jordan Avery
Crawford, Laura D. Bonser
Crawford, Lois J. Turi
Crawford, Richard K.
Crawford, Annie L.
Crawford, David L.
Crawford, Megan Leigh
  Phares
Crawford, Penelope Lielous
Crawford, Dennis Michael
Crawford, Carson Michael
Crawford, Tariogh N. Redmon
Crawford, Richard N.
Crawford, Melissa Neill
Crawford, Robert P.
Crawford, James R.
Crawford, Burton
Crawford, Geoffrey
Creadick, Susie
Creaturo, James J.
Creaturo, John T.
Creech, Richard
Creed, Lee Adair Haring

Rowzee
Corcoran, Douglas M.
Corcoran, Zachary Scott
Corcoran, Earl
Cresson, Richard H.
Crichton, Peggy A. Rogers
Crichton, Betty Jean Altfather
Crichton, John W.
Crickard, Enid Harper
Crickard, Charles J.
Crickard, Richard Leo
Crickard, Richard N.
Crickard, Hyldred W.
Crider, Derek George
Crigger, Charles David
Crines, William P.
Crisci, Sherri L. Haddix
Crisp, Martha Tibbels
Crist, Penny
Crist, Kyle
Critchfield, Donna
Crites, Patricia A. Koehler
Crites, Kay E. Moorman
Crites, Brenda L. Butler
Crites, Fay O.
Critton, Gregory John
Croce, Nicholas J.
Crockarell, Jeffery E.
Croes, Louis
Cromer, Mary B.
Crompton, Sally
Cromwell, Dorothy L.
Cromwell, Owena Sanderson
Cronin, Diane E. Whetsell
Cronin, Jefferson S.
Cronin, Virginia Smith
Crooks, A. Charlene Winans
Crosby, Joseph E.
Crosby, Clarence F.
Crosby, Donovan P.
Crosen, Carmella Montoney
Crosier, Douglas D.
Cross, Michael A.
Cross, Susan Elaine Henninger
Cross, Rachel Erin
Cross, Harvey H.
Cross, Gillian I. Skimins
Cross, Kenneth L.
Cross, Kenneth L.
Cross, Ronald L.
Cross, Ernest L.

Cosic, Ante
Cosner, Brent Elwood
Cosner, Mandy L.
Cosner, Angela M. Evans
Crossland, Kelley A.
Crossland, Alisha Nicole
Crossland, Sandra Sue
  Hershberger
Crosston, Kristin Brianna
Crosston, Kory C.
Crosston, Linda L. Calain
Crosten, Gregory A.
Crosten, Kellie Gail Philli
Croston, Edna E.
Croston, Tracy Rebecca Fill
Croston, David Scott
Crouch, Mary W. Pence
Crouch, Evelyn
Crouse, Kathy A.
Crouse, Dorene Clawson
Crouse, Joanne Gellas
Crouser, Mildred Steever
Crovo, Linda L.
Crow, Virginia Anne Farm
Crowder, Jennifer R. Mole
Crowell, Karen Elizabeth
  Marcus
Crowell, Douglas Sturteva
Crowl, James W.
Crowley, James W.
Croy, Charles A.
Croy, Roy R.
Cruickshank, Dimsoy
Crumm, Henry G.
Crump, George A.
Crump, Karen L.
Crump, Bajz-Marie Ogden
Crump, Kevin Walter
Cruse, Donald R.
Cruse, Dale R.
Cruse, Linda W
Crutchfield, Thomas L.
Cruz, Joseph Maria
Cruza Dominguez, Carlos
Csemez, Matthew Steven
Cubbison, Paul V.
Cudworth, Barbara
Cuellar, Rafael
Cugler, Meghan Nicole Forb
Culbertson, Martha Ellis
Cullen, Chris F.

Coyle, James B.
Coyner, Evelyn K.
Cozzolino, Samantha Marie
Crabtree, Philip G.
Cumberworth, Craig A.
Cummings, Marcia Bishop
Cummings, Amy E.
    McDonald
Cummings, James H.
Cummings, Tonya Marie
Cummings, Savanna Marie
Cummings, William O.
Cummings, Shelly R.
Cummings, John T.
Cummings, Patricia
Cummings, Miranda
Cunningham, Marvin A.
Cunningham, Nancy A.
Cunningham, Wanda Gum
Cunningham, Michael I.
Cunningham, Joy L. Kuhn
Cunningham, Debra L.
Cunningham, Ashley Lynn
Cunningham, Beryl Marshall
Cunningham, Veronica
    May Fragmin
Cunningham, Ruth Payne
Cunningham, Lillian Preys
Cunningham, Joseph W.
Cunningham, Perry
Cunningham, Amy
Cunningham, Krysten
Cuonzo, Marilynn
Cupp, Jaime Sue McGee
Cuppett, Rebecca L. Railey
Curcio, Susanne L. Czyborra
Cure, Paul D.
Curran, Elizabeth A. Smolski
Curran, John A.
Curran, Sarah Brock
Curran, Irma Crosier
Currence, Peggy A.
Currence, Homer C.
Currence, Rebecca C.
Currence, Marvin D.
Currence, Jessica Diane
Currence, William H.
Currence, David J.
Currence, Crystalin Jill Fox
Currence, Rebecca L.
    Fincham

Creed, George J.
Creighton, Ruth C. Wyand
Crenshaw, Scott T.
Cresser, George W.
Currence, Wanema Pauline
    Cross
Currence, Jennifer S. Kennedy
Currence, Emerson
Currence, Ford
Currence, Matthew
Currence, Mike
Curry, Craig D.
Curry, Kris L. Horvat
Curry, Edwin Lee
Curry, Kelsea Marie
Curtin, Charles H.
Curtis, Pauline Enlow
Curtis, Sydney Faith
Curtis, Tandra Joyce Linger
Curtis, Taylor L.
Curtiss, Philip B.
Curtiss, Barbara Jane Cross
Cushing, A. Lynn Weidner
Cushman, Pauline Keppel
Cussen, Remington J.
Cutlip, David Edwin
Cutlip, Jane Fox
Cutlip, Billie Jane
Cutlip, Loretta K.
Cutlip, Heather Lynn
    Amburgey
Cutlip, Penny N.
Cutlip, Joann
Cutright, Barbara Blackwood
Cutright, Reba Danielle
Cutright, Eva Goddin
Cutright, Sherry Hewitt
Cutright, Janet L. Harper
Cutright, Christina M.
Cutright, Heather Marie
Cutright, Paul R.
Cutright, Thaddius
Cutright, Randall
Cutshaw, Otis Henry
Czerepinski, Frank
Dabney, Michael
Dadisman, Barbara A.
Daetwyler, Bernard A.
Daetwyler, Richard E.
Daetwyler, Martha Leonard
Daft, Joseph Beau

Cross, Eula M.
Cross, Lynnette Marie
Cross, Jacquelyn S.
Cross, Harold W.
D'Agostino, Cherie Lynn
    Tsoplakis
Dahmer, Gaynelle Crosier
Dahmer, Charles G.
Dai, Huiying
Daiger, Christopher H.
Dailey, Francis C.
Dailey, Josephine Fiorentino
Dailey, Charmalea Gibson
Dailey, Brenda K.
Dailey, Robert W.
Dakan, Margaret Kelly
Dakes, Michael G.
Dale, Roger A.
Dale, Steven W.
Daley, Lori A. Ford
Daley, Peter Henry
Daley, Mark J.
Daley, Karen Knowlton
Daley, Kathy R.
Dalton, Scott J.
Dalton, Robert
Daly, Jennifer Marie Smith
Daly, Brian P.
Daly, Brian W.
Daman, Terry S.
Dambach, Vicki L.
D'Ambrosio, Paul J.
Dameron, Brenda Baker
Damiano, Charles A.
Damick, Elizabeth A. Isleib
Damon, Shauna Ann
D'Angelo, Sarah Jane
D'Angelo, Doris L. White
Daniel, Jeffrey K.
Daniel, Frank L.
Daniell, Dawn M. Rudolph
Daniels, Kathleen A. Kyser
Daniels, Debbie A. Venettone
Daniels, Lisa A.
Daniels, Debra Ann
Daniels, Patrick D.
Daniels, Margaret Elizabeth
    Long
Daniels, Amanda G.
    Armstrong
Daniels, Mary Hinzman

Cullen, Shaun Francis
Culler, Mitchell D.
Culoso, Monica Lynne Quinn
Culp, Martha Barnard
Daniels, Elva L. Zickefoose
Daniels, Bryan L.
Daniels, Lori L.
Daniels, Kathy L.
Daniels, Anthony Maurice
Daniels, Carole N. Tacy
Daniels, Gene Neil
Daniels, Cathy P.
Daniels, Mae Poling
Daniels, Pamela Sue
Daniels, Joseph W.
Daniels, Daniel W.
Danitz, Winifred Neale
Danley, Robert A.
Dansby, Virginia Prichard
Dant, Allison Leigh
Dant, Nicole Marie
Dantzic, Sidney P. Collett
Danvers, Harry T.
Danz, David H.
Danz, Jane V. Watson
Dareing, Michael A.
Darkey, James R.
Darling, Margaret Adamson
Darling, Nina Elaine
Darling, Houston Taylor
Darling, Russell
Darnell, David L.
Darrow, Paul B.
Dashiff, Cary F.
Datesman, Daniel T.
Dattilo, Jill H.
Daube, Nathan Owen
Daugherty, Pamela A. Kelly
Daugherty, Richard A.
Daugherty, Melodie A.
Daugherty, Eugene B.
Daugherty, Douglas D.
Daugherty, Tammy D.
Daugherty, Heather E. Knapp
Daugherty, Elizabeth M.
Daugherty, Danielle Marie
    Perry
Daugherty, Kaitlyn Marie
Daugherty, Keith W.
Davenport, Churchill Gibson
Davenport, Sara Michelle

Currence, Robert L.
Currence, Jacob Steven
Currence, Lucille V.
Currence, Douglas W.
Davidson, Kimber Earl
Davidson, Irene Goode
Davidson, John J.
Davidson, Mary Louise
 Fortmann
Davidson, Lori M. Forman
Davidson, Richard Stanley
Davies, Jonah A.
Davies, Barbara J. Schranz
Davies, Melva Kay
Davies, Valentine M.
Davies, James N.
Davies, Robert S.
Davies, Ronald V.
Davis, Kelly A. Nagel
Davis, James A.
Davis, Thomas A.
Davis, Lisa A.
Davis, Michael A.
Davis, Loran Adelle
Davis, Glenn Albert
Davis, Lalian Alexandra
Davis, Mark B.
Davis, Sherry B.
Davis, Lauren B.
Davis, Joshua Brandon
Davis, David C.
Davis, Katherine C.
Davis, Morris Caleb
Davis, Anne Conner
Davis, Mariah Cynthia
Davis, Erica Dawn
Davis, Tamara E. Lambert
Davis, Christina E. Robinson
Davis, Brent E.
Davis, Douglas E.
Davis, Bruce E.
Davis, Thomas E.
Davis, Mary Elaine Wheeler
Davis, Ashley Elizabeth
Davis, Mary F. Ketterman
Davis, Susan F.
Davis, Carol Findley
Davis, Andrew Glenn
Davis, Crystal I. LaNeve
Davis, Robert J.
Davis, Conn Jay

Daft, Anthony
Dagitz, Alex R.
D'agostin, Lara K. Rutherford
Davis, Monica L.
Davis, Rosemary L.
Davis, Matthew L.
Davis, Johnnie L.
Davis, Heather LaDawn Foley
Davis, Camilla Laureen
 Dixon-Haynes
Davis, Deborah Leah Behm
Davis, Samantha LeAnn
Davis, Christopher Lee
Davis, Ryan Lee
Davis, Emma Louise
Davis, Donna Lynn
Davis, Stacie Lynn
Davis, Diana Lynn
Davis, Virginia M. Howell
Davis, Clara M.
Davis, Elwood M.
Davis, T. M.
Davis, Michael M.
Davis, Eric M.
Davis, Nicole Marie
Davis, Rachael Marsh
Davis, Brian P.
Davis, Sidney P.
Davis, Katrina R. Mallow
Davis, Charles R.
Davis, Timothy R.
Davis, Sara Rachelle
Davis, Jason Ryland
Davis, Norma S.
Davis, Peggy S.
Davis, Matthew T.
Davis, Jeremy Thomas
Davis, James Tyson
Davis, James W.
Davis, Mark W.
Davis, Genevieve Yosia
Davis, Kenneth
Davis, Murdock
Davis, James
Davis, Cara
Davis, Rebekah
Davison, Frank A.
Davison, M. B.
Davis-Taylor, Cynthia M.
Davy, Richard Michael

Daniels, Shirley J. Chenoweth
Daniels, Brenda Johnson
Daniels, Deborah K. Hatfield
Daniels, Ivan L.
Dawson, Jared N.
Daxon, Andrew M.
Day, Gene G.
Day, Lloyd H.
Day, Casey J.
Day, Debra K. Norman
Day, Virginia Lee Myers
Day, Ashley Lynn
Day, John R.
Day, James R.
Day, Gorman
De Esso, Robert Anthony
de Klerk, Willem Floris
de la Bay-Coffie, Ebele Rene
Deacon, Donald B.
Deacon, Jeffrey R.
Deal, Thomas F.
Dean, Roger A.
Dean, Dewaine C.
Dean, Laura C.
Dean, Forrest D.
Dean, Amy E. Zidow
Dean, Nancy J.
Dean, David L.
Dean, Sandra Lee
Dean, Betty Lou Garrison
Dean, Wanda M. Hart
Dean, Howard R.
Dean, Deborah S.
Dean, Andrew
Dean '19, Megan Rae
Deane, Edith Kramer
DeAngelis, Dianne L. Johnson
Dearborn, Philip M.
Dearborn, Amanda N. Cooper
Dearth, Clark Baird
Dearth, Patricia Sterling
Deavers, Sharon E.
DeBaets, Lucylle Chambers
DeBaets, Michel P.
DeBarr, Jean Malcolm
DeBease, John G.
DeBease, Linda L. Voyt
DeBease, Brian P.
DeBerry, Michele D.
DeBerry, Sherry
DeBevoise, Dorothy Virginia

Davey-Karlson, Matthew
 Michael
David, Janet Kay Lanham
Davidson, Carrie Ann Carr
DeBroy, James A.
DeCanio, Angela R. Bentley
Decastro, Ivan
DeCerbo, Sandra Schroeder
Decker, Pamela A. Malkmes
Decker, John C.
Decker, Clifford J.
Deckers, Louis F.
Decoux, Joanne M. Donnelly
Deebo, Jeanette F. Poe
Deebo, George Thomas
Deeck, Kimberly J.
Deegan, Kenneth A.
Deel, Lisa McLaughlin
Deely, Nancy D. Moore
Deem, Rebecca Lewellen
Deem, Carla Nicole
Deemer, Jay C.
Deemer, Craig K.
Deemer, Judith L. Forbes
Deemer, Pamela Matters
Defibaugh, Debra Denise
Defibaugh, Christina M. Be
Defibaugh, Whitney Reanee
Defiore, Linda Ann
DeFontes, Marilyn Backofen
DeFontes, James R.
DeFontes, John
DeFreitas, Mark Errol
Defrino, John A.
Degarno, Joshua
Degenhardt, Cara
Degraffenreid, Larisa A. Perez
deGruyter, Eric F.
Deir, Brian G.
Deitsch, April L.
Dejean, Elizabeth Catherine
 Louise
DeLaCruz, Lorena G.
Delahey, Donald K.
Delahoussaye, Linda S.
DeLand, Margaret L.
Delaney, Earl J.
Delaney, Michael J.
Delaney, Beth Johnston
DeLange, Marilyn R. MacKa
DeLanoy, William W.

Davis, Samantha Jo Tallman
Davis, Suzanne L. Benton
Davis, Lorna L. Gabriel
Davis, Patricia L.
Delavigne, Dorsey H.
DelConte, John F.
Delconte, Bonnie P. Blasko
Delconte, Vincent Richard
DeLisser, Julia Ann Kenyon
DeLisser, Richard L.
Dell, Richard
Dellafiora, Richard A.
Dellafiora, John A.
Dellicker, Samantha
  Brooke Adkins
DelliSanti, Michael A.
Delnat, Gregory C.
Delorenzo, Richard B.
DeLorenzo, Katharene R.
  Masters
DelRosario, David
DeLuca, Mary Ann
DelValle, Francisco
Demakos, John D.
DeMarco, Gwendolyn A.
Demario, Feore
DeMartini, William V.
DeMasi, Ann Marie
DeMatteo, Anthony
Demchik, Sophie M. Long
DeMetrovich, Cynthia Cahill
DeMotte, Elizabeth Sheeley
DeMotto, Mark A.
DeMotto, Jacob Michael
DeMotto, Jessie Roberson
DeMotto, Dianne Sanders
Dempsey, Seth Austin
DeMundo, Melinda L.
Denbigh, John H.
Deneroff, Michael Lewis
Denise, Melissa Beth
Denise, Rene Gabrielle
Denison, Dorothea Niman
Denison, Robert S.
Denna, Anthony Lynn
Denning, Tatiana R.
  Konchesky
Dennis, Natalie Elizabeth
  Poling
Dennis, Derek
Dennison, Keri Lynn

Dawood, Mohammed
  Abdulaziz Mohammed
Dawson, John B.
Dawson, Amie Michele
Densmore, Leela Ann
Denton, Peggy Harms
DePew, Robert C.
DePoy, Jack F.
Deppenbrock, Bonnie
DePriest, Zandy D.
DePriest, Susan Jane
  Hasbrouck
Derienzo, John
Deriugini, Aleksandre
Derrickson, Pamela
Deshayes, Jamie Leigh Ratlilff
Deshinsky, Patricia
  Mountfield
Deshinsky, George
DeSouza, Helio J.
DeSpain, James R.
Detjen, Sara Jane Reid
Detmer, Jodi B. Sabo
Dettinger, Brennan
Deutsch, Mark J.
Deutsch, Gary P.
Devaney, Matthew J.
DeVault, Lawrence Grahm
DeVenney, Sharon D. Myers
Dever, Connie B. Sparks
Dever, Allie K.
Devereaux, Meredith Ann
  Kelly
Devery, Michael Joseph
DeVille, Olivia Christine
Devine, Paula J.
Devine, Carl T.
Devine, Lela
DeVoss, John D.
DeWeese-Gatt, Daisy Lynn
Dewey, Karen Kerbel
Dewitt, John O.
Dexter, Wilburta W. Cornwell
d'Hedouville, Jeffrey Tyler
Di Girolamo, Alberto
Di Iorio, Amy N. Miller
DiAngelo, Dorothy A. Smith
Dianna, Kayla Nicole
Diaz, Robert P.
Diaz, Leon
DiBacco, Kathy E.

Debiase, Susan L.
DeBlecourt, Cheryl L.
  Novoshielski
DeBroske, Arlene Carty
DiCesare, Joseph V.
Dick, Emilie Ann Brodisch
Dick, Eric D.
Dick, Dennis G.
Dickens, Cassidy Kaitlynn
Dickens, Clyde
Dickerson, Richard Alphonsia
Dickerson, Alvin L.
Dickey, C. David
Dickison, Frank H.
Dickson, Arin Fincham
Dickson, Holly Marie
Diebold, Chandra Dee Auville
Diefenderfer, Bruce G.
Diefendorf, Donald T.
Dieffenbach, Chris
Diegmann, Scott R.
Dielman, Scott Franklin
Dieringer, Rita Cuff
Dieringer, Stephen W.
Dierlam, Amy R. Warren
Digiacomo, Felix A.
DiGiovanni, M. Rebecca
  Hellems
DiGiovanni, Louis P.
Diglio, John T.
Digman, Lisa A. Valentine
Digman, Twila Carr
Digman, Jerry E.
Dilcher, Kimberly E.
Dilettoso, Diane M. Davidson
Dilley, Brenda K.
Dilley, Donna L.
Dilley, Leann Nicole
Dilley, Marvin R.
Dilling, David Jeffrey
Dillinger, Megan Elizabeth
  Dulik
Dillinger, Cory James
Dillon, Christopher C.
Dillon, Susan Grimes
Dillon, Kate Irwin
Dilly, Belva A. Goss
Dilly, Teresa L. Rudd
Dilly, Eugene P.
DiMario, Priscilla Carolyn
  Weaver

Delauder, Roy A.
Delauder, Kimberly J.
  Helmick
DeLauter, Hilary L. Cook
DiPasquale, Michael A.
DiPasquale, Danielle L.
  Cutright
DiPiano, Michael A.
DiPiano, Rosemary K. Bell
Disharoon, Frank Woodland
DiSilva, Joan
Disney, James G.
Diston, Dolores A. Lynch
Ditcheos, Nicholas
Ditty, Thomas P.
Dix, Susan E.
Dix, James Melvin
Dixon, Philip A.
Dixon, Brian Donnell
Dixon, Keith E.
Djordjevic, Luka
Dobbs, Lee F.
Dobyan, Dennis C.
Dochez, D'Armand W.
Dockery, Mildred J.
  Williamson
Dockery, Jennifer
Dodd, Devyn Alexander
Dodd, Tiffany Mary Frances
Doderer, Hans F.
Dodge, James W.
Dodrill, Anna Hogan
Dodson, Ryan Anthony
Doe, James H.
Doeblin, Ronald G.
D'Oench, Nancy Esther
  Malone
Doerr, Carolyn Channell
Dogrul, Demir M.
Doherty, Katherine I.
Doig, Thomas M.
Doig, Kathleen Patterson
Doig, Andrew T.
Dolan, William F.
Dolan, Evelyn M. Lanham
Dolan, Peter T.
Doleschal, Robert R.
Dolfie, Douglas L. Sibbald
Dolly, Robin A.
Dolly, Meghan B.
Dolly, Mary Ellen Flint

Dennison, Richard Wayne
Dennison, Sarah
Denniston, Jeffrey Scott
Denniston, Marlene Wilmoth
Dominic, Stephen V.
Domoto, Manatsu
Donahugh, Richard S.
Donaldson, Robert B.
Donaldson, Robert C.
Donaldson, Joan Goode
Donaldson, C. H.
Donaldson, Bruce O.
Donatelli, Gregory C.
Donchez, Ryan Anderson
Doner, Harry
Donev, Damjan
Donley, Martha Ann Clark
Donnahoe, Sarah P.
Donnelly, Joseph E.
Donnen, Christine Lea
Donniez, Richard L.
Donofrio, Arthur F.
Donohoe, Michael
Donovan, Katie Ann
Donovan, Wesley J.
Donovan, Carolyn L.
Doran, John G.
Doran, Krista Prussak
Doremus, Nancy J. Kelshaw
Dornhart, Adam J.
Dorsey, Dixie Lee A.
Dorsey, Owen H.
Dorsey, Cynthia Nelson
Dortmund, Jennifer Kuhns
Dortmund, Paul Lee
Dortmund, Charles M.
dos Santos, Vitoria Issaho
Dosch, William H.
Doss, Kelli Elizabeth Perry
Doss, Katherine Jewell
Dotson, Hellen E.
Dotson, Jennifer J.
Dotson, Margaret M.
Dottellis, Laurel L. Proudfoot
Doucet, Rene
Dougall, Carolyn Black
Dougherty, Peter H.
Dougherty, Sandra Lee
  Helsel
Dougherty, Constance
  Mallett

Strawderman
DiBona, G. Fred
DiBrandi, Paris P.
DiCenzo, Joseph G.
Douglas, Harry B.
Douglas, Robert E.
Douglas, Sally Harrison
Douglas, Raymond J.
Douglas, James M.
Douglas, V. Ruth Summers
Douglas, Rebecca
Douglas, W.D.
Douglas, Troy
Douglass, Helen Doscher
Douglass, Susen E. Wolford
Douglass, Thomas Edward
Douglass, Louis J.
Douthett, Quillma Beecher
Douthett, Russell M.
Dove, Seylon
Dowe, Larry
Dowler, D. Drake
Dowler, Joe E.
Dowler, Jennifer Jo Klasan
Dowler, Jack T.
Down, Edward L.
Downen, Richard D.
Downen, Barbara Jean Hansen
Downes, Sheldon Canfield
Downs, Tara L.
Downs, Henry
Doyle, Karen A. Goerlich
Doyle, William A.
Doyle, Judson C.
Doyle, Robert F.
Doyle, Vicki J. McWilliams
Doyle, Eric John
Doyle, Dennis K.
Doyle, Chad R.
Doyle, Patrick W.
Drain, Robert B
Drain, Elizabeth Lorraine
Drain, Joshua
Drake, Marshall M.
Drake, Robin M.
Drake, Ed
Draney, Kevin J.
Dransfield, Laura
Dreibelbis, Georgina Jane
  Peiser
Dreibelbis, Eric P.

DiMario, Michael F.
Dimit, Roger H.
DiNola, Diane
Diorio, Daniel J.
Drobins, Barbara Jill
Droll, Jeff A.
Droppleman, Anna Dibacco
Droste, Ronald
Drucker, Claire
Drumheller, Harold K.
Drumm, Taylor Noelle
Drummond, James E.
Dubiel, Kristin Noel Justice
Dubiel, Treavor Stewart
Dubois, Susan
Dubreuil, Joseph R.
Duckworth, Jennifer D. Poling
Duckworth, Celeste Nichole
  Yardley
Duckworth, Fredrick W.
Dudiak, Neil B.
Dudik, Ruthanne Kron
Dudley, Margaret T. Kopfle
Duffey, David K.
Duffus, Kathleen Breslin
Duffus, Matthew Colin
Duffy, Richard M.
Dugalic, Branko
Dugan, Eleanor L. Kisner
Dugan, James L.
Dugan, Jeremy P.
Dugan, Charles R.
Dugan, Cindy Troutner
Duger, Raymond D.
Duggan, H.L.
Duke, Mary A. Hahn
Duke, Charles I.
Dukes, Aliyah Gabrielle
DuLac, Gregory Scott
Dulaney, Klara K.
DuLaney, Carla
Dumas, Julia Ann
Dumire, Jerica Dawn
Dumire, Lois E. Wolfe
Dumire, Freda G. Roy
Dumire, Ethel G.
Dumperth, Elizabeth J.
  O'Brien
Dunbar, John Albert
Dunbar, Heather Lynn
Dunbar, Howard R.

Dolly, McNeer K.
Dolly, Willis L.
Domenack, Janet Kay Hasm
Domenick, Lewis A.
Duncan, Wendy L.
Duncan, William Wilson
Duncan, Robert
Duncanson, Patricia A. Eg
Duncanson, Gregory S.
Dunetz, Bryant R.
Dunkle, Sarah Stephens
Dunlap, Sam C.
Dunlap, Ara J.
Dunn, Florence Corley
Dunn, Robert E.
Dunn, Carissa Janette
Dunn, Patricia Louise
Dunnagan, Patrick Lowell
Dunne, Mimi L. Birkenba
Dunsmore, Diane Eileen
  Heintz
Dunsmore, John W.
Dunstan, Barbara Ann
Dunstan, Ralph F.
Dunston, Anthony Malik
Dunton, Brian T.
Dunville, Robert M.
Dunz, Tanika Kay
DuPlessis, Eric F.
DuPlessis, Jennifer McCarth
Duran, Carole J.
Duran, Alicia
Durante, Christina
Durham, Jessica Kay Brad
Durkee, J. Suzanne Grandi
Durkin, Kathleen
Durrett, Harold L.
Durrett, Ralph
Dusch, James E.
Dusenberry, Jill
Dusenbury, Joseph F.
Dutra, Tracey A.
Dutton, Raymond Jesse
Duvall, Christopher J.
Duy, Pierre V.
Dyck, Matthew James Kale
Dyckes, Jacqueline Power
  Dionne
Dye, Dina Banda
Dye, I. K.
Dye, D. L.

Doughty, Thomas E.
Douglas, Barbara A.
  Workman
Douglas, Carol Ann
Dyer, Nicole Lydzinski
Dyer, Michael P.
Dyer, Charles
Dyer, Duane
Dyke, Sharon Patricia
Dzuback, John C.
Eades, Carolyn R. Paretti
Eadson, Judith
Eagle, Diane Mastrobattista
Eakin, Kathryn M.
Eakin, Robert W.
Eakle, Shane M.
Earle, Elizabeth A. Whetsell
Earle, Richard D.
Earle, Jennifer Rebecca
  Henderson
Earles, David Keith
Early, Jeb Ryan
Earnest, Roy F.
Eary, Verla O.
Eash, Cassidy Jordan
Easter, Kassidy Denise
Easterbrook, John C.
Eastin, Bragg Matthew
Eastman, Philip Carl
Eastmond, Wayne S.
Easton, Tanya Kittle
Easton, Garrett
Easton, John Brent
Easton, Edward
Eaton, Andrea M. Lookhart
Eaton, Richard M.
Eavey, Cathy P. Cosner
Ebaugh, Amy Marie
Ebaugh, Melissa Nicole
Ebersole, Joshua A
Ebert, Richard D.
Eby, Leroy Eugene
Eccleston, Raymond V.
Eckart, Linda L. McDonald
Eckerd, Kayla Lee
Eckert, Dorothy L. Hill
Eckhardt, Bridget Jessica
  Lynne
Eckles, John R.
Eckley, Caryn Seward
Ecklind, Jerrold R.

Drenkard, Allan A.
Drew, Randall J.
Driscoll, Pamela A.
Driver, Juanita L.
Edgell, Jeannette Rachel
Edgemeyer, Marion Burke
Edings, Williams D.
Edings, Aaron
Edminster, T. Ross
Edmond, Nola Elaine Stone
Edmondson, Elma Weimer
Edwards, Alexander A.
Edwards, Valerie Ann Heller
Edwards, Kelly Ann
  O'Donnell
Edwards, Robert B.
Edwards, Alyssa Brooke
Edwards, Michelle Davis
Edwards, George Edmund
Edwards, Melanie Gosnell
Edwards, John H.
Edwards, Susan Kabert
Edwards, Nicole Leigh
Edwards, Mark O.
Edwards, Richard S.
Edwards, Gary S.
Edwards, Timothy S.
Edwards, Patricia Williams
Edwards, Amy
Egeland, Richard R.
Eger, Carol Sue Lynch
Egger, George F.
Egger, Robert I.
Eggleson, Amanda C.
  Vanscoy
Eglinger, Jane McClintock
Egress, Carrie Lee
Ehtesham-Zadeh, Timor
Eib, Charles
Eichhorn, Mary Rodgers
Eichler, Leslie J.
Eidell, Daron C.
Eidell, Shasta L.
Eidell, Carolyn Pennington
Eidell, Thomas R.
Eidell, Thomas R.
Eidell, Linlee R.
Eilenburg, Thomas R.
Eilers, Hayes R.
Elam, Laura A. Gianettino
Elbon, Linda L. Hogue

Dunbar, Madge Tolbard
Duncan, Stacy Elizabeth
  McKeown
Duncan, Laurie Ellen
Elgin, Betty J. Steele
Elgrim, Kristen Lynn
Elias, Sheldon C.
Elias, Jane Chandler
Elias, Joseph L.
Elias, Michael T.
Eliason, Kevin Matthew
Eliason, Emma Nicole Wolfe
Elkin, Kimberly
Elkins, Mark J.
Elkins, Thomas L.
Ellefson, Lisa A. Whitlatch
Eller, Mary F.
Ellifritz, Mary H.
Ellifritz, Amelie M. Cormier
Ellingwood, Audrey A. Kesler
Elliott, Walter D.
Ellis, Kimberly A.
Ellis, William E.
Ellis, William G.
Ellis, Sharon Hensley
Ellis, Melanie June Butcher
Ellis, Tillman L.
Ellis, Ashley Marie
Ellis, Julia Millar
Ellis, William R.
Ellis, Leonard W.
Ellisen, Mitchell P.
Ellison, Shania Jane
Ellison, Carley
Ellyson, Erma C. Kisner
Elmer, Lauren Rachelle
Elmore, Misti Dawn
Elmore, Louise Jarvis
Elmore, Rodney L.
Elmore, Christopher L.
Elmore, Morgan Makayla
  Gooden
Elmore, Anna Marie
  Riggleman
Elmore, Jason Ray
Elswick, Raymond L.
Elward, Joseph
Ely, Richard W.
Elza, Elizabeth Brooke
Elza, Linda D.
Elza, Sandra J.

Dye, Kenneth R.
Dye, Mary W. Chambers
Dye, Richard W.
Dyer, Virginia L.
Elza, Linda S. Mullennex
Elza, James T.
Elza, John T.
Elza, Brennan
Elza-Wilkie, Kimberly Dawn
Ema, Ryoka
Emanuelli, Peter L.
Emberley, Paul G.
Emerson, Harriet A.
Emerson, Mark A.
Emery, Meaghan Renae
Emes, Robert J.
Emme-Pingley, Danielle
Emmer, Robert S.
Emmerson, Dennis Michael
Emmons, Lynn Ora
Emmons, Kenneth R.
Emory, Heidi
Encarnacion, Karen
  Dickenson
Encarnacion, Ethany
Enda, Tomorohiro
Enders, Frank R.
Endo, Akiko
Engel, Susan Siegrist
Engelberger, Arthur William
Engelkemier, Phillip Charles
Engelkemier, Benjamin Kyle
England, Earlene R.
England, Heather Renee
Engle, Rogers C.
Engle, Stephen E.
Engleman, Catherine N.
  Garnett
Engleman, H. Flint
English, Helen C.
English, Trevor Dominique
English, Deanna L. DeWeese
English, Sallie L. Hamilton
English, Sue M.
Englishman, Allen K.
Englishman, Herbert N.
Enix, Kali Marie
Enke, Jenna Jo
Ennis, Robert M.
Enriquez, Falicity Dawn
  Wallace

Eckman, Tricia A. Demmy
Eddy, David A.
Eddy, David H.
Edgell, Amy Jo
Epp, Lori Marie
Epperson, Patricia C.
Epperson, Taylor Leigh
Eppright, Craig M.
Eramo, Louise Preysz
Erdie, Emily Layne
Erhard, Lloyd
Erickson, Barbara J.
Erickson, Karla L.
Erickson, Nancy
Eriksen, Amanda Lorraine
Erler, David G.
Erskine, Stacie L.
Ertter, Tammy Lynn
Ervin, David E.
Ervin, Dana R.
Ervine, Charlotte M.
Ervine, Jessica ReAnn
Ervine, Joseph W.
Erwin, Donald L.
Escotet, Maria Mercedes
Eskew, Charlotte A.
  Vierheller
Eskew, Breanna L.
Eskew, Amy Ren'ee Cosner
Espinal, Rodrigo
Essex, Paul D.
Essex, Judy Margaret Towne
Estep, Lyndsay Marie Bauer
Estes, Katie Ann
Estes, Carol Herron
Estes, Elizabeth Noel
Estes, Sally W. Perry
Estler, Nancy Cook
Estler, Paul F.
Etter, Lisa Bernzott
Etuknwa, Ekong T.
Evangelista, Andrew D.
Evangelista, Nan Guarducci
Evans, Caroline A. Geroski
Evans, Denise A. Marsh
Evans, Mary Astorino
Evans, Craig B.
Evans, John B.
Evans, Irene Chenoweth
Evans, Keith E.
Evans, Richard H.

Elbon, Katina M. Dixon
Elbon, Harold R.
Elder, Harry
Elekes, Michael
Evans, Alison K.
Evans, Doris L. Nelson
Evans, Renea L.
Evans, Barbara Lantz
Evans, Hannah Marie
  Lancaster
Evans, Joshua O'Neil
Evans, Gary R.
Evans, Amanda Rae
Evans, Ted W.
Evans, Milan
Evans, S. Clark
Evans, Jillian
Evans-Bennett, Nancy
Evenden, John Anthony
Evenden, Nancy Wilson
Evens, Charles David
Everett, Gerard R.
Everett, Priscilla T.
Everett, Janice
Everhart, Debra Ann Stark
Everhart, Michael E.
Everly, Margaret Baller
Eversole, Laura Tinsley
Everson, Lisa A.
Everson, Sheila K. White
Everson, Valerie M. Veith
Evick, Susan A. Fincham
Evick, Jill Elaine
Evick, Ancile W.
Ewing, John R.
Ewing, Gary W.
Ewy, Kimberly A. Gloistein
Exline, Opal N. Perry
Eye, Lisa Ann
Eye, Olin E.
Eye, John E.
Eye, Raymond J.
Eye, Robin M.
Eye, Ruth Simmons
Eye, Jessica
Eyler, Pauline Payne
Eyster, Kathleen J. Weston
Eyzaguirre, June Gallaher
Faber, Meta K. Loudermilk
Faber, Bryan R.
Fagan, Michael J.

Elza, Casey Jefferson
Elza, Deborah K.
Elza, Tracey L. Taylor
Elza, Chantal Marie
Fairman, Nancy
Fakhouri, Fouad E.
Falconer, David P.
Fallon, Richard A.
Fallon, Christine Frances Laird
Falls, Gregory L.
Falls, David W.
Falvo, Gregory G.
Fama, Makayla Elayne
Fanning, John Pat
Fannon, Matt Stephen
Fansler, Elizabeth Burke
Fansler, Everett D.
Fansler, Janie L. Dacal
Fansler, Gladys L. Ferguson
Fansler, Otis L.
Fansler, Lonnis O.
Fantasia, Dawn M.
Fantry, Timothy Ryan
Farhi, Wendy L. Brewer
Farino, Pamela Sue Young
Faris, Chelsea Alyssa
Farley, Gary A.
Farley, Cristin Gaye
Farley, Fred P.
Farley, Kelly Patrick
Farlow, Eldred E.
Farmer, Sherrie A. Trumble
Farmer, John D.
Farmer, Charles J.
Farrell, Martha Comisky
Farrell, Kevin D.
Farrell, Stephanie Perry
Farrelly, Ralph C.
Farringer, Carol D. Dapp
Farrow, Gerald W.
Farry, Kimberly M.
Fath, Stetson Hunter
Faulconer, C. Newman
Faunce, David D.
Fausel, Donald E.
Favre, Winona C. Harrison
Favre, Niels S.
Faw, John Edward
Fayer, Zachary Edward
Fayez, Mohammed
Fealy, Taylor Raye

Enriquez, Caleb Joshua
Enterline, Ashley Nicole
Entzminger, John
Epler, Irene D. Craig
Feather, Chasity Inez
Feather, S. Margaret Jeffers
Feather, Holly Lynne
Feather, C. W.
Featherngill, Paul
Featherstone, Guy R.
Fedak, Whitney
Federico, Jacqueline A.
  Kearney
Federovitch, Gertrude
  Crawford
Federovitch, John L.
Fedik, Joyce Fencl
Fedor, Gerald James
Fee, Eugene A.
Fee, Harry A.
Fee, Jeanne Greves
Fee, Harry R.
Feeley, Dorothy Ann
  Somerville
Feeley, Robert
Feglar, Paul
Feick, George
Feingersch, Allen
Felber, Everett Craig
Felber, Claudia Waters
  Weaver
Fellenstein, Barbara Elaine
Felley, James R.
Felton, Marie Bishoff
Felton, Lora M. Peek
Fendley, Jeremy Adam
Fenn, Walter P.
Fenstermacher, Adrianna
  Marie Gibson
Fenton, Ruth Ann Sorice
Fenton, Robert C.
Fenton, Judy Ciocca
Fenton, Gwenyth Paige
  Davenport
Fenton, Jon R.
Fenton, Harry Walter
Ferebee, MaQuasia Masean
  Chyanne
Ferguson, Kristy D.
Ferguson, Laura J.
Ferguson, Brian K.

Evans, David Hubert
Evans, Evan J.
Evans, Autumn Jade Bonner
Evans, Amber Joanne
Ferguson, Susan Lambert
Ferguson, Heidi Lee
   Jacqueline
Ferguson, Jerry R.
Ferguson, Suzanne R.
Ferguson, Bertha Yeager
Ferguson, Eugene
Fermosel Sancho, Laura
Fernandez, Frank Joseph
Fernandez, Joseph P.
Ferrara, Laura Katharine
   Wetzel
Ferrari, Annette E. Lent
Ferreby, Paula Hazard
   Ingram
Ferreby, David William
Ferreira, Rildo P.
Ferrell, Petra C.
Ferrell, Robert
Ferrese, Richard Scott
Ferris, Michelle E. Walker
Ferris, Mary R. Terry
Ferrise, Bernard A.
Ferruso, Orlando Alfred
Ferzoco, Christopher C.
Fest, Lorraine Woodford
Fetter, Shawn C
Fidler, Kathleen Davis
Fidler, James E.
Fidler, Kathryn Perry
Field, Barry L.
Fields, David B.
Fields, Justin Bradley
Fields, Ruth Jeffers
Fields, Charles L.
Fields, Robert L.
Fields, Thomas L.
Fields, Kathy S.
Figari, Lewis A.
Figueroa, Sarah Renee
Fike, Marlee D. Smith
Fike, Cecelia E. Hile
Fike, Earl E.
Fike, Debra L. Sturms
Fiks, Leslie
Filer, Joseph E.
Filiatrault, Pierre

Fahoury, George
Fair, Kevin M.
Fairbanks, Clyde Richard
Fairbanks, Lela W.
Finafrock, Jennie E.
Fincham, Jordan Alexandra
Fincham, Kermit E.
Fincham, Leenette Eileen
Fincham, Amy Elaine
Fincham, Abby Jean
Fincham, Karen Savage
Finch-Rosa, Heather Sue
Fincken, Barbara Donaruma
Fincken, Frederick J.
Findlay, Dwight S.
Findley, Nicole Denise
Findley, Jennifer K.
Fine, Jules
Finegan, Robert E.
Fink, Morgan A.
Fink, Robert Bosworth
Fink, Judy C.
Fink, Parker D.
Fink, Joseph W.
Fink, C. B.
Finkbeiner, Wayne J.
Finkelstein, Daniel A.
Finley, William Jarrell
Finley, Timothy M.
Finley, Ralph R.
Finley, Dirk R.
Finn, Edwin D.
Finn, Matthew
Finnegan, Ryan Michael
Fiore, Cailin A.
Fiore, Carla L. Baver
Fiorentino, Frank
Fiorentino, Claire
Fiori, Clayton J.
Firl, Carleen Fay
Firth, Edward G.
Fischer, Lyle R.
Fischer, Lanelle S.
Fischer, James W.
Fischer, Cecilia Zoe
Fish, Barbara M.
Fishel, James L.
Fisher, Carole Ann Payne
Fisher, Paige Dakota
Fisher, Richard E.
Fisher, Anne E.

Fearey, Victoria Anne
Feaster, Richard N.
Feaster, Donald V.
Feather, Alice A.
Fisher, Kathy J.
Fisher, Albert J.
Fisher, Colby James
Fisher, Alan L.
Fisher, John M.
Fisher, Christopher Michael
Fisher, Travis R.
Fisher, Genie Ramsey
Fisher, Max Ray
Fisher, Kathleen Suzanne
   Brusso
Fisher, Zachary Thomas
Fisher, Matthew W.
Fisher, Richard
Fisher, Beth Ann
Fishpaw, Jarrett K.
Fiske, Kelly
Fite, Thelma R. Clark
Fitting, Robert G.
Fitts, Pauline
Fitzgerald, Michael Dale
FitzGerald, Ada M. White
Fitzgerald, Lisa M.
Fitzgerald '21, Connor
FitzGibbon, Donald S.
Fitzpatrick, Joseph A.
Fitzpatrick, Nancy J. Fish
Fitzpatrick, Sean M.
Fitzpatrick, Eve
Fitzsimmons, Gilbert J.
Fitzsimmons, Susan Kay
   Hodgman
Fitzwater, Glenda J. Foy
Fitzwater, Marlin J.
Fitzwater, Robert J.
Fitzwater, Virginia Lantz
Fitzwater, Lila M. Brady
Fitzwater, Chandler Morgan
Fitzwater, Clarence T.
Flage, Richard A.
Flanagan, Denise Alice
   Bowker
Flanagan, Talladaga
   Charolette Pennington
Flanagan, Edwin F.
Flanagan, Ryan James
Flanagan, Virginia M.

Ferguson, Anita L. Delauder
Ferguson, Catherine L.
   Sanders
Ferguson, Elwood L.
Flatt, James G.
Fleischmann, Lisa Glover
Fleischmann, Joseph M.
Fleming, Perryn B.
Fleming, Marilyn Brokering
Fleming, Betty D. Dye
Fleming, Suzanne Marie
Fleming, Fred P.
Fles, Jonathan T.
Fleschner, Sharon
Flesher, Dorothy
Flesher, James
Fleshman, Bruce E.
Fletcher, Gail A.
Fletcher, Steven D.
Fletcher, Andrea Diane Adams
Fletcher, Brettie E. Ramsey
Fletcher, David E.
Fletcher, Charles H.
Fletcher, Robert J.
Fletcher, Victoria Louise
Fletcher, Thomas Morgan
Fletcher, John P.
Fletcher, Sarah Thompson
Flick-Ttee, Donna J. Durrett
Fliess, Rexford A.
Fliess, Claire J. Rehill
Fling, John Bosworth
Flinn, Molly Marie
Flinn, Thomas W.
Flint, Quin D.
Flint, Karen E.
Flint, Eliza
Flint, Robert
Floch, Jason D.
Floor, Debra McDonald
Flora, Alphonse R.
Flora, Flora Tabscott
Florence, Wendy Dawn
   Pittman
Florence, Donald Watson
Florich, Sherry Scardilli
Flory, Derek Christian
Flowers, Charlotte M.
Flowers, Leola W.
Floyd, Alma E.
Floyd, Heidi M.

Filippi, Eugene V.
Filler, James Edwin
Filosemi, Michael A.
Filsinger, Jennifer L.
Foehr, David C.
Foell, Thomas F.
Fogg, Gordon G.
Fogg, G. Lynne Martin
Fogle, Dorothy C.
Foley, Christine Elizabeth
Foley, John P.
Folino, Mary Lou Mashione
Follansbee, Walton A.
Follensbee, Jennifer Lynn
Folley, Denise Virginia
Folmer, Derek J.
Fondelier, Charles R.
Fong, Daisy L.
Fonorow, Robert E.
Foote, Edward H.
Foote, Mary Lou Beatty
Foote, Richard W.
Forbes, Mark C.
Forbes, Warner C.
Forcier, Mary
Ford, Layne H.
Ford, Matthew S.
Ford, Andrew Thomas
Ford, Marc
Fore, Lisa M. Beam
Forinash, John B.
Forinash, Nancy Louise
Formal, Dean Martin
Fornabai, Wilma Sue
    Schroeder
Forner, Reita M. Patterson
Fornwalt-Bedard, Kelly
Forrest, Robert A.
Forsberg, Danual E.
Forsythe, Alasdair John
Fortino, Vanessa Kesner
Fortino, Steven Michael
Fortner, Cynthia Anger
Fortney, James Albert
Fortney, Robert Allan
Fortney, Nicole Ann
    Davenport
Fortney, Anita C. Steerman
Fortney, Edwin C.
Fortney, Loren D.
Fortney, Ellen D.

Fisher, Christine F.
Fisher, William H.
Fisher, Vicki J. Clark
Fisher, Carol J. Duttweiler
Fortney, Jessica Enin Maradei
Fortney, Thelma Shreve
Fortunato, Carla DeJohn
Fortunato, Leonard M.
Foss, Hetrick
Foster, Jill Ann Harlan
Foster, Robert B.
Foster, Gerald D.
Foster, Tonya Dai
Foster, Ashley Dawn
Foster, Candida Dawn
Foster, Dianne Dolly
Foster, David E.
Foster, Anita Faye
Foster, Arnold L.
Foster, Andria L.
Foster, Jackie Lyn
Foster, Debora Lynn
Foster, Paul R.
Foster, Adelheide Shuster
Foster, Anna Teresa Tavolacci
Fotheringham, Ruth Cattelle
Fowler, Daniel B.
Fowler, Donald E.
Fowler, Bobbie M.
Fowler, Katrina Mae
Fowler-Righman, Larissa
    Dawn
Fox, Natalie Dawn Mason
Fox, Richard J.
Fox, Leah Jane
Fox, Kimberly K. Vance
Fox, Fred L.
Fox, Janet L.
Fox, Kara L.
Fox, Robin Lenore Nilsen
Fox, Anna M. Friel
Fox, Jessie M.
Fox, Charles Marshall
Fox, Vicki S.
Fox, Mason Scottie
Fox, Dorothy Wilson
Fox, Nancy Winifred Stein
Fox, Alan
Fox, Mary Beth
Foxwell, Carolynn Chlada
Foy, Hayward W.

Flanagan, Sean T.
Flanagan, Mary Virginia
Flanagan-Smith, Deborah
Flanigan, Ryan P.
Fralick, Elizabeth Rouse
Frambes, Todd A.
Frame, Joan B. Williams
Frame, Mary L.
Frame, Jason
Frame, Leah
France, Steven C.
France, Rhiannon M. Day
Franciose, Kenneth Joseph
Francis, Meredith D.
Francis, William E.
Frank, Jeffrey B.
Frank, Jean J. Bowers
Frank, Ruth M. Wagner
Frank, John W.
Frankhauser, M. Scott
Franklin, Erin Elyse
Frantz, Elisabeth D.
Frantz, William Frederick
Frase, Jason
Fraser, John A.
Fraser, James Eric
Fraser, Alan G.
Fraser, William O.
Frasher, Deborah A. Leaf
Frasier, James H.
Frasier, Dawson M.
Fratello, Lawrence J.
Fratt, Heather M.
Frawley, Michael J.
Frazee, Eleanor D.
Frazier, Robert Betts
Frazier, Endi Martise
Frazier, Anthony
Fredell, Jennifer Marie
Fredlock, Stanley R.
Fredrick, Robert C.
Fredrick, Kathy Jackson
Free, John Charles
Freed, Harry L.
Freed, William L.
Freed, Asheli Nicole
Freed, V. R.
Freedman, Meredith Anne
Freeman, George A.
Freeman, Anita Beth
Freeman, John H.

Flynn, Christi Ann
Flynn, Penny D.
Flynn, Scott T.
Flynn, Mark W.
Freeman, Katherine
Freiberg, James A.
Frelick, Emily J.
French, John D.
French, Catherine M.
Frey, Nancy A.
Frey, Janet E. Lambert
Frey, Jane McManus
Frey, Lacey
Fricke, Dennis Willam
Friday, Ruth A.
Friddle, Stacie Elaine Yeage
Fridley, Cheryl L. Hamrick
Frieder, Arthur R.
Friedman, Vanessa D.
Friel, Eugene A.
Friel, Ellen L.
Friel, Clay Robert
Friel, Jack S.
Friend, Warren A.
Friend, Loretta A.
Friend, Emilee Jo Frazee
Friend-Lantz, Rachel Rene
Fritts, Bradford H.
Fritz, Roger G.
Fritz, Heather K. Ulrich
Fritz, James Z.
Fritzius, Kauren Kimberle
    Nordstrom
Frohnapfel, Katherine Jea
Frome, Richard J.
Frome, Anna Psihountas
Fromm, Thomas Glenn
Frost, Sara Elisabeth Hunt
Fry, Joseph A.
Fry, Margaret Elizabeth
Fry, Matthew Justin
Fry, Mary K. Collett
Fry, Cora Lee
Fry, Raymond R.
Fry, Sandra Sweitzer
Frye, Kari Virginia
Frymyer, Angela Melissa
Fuentes, Gilbert R.
Fuhrman, Susannah L.
Fuhrman, Brandon
Fulcher, Sarah C.

Fortney, Nathan Dean
Fortney, Dustin Donald
Fortney, Kristi E.
Fortney, Patricia S.
Fuller-Carpenter, Molly E.
Fulmer, Audrey Ann Scott
Fulmor, Edgar
Fulton, Alexis Brooke
Fulton, Ellis W.
Fultz, Tracy Diane Rosencrance
Funk, John N.
Funk, Paul R.
Funk, Kimberly S.
Funkhouser, Rebecca J. Davis
Furby, Hannah Aileen
Furby, Gerald C.
Furby, Gerald Camden
Furby, Traci L. Weese
Furby, Tristen Marra
Furgurson, Ernest B.
Furis, Christopher W.
Furrow, F. DeWitt
Fusco, Samuel T.
Futral, Michael
Futrell, Patrick H.
Fyock, Sarah Lorraine
Gaaserud, Alexander David
Gaaserud, Charlotte J. Polino
Gaaserud, David P.
Gabel, Jonathan Dmitri
Gabriel, Julie J.
Gadacz, Alissa L.
Gadd, Penny Allison
Gadd, Carla J. Primavero
Gadd, William J.
Gadd, William P.
Gadd, Inetta Rossey
Gadd, Michael S.
Gadd, Kasey
Gadek, William V.
Gaffron, Eduardo
Gagliano, Lisa D. Ferguson
Gagliardi, Tracy Dawn
Gahres, Matthew Paul
Gainer, Willis G.
Gainer, Debra L. Hart
Gainer, James L.
Gainer, Jessica Leanne Eddy
Gainer, Janet Marker

Fragale, Ronald A.
Fragale, M. Deborah Payne
Fragmin, Shannon Lynne Johnston
Gaines, Carol Marie
Gaiss, Herbert G.
Galbreath, John L.
Galen, Josephine Manne
Galford, Hubert
Galindez, Jose R.
Gallagher, Richard B.
Gallagher, Michael F.
Gallagher, Sean P.
Gallagher, Dennis
Gallier, Monica A. Minix
Gallier, Richard Bowman
Gallo, David A.
Gallo, Joseph H.
Gallogly, Michael P.
Gallopo, Andrew S.
Galloway, Lori Anne Salo
Galloway, Donald G.
Gallup, Anna Ruth
Galusky, Ernest S.
Galvin, Robert L.
Gandee, Jennifer L.
Gandee, Nicola Smith
Gandica, Esther Henry Alcheh
Gangi, Vincent C.
Gank, Marlene J.
Garamone, Marjorie Utter
Garb, Charles H.
Garcia, Kimberly A. Coontz
Garcia, Manuel A.
Garcia, Maria C.
Garcia, Robert L.
Garcia, John Paul
Garcia, Deyanira
Garcia-Reyes, Ron Emmanuel
Garde, Richard E.
Gardella, Edward A.
Gardiner, Kimberly A.
Gardiner, Mark W.
Gardner, Dale A.
Gardner, Virgil F.
Gardner, Harold W.
Gardner, Scarlett
Garfield, William R.
Garland, Karl J.
Garner, David C.
Garrabrant, Kellie A.

Freeman, Carol J. Martin
Freeman, Mary L. Parsons
Freeman, Leonard L.
Freeman, J.P. LadyHawk
Garrett, Guy R.
Garrett, Chris
Garris, Lisa C. Newton
Garrison, Aubry A.
Garrison, Sean C.
Garrison, Justin D.
Garrison, Edith D.
Garrod, Robert W.
Garry, Patricia A.
Gartelmann, Richard W.
Garten, Thomas Trammell
Garten, Joseph Tucker
Gartland, Dorothy J.
Gartmann, Alexander M.
Garton, Whitney Jade
Garvin, Jo Ann Adamson
Garvin, Shirley K.
Garvin, Cynthia Mabel Camp
Garvin, Sarah
Gass, Thomas E.
Gassert, Phyllis Ann Meals
Gateless, Kirsten Linnea
Gatt, Jason J.
Gattis, William Dudley
Gaunt, Katie
Gaunt, Virginia
Gauvreau, Loretta Julia
Gawenus, Mary B.
Gay, James A.
Gay, Deborah E. Greenham
Gay, Lacy Jean
Gay, Grace Mauzy
Gay, G. P.
Gay, Karen Trautman
Gay, Gary W.
Gazza, Ashley L. Uberty
Gazza, Evan Michael
Gear, Charles G.
Gear, Macel Greene
Gear, Timothy Joseph
Gear, James L.
Gear, Michael L.
Gear, Clarence L.
Gear, Catherine Louke
Gear, Felix
Geary, Mark C.
Geary, Mary Jane Smith

Fulcher, James Paul
Fuller, Barbara A. Feaster
Fuller, Judith L.
Fuller, David W.
Geier, Timothy D.
Geier, Ione Kotch
Geier, Hazel Moore
Geiger, Ann E. Joyce
Geiger, Clifford T.
Geismar, Deborah J.
Geiss, Arthur A.
Geissinger, John A.
Gelber, Michael C.
Gelfer, Arnold H.
Gennantonio, John A.
Gennett, Robert E.
Genther, Robert A.
Gentile, Nicole N.
Gentry, Cynthia D. Lewis
Gentry, Louise E. Figula
Gentry, Jean E. Shoaf
Gentry, Robert T.
Geohagan, Daniel
George, William A.
George, Charles A.
George, Teresa A.
George, Kathryn B.
George, Michele C. Armstrong
George, John C.
George, Michelle Dawn
George, Devin Edward
George, Ann Elizabeth Urban
George, Philip G.
George, Stephanie Jo
George, Sabrina Jo
George, Rick L.
George, Charles L.
George, David L.
George, Susan M. Hamrick
George, Denise M.
George, Terrence Mack
George, JoAnna Michaelle Summerfield
George, Breanna R. Wamsley
George, Christopher R.
George, Tochukwu
George, Frances
Georgeson, Neva Paul
Georgeson, Robert
Georgiadis, Laura S.

Gibson, Nancy King
Gibson, Amber Marie
Gibson, Silas Parker Chase
Gibson, Glenna
Goldstein, Susan Binder
Goldstein, Scott S.
Goldstone, Gerald
Golia, Michael A.
Goller, Peter H.
Golomb, Lisa
Golston, Jeremy Abady
Golub, Angela Lauren
Gombert, Michael F.
Gomer, Tammy Gail
Gomez, Anahi
Gonsman, Lindsay Renee
Gontarski, Mathilda Soliday
Gonzalez, Miguel L.
Gonzalez, Ander
Good, Michael Duran
Good, Susan Krakoff
Goodall, Karen J.
Goodarzi, Manucher A.
Goodarzi, Bijan Joseph
Goodarzi, Kathryn L. Elward
Goode, Rudyard B.
Goode, Paul C.
Gooden, Jenna Lea Hanifan
Gooden, Idress M.
Gooden, Helen O.
Goodger, Lisa M.
Gooding, Danielle Caroline
Goodman, Jefferey David
Goodman, Jesse L.
Goodman, Emilee Marie
Goodrich, Amber L. West
Goodwin, Robin Louise
Goodwin, Debra P. Ware
Goodwin, Angelea Ruby
Goodwin, Olive
Gopel, Warren P.
Gorbea, Kristopher Michael
Gordon, Margaret B.
Gordon, Eric Francis
Gordon, Joanne Fusca
Gordon, Leslie Gordon
Gordon, Phyllis Harvey
Gordon, Ellen J.
Gordon, Kimberly Lynn
   Hinebaugh
Gorham, George J.

Gilmore, Tamela F. Bennett
Gilmore, John F.
Gilmore, Michael G.
Gilmore, Flo H. Stalnaker
Goss, Violet B. Long
Goss, Leah Jo
Goss, Irene W.
Goss, Ronald W.
Gossette, Inga M.
Gostomski, Rachel Christen
Gott, Eugene Cissell
Gott, Edwin H.
Goughneour, John R.
Gould, Edith C. Scott
Gould, Eleanor C.
Gould, Barbara E. Brown
Gould, Jessica F. Woy
Gourley, Mary Best
Gover, Charles H.
Gow, Patricia A. Wagner
Gow, Elizabeth Kadel
Gow, Betty
Gower, Rebecca Denise
Gower, Mary L. Wharton
Grabau, Marlene M.
   Klotzmann
Grabe, Pamela Verner
Grabe, Charles
Graber, Gail Marie Rasor
Grable, JoAnna Priest
Gracey, Jonathan B.
Gracey, Jane M. Renner
Gracey, Cynthia Wands
Gracey, Robert William
Grady, Jessica E.
Graeb, Charles A.
Graeb, Ronald V.
Graefe, Martin
Gragg, Jeanne H.
Gragg, Cheryl Kay
Gragg, James L
Graham, Rebecca A.
Graham, Morgan Alisha
Graham, Kellie Dawn
Graham, Chelsea Denee
Graham, Susan E.
Graham, Fay H.
Graham, Jennifer L. Cacka
Graham, Kenneth M.
Graham, Delmos Roy
Graham, Robin Sue

Glover, Samuel E.
Glover, Elizabeth K. Massi
Glover, Christopher S.
Glover, Lynne Sharpe
Grahame, Morgan Sarah
   Marie
Grandusky, Sharon Lamb
Granger, Douglas W.
Grant, Kevin C.
Grant, Douglas H.
Grant, Ryan Jae-Thomas
Grant, Sarah R. Flagg
Grant, John W.
Grasis, Sylvia A.
Grassgreen, Martin A
Gratias, Kevin Eric
Graul, Robert L.
Gravely, Nicholas Tanner
Graves, Jennifer R.
Gray, Jonathan Davies
Gray, Gerald F.
Gray, Richard H.
Gray, Colletta J.
Gray, Nickolena L. Myers
Gray, Vevica L.
Gray, Sharyn Lorraine Maurer
Gray, Robert P.
Gray, Arthur Patrick
Gray, Theodora R.
Gray, Glenn Thomas
Gray, Jeffery W.
Grayson, Michael O.
Grayson, Sara V. Ludwig
Graziani, Jerilynn E. Hamilton
Graziani, Philip J.
Graziani, Philip James
Greathouse, Paige Nicole
Greaves, Charles Flint
Grebenstein, Barbara Ann
   Stover
Grebenstein, Ed B.
Green, David Allen
Green, Beckey Ann
Green, Tressa B. Smith
Green, N. Bayard
Green, Shannon D.
Green, Elizabeth Fling
Green, Nancy J. Catterall
Green, Jess M.
Green, Richard M.
Green, Natalie Mae

Goldie, Paul K.
Goldman, Hannah Goldberg
Goldman, Luke Sander
Goldring, David A.
Green, Milson T.
Green, James W.
Green, John
Green, Shaun
Greenberg, Robert J.
Greene, Barry A.
Greene, John H.
Greene, Virginia M. Weese
Greene Campbell, Rhonda L.
Greenlief, Kennetha Kidwell
Greenlief, Alexa Lee
Greenway, Gail Ann Davis
Greenwell, William
Greenwood, Barbara J.
Greer, Nancy Hugart
Greer, Robert
Gregg, Krysten Deanne Welke
Gregg, Gary L.
Gregg, Savannah
Gregg-Weber, Betti-Ruth
Gregis, Rachel Ann Porter
Gregoire, Sheila A. Richards
Gregory, Malcolm D.
Gregory, Gloria Jean Holcomb
Gregory, Robert Taylor
Greiner, Nick G.
Greives, Meredith
Grenci, Charles J.
Gresak, Mia Rae
Gresh, Kathy L. Strasburg
Grey, Roberta Dawn
Grey, Chasdity Lee Taylor
Gribb, Cassandra A. Muscara
Gribble, Glenna Claudine
   Shaffer
Gribble, Bethany Ellen
Gribble, Pauline Hughes
Grieder, Franklin J.
Grier, Wendy J. Smith
Griffin, L. Vernie E. Craig
Griffin, Ann Mechile Collins
Griffin, Richard T.
Griffith, Wayne Bennett
Griffith, Richard D.
Griffith, Troy E.
Griffith, James F.
Griffith, Kylee L.

Gorman, Patricia M.
Gormley, William J.
Gorstein, Stacey Jean Scott
Gortari, Juan R. Alonso
Griffiths, Margaret N.
  Williams
Grilliot, Brent A.
Grim, Angella S.
Grimason, William V.
Grimes, Martha J.
Grimes, Olivia Paige
Grimes, Paul
Grimm, Beth Bachand
Grimm, Alfred D.
Grimm, Megan Marie
  Winterton
Grindle, William H.
Grindle, William Paul
Grindle, Barbara Phillips
Grindle, Paul R.
Grinnan, Kimberly E.
Griswold, Bryan William
Griswold, Sheppard
Grocki, John P.
Grogg, Marshall
Groman, Daniel E.
Grominger, Howard M.
Grose, Linda C. Branch
Grose, Gary D.
Gross, Caralea Elizabeth
Gross, Allen J.
Gross, David L.
Gross, Jennifer L.
Gross, Stephen M.
Grosse-Puppendahl, Lukas
Grossman, Alan
Grote, Robert A.
Grote, Neil W.
Grotefend, Richard F.
Grotefend, Telete Richards
Ground, Edmund B.
Grove, Lester R.
Groves, Ronald E.
Groves, Okey Lee
Groves, Katrina Lewellian
  Mullenax
Groves, Cecily P.
Groves, James
Gruber, Frank F.
Gruber, Alfredo H.
Gruelich, Helen Digiacomo

Graham, Whitney Taylor
Graham, James
Graham, Tonya
Grahame, Allan R.
Guerra, David G.
Guerrero, Rebecca F. Hipkins
Guerrieri, Joyce L.
Guichon, Nicholas Thierry
Guida, Richard G.
Guinan, Walter Dennis
Guire, James A.
Guire, Anita V. Davis
Gulley, Beverly A. Howell
Gulley, Ronald E.
Gum, Frances A. Hogshead
Gum, Filcer C.
Gum, Brandy Lynn
Gum, Ruth Malson
Gum, John Wesley
Gum, Vernon
Gunn, Andrew C.
Gunning, Cynthia Cole
Gunning, John R.
Gurd, Doris Anne Smith
Gurd, Bruce
Gurtler, Katherine
Gurung, Sunam
Gury, William E.
Gustafson, Sarah Marie
Gustely, Kristin
Gustitis, Victoria Leigh
Guthrie, Fred F.
Guthrie, Tivius
Gutierrez, Artemisa Michelle
Gutierrez, Ana T.
Gutmann, Dixie Goff
Gutshall, Neil A.
Gutshall, Mildred E. White
Gutshall, Meade L.
Guttzeit, Alice B.
Guy, Justin Andrew
Guye, Grady F.
Guyton, William Fay
Gwaltney, James Benjamin
Gwinn '20, Cody Dale
Gyongyosi, Megan Elizabeth
Habers, John A.
Hackenbrack, Karl Edward
Hackman, Thomas I.
Hackman, Rebecca Susan
  Smith

Green, Don O.
Green, Fred R.
Green, Jill S. Bowser
Green, Linda S.
Haddix, Tyler Grant
Haddix, Connie L.
Haddix, Gabrielle L.
Haddix, Amie M. Weese
Haddix, Brittanni Marie
Haddix, Ella Thompson
Haddix, Lucille
Haddix, D. Parker
Haden, Juanita
Haderman, Albany C.
Haderman, Christine Danielle
Haderman, Janie Laine
Hager, William D.
Hager, Katie Lauren
Hager, James M.
Hagerich, Todd A.
Hagerman, David Putnam
Haggerty, Frank L.
Haggerty, Alizabeth
Hagner, Jon W.
Haher, Kimberlee
Hahon, Nicholas
Haigh, Lyndon W.
Hailes, Roger P.
Haines, Lori A. Robinson
Haines, Gregory A.
Haines, Michael A.
Haines, Shawnee Amber
Haines, Karen DiSapio
Haines, Amy Jean
Hairston, David A.
Hairston, Jennifer Rose
Haislip, Anne E.
Hajek, Debra Juskowich
Hakami, Anwar Hadi
Hakami, Abdulaziz Khaled
Hakami, Sami
Hakimoglu, Robert A.
Halad, Laura D. Hickey
Halad, Michael J.
Hale, Alan D.
Hale, Sherry L. Harford
Hale, Katye R. Whitaker
Hale, William R.
Hale, Amanda Shea
Hall, Frederick B.
Hall, Megan Danielle

Griffith, Gail Lynn Carr
Griffith, Mark P.
Griffith, Patricia Yahn
Griffith, David
Hall, Richard H.
Hall, N. I.
Hall, Doris Jean White
Hall, Frank Joseph
Hall, Jacqueline K. Goff
  (Burner)
Hall, Deborah Kay Holbro
Hall, Michael L.
Hall, Roger Leland
Hall, David R.
Hall, Allen Ray
Hall, April Rolanda Matthev
Hall, Marilyn Ruth
Hall, Diane S. Wendland
Hall, Rolondo
Hall, Goldie
Halldorson, James R.
Hallem, Kayla Renee Barr
Haller, Richard D.
Haller, Ethyl McDonald
Haller, Mary R.
Hallett, Aaron J.
Halloran, John J.
Hall-Spry, Mary L. Phillip
Halpert, Stephen A.
Halpin, James P.
Halterman, Tina V. Jones
Hamada, Jaia
Hamelman, Marilyn
  Catherine Brown
Hamelman, David
  Christopher
Hamelman, Paul W.
Hamill, Richard F.
Hamilton, Howard Craig
Hamilton, Deborah J. Sno
Hamilton, Harold J.
Hamilton, Adrienne Kuenz
Hamilton, Irene Moore
Hamilton, William N.
Hamilton, Lela Tyre
Hamilton, Harry W.
Hamilton, John Z.
Hamm, Rachel Alene
Hammack, Jennifer L.
Hammack, Mary
Hamman, Roy

Gruen, Patricia L.
Gsell, Audrey J. Wieben
Gudz, Walter A.
Guenther, Chris Palmer
Hammer, Mary Lee
Hammer, Kimberly S.
Hammer, Rolf T.
Hammer, Linda Work
Hammer, Dorothy
Hammerton, Joshua Thomas
Hammond, Scott E.
Hammond, Nicholas Earl
Hammond, Karen L. Spahr
Hammond, Michelle L.
    Winans
Hammond, Victoria Lynn
    Campbell
Hammond, Braden
Hammons, Jennifer Brooke
Hamner, Carla J. Hanna
Hamon, Vincent Luc
Hamons, Brandon Lee
Hampel, Joseph F.
Hampton, Maria Antoinette
    Hopp
Hamrick, Sallie Ann
Hamrick, Alison Beth
Hamrick, Jamie Erin Gum
Hamrick, Bobby J.
Hamrick, Lacy Jane Lynn
Hamrick, Cathy Mae McCoy
Han, Catherine S. Barclay
Hancock, Keith Daniel
Hancock, William E.
Hancock, Julia Marie
Hancock, James W.
Handrahan, Joshua Zackary
Haney, Peggy Bear
Haney, Edward S.
Haney, Douglas
Haney, Natisha
Hanger, Dale A. Hart
Hanger, Dale A.
Hanifan, Hannah
Hanks, Fiona Susan
Hanna, Barbara Ann Sanders
Hanna, Alyssa
Hannah, Porter A.
Hannah, Sally A. Virginia
    Chenoweth
Hannah, Brittany Denise

Haddad, Jon
Haddix, Abigail Beth
Haddix, Jenna Brooke
Haddix, Linda G. Spencer
Hannon, Kathleen A. Blaum
Hannum, William J.
Hanselberger, Francis
Hansen, Randall S.
Hansford, Rowland C.
Hansford, Fred
Hanshaw, Zachary Ryan
Hanson, Gregory A.
Hanson, Anne Bartholomew
Hanson, Janis C. Price
Hanson, Robert W.
Hanson, Eugenia Yarbrough
Hanson, Ray
Haq, Ehsanul
Harbert, Frank B.
Harbert, Bert L.
Hardesty, Sheila Ann
Hardesty, Wendy Lea
Hardey, Robine K. Brining
Hardin, Tegan Desiree
Hardin, Robert E.
Harding, Joan B.
Harding, Bertrand M.
Harding, Mildred
Hardman, Denise L.
Hardy, Mallory Ames
Hardy, Crystal D.
Hardy, Brittany L.
Hardy, Tane
Hare, Patricia A.
Harford, Kristopher
Harkowa, Christal Dawn
    Woods
Harkowa, Brian W.
Harlacher, Donald S.
Harlan, Christina Faith
Harlan, Tracy Lea Shomo
Harlan, Melissa R. Bonner
Harley, Nina Jo
Harling, John Henry
Harlowe, M. Gwynn
Harman, Hazel A. Jordan
Harman, Cambria B
Harman, Mary Carwell
Harman, Frederick D.
Harman, Edith G. Harper
Harman, Sarah I.

Hall, Roland E.
Hall, Mark Evens
Hall, William Ewing
Hall, James F.
Harman, Pauline Ruddle
Harman, J. Robert
Harman, Nina
Harman, John
Harmon, Dorothy Kay
    Thurston
Harmon, Betty M.
Harmon, Mildred Stalnaker
Harmon, David
Harned, John L.
Harness, Phillip K.
Harnett, Owen Arthur
Harper, Macel A. Pennington
Harper, Kimberley A. Spaid
Harper, Linda C. Thompson
Harper, Heather Corrinne
    Wilson
Harper, Enid E.
Harper, Heather Ellen
Harper, Bardon H.
Harper, William H.
Harper, Edith L. Smith
Harper, Angela Michelle
Harper, Elizabeth Perry
Harper, James R.
Harper, Sara Renee
Harper, Jeremy S.
Harper, Richard Steven
Harper, Bryant T.
Harper, Winifred Triplett
Harper, Don
Harper, Woodrow
Harper, Robert
Harper, Stellman
Harpold, John Clement
Harr, Philip E.
Harrell, Denise A.
Harrell, Loy S.
Harrelson, Martha A.
Harriman, Robert B.
Harriman, Andrea P. Crabill
Harrington, Myrtle Purdum
Harris, Frederick A.
Harris, Vernon B.
Harris, William B.
Harris, Susan B.
Harris, Roscoe C.

Hammell, Bernard J.
Hammer, Elisabeth H.
Hammer, Rebecca J. Hoffman
Hammer, Robert L.
Harris, Michael D.
Harris, Sarah E.
Harris, Rhonda E.
Harris, John Edward
Harris, John F.
Harris, Robert I.
Harris, Stephanie J. Hayes
Harris, Michael L.
Harris, Michael L.
Harris, Melissa Lee
Harris, Robin Leigh Davis
Harris, Bari Lynn Pickens
Harris, Anna M. Davis
Harris, Jayne M. Wood
Harris, Kaitlyn Marie
Harris, Susan Marlene Weaver
Harris, Joe Merle
Harris, Pauline R. Goff
Harris, Kaylee Rae
Harris, Lesley Renee
Harris, William W.
Harris, Kathy Winemiller
Harris, Ann Woodling Knotts
Harris, Reva
Harrison, Brandi A. Beigay
Harrison, Deirdre Anne
Harrison, Richard Bixby
Harrison, Michael Dunham
Harrison, William H.
Harrison, Rebecca J. Smith
Harrison, Scott James
Harrison, Cynthia Kretsinger
Harrison, Lainey Marie
Harrison, Clarence R.
Harrison, Virginia Zinn
Harrold, Cleva Hart
Harrold, David I. Lowther
Harrold, Edgar R.
Harron, Brianna Faye
Harsh, Melissa A.
Harsh, Nancy L. Reckart
Harshbarger, William L.
Harshbarger, E. V.
Hart, Beth A.
Hart, Jenny Brooke
Hart, David C.
Hart, Barbara Ellen Brown

Hannah, A. Clyde
Hannigan, Rebecca L. Dearborn

Hart, Janice M.
Hart, Teresa Marie
Hart, Jodi Marsh
Hart, Danielle Nicole
Hart, Virgil S.
Hart, Cecelia S.
Hart, Benjamin Seth
Hart, Lisa Shaw
Hart, Winifred Steele
Hart, Lucinda T. Wood
Hart, Kenneth T.
Hart, Aimee W. Hadfield
Hart, Robert X.
Hart, Robert
Harte, David Harriman
Hartfield, Kayla Maire
Hartley, Sheryl J. Harman
Hartley, Bruce M.
Hartley, Danielle N.
Hartman, Jeffrey A.
Hartman, Michael E.
Hartman, William Gordon
Hartman, Stephanie J. Turner
Hartman, Ivan L.
Hartman, Tamra L.
Hartman, David M.
Hartmann, Kathryn R. Owsianiecki
Hartung, Barry
Harvey, Robert Asa
Harvey, Judith Brill
Harvey, Patty Elaine Ketterman
Harvey, Deborah J.
Harvey, Roberta M.
Harvey, Steven M.
Harvey, Lauren Patrice
Harvey, T. Richard
Harward, Reba Violet
Harwood, Timothy J.
Hasbrouck, Walter Hughson
Hasegawa, Takami
Haselberger, Francis
Hashagen, Donald C.
Hashagen, Jean Elizabeth
Hasiuk, Michael H.
Haskiell, Nathan

Harman, Elma K.
Harman, Cynthia K.
Harman, Tracy Lee Coberly
Harman, Peggy Proudfoot
Hatcher, Susan L.
Hatchett, Peter Clark
Hatefi, Youssef
Hathaway, Robert H.
Hatheway, Alison Trojan
Hatrak, Michael F.
Hatton, Rondo
Hauck, Catherine Ann Brooks
Hauck, Donald E.
Hauck, Elizabeth J.
Haufe, Anette E.
Haug, Micheal
Haught, Thomas R.
Haun, Joshua K.
Haupt, Norris Harkness
Hauser, Marcia Dawn Powell
Hauser, Rebecca Louise Klotz
Havasy, Ray Ann De Prisco
Havenner, Rosalie Blacka
Havenner, George
Hawkins, Barbara E. Smith
Hawkins, Steven Edward
Hawkins, Laura Elaine
Hawkins, Issac K.
Hawkins, Scott P.
Hawkins, Joyce R.
Hawkins, Richard W.
Hawkins, Erika
Hawley, Juanita Grimes
Hawley, Albert M.
Hawley, Albert M.
Hawley, Lucille Talbot
Haworth, Judy Miklos
Hawthorne, Cynthia F.
Hayes, Whitney Anne Parsons
Hayes, Glenna Barnes
Hayes, Pamela Bradberry
Hayes, William C.
Hayes, Richard Drake
Hayes, Curtis F.
Hayes, Kimberly J. Tyre
Hayes, Amber Nicole
Hayes, Richard P.
Hayes, Susan Starks
Hayes, Michael T.
Hayes, Robert
Hayes, David

Harris, Stephen C.
Harris, Norma C.
Harris, Jeffrey C.
Harris, Judith D.
Haynes, Nicholas R.
Haynie, James D.
Hays, Alma Davita C. Jett
Hays, Joshua Steven
Hays, Andrew W.
Haywood, Thomas David
Hazel, Jonienne
Hazinski, Linda Kay Snyder
Headley, Jason M.
Healy, Sheela Kaye
Healy, Daniel T.
Heaney, James Andrew
Heaney, Elizabeth Carlene
Heaney, Mary Margaret Carmona
Heap, Ann E.
Heaps, David P.
Heard, Stephen J.
Heard, Jonathan
Heasley, Carolyn Ekins
Heater, Ann Hickman
Heath, Clydetta Ann Hartman
Heath, Kimberly D. Linhares
Heath, Thomas M.
Heatwole, Megan E.
Heavener, Carolyn M. Collett
Heavner, George R.
Hebach, Lawrence M.
Hebb, Teresa A. Ricottilli
Hebb, Jennifer E. Ashby
Hebb, Joyce Elmore
Hebb, Melondy L. Curry
Hebb, Sarah M. Barbe
Hebb, Nina Margaret Sharp
Hebb, Donna Michael
Heck, Mary A.
Heck, Charles E.
Heck, Charles E.
Heck, James
Heckel, Patricia A.
Heckel, Lloyd A.
Heckel, William R.
Heckel, J. Renee Teter
Heckelman, Fern H. Biser
Heckler, Susan A Bava
Heckmann, Conrad
Hedemark, Fredrik Nyborg

Hart, Edward F.
Hart, Suzanne H.
Hart, John H.
Hart, Bertie L.
Hedrick, Macey Alexandria
Hedrick, Geneva B. Carr
Hedrick, Melanie B. Evans
Hedrick, Michelle D.
Hedrick, Carl E.
Hedrick, Carl E.
Hedrick, Vonda F.
Hedrick, Virgil G.
Hedrick, Pauline H.
Hedrick, Leonard K.
Hedrick, DeAnn L. Stalnaker
Hedrick, Lora L. Teter
Hedrick, Terrie L.
Hedrick, Tamara L.
Hedrick, Kristen Rae
Hedrick, Jamie Roberta
Hedrick, Matthew Sheldon
Hedrick, Frank Spessart
Hedrick, John T.
Hedrick, Roy
Heermance, Jeanne E.
Heffernan, Michelle A. Kerwood
Heflin, Eujeania K.
Heflin, Susan R. Hayes
Heflin, Marilyn S.
Hefner, Mary Ann Dean
Hehle, Joseph P.
Hehn, Charles F.
Hehn, Suzanne Olivia Halloc
Heide, Candace Jo Tice
Heill, Jane S.
Heimall, Kristin Pfahler
Heiman, Aberigel V.
Heiman, Henry
Heinke, Nils A.
Heinke, Paula Hepler
Heinly, Barbara D. Stephan
Heintzelman, Patrick
Heinzman, Karl D.
Heisey, Irina Wooden
Heishman, Paul F.
Helbig, Kimberly D.
Helbig, Terry Richard
Heldman, Arthur C.
Heldman, Betty Lou Faulkner
Helfenbein, Chad Mitchell

Haslam, Paul G.
Haslett, Elizabeth Jean
Hatch, Jearline Heltzel
Hatch, William P.
Heller, Thomas E.
Heller, Christopher E.
Heller, Gary L.
Heller, Shelley Lyra Burr
Heller, Alexander R.
Heller, Alan W.
Hellier, James N.
Hellings, Clifford S.
Helm, Elizabeth A. King
Helmick, Kathy A.
Helmick, Angie D.
Helmick, Samantha Dawn
Helmick, Tina E. Carr
Helmick, Kylie Elizabeth
    Hatfield
Helmick, Judith L. Phillips
Helmick, Bernard N.
Helmick, Megan
Helms, Sharon M.
Helmstetter, Amanda M.
Helmuth, Kimberly Michelle
Heltzel, Carl K.
Helzer, Derrick Dale
Hemmis, Diana
Henderson, William Blades
Henderson, Clio C.
Henderson, Nancy D. Hosey
Henderson, Jacqueline
    Diane Belon
Henderson, John F.
Henderson, Jean Hyde
    Humason
Henderson, William K.
Henderson, Zachary L.
Henderson, David Lee
Henderson, Juanita M.
Henderson, Rachelle Marie
    Sprenkle
Henderson, Janesa R.
    Wilfong
Henderson, David S.
Henderson, Nancy Susan
    Rath
Henderson, William V.
Henderson, Harry W.
Henderson, Wayne
Hendler, Alvin J.

Hayhurst, Freda B. Wamsley
Haynes, Danielle Angelene
Haynes, Virginia Elise
Haynes, Lori Grimes
Hendrick-Dillon, Shari Ann
    Dillon
Hendricks, Jackie M. Davis
Hendrickson, Ralph A.
Hendrix, Bethany Grace Fulk
Hendrix, Paul Wesley
Henline, Shana Keller
Henline, Lisa Marie
Henline, Kelsi Renee'
Hennen, Mary F. Mary
Hennessey, Diego
Hennessy, Cheryl A.
    Matthews
Henney, Paul E.
Henrie, Rachnee L. Coberly
Henrie, Justice Marie
Henrie, Morgan T.
Henriksen, Edward J.
Henry, Jacob Brian
Henry,   Trisha   Brittnee
Heather Higgins
Henry, Amy Christine Troastle
Henry, Steven J.
Henry, Virginia Loop
Henry, Jennifer Noel
Henry, Glen Patrick
Henry, Lillian Poling
Henry, Ted R.
Henry, Harold
Hensil, Henry H.
Hensil, Mabel L.
Hensley, Ronda J. Snodgrass
Hensley, Lauren Raeshel
Hensley, Ralph
Henson, John H.
Hepburn, Richard F.
Hepburn, Julia Petra Wilson
Hepler, Patricia Ann Bennett
Hepler, Markia Denea
Hepler, Ruth M.
Hepler, Mark
Heptonstall, Myrtle Goddin
Herbel, Duane K.
Herder, Suzanne
Hergert, Richard H.
Herholdt, John F.
Herklotz, Richard A.

Hedji, Elvis Junior
Hedman, Susan Robers
Hedrick, Joseph A.
Hedrick, Frank Albert
Hermanson, Brenda J.
    Woodson
Hermanson, Herman J.
Hermanson, Chrisantha
    Lynette Frederick
Hermanson, Gordon R.
Hermanson, Robert William
Hern, Dustin Kevin
Hern, Shanna M.
Hern, Tyler Russell
Hernandez, Maria E. Buxade
Hernandez, J. H.
Hernandez, Silvia
Herndon, Geraldine Morgan
Heron, David J.
Heronemus, William J.
Herr, Wendy Garrison
Herr, Dana L.
Herren, Elizabeth S.
Herrick, Phyllis A. Stout
Herrick, Calvin P.
Herrick, John P.
Herring, Jennifer Ann Jones
Herrington, Kathleen L.
Herrmann, Barbara D.
Herron, Michael E.
Herron, Warren G.
Herron, Stephen L.
Herron, Erin N. Cutright
Hershberger, Betty J. Miller
Hershelman, Connie Louise
    Howe
Hershey, Michael David
Hershey, Patsy J. Tingler
Herter, Judith R.
Hertig, Willis H.
Herzog, William P.
Heskett, Tonya L.
    Sommerville
Hess, Oliver A.
Hess, Kathryn B.
Hess, Wayne B.
Hess, Kayla Lynn
Hestad, Simon
Hester, John E.
Hester, Shirley Taylor
Hevener, Leon H.

Helfenbein, Jennifer S.
    Zullinger
Helfrich, Christopher R.
Helgerman, David J.
Hiatt, Kathleen Summer
    Lovejoy
Hiatt, Nicholas
Hibbs, Sasha M.
Hickey, Nora H. Grace
Hickey, Jean Rae Wesley
Hickling, Anne F.
Hickman, Garland Butcher
Hickman, John Gregg
Hickman, Shasta R. Wolford
Hickman, Burley
Hickok, Sheri L.
Hicks, Jamie Cecile
Hicks, Reginald Edward
Hicks, M. Louise Head
Hicks, Jazman Jerome
Hicks, Shelby Kay
Hicks, Chasity LaDawn
Hicks, Brittany Rene
Hicks, Henry W.
Hicks Clingerman, Terry
    Marie
Hicks Hall, Linda Beverly
Hidalgo-David, Yanery
    Yesmaira
Hiebert, Steven M.
Hiester, Madeleine Nancy
    Truesdell
Hiester, David
Higashide, Mari
Higgins, Michael Richard
Higgins, Caitlin Rose
Higgins, Rebecca Ruth
    Kaposy
Higgs, Joseph F.
Highfield, Beverly G. Williver
Highfield, Harry W.
Hight, Ronald H.
Hight, Ricky Z.
Higy, Charles A.
Higy, Anita K. Davis
Hilaire, Kristina L. Roe
Hilaire, Sheldon
Hilbert, Karl A.
Hilbert, Jill N.
Hildebrant, Floyd
Hildenbrand, Jeanne E. Carey

Hendler, Stuart
Hendon, Kurstie Ann
   Strothers
Hendon, Carol Evans
Hill, Rebecca Ann Marie
Hill, Cecil C.
Hill, Michelle D. Goss
Hill, Marina Danielle
Hill, Meredith Dawn
Hill, Laura E.
Hill, Fred G.
Hill, Mark G.
Hill, Margaret Glenn
Hill, Evelyn J.
Hill, Harry J.
Hill, Peggy J.
Hill, Sara Kathryn
Hill, Alexander L.
Hill, Randall Lee
Hill, Richard M.
Hill, Katherine Marie Posey
Hill, Lauren Marie
Hill, Ashley Nicole
Hill, Jennifer Noelle
Hill, Lycurgus P.
Hill, Shalisa S
Hill, Neil W.
Hill, James W.
Hill, Bruce W.
Hill, Heather
Hill, William
Hilliard, Douglas C.
Hilliard, Michael H.
Hilliard, Ruth L. Orr
Hilling, Karen S. Nicholson
Hillman, Janice
Hills, Amy L. Garrett
Hillyard, Charles G.
Hillyard, William M.
Hilmer, Wayne J.
Hiltgartner, Jennifer S.
   Dulany
Hilton, Beatrice G.
Hiltz, Paul F.
Hilzinger, Fred Glen
Hilzinger, Beth Louise
   Lohman
Himes, Stuart A.
Himes, Eleanor J. Harper
Himes, Kenneth R.
Hinchcliffe, Beckie Kaye

Herman, Judith R. Gallagher
Herman, Robert R.
Hermanson, Katherine
   DeLena Phillips
Hinchman, Robert L.
Hinchman, Harold R.
Hinchman, G. Michael
Hiner, Nancy Ellen Dassdorf
Hiner, Clara G.
Hiner, Ben H.
Hiner, James Stephen
Hines, Neal K.
Hines, Brittany Lynn
   Anderson
Hines, Martin P.
Hines, Bryant Scott
Hines, Lance William
Hinett, Robert T.
Hingel, Robert E.
Hinkle, Charlotte A.
Hinkle, Kacey Ann
Hinkle, Russell B.
Hinkle, Sandra B.
Hinkle, Virginia D
Hinkle, Firman D.
Hinkle, Ruth E. Collins
Hinkle, Snoden E.
Hinkle, Wayne E.
Hinkle, Coline F.
Hinkle, Willetta Goddin
Hinkle, Angellea Grace
Hinkle, Betty Johnston
Hinkle, Phyllis Jones
Hinkle, Russell L.
Hinkle, Ronald L.
Hinkle, Samantha L.
Hinkle, Verr M.
Hinkle, Anna Mae Harper
Hinkle, David Moyer
Hinkle, Nana R.
Hinkle, Nicole R.
Hinkle, Lisa Rogers
Hinkle, Paul S.
Hinkle, Benjamin Scott
Hinkle, Bobbie Sue
Hinkle, Zeola V.
Hinkle, Carl
Hinkle, Clark
Hinterer, Shayla Lou
Hinton, Ella Glenn
Hinzman, Tiffany Alexander

Hewitt, Matthew David
Hewitt, John Kenneth
Hewitt, Pamela S. Isner
Heyl, Helen J. Humphrey
Hinzman, Franklin W.
Hinzman, Daniel
Hirsch, Julius A.
Hirshey, Arthur S.
Hiser, Helen F.
Hiser, Norma Nelle Hardy
Hiser, J. Keith
Hiserman, Richard H.
Hitchins, Walter A.
Hitchner, William R.
Hitt, Teresa Dawn
Hively, Ashley J. Painter
Hixson, Matthew R.
Hoag, David S.
Hoagland, David A.
Hoagland, Terri R. Colwell
Hobbie, Norman J.
Hobbs, Roland L.
Hockenberry, Idell G.
Hockenberry, Charlene H.
   Mason
Hockenberry, Richard
Hockman, Mary Francis
   Hockensmith
Hockman, Ronald L.
Hodges, Allen T.
Hodgson, Joan
Hodill, Kevin
Hoehn, Julia Katharina
Hoeper, Deborah Harker
Hoernel, Paul W.
Hofer, Renee A.
Hofer, Genevieve
Hoff, Linda Sue
Hoffa, Clyde W.
Hoffman, Rita A. Hammer
Hoffman, Elaine B. Friend
Hoffman, Robert B.
Hoffman, Gary C.
Hoffman, LaDonna D.
Hoffman, Norman D.
Hoffman, Elsie F. King
Hoffman, Chrystal Gale
   Lower
Hoffman, Richard Lee
Hoffman, Bryan Marcus
Hoffman, M. Lynne Motley

Hildenbrand, Bruce G.
Hile, Pearl L.
Hill, Beatrice Adderley
Hill, Wyatt Alan
Hoffman, Howard W.
Hoffman, James
Hoffmann, Briana Elise
Hogan, Jeanne Keefe
Hogan, Michelle Lynn
   Arbogast
Hogan, Robert M.
Hogan, Gregory P.
Hogeland, Norman H.
Hogg, Charles C. "Trey"
Hogg, Emily Lynn
Hohing, Karl T.
Hohman, Richard A.
Hohman, Garield Mark
Hohman, Charles S.
Hokman, William
Holbert, Jeana Beth Carr
Holbert, Kathy Chiado
Holborow, Virginia Smith
Holcomb, Michael Scott
Holden, Robert B.
Holden, David B.
Holden, Nancy Ellen Byru
Holden, Phillip G.
Holden, Kenneth P.
Holgin, Richard P.
Holland, Bonnie Jean
Holland, Gregory
Holliday, Robert Asa
Holliday, Stephanie Dawn
Holliday, Lindsay Diane
Hollier, Alexandria Daniel
Hollingsworth, Samuel D.
Hollingsworth, Jennifer M
   Raley
Holloway, Theodore James
Holmaas, Julia
Holman, Andrew A.
Holman, Marion Walsh
Holmberg, Charlotte
   Estabrooks
Holmberg, Edwin J.
Holmes, Nancy Louise Wa
Holmes, Kathryn R. Cain
Holmes, Stanley R.
Holmes, Robert Thomas
Holmes, Kevin V.

Hinchman, Norma A. Swink
Hinchman, Barbara J. Bucy
Hinchman, Ronald J.
Hinchman, Carla J.
Holst, Mark A.
Holstein, W. J.
Holstein, Michael William
Holt, Philip A.
Holt, Kristie A.
Holt, John D.
Holt, Carol L. Clark
Holt, Charles R.
Holt, David Richardson
Holt, Thomas Russell
Holt, Janet Rykert
Holt, Miriam W. Reed
Holt, Nancy Wolfe
Holtermann, Henry J.
Holton, Harry L.
Holton, Jacqueline Madama
    Hudson
Holtzworth, Jennifer C.
    Raffaele
Holz, Rebecca P. Arnold
Holzer, Robert F.
Homer, Douglas A.
Hommes, Amber
Honaker, Mary A.
Honeycutt, Tyler Vann
Hood, Stephanie Dawn
    Flanagan
Hood, Leonard L.
Hood, Robert W.
Hoofnagle, James G.
Hook, Marion Kosa
Hoops, Jeffery A.
Hoos, Dana Gail Kreutzer
Hoos, Bryan S.
Hoots, Madeline Vick
    Hechenbleikner
Hoover, Nancy A. Spindle
Hoover, David Allen
Hoover, Melissa D. Warner
Hoover, Sam R.
Hopkin, Scott
Hopkins, Gerard A.
Hopkins, Kenneth L.
Hopkins, Ellis M.
Hopping, Crystal Ann
Hopwood, Walter A.
Hopwood, Cary Muldoon

Hinzman, Vickie Butcher
Hinzman, Robert E.
Hinzman, V. Christine Hester
Hinzman, Tammy L. Shiflett
Horn, Alfred D.
Horn, John Douglas
Hornbeck, Michael Shane
Horne, Geoffrey
Horner, Joan Carol Rushton
Horner, Iva Hedrick
Horner, Eleanor K.
Horner, Tracy L.
Hornick, Timothy J.
Hornick, Mary R. Vest
Hornick, Ashleigh Renee
Hornick, Dixie S.
Hornish, Samantha Jean
Hornor, Debra Lou
    Burkhammer
Horowitz, Jeffrey S.
Horre, Robert W.
Horsey, Ruth P.
Horsham, Donald
Horvath, Michael A.
Horvath, Gary
Hosbach, Neva T.
Hosey, Carolyn Ruth Davis
Hostettler, Alfreda
Hotaling, Kimberly J. Cash
Hotetz, Deron C.
Hott, Owen Chandler
Hottel, John L.
Houchin, Rex
Hourigan, William J.
House, Thor R.
Houser, Casey A.
Houseworth, William A.
Houseworth, Joanne G.
    Funsten
Houseworth, Martha V.
Houston, Rutherford R.
Houston, Susanna
Hover, Karen L.
Hovland, James M.
Howard, Jennifer April
Howard, Angela D. Helmick
Howard, Cynthia D.
Howard, Janine Hardy
Howard, Rebecca J.
Howard, Sharon R.
Howard, Kathryn Rae Brown

Hoffman, Eugene R.
Hoffman, David R.
Hoffman, Maya Rhudy
Hoffman, Elizabeth V.
Howard, George W.
Howard, Evelyn
Howard O'Brien, Sara Ann
Howd, Deborah A. Maquire
Howd, Anthony D.
Howe, Jonathan D.
Howe, Kelli N. Rexrode
Howell, Patricia Alkire
Howell, Teri Ann Ford
Howell, Amanda Beth Tingler
Howell, Harry E.
Howell, Michael E.
Howell, Leonard E.
Howell, Kaitlin Elizabeth
Howell, Sherry Elizabeth
    Ann Weasenforth
Howell, Howard G.
Howell, Evelyn J. Burky
Howell, Shanda Jane
Howell, Kimberly Nicole
Howell, Beulah P.
Howell, Charles P.
Howell, Caleb Riley
Howell, Ronda S. Huffman
Howell, Andrew S.
Howell, Gregory T.
Howes, George A.
Howes, Laura Ashley
Howes, Victoria D.
Howes, Elizabeth J. Ratliff
Howitt, Neil
Howland, Nancy Cummings
Howsare, Anne S.
Hoxmeier, Jane Hinchman
Hoy, Glenn D.
Hoy, Sean Michael
Hoy, Gilbert Richard
Hoyer Barcinas, Lisa Y.
Hoyt, Joseph E.
Hoyt, Nancy Joyce Drake
Hoyt, David L.
Hozumi, Natsuko
Hruska, Joseph A.
Hruska, Daniel G.
Hsu, Donald
Huang, Brandon Liang
Hubbard, Marla L. Prather

Holsberry, Frances Mary
    Wilmoth
Holsclaw, Frank Sorrell
Holsclaw, Gail Wollaston
Hubsch, Jessica Kailee
    Williams
Huck, Elizabeth C.
Huck, Julie Joyce
Huckaby, Kayla Snow
Hudacek, Christopher M.
Hudnall, Sabrina Anne
Hudok, Phylicia LeeAnn
Hudok, Lynn W. Simcoe
Hudson, Patricia E. Greene
Hudson, John E.
Hudson, George N.
Hudson, Judson R.
Hudspeth, Kathryn A. Wolfe
Hudspeth, Harold S.
Huet, Gregory McCaslin
Huey, James H.
Huey, Jo Ellen Harris
Huey, James Q.
Huff, Renton B.
Huff, John C.
Huffaker, Almeda Shimer
Huffman, Susan A.
Huffman, Deborah Carr
Huffman, Katlyn Dawn
Huffman, Nathan James
Huffman, Sierra Katlyn
    Yowell
Huffman, Alta McDonald
Huffman, Gerald Ralph
Huffman, Jeremy
Huffnagel, Lorena
Huffstutler, Rafe N.
Huggins, Richard L.
Huggins, Joyce Scott
Hughes, William Barry
Hughes, Lloyd D.
Hughes, Ava E. Loudin
Hughes, Mary Ellen Wilt
Hughes, Jamie Lynn
Hughes, Michael Martin
Hughes, Joseph R.
Hughes, Margaret T.
Hughes, Jay W.
Hughes, Archie
Hughes, Daniel
Hui, Chitman C.

Hopwood, Kollin Sheppard
Horan, Michael J.
Hori, Martha L.
Horisk, Peggy Rice
Hulbert, Judith W. Gilbert
Hull, Robert B.
Hull, Paul E.
Hull, Forrest H.
Hull, George H.
Hull, Jeffrey H.
Hull, Tammie L. Ketterman
Hull, Bevin Rae
Hull, Hudson
Hullstrung, Robert E.
Hulsen, Robert W.
Hultquist, Kathryn Cordero
Hulver, Sherri L. Swecker
Humbert, Janice Louise
Hume, Thomas D.
Hume, Mary E. Tyre
Humes, Emilie Rebecca
Hummel, Michelle M.
Hummel, James Richard
Hummer, Nancy J. Hess
Humpe, Jocelyn Renee
Humphrey, Julie A. Hooton
Humphrey, Angela
    Danielle Kisamore
Humphrey, Susan M.
    Beardsley
Humphrey, Madalyn Marie
Humphreys, William Walter
Humphreys, James West
Hunt, Wilbur A.
Hunt, Lawrence Barrett
Hunt, Sarah G.
Hunt, Edward J.
Hunt, Brenda Wymer
Hunter, Edward B.
Hunter, Tracy E.
Huntington, Marilynn Arthur
Huntington, Joel
Huntley, Robert D.
Hupp, Virginia Fistick
Hupp, Dennis J.
Hurley, Taylor LeAnn
Hurst, Douglas A.
Hurt, Michael
Husfelt, James C.
Husing, G. William
Hussion, John J.

Howard, Jesse S.
Howard, Patricia W.
    Dougherty
Howard, Boyd W.
Hutchison, Claire Elaine
    Sainato
Hutchison, William Rowan
Hutchison, John S.
Hutchison, Nancy S.
Hutson, Howard H.
Hutson, Nicole Lynn Rowan
Hutson, Josephine Miller
Hutson, Clyde P.
Huttel, Ernest A.
Hutten, Joan Rothenmeyer
Hutton, John A.
Hutton, Henry C.
Hutton, Eugene E.
Hutzell, Amy M. Arbogast
Huyck, Robert W.
Hylton, Akil M.
Hylton, Claude Swanson
Hyre, Patricia D. Hart
Hyre, Peggy D.
Hyre, Leslie Jayne Wilfong
Hyre, Carole L.
Iannacone, Douglas G.
Ice, Jennifer E. George
Ice, David L.
Ice, David L.
Ice, Leesa Lorrayne
Ice, Mary Pingley
Ice, Jeanne Riggleman
Ice, Philip
Ichikawa, Akemi
Ickert, Patricia Nelson
Ickes, Shane Kyle
Iden, Deborah L. Mayo
Ideozu, Sonny E.
Idzal, June Marie
Ihle, Bruce R.
Iijima, Mami
Ijiogu, Julius C.
Ikirt, Frank B.
Ilboudo, Issa
Iles, Jeane Bulkley
Illig, William B.
Illmensee, Thomas
Inaba, Maki
Indyk, Charles
Ingemie, Matthew D.

Hubbard, Jeremiah W.
Huber, Jillian M.
Hubley, Cameron John Theirs
Hubsch, Guilherme Condolo
Ingram, Herbert L.
Ingram, Lester P.
Ingram, G. William
Intemann, Barbara Anne
    Woodford
Intemann, Betty Liles Little
Intemann, Edgar
Inter, Amy J.
Inter, Frederick John
Intriere, Donald
Inzillo, Maureen M.
Ireland, Deborah G.
Iriarte, Carlos F.
Irons, Earl L.
Irons, Neil Leon
Irons, Robert P.
Irons, Inez Rossey
Irons, Exie Singleton
Irons, Linda Teter
Irvin, William J.
Irvin, Cecil Paul
Irvine, David T.
Irvin-Parsons, D. Darlene
Irwin, Robert S.
Irwin, Arthur Samuel
Isabell, Joseph Anthony
Isch, Rose F.
Isele, Dorothy G.
Iseli, Kerri C.
Iseli, Robert N.
Iseli, Kayla Paige
Iseli, W. Kenneth
Ishii, Kenji
Ishikawa, Sotoko
Isiminger, Shelli R.
Isner, Robert B.
Isner, Russell David
Isner, Virginia Earle
Isner, Rennix J.
Isner, Willa L. Brown
Isner, Ashley Lee
Isner, Nellie M.
Isner, Amanda S.
Isner, Alva T. Stalnaker
Isner, Patricia Y.
Itnyre, Lena Bradley
Ito, Osamu

Hui, Christina
Hui, Chiton
Huke, Joan Larkin
Huke, G. Ed
Izziddin, Fawaz H.
Jaber, Ernest G.
Jack, Jerome Daniel
Jack, Marguerite I.
Jack, Judy K. Mewha
Jack, Tharon L.
Jack, Tharon L.
Jack, Kayla Louise
Jack, Alvin R.
Jack, L. W.
Jackson, Bryan A.
Jackson, Jacob A.
Jackson, Molly Ann
Jackson, Cecil B.
Jackson, Velma C.
Jackson, Meredith Duval
Jackson, Jelani G.
Jackson, Becky Jean
Jackson, Charles L.
Jackson, Jennifer Leah Deit
Jackson, Phyllis Lee Scott
Jackson, Cynthia M.
Jackson, Jacqueline Nicole
    Brubaker
Jackson, Rosemarie Perry
Jackson, Macy Rose
Jackson, Mildred Suesli
Jackson, Todd T.
Jackson, Geoffrey Tyler
Jackson, Thomas W.
Jackson, Nicole
Jackson, Matthew
Jaco, David Lee
Jacobs, Alyssa Ann
Jacobs, Edward F.
Jacobs, Jack
Jacobsen, Kendall Jacqueline
Jacobson, Yorke
Jacome, Danilo M.
Jadoo, Chelsi Cherise
Jaeger, Emmett Isaiah
Jaffe, Matthew A.
James, Lindsie A. Frase
James, Donald D.
James, Thomas E.
James, Amber Elisa Bowman
James, William K.

Hutchison, Janice A. Kemp
Hutchison, John Allen
Hutchison, Pamela Husby
Hutchison, Holley Nicole
James, Kenneth
Jamison, Charlotte I.
Jamison, Philip Nelson
Janecek, Joseph C.
Janes, Robert Glenn
Jang, John L.
Janicki, Lori A. Hlopak
Jankovic, Scott
Janof, Eric L.
Janowski, Jon C.
Jansson, Karl Christian
Janushevich, Alexis A.
Jaquith, Iris C. Babayan
Jaramillo, Celia R.
Jarboe, Jacob Noah
Jarman, Grace Marie Cyphert
Jarmow, Betty Martin
Jarrele, Tianna Danielle
Jarrell, Daniel Matthew
Jarrett, Kimberly A.
   Humphrey
Jarrett, Robert M.
Jarrett, William Scott
Jarvis, Aerial Ann
Jarvis, Felicia Ann
Jarvis, Suzanne Browning
Jarvis, Leslie C. Tate
Jarvis, Earl F.
Jasin, David D.
Jauchem, Philip W.
Jeannette, Anna M.
Jeffery, Allyson Jane Mattson
Jeffery, Peter MacDonald
Jeffries, Sam B.
Jeffries, Sam B.
Jeffries, Irma C.
Jeffries, Kimberly S. Wray
Jenkins, Mary Burner
Jenkins, John E.
Jenkins, David E.
Jenkins, James J.
Jenkins, Richard L.
Jenkins, Susan Lily
Jenkins, Alta M. Harper
Jenkins, John M.
Jenkins, Deborah Moler
Jenkins, Leo

Ingham, Larry S.
Inglee, Philip Scott
Ingraldi, Sam J.
Ingram, Helen G. Butcher
Jennings, Alan K.
Jennings, Jodi Lynn
Jennings, Donald
Jensen, Falina Marie Holbrook
Jester, John H.
Jeter, Jennifer Kirby
Jeter-Burgette, Debora
   Mechell
Jett, Darrell E.
Jewell, Teonna Denise
Jezik, Sharron Burdette
Jezik, William J.
Jimenez, Marta E.
Jimenez, Alesia J. Harris
Jobe, Nancy L. Darling
Joe, Elise McKenna Reed
Joh, Fredrick
Johannsen, Robert P.
Johanson, Gerald F.
Johanson, Andrew H.
Johansson, Ove
John, Daniel C.
John, Claude D.
Johnkoski, Lillian Heltzel
Johnkoski, Phoebe Hickman
Johns, Keith G.
Johns, Stephen P.
Johnson, Kimberly A. Kniley
Johnson, Pamela A. Poling
Johnson, Richard A.
Johnson, Josef Alexander
Johnson, Phyllis Ann Hager
Johnson, Elizabeth Ann
Johnson, Joseph B.
Johnson, John B.
Johnson, Taylor B.
Johnson, Virginia Blair
   Simons
Johnson, Carolyn C. Walsh
Johnson, James C.
Johnson, Casey Carla
Johnson, Matthew Cole
Johnson, Susan D.
Johnson, David D.
Johnson, Tara D.
Johnson, Joseph D.
Johnson, Henry E.

Ivanic, Mile
Iverson, Dana Lynn Drust
Ivis, Paolo
Ix, Jane Earle Taylor
Johnson, Peggy J. Hickman
Johnson, Carl J.
Johnson, Katherine Jane
   Glotfelty
Johnson, Peggy Jean Gerard
Johnson, Jennifer Jill Moore
Johnson, Sheila K. Fincham
Johnson, Mary Kathryn
   Shumaker
Johnson, Juanita Kay Bodkins
Johnson, Kari L. Medcalf
Johnson, Terry L.
Johnson, Donna Lotus
Johnson, Rita Louise Findley
Johnson, Stephanie Lynn
   Masters
Johnson, Ann M. Chambers
Johnson, Christina M. Riley
Johnson, Diane M. Skillman
Johnson, Steven M.
Johnson, Morgan Marie
Johnson, Danielle Marie
Johnson, Jeremy Michael
Johnson, Sasha Monae
Johnson, Robert N.
Johnson, Ralph N.
Johnson, LaMeekiaa Nadine
   Horton
Johnson, Henrietta P.
Johnson, Lawrence P.
Johnson, Madeline Poling
Johnson, Donna R. Shearer
Johnson, Virginia R. White
Johnson, Carl R.
Johnson, Stephanie Rae
   Chenoweth
Johnson, Ebbonie Riner
Johnson, Diane S. Adger
Johnson, Andrew S.
Johnson, Bradley S.
Johnson, Hazel Stalnaker
Johnson, Rebecca Stollar
Johnson, Harold W.
Johnson, Donald W.
Johnson, Erik Wayne
Johnson, Annabel Williams
Johnson, Pinkney

James, Joseph L.
James, Robin Lynn Bozic
James, Kayla Sierra
James, Megan Turske
Johnson, Angela
Johnston, Michael F.
Johnston, Yvonna G. Akers
Johnston, Rose Mary Isner
Johnston, Robert J.
Johnston, Elizabeth Lucile
Johnston, Britteny Nicole
Johnston, Misty R.
Johnstone, Gladys M. Snyder
Johnstone, A. R.
Jones, Barbara A. Griffin
Jones, Wes A.
Jones, William A.
Jones, Charles A.
Jones, Cleder A.
Jones, Carmin Ann
Jones, Kimberlie Anne Benn
Jones, Hope Armstrong
Jones, James B.
Jones, Jean Barnard
Jones, Kirk Brian
Jones, Mable C. Mauzy
Jones, Richard C.
Jones, Gregory C.
Jones, Matthew C.
Jones, Jessica C.
Jones, Brian Carter
Jones, Colleen D. Callahan
Jones, Kimberly D. Marsh
Jones, James D.
Jones, Thomas E.
Jones, James E.
Jones, Prior E.
Jones, Thomas E.
Jones, Judith Ellen Arbogast
Jones, Dylan Erick
Jones, William F.
Jones, Isaac F.
Jones, Beverly Fells
Jones, Darin G.
Jones, Angelique J. Dingman
Jones, Donalda J.
Jones, Linda Jean Ball
Jones, Shannon Jill Pastine
Jones, Dorothy Joan Gerhardt
Jones, Pamela K. Carter
Jones, Monique Karin

Jenness, Margreet K.
Jennings, Maurice Antion
Jennings, Brigid E. Farley
Jennings, Timothy E.
Jones, William L.
Jones, Tina L.
Jones, Jennifer L.
Jones, Sherry L.
Jones, Alison L.
Jones, Thomas M.
Jones, Glenda M.
Jones, Alanna Marie
Jones, Amy McFarlane
Jones, Shane Michael Alan
Jones, Andrea Morgan
Jones, Ralph N.
Jones, Britainey Nicole
  Kisamore
Jones, John Oliver
Jones, Rachel Paige
Jones, Robert R.
Jones, William R.
Jones, Roger R.
Jones, Edgar R.
Jones, Grant R.
Jones, Spring Rae
Jones, Anita Rubianto
Jones, Dixie Singleton
Jones, Scott Thomas
Jones, I. Jewell Updike
Jones, John W.
Jones, Martin Wayne
Jones, Benjamin William
Jones, Lisa Wright
Jones, A. Pierre
Jonese, Makeia Raine
Jonese, Lakota Rand
Joness, William W.
Jordan, Christina A.
  Newhouse
Jordan, Philip B.
Jordan, Joseph B.
Jordan, Mary Bethune
Jordan, Philip D.
Jordan, Dale E.
Jordan, Ruth E.
Jordan, Charles F.
Jordan, Valerie Jean
Jordan, Cheryl L. Romesburg
Jordan, Robin L.
Jordan, Grace Lee

Johnson, Mary E.
Johnson, Kristen Elaine Kulick
Johnson, Michael H.
Johnson, Lillian Harris
Jordan, Deirdre
Jordon, George W.
Jorewicz, Ada M. Green
Jorge-Blanco, Joaquin
Jorgensen, Claudia C. McKay
Jorgensen, John C.
Jorgensen, Michael W.
Joseph, Charles D.
Joseph, Julie M. Toutant
Josimovich, Natalie Catherine
Josimovich, Peter Wright
Joyiens, Allen J.
Jozwicki, Edward M.
Juback, Robert J.
Judd, Thomas Oliver
Judd, Erik Richard
Judge, Marlo A.
Judge, Michael R.
Judge, Gregory W.
Judson, Kenneth L.
Judy, Jacie A.
Judy, Whitney Alexandra
Judy, Cody Allen
Judy, Deborah Cross
Judy, Randall D.
Judy, Heather Lenora
Julian, Arlow A.
Julin, Jill L.
Junker, John R.
Kaasik, Hillar G.
Kabbash, Roger H.
Kabiru, Kennedy
Kadel, Karen Reynolds
Kadel, Richard W.
Kader, Jean Ann Good
Kader, Michael S.
Kadota, Miwa
Kaechele, Corey James
Kaelin, Michael H.
Kahley-Wolf, Mary J.
Kahrs, Judith McCullough
Kaiser, Mads Flemming
Kaiser, Gary J.
Kaiser, Julie L. Shamblen
Kalament, Jennifer L. May
Kalar, Catherine S. Gainer
Kalinosky, Joseph

Johnson, H. Gordon
Johnson, Paula
Johnson, Gregg
Johnson, Stuart
Kaminsky, Robin Jean
  Schumann
Kammer, Kristin M.
Kampf, P. B.
Kanagy, Alvin C.
Kane, Barbara A. Feudale
Kane, Carl J.
Kane, Bradley P.
Kanouff, Rebecca Ann
Kapnicky, Tiona Lynn
Kapp, Marvin J.
Kapust, Thomas Peter
Karamanol, Deborah A.
  Rodgers
Karas, Robert A.
Karcher, Kenneth J.
Karcher, Frank W.
Karg, Eric R.
Karickhoff, R. Thomas
Karlen, Susan L.
Karn, Beverly J.
Karp, Tyler
Karr, Elliott Jay
Karson, David Michael
Kata, Edward J.
Katano, Kosuke
Kataoka, Nagisa
Katenda, Ntumba M.
Kater-Hurst, Kaia Myra
  Florence
Kates, Susan H. Curran
Kates, William J.
Kato, Yuko
Kato, Yumi
Kaufman, Beverly A.
Kaufman, Ronald D.
Kaufman, Rosemary P.
Kaufmann, M. Bruce
Kautz, Eric T.
Kavulich, Michael J.
Kawahara, Nami
Kawakami, Mondo
Kawakubo, Misa
Kawashima, Yuka
Kawata, Eita
Kay, Jennifer Courtney Martin
Kay, Stacy L.

Jones, Brian Keith
Jones, Betsy L. Corbin
Jones, Terri L. Fridley
Jones, Sondra L. Murphy
Kazianis, Spyridon
Kazlo, John T.
Keatley, Brett Colin
Keaton, Karen A.
Keaveny, Billy J.
Keck, Ruth Ann Lautenbac
Keck, Harold F.
Keddle, Leigh W.
Kee, Robert E.
Keebler, Miyoshi Udagaw
Keech, Melissa L. Urban
Keech, Andrew M.
Keedy, Gary L.
Keefe, Dorothy C. Dann
Keefer, Victoria V. Anthon
Keefover, David L.
Keeling, Nathan Andrew
Keeling, Tommy
Keelips, Christopher G.
Keels, Patricia A.
Keenan, Cornelius E.
Keenan, Melodie Porch
Keene, Kelsey Danielle
Keeney, Marjorie Ann Wood
Keeney, Robert D.
Keeney, Sally Higginbotham
Keesee, Cory Scott
Keesee, Zachary
Keffner, Albert G.
Keffner, Margaret Saling
Kegerreis, Dona L. Shipp
Kegley, Mary R.
Kehl, Tania L. Gooden
Kehr, Joshua Alexander
Keim, Jennifer L.
Keith, Kathern Nicole
Kellar, Deborah M.
Kellaway, Joseph C.
Keller, Riann Brooke Holl
Keller, Jodi E. Jashinski
Keller, James E.
Keller, Vickie F.
Keller, Charles M.
Kellers, Laura M.
Keller-Zierold, Linda Lee
Kelley, Skylar Alaine
Kelley, Justin Andrew

Jordan, Cedric Legrand
Jordan, Jamie Roberta
  Winans
Jordan, William Travis
Kelley, Donald H.
Kelley, Karen J.
Kelley, Katrina Jacklyn
Kelley, Matthew Joseph
Kelley, John K.
Kelley, Thomas K.
Kelley, Debra L.
Kelley, Paula Lee
Kelley, Kazelyn LeNae
Kelley, Sierra Lynn
Kelley, Granada M.
Kelley, Dennis P.
Kelley, Anne T. Marshall
Kelley, Wilburt W.
Kelley, Francis
Kelling, Carole L.
Kelly, Pamela A.
Kelly, William A.
Kelly, Shana A.
Kelly, John Anderson
Kelly, Raymond C.
Kelly, Howard D.
Kelly, Doris E. Dye
Kelly, Gail E. Stewart
Kelly, Gary E.
Kelly, Virginia E.
Kelly, John F.
Kelly, Janet Faye Phillips
Kelly, Jack G.
Kelly, Paulette G.
Kelly, John J.
Kelly, Zandra Jade
Kelly, Melanie L. Bava
Kelly, Nancy L.
Kelly, Gary L.
Kelly, Margaret Meredith
Kelly, Joseph P.
Kelly, Sean Patrick
Kelly, Donna S. Wasson
Kelly, Asher W.
Kelly, Doug W.
Kelly, Donna W.
Kelly, Sheila Weedon
Kelly, Johnelle Young
Kelly, James
Kelly, J. Mark
Kemble, John V.

Kalista, Scott Michael
Kaltaler, Robert E.
Kalthoff, Wendy B. Lerner
Kamara, Shuaib
Kendall, Forest H.
Kendall, Ralph L.
Kendall, Mary Lingamfelter
Kendall, Steven Mitchell
Kendall, Oscar
Kenderdine, David A.
Kendrick, Patricia Ballard
Kendrick, Robert J.
Kendrick, James William
Kengne Mouafo, Issa Franck
Kenlock, Malcolm Emmanuel
Kennan, Judith King Stephens
Kennard, Ruby A. Phillips
Kennedy, Warren B.
Kennedy, Alice H.
Kennedy, Colette M. Webb
Kennedy, Sean Martin
Kennedy, Tonya S. Chewning
Kennedy, Christopher S.
Kennett, Walter L.
Kenney, Lloyd B.
Kenney, Robin L.
Kennon, Jenifer Nicole
Kennon, Megan
Kent, Kathleen Wilson
Kent, L. Daniel
Kenzleiter, Joanne R.
Kepner, Myrl J.
Keppler, Thomas R.
Kerbel, E. Kathryn
Kerens, Malisa L. Armentrout
Kerns, Phyllis A.
Kerns, Lisa Adkisson
Kerns, Grover G.
Kerns, Dorothy Heck
Kerns, Rueben James
Kerns, Barron L.
Kerns, Charles Lester
Kerns, Ruth Marie Quinn
Kerns, Tiffany Marie
Kerns, Bobbie Moran
Kerns, Jessica Nichole
Kerns, Kathryn Rosencrance
Kerns, Allen W.
Kerns, Robert W.
Kerns, R. Michael
Kerr, Jennifer Ann Nelson

Kay, Christopher T.
Kaynor, William K.
Kays, William L.
Kazan, John
Kerr, Jeanette L.
Kerr, Lynn
Kerr Beckwith, Margaret A.
Kershner, Ruth E.
Kershner, John W.
Kerzel, Chase
Keskkula, Henno
Kesner, Amber Lynn
Kessel, Katharyn
Kesslar, Todd Peter
Kessler, Lois Ellen Irons
Kessler, Ellen M.
Kessler, Stowell V.
Kester, C. Doyle
Kesterson, Mary L. Ogle
Ketchem, Phyllis Moore
Ketterer, Melynnie F. Sikora
Ketterman, Kristina Dawn
Ketterman, Virginia R.
Kevech, Pamela J. Polan
Kewitt, David B.
Key, Roy C.
Key, Roy C.
Keyes, John J.
Keyser, Debra K. Hannan
Keyser, Edna N. Hostettler
Khalilov, Shahin
Khan, Roohi S.
Khan, Zainab
Khashugjee, Sultan Sameer
  Abdulmohsen
Khosrow, Ardalan
Kidd, Harold R.
Kidwell, Jason O.
Kieffer, Harold Scott
Kier, Deborah S. Elias
Kiess, Jeffrey C.
Kiess, Sharon J. Isner
Kiewitt, Gregory D.
Kiewitt, Lisa K. Williams
Kiger, Cynthia Sue
Kight, Lucille Dumire
Kilby, Jason D.
Kilduff, Vincent D.
Kile, Patricia M.
Kilgore, Kevin F.
Kilpatrick, Jyanla Da'jour-Rae

Kelley, Daytana Cheryl Weese
Kelley, Roger Dillon
Kelley, David F.
Kelley, Jeffrey Gail
Kimberl, Tiechea J.
Kimble, Susan C.
Kimble, Kourtni Dawn
Kimble, Edgar L.
Kimble, Ashley Lynn
Kimble, John
Kincaid, Jack B
Kincaid, Judith J.
Kincheloe, James
Kinder, Lindsey Ann
Kinder, Renee S.
Kines, Whitni L. Freeman
King, Deborah A. English
King, Martha A. Fenn
King, Loretta A.
King, Patricia A.
King, Nicole Alexandra
King, Robert E.
King, Colleen E.
King, Joann Eckard
King, Dorothy Elane Mick
King, Robert Eugene
King, Hazel Evans
King, Stephen H.
King, Regina I.
King, Paula King
King, Donald L.
King, Angela Lynea
King, Elizabeth Martin
King, Susanne McCutcheon
King, Jeffrey P.
King, Kenneth R.
King, Emmons T.
King, Mildred
King, Clarence
King, Allie
Kinger, C. J.
King-Gore, Kamal Attia
Kingsolver, Florence Yates
King-Talbott, Martha J.
Kinney, Joseph J.
Kinni, Patrick T.
Kinnison, Virginia M.
Kinsley, Francis T.
Kipp, Autumn K. Tonnesen
Kirby, David Clifton
Kirby, Viodelda Ivonne Teano

Kittle, Elizabeth Guye
Kittle, Mildred Hinchman
Kittle, Shirley J. Shreve
Kittle, Franklin L.
Krantz, Arthur E.
Krasnican, Janet L.
Krechel, Grace Ellen Gray
Krechel, Glenn Richard
Kreh, Susan E.
Kreit, Bruce L.
Krentz, David M.
Kreps, Gary L.
Kresser, Herbert J.
Kriebel, John Duncan
Krietz, Kaylee
Kristofik, Dean D.
Krizan, Jeffrey F.
Krogel, Joann W. Shaver
Krogel, Thomas W.
Krogel, Paul
Kron, James E.
Kron, Sandra N. Sauper
Kroncke, Reed R.
Kroon, Tanya Ann
  Moering-Weiner
Kruger, Albert
Krum, Bonnie Cook
Krum, Jacqueline Elizabeth
Krum, Rachael Elizabeth
Krystynak, Victoria
  Elisabeth
Kubichek, David Lee
Kubichek, Marguerite
  Louise Gilmore
Kubick, John J.
Kubota, Mildred Elizabeth
  Phares
Kuchar, Elizabeth A.
  Brammer
Kuchar, Edward J.
Kuchta, John E.
Kuehn, Carl E.
Kuhar, Christine J.
Kuhl, Peter M.
Kuhns, Doris J. Darkey
Kuipers, Leah Icen
Kuipers, Christine Louise
  Vonderahe
Kukoly, Joseph
Kukor, David K.
Kulevich, Christopher J.

Marshall
Knittel, J. Gregory
Knoche, Jeffrey A.
Knodel, Mamie Mary
Kuntz, Elizabeth A.
  Biederman
Kuntzleman, Lois Springer
Kuponiyi, Cheryl A. Kosak
Kuponiyi, Peter T.
Kurgan, Mary Ann
Kuroshima, Satomi
Kurtz, Susannah Boal
Kurtz, David Lee
Kurtz, Robert W.
Kurz, Burton E.
Kurz, John W.
Kushay, Richard L.
Kvidahl, Glenn D.
Kwafo, Jordan Michole Hall
Kwafo, Daniel Ofori
Kyle, Deborah A. Bullock
Kyle, Judith A.
Kyle, George C.
Kyle, Clyde C.
Kyle, Alistair Cameron
Kyle, Ronald H.
Kyle, Victoria Rochelle
Kyle, Carl W.
Kyle, Rosemary
Laari, Barbara Honoria
  Nordeck
Laaveg, Nancy V. Coffman
LaBille, Amber Kristine
Lacey, Pierre Morice
Lacey, David R.
Lacouette, Louis F.
Lacour, Kaitlyn Anastasia
Lafayette, Helen Cappadony
Lafayette, Hugh
Laffidy, Tracy Lynelle Sarvis
LaFollette, Bryan Russell
Lahaza, Jessica Mae
Lahman, Nicholas N.
Laine, Jennifer Hanes
Lainhart, Alice Hart
Lainhart, John W.
Lajterman, Abe D.
Lajterman, Donna MacGregor
Lake, Anthony A.
Lake, Ronald E.
Lake, Nellie L. Isch

Kolb, Charles R.
Kolb, Alexander William
Kolcun, Joseph M.
Kolesar, William
Lamagna, John D.
Lamar, Lucius Q.C.
LaMarca, Thomas J.
LaMaster, James M.
Lamb, Steve
Lamberson, Bart
Lambert, Woodrow Achilles
Lambert, Randy Allen
Lambert, Deborah B.
Lambert, John E.
Lambert, Deborah Elaine
  Swecker
Lambert, Audra G.
Lambert, Rella H.
Lambert, Jessica I.
Lambert, Kumar Jason
Lambert, J. K.
Lambert, Winifred L. Sites
Lambert, Emmett L.
Lambert, Mary L.
Lambert, Melinda M. Skeens
Lambert, Amy Nichole
  Rhodes
Lambert, Tiffanie Nicole Toler
Lambert, Naomi R. McVicker
Lambert, Nellie R.
Lambert, Chelsea Renee
Lambert, Norman W.
Lambert, Kevin W.
Lambert, Curtis
Lambert, Stephanie
Lamborne, Kathy M.
Lamfon, Moayad Nabeel
Lamon, Ashley Lynne
  Yuschak
LaMora, Susan Anne
  Beekman
LaMora, Raymond Kenney
Lancaster, Jacob Wilson
Lance, Richard J.
Lancy, Leslie E.
Landgraf, Robert A.
Landis, Julie A. Trawick
Landis, Lucinda Marie
Landis, Kimberly Sue
Landolt, Kendra Jane Cole
Lane, Rudy Ashton

Krammer, Mary E. Collins
Krammer, Kurt
Kranch, Kathleen L.
Kranik, Frank
Lane, Virginia Martin
Lane, James Todd
Laney, Zack G.
Laney, Arthur R.
Lanford, Mary F. Broschart
Lanford, Terry J.
Lang, Nancy Armentrout
Lang, Bretsel M.
Lang, Guy N.
Lang, Halfred P.
Lang, Brandon Scott
Lange, Richard R.
Langford, Robert G.
Langley, Kelvin C.
Langley, Albert L.
Langley, Mary Lynn Vine
Langolf, Edward T.
Lanham, Perry A.
Lanham, James B.
Lanham, Jean Clara Jennings
Lanham, Samuel E.
Lanham, Mark Eugene
Lanham, Cindy Leigh Graves
Lanham, Olivia Marie
Lanham, Catherine R. Lay
Lanham, Wyatt
Lannon, Yvonne Valembois
Lantz, Cassie Annette Phillips
Lantz, Amanda Dawn
Lantz, Kimberly Dawn
Lantz, Jean Hunter
Lantz, Janice K. Hedrick
Lantz, Leonard L.
Lantz, Orden L.
Lantz, Janet L.
Lantz, Bertha Nine
Lantz, Carolyn R.
Lantz, Sherry Renee Smith
Lantz, Joseph S.
Lantz, Jo Tetrault
Lantz, Carrie V. Wilt
Lantz, Raymond
Lantzounis, George
Lanza, Joseph A.
Lanzi, Leslie A. Pittman
Lapallo, Alexandra Ruth
Lapeer, Darlene M. Raines

Kulp, Dana H.
Kump, Cyrus Kerr
Kump, Agnes Mae Dick

Larese, Virginia Stalnaker
Larese, Joseph William
Larew, Jarrell Simmons
Largie, Karl A.
Larkin, Deborah A. DeNitto
Larkin, Amanda Rae
  Chadwick
Larkin, Joshua Taylor
Larrivee, Andrea D. Dalen
Larry, Brooke Rodgers
Larsen, John N.
Larsen, Barbara Norton
  Laing
Larson, Craig P.
Larsson, Arthur H.
Larsson, Anders H.
Lascala, Michael S.
Lashley, Ian Fernando
Lashley, Linda Lee
  Singalewitch
Lasota, Caitlin Jayne
Lassiter, William Eric
Lassiter, Daya Louise Perkins
Latif, Jawad
Lattner, Valarie L.
Lauderbaugh, George
  Monroe
Lauderbaugh, Susan Wells
  Salisbury
Laufer, Joseph J.
Laughton, Walter P.
Launtz, Dora Moreland
Laurora, Justine R.
Lautenklos, David A.
Lauvara, Lynn A.
LaValla, Nathan R.
LaValla, Kathryn Tipton
LaValla, Kathryn Ward
LaValla, Patricia
Lavery, Donna J. Moore
Law, Carol A. Gaines
Law, Elizabeth Butt
Lawler, Margaret Heckel
Lawler, Karen S. Wilson
Lawless, Gale Robinson
Lawless, Maureen
Lawnicki, Lucy F.

Lake, Harley W.
LaKernick, Frances Ward
Lakhani, Arman
Lally, Michael R.
Lawrence, Matthew John
Lawrence, Terri L. Petrice
Lawrence, Rebecca S.
  Mantheiy
Lawrence, Gerald S.
Lawrence, Gerald Samuel
Lawrence, Jean Scott
Lawrence, Texie Wolford
Lawrence, Courtney
Lawson, Katherine G.
Lawson, Vera Katherine Keim
Lawson, Jordan
Lawton, Geraldine Kisner
Layfield, Melanie Cora
Layfield, Michelle Diane
Layfield, Nicole Marie
  Dickson
Layman, Cecil G.
Layton, Catherine Hanley
Layton, Cody
Lazari, Sara Gartmann
Lazari, Andreas
Lazarsky, Christopher J.
Lazarus, Ephraim
Leach, Denise A.
Leach, Leona Harper
Leach, Samuel Kenton
Leach, Jeffrey S.
Leach, Scott Thomas
Leaird, Jennifer L. Blair
Leake, Vivian Scallon
Leamon, Ralph A.
Leamons, Susan P. Barber
Lear, Randy L.
Leard, Jordan Michael
Leary, John B.
Leary, Francis H.
Leary, Richard J.
Leary, Charles R.
Leather, Robert G.
Lecker, Gregory James
Ledden, Camille Elizabeth
Lederer, Robert A.
Lee, Denise A. Sterro
Lee, George Barstow
Lee, John C.
Lee, Richard K.

Lane, Taryn Bohon
Lane, Hannah Faith
Lane, Daniel J.
Lane, Sherry L. Solon
Lee, David P.
Leeb, Burton O.
Leech, Matthew A.
Leeson, Dawn L.
Leet, Bonnie Macgregor
Leete, Douglas A.
Lefcourt, Arthur M.
Lefkowitz, Phillip
Legaspi, Luciana Marie
Legg, Courtney Dawn
Legg, Betty J. Lewis
Legg, Leah Kate Pniewski
Legge, Erin
Leguizamon, Juan Sebastian
Leibowitz, Joan C. Gordon
Leibowitz, Mark L.
Leidel, Henry C.
Leighty, Martha L.
Leighty, Hugh
Leiman, John C.
Leipold, Elizabeth E.
Leist, William Alexander
Leitzel, Steven E.
Lemke, Virginia Bibinger
Lemons, Jean I.
Lemos Cabral, Gustavo
Lempke, Charles T.
Lemus Perez, Gloria
  Magdalena
Lenar, Sharon M. DeFiore
Lenhart, Debra J.
Lennon, Kimberly Ann
  Balcarczyk
Lennon, Edward
Lennox, Robert S.
Lent, Lori A.
Lent, Norma L. Veazey
Lentino, William J.
Lentz, Alicia Jean
Leo, Susan Antolini
Leon, Miguel Vicente
Leonard, Mary Anne Rullo
Leonard, Charles F.
Leonard, Charles L.
Leonard, Paula Sue Kyle
Leonard, David Wayne
Leonard, James

Lapen, Richard R.
Lapp, Edwin C.
Lappen, Zachary H.
Lara, David W.
Leskuski, Walter John
Leskusky, John
Lesley, Aurilla R. Scherbaur
Leslie, Ramona Mae Peterso
Lesofsky, James A.
Lessard, Melissa Lynn Ray
Lessard, Christopher
Lesser, M. Leann White
Lessner, Madeline Mae
Lester, Sarah Graves
Levenson, Janice S.
Levenson, Erin
Leventis, Victoria L. Byrd
Levering, Lee D.
Levering, Lacy Laurene
Levy, Albert G.
Lewandowski, Penny Elle
  Goddin
Lewis, Maura A. Hofer
Lewis, Susan Ann McRae
Lewis, Michael D.
Lewis, Lisa Irene Collett
Lewis, Janet K.
Lewis, Eileen King
Lewis, Pamela L. Butler
Lewis, Donna L. Moore
Lewis, Mary L. Taylor
Lewis, Rebecca L.
Lewis, Chelsey Leigh-An
Lewis, Junele Lynn
Lewis, Janice M.
Lewis, Barbara M.
Lewis, Tesla Marie
Lewis, Sherry Mullins
Lewis, Charles N.
Lewis, Janella Nitz
Lewis, Mary Pauline Rhoad
Lewis, Brenda S.
Lewis, Tamara Sue
Lewis, Marsha Thompson
Lewis, Christopher W.
Lhota, Judith Alinovi
Li, Conway
Libby, Herbert J.
Libby, William R.
Libby, Richard Sperry
Lichtenstein, Jean

Lawrence, Maggie A.
Lawrence, Matthew Calvin
Lawrence, Robert E.
Lawrence, Wendy E.
Liggett, Sarah E.
Liggett, Jesseka Elaine
Liggett, Bassell
Liggio, Stelio V.
Light, Randall E.
Light, Keyolan G.
Lightfoot, Kimberly D.
Likins, Sherry L.
Liller, Edwin L.
Lilly, John F.
Limer, Twila P.
Linaburg, Sara Elizabeth
Linane, Kristi L. Nidiffer
Lincicome, Tabitha Anne
Lind, Joy Filiatrault
Lind, Daniel J.
Lind, Karen L. Hood
Lindemann, Matthew S.
Linder, Robert C.
Linder, Michele L. Groff
Linder, Sandra Romanell
Lindholm, Roxanne R.
   Davis
Lindholm, Victor
Lindner, Charles H.
Lindner, William L.
Lindner, William R.
Lindner, Carol Wilson
Lindsay, Bruce H.
Lindsay, James J.
Lindsay, Ryan John
Lindsay, Michael S.
Lindsay, Darlene Y. Cool
Lindsey, Steven Christopher
Lindstrom, Nancy Mitchell
Line, Robert A.
Lineweaver, Debra Kay
Lineweaver, Hans
Ling, Bradley F.
Ling, Dorothy J. Garner
Ling, Thomas Y.
Linger, Patsy Javins
Linger, Russell
Linger, Russell
Linhart, Patricia Brock
Linhart, Margaret L. Sleeman
Linhart, William

Lee, Olga Kosciukiewicz
Lee, William L.
Lee, Nancy Nicoll
Lee, LaSharon P. Bullock
Linn, Meghan Elizabeth
   Chandler
Lint, Duncan Gogol
Liong, Tina Alt
Lipkin, Amy Goodwillie
Lippincott, Herbert M.
Lipps, William A.
Lipps, Harry E.
Lipscomb, Nettie G.
Lipscomb, Susan Lee
Lipscomb, Gennifer LouRay
Lipscomb, Hollis Neil
Lipscomb, Kimberly Norman
Lipscomb, Kathleen
Liptrap, Elizabeth Faith
Lisko, James R.
List, Jacob P.
Liston, Mary Ann
Liston, Melissa D.
Liston, Sheena M.
Litman, Mary Lipscomb
Little, John A.
Little, Martha Anne Woodford
Little, Raymond C.
Little, John Calvin
Little, Gladys Elizabeth
Little, Katharine Jane
Little, Donald S.
Little, Bryan W.
Littlecott, Kimberly Diane
   Peterson
Littlecott, Harry R.
Littleton, Martha C.
   Townshend
Lively, Michael
Livingston, Jennifer L. Gross
Livingston, Robert P.
Livingston, Matthew Robert
Livingston, Kenneth S.
Lloyd, Ray A.
Lloyd, Jim Blake
Lloyd, Gregory D.
Lloyd, Marcy D.
Lloyd, Haley Dawn
Lloyd, Rebecca K. Walters
Lloyd, Marsha K.
Loane, M. Scott

Leonard, W. Parker
Lepley, May A.
Lepson, Bonnie Horn
Lesher, Theresa A. Chomas
Lobdell, Barbara Louise
   Kennedy
Locke, Nancy Bohne
Locke, Alan Charles
Locke, John P.
Locke, Stephen Walter
Lockhart, Jeffrey A.
Lockhart, Kathy Ann Collett
Lockhart, Stephen D.
Lockhart, Daniel Eugene
Lockwood, Garret K.
Loew, Josie M.
Logan, Justin Charles
Logan, William F.
Logan, Pamela Faye
Logan, Kevin P.
Logar, Jody Michelle Park
Loges, Deborah L.
LoGreco, Emily J.
LoGreco, Lorin Rose
   Shellhamer
LoGreco, William Vincent
Logue, Jessie Nethken
Logue, Kane Raymond
Logue, Dennis
Lohman, Robert Good
Lohn, Norman L.
Lohne, Helen M. Hepler
Lohr, Katherine Bradley
Lohr, John W.
Lollot, Patricia Charlotte
   Saborido
Lomauro, Joanne Teresa
London, David J.
Long, Joseph A.
Long, Scott A.
Long, Ann E.
Long, Marissa Jo
Long, Lona K.
Long, Fred K.
Long, Tina L. Shaver
Long, Edwin L.
Long, Cecilia M.
Long, Stephen P.
Long, Stephanie Paige
Long, Rachel Renee
Long, Karen S. Cowen

Lichti, Sandra J. Slane
Lichtner, William Ryan
Liddane, Mark
Liggett, Mary B.
Lonon, Aaron Lamar
Looney, Karin
Loop, Justine M.
Lopez, David B.
Lopez, Lisa M.
Lopez, Joshua Pete
LoPresto, Kevin A.
Lord, Sharon E.
Losh, Carol J. Hinchman
Lothes, Gregory Alan
Lothes, Charles D.
Lothes, Rebecca Dawn Tacy
Lothes, John E.
Lothes, Gail Y. Swick
Louder, Jennifer Lauren
   Maczynski
Loudin, Gordon F.
Loudin, Nicholas G.
Loudin, Howard M.
Loudin, Angel M.
Lough, Carolyn June
Loughlin, Karen Schnepp
Loughry, Lisa L.
Louk, Rosemarie Casanova
Louk, Ronald D.
Louk, Terry D.
Louk, Tori Don
Louk, Rita May
Louk, Sarajane Ponder Heckel
Louk, Christopher Randall
Louk, Tyler Wayne
Louke, Catherine E.
Lourie, Carrol L. Garner
Louse, Amy Benhoff
Loutfi, Carla Sue
Louther, Tracy M.
Louzy II, Paul Joseph
Love, Raymond C.
Love, Norval L.
Love, Jeffery W.
Lovelace, Sunceria J. Walker
Loveland, Amanda Marie
Lovenberg, Richard McKay
Lovenstein, Leonidas K.
Lovern, Stephanie C.
Lovins, Roger M.
Lowe, Michele A. Campbell

Link, Candace Dawn Auville
Linkovich, Mike
Linley, Jacob J.

Lowman, Marianna
    Wodzinoki
Lowrie, Patricia A. Hayes
Lowther, Tammy A.
Lowther, John Sammuel
Lowther, Elizabeth
Loy, Mary B.
Lozman, Harvey
Lubert, Susan D. Byrd
Lubin, Todd Daniel
Lubran, Yuri B.
Lucas, Gregory Dean
Lucas, Robert J.
Lucas, Trent James
Lucchesi, Eli Benjamin
Luce, Melissa Hambrick
Luce, Ray P.
Luchs, Martin L.
Lucia, Louis A.
Lucke, Jessie
Luddington, Robert T.
Ludemann, John H.
Ludwig, Alyssa Marie
Lugar, Shirley Martin
Lugo-Rigau, Ruben
Luker, James Cody
Luloff, Donald A.
Lum, Christopher E.
Lumm, Megan Elizabeth
    Bush
Lunde, Norman A.
Lunde, Anna Jean Daetwyler
Lunde Rodriguez, Vicki
Lunemann, Lauren Elizabeth
Lunn, Madonna Lynn Hart
Lunoe, William E.
Lupi, David P.
Luque, Sebastian P.
Lutman, Jacqueline Gail
Lutman, Kathleen P.
Lutness, Carole Leland
Lutz, Opal M.
Lutz, Timothy R.
Lutz, Neil T.
Lutz, Owen W.
Lutz, Preston
Luvara, Lynn A.

Loar, Orpha B.
Loaring, Tiffney A.
Lobdell, David Leslie
Lobdell, Donald R.
Lybrand, Lynn B. Leatherman
Lyburn, Danita Leslie
    Garrison
Lykes, Jorden Nicole
Lyles, Victoria Antoinette
Lynch, John C.
Lynch, Ada H. McCauley
Lyons, Larry A.
Lyons, Earl K.
Lyons, Izetta McQuain
Lyons, Benjamin Scott
Mabiza, Kudakwashe
Macapinlac, Rachel Morgan
    Landfried
Macbeth, Bruce A.
MacCartney, Jarett A.
MacCartney, Darren J.
MacDonald, Christine Anne
    Brenner
MacDonald, Ronald F.
MacDougall, Ellis C.
Mace, Charles D.
Mace, Guy E.
Mace, Judith M.
Mace, Taylor Nicholas
Maceira, Domingo
Macey, Carter M.
MacFadyen, Kenneth J.
MacFadyen, Barbara Jacobitti
MacGabhann, Kevin L.
MacGregor, Kathleen E.
MacGregor, Donald M.
Macioce, Mary A. Woodburn
Mack, Thomas W.
MacKay, George R.
Mackey, Traci K. Payne
Mackey, Melvin L.
Mackey, Jane Strickler
Mackey, Richard W.
Mackey, Bethany
Macklin, Paul R.
Macko, Jane Irving
Macko, Stanley J.
MacLachlan, Jean Gross
MacLean, Melissa H.
MacMillan, Stuart W.
MacNamee, Daniel F.

Long, Eric S.
Long, Luvine W. Fowles
Longo, Arthur
Lono, Kauluwehi
Macon, Brandon C.
Macpherson, Janet Powers
MacPherson, Patrick
MacSherry, Beverly A. Small
Macsherry, Stewart
    Woodruff Smith
Macurdy, Melody
MacVean, Margaret L.
MacVean, Timothy M.
MacVean, Mary Meador
MacVicar, Scott C.
Madan, Peter K.
Madan, Cynthia Pazos
Madden, Robert C.
Madden, Marina Eliza
Madden, Edward F.
Madden, Elizabeth Hughes
Madden, Joseph J.
Maddox, Matthew C.
Maddox, Carolyn F. Camp
Madeheim, Huxley Thomas
Madison, Georgia D.
Madison, Angela E.
Madonis, John D.
Madriz, Carlos L.
Madzimure, Thabo
Maeso, Daniel Enrique
Maffei, Frank A.
Maffucci, John Anthony
Magallanez, Ashley Marie
Magee, Rebecca Cox
Magee, Kerry P.
Maghrabi, Mohammed
    Nabeel
Magos, Mary C.
Maguire, Kelly Ann
Mahakusol, Panadtorn
Mahamedi, Manucher
Mahlman, Thomas V.
Mahon, Daniel A.
Mahoney, Catherine Ann
    Glessner
Mahoney, Gregory B.
Mahoney, George E.
Mahoney, Jon Kurtis
Mahoney, Barbara L. Butcher
Mahoney, Mary P. Gibbons

Lowe, Sandra E.
Lowe, Jana Marie
Lowe, Danielle
Lowery, Bette L. Rowe
Maillefert, Abigail J.
Mailloux, Catherine M.
Main, Glenn A.
Main, Joyce Delain
Main, Austin Leroy
Main, Roger Lewis
Main, Darla Sturm
Main, David W.
Mainiero, Raymond J.
Maio, Belinda
Maitan, Robert Bruce
Maitan, Beverly Hansgen
Maitland, Kenneth B.
Majette, Ronald M.
Majkowski, Deven J.
Major, William D.
Makar, Robert D.
Makepeace, Ruth Marie
    Phelps
Makino, Yon Wayne
Malave, Harry
Malcolm, Mae
Malcomb, Vanessa Ann
Malfi, Andrew J.
Malfi, Alice Sigler
Mallery, William
Mallisee, Jessica Lynn
Mallonee, Gary
Mallow, Harding A.
Mallow, Jedidiah Davidson
Mallow, Hope H.
Mallow, Sabrina Janaye
Mallow, Clayton Keith
Mallow, Marlene L.
Mallow, Amy L.
Mallow, Chelsea Mae
Mallow, Jayson Thomas
Mallow, Jessica
Malloy, Kathleen Ann
Malm, Richard L.
Malmo, Kristian
Malone, Michael S.
Mamalis, Patti L. Hughes
Mams, Joseph E.
Mams, Carl F.
Mams, Geneva Myer
Manchin, Kathleen M.

Luxsitanonda, Rungsrid
Luzier, Gladys
Luzzatto, Rudolph G.

Mangold, Kimberly
  McCroskey
Manley, Sara J.
Manley, Jewell Y. Revels
Mann, Lacy A.
Mann, Leslie B.
Mann, Dianne C.
Mann, John K.
Mann, Janice M.
Mann, Robert R.
Mann, J. Donnie
Manning, Elizabeth T.
  Bullivant
Manning, Lou Anne
Mannon, Jameson Pate
Mano, Sachiko
Manolakos, Stavros
  Emmanuel
Manolidis, Delane R.
  Simmons
Manolidis, Crystal
Manor, Katharine Taylor
Manson, Katlyn Brooke
Manson, Christopher G.
Mansour, Sandrine Garceran
Mansour, Serge
Mantheiy, Christina Marie
  Oldaker
Manuel, Ellyson Anne
  Schumacher
Manuel, Brian K.
Manuel, Daniel R.
Manuelian, Peter J.
Manz, Barry F.
Manzo, Deborah S. Teets
Maples, Alliene C. Johnson
Maradei, Robert Anthony
Maravich, Peter
Marcell, Joyce A. White
Marchand, Frank W.
Marchewka, Cindy S.
Marchitelli, Stacy M.
Marcinkowey, Bernard G.
Marcinkowey, Evelyn P. Hill
Marco, Jerry A.
Marco, Paula D. Jones
Marcolina, Laura M.

MacNichol, Dian Metzger
Macomber, Monna M.
  Channell
Macomber, James W.
Mariniello, Elizabeth A.
Marino, Tiffany Diane Wenzel
Marion, Stacy Lynn
Mariotz, Elizabeth L. Spinella
Marissael, Peter A.
Markle, Eileen Dennis
Markle, George Donald
Markle, John E.
Markle, Kelsey Marie
Markley, Robert A.
Markley, Jacqueline D.
Markley, Mikayla Grace
Markley, Eva L.
Markley, Elaine R. Bell
Markley, Carson W.
Markley, Jo Ellen
Marks, Sarah Jane
Marks, Susan Marie
Marks, Lindsay Rose
Marlow, Michael F.
Marlow, Lisa Marie
Maros, Andras L.
Marple, Dorsey A.
Marple, Melissa Dawn Phares
Marple, Steven L.
Marple, John R.
Marple, Wanda Smith
Marra, Judy C.
Mars, Ronald S.
Marsden, Cynthia J. Ryan
Marsh, Charles A.
Marsh, James A.
Marsh, Cynthia Ann Hughes
Marsh, Rebecca Ann
Marsh, Sarah Joyce
Marsh, Roberta L. Johnson
Marsh, Linda Lou Baker
Marsh, Michelle Lynn
Marsh, Donna M. Dennison
Marsh, Linda M.
Marsh, Amy Marie Skidmore
Marsh, Jean P.
Marsh, Angela S. Bibey
Marsh, Phillip S.
Marsh, Katheryn Sue
  Pennington
Marsh, Eleanor Sue

Mahoney, Derek S.
Maiden, Betsy J. Forsha
Maiden, Michael S.
Maier, Katie A.
Marshall, Sheila C. Wiseman
Marshall, Mendy G. Alt
Marshall, Douglas Gregory
Marshall, Ben Jordan
Marshall, Sarah Katharine
Marshall, Amanda Leigh
  Fewster
Marshall, Herbert P.
Marshall, Herbert T.
Marson, Randy J.
Marstiller, Sherri E. Bennett
Marstiller, Clifford Earle
Marstiller, Barbara J. Varner
Marstiller, James K.
Marston, John C.
Marteney, David C.
Marteney, Ross E.
Martens, Charles H.
Martens, Etta Rosenzweig
Martielli, John J.
Martielli, Claire Mae
  Belsinger
Martin, Samantha A.
Martin, Norma Jean B. Ryan
Martin, Willard Blaine
Martin, David Bruce
Martin, Henry C.
Martin, Bruce C.
Martin, Timothy C.
Martin, Joan Carder
Martin, Colleen D.
Martin, Bradley D.
Martin, Diane Deininger
Martin, Brent Douglas
Martin, Kristin E. Gulbransen
Martin, Mary F. Shaver
Martin, Daisy Ferguson
Martin, Theresa Gainer
Martin, Rose Godlove
Martin, James H.
Martin, Bobbi J. Carr
Martin, Thomas J.
Martin, Freda Kerens
Martin, Linda L. Irving
Martin, Sharon L.
Martin, Sharon L.
Martin, Richard L.

Mancine, Diane S.
Mancuso, Domenica
Maner, W. Lawton
Mangold, Christopher S.
Martin, Nancy Oleson
Martin, Arch P.
Martin, Cameron Paul
Martin, Roscoe R.
Martin, Thomas R.
Martin, James R.
Martin, Kelle Rose Kraus
Martin, John S.
Martin, Lois Stein
Martin, Charles W.
Martin, Leonard W.
Martin, Sharon
Martin Vernon, Sabrina D.
Martinez, Deborah A.
Martinez, Jose Carlos
Martinez, Sandra E. Charity
Martinez, Bruce P.
Martinez, Gabriel
Martinez, Felipe
Martirano, Joseph C.
Martone, Kelly L. Farmer
Marzolf, Richard A.
Marzolf, Dana M.
Marzullo, Franklin Patrick
Mascolo, Philip R.
Masessa, Carmen G.
Mashburn, Natasha Caitlin
Mask, Robert H.
Mason, Janet B.
Mason, Tyler James
Mason, Jonathan W.
Mason, Kent W.
Mason, Cecil
Mason, Vivian
Masoncupp, Lucile H.
Masoud, Abdulaziz Saud
Masoud, Mohammed Saud
Mass, Lloyd G.
Massa, Patrick Joseph
Masse, Marissa A.
Massimino, Jessica Leigh
Masters, Jessica Lauren
Masters, Kayla Sue
Masterson, Kathleen N.
Matanic, Vincent P.
Matarante, Richard A.
Mataset, Elizabeth J.

Margenat Dordas, Laia
Margrey, Margaret B. Young
Marin, Carmen Pinto
Marin, Valentin
Mather, Judith Walker
Matherly, Thomas Andrew
Mathers, Dustin Charles
Mathes, Savannah C.
Mathews, Cheryl A.
Mathews, Joseph G.
Mathews, James M.
Mathews, Janet
Mathias, Suzanne M.
Mathiesen, Hans S.
Mathieson, Carol E. Hay
Mathus, John F.
Matlack, Stephen R.
Matsumoto, Mizue
Matsumoto, Miyuki
Matthew, Nicole A.
Matthew, Sharon R. McGee
Matthews, Anne Clay
Matthews, Howard E.
Matthews, Herbert J.
Mattice, Phylis Hasselberger
Mattice, Robert J.
Mattingly, Carol S.
Matuszek, Mallory Kara McCartney
Matyus, Stephen A.
Matz, Alicia A. Shellhammer
Matz, Richard
Mauck, Lance D.
Mauller, Willard L.
Mauller, Willard L.
Maurer, Theodore Rix
Maurhoff, Carl N.
Mauriello, Joseph M.
Mauro, Sara
Maus, Bryan Jeffrey
Mauzy, John C.
Mauzy, Jacob K.
Mauzy, Twila V. Harman
Mauzy, Bridget
Mavila, Julio
Maxson, Kathryn A.
Maxson, Sheila J. Roy
Maxwell, Kenneth A.
Maxwell, Jane Armentrout
Maxwell, Samuel Arthur

Marsh, William T.
Marsh, Dana Washburn
Marshall, J. B.
Marshall, Craig D.
Maxwell, Linda Anne Dejong
Maxwell, Earl Wilson
Maxwell, Jack
May, Elizabeth Hart
Maybury, Mary Anne Murphy
Maybury, Stephen E.
Mayer, William Christopher
Mayer, Maryann Davis
Mayer, Kristen
Mayle, Rosa Ann
Mayle, Whitney B.
Mayle, Catherine F. Ware
Mayle, Dennis H.
Mayle, Jennifer Lynn
Mayle, Damon
Mayle, Amy
Maynard, Fay Devier McGee
Maynard, Gerald J.
Maynard, Eileen Theresa Mumme
Mayner, Irvina J. Franklin
Mayo, Robert A.
Mayo, Wilbert B.
Mayo, Kristina Ruth
Mayo, Clee
Mays, Charles D.
Mays, Kristine D.
Mays, Corey Daniel
Mays, Richard P.
Mays, Robert
Mays, Juliette
Maza, Robin J. Walker
Mazumdar, Madhulika
Mazurik, Anita
Mazzone, Patricia Guy
McAllister, Sheena Helen
McAllister, Ladecca L.
McAninch, Cassandra Elise
McArthur, Prescott Briggs
McArthur, Benjamin J.
McArthur, Kathleen Mae
McArthur, Jonathan Richard
McAtee, Paula A.
McAtee, William H.
McAtee, Marsha
McAveney, Steven F.
McAvoy, Peggy L. Rothman

Martin, Lonnie Lloyd
Martin, Jaime Lynn
Martin, Danelle Marie
Martin, Dorotha Moore
McCalip, Gregory
McCall, Debra K.
McCallister, Mrs. William (Louise) Everhart
McCallister, Martha
McCallum, Paul K.
McCallum, W. Barbara Vanscoy
McCamant, Pamela A. Wadding
McCamant, Richard E.
McCammon, Mark
McCann, Bridget L.
McCarley, Julian E.
McCarley, Leonora R. Smith
McCarthy, William Thomas
McCartney, Alexa Jade
McCarty, Sondra W. Ziegfield
McCaslin, Donald Scott
McCauley, Sally A.
McCauley, Shelby Amber
McCauley, Virginia C.
McCauley, Laurie D. Jensen
McCauley, Courtney Diana
McCauley, Hannah Faith
McCauley, Diana L.
McCausley, Rachel Crites
McClain, Deborah L. Betting
McClain, Edward Morgan
McClanahan, William J.
McClane, Katherine Davis
McCleery, Janice J. Scherling
McClellan, Doris E.
McClellan, Evelyn H.
McClelland, Sean K.
McClelland, Amanda-Faye Pauline
McCleneghen, Robert
McClintic, Andrea A. Forbes
McClintic, Charles
McCloud, Grace
McClung, Glen A.
McClure, James B.
McClure, Mary J.
McClure, Kevin M.
McClure, Shannen Marie
McClure, Romaine V. Reid

Mathaney, Craig E.
Matheny, Alice A. Larew
Matheny, Eric Tyler
Mather, William W.
McCollough, Austin E.
McCollough, Martha Jean Kimmel
McCollum, Miles L.
McComas-Wood, Matthew Robert
McCombs, Julia A. Boggs
McConnel, John S.
McConnell, Barbara J. Bow
McConnell, David L.
McConnell, Martha Moats
McCook, Charles F.
McCord, Elizabeth Ellen Pe
McCord, Sandra K.
McCorkle, Karen A. Schumann
McCorkle, Andrew R.
McCormack, Marilyn Palm
McCormick, Joann C.
McCormick, Alan K.
McCormick, Robert M.
McCormick, Scott
McCourt, Jessica Lee
McCourt, Evelyn Lucille
McCown, Walter R.
McCoy, Bruce A.
McCoy, Steven E.
McCoy, Nancy Ellen Hays
McCoy, William H.
McCoy, Jo-Anne Jenkins
McCoy, Mary L. Hahn
McCoy, Eileen L. Wehrle
McCoy, Martha L.
McCoy, Donell Lee
McCracken, John
McCready, James L.
McCreery, Patrick W.
McCrobie, Brandon Scott
McCrum, Kimberly Leigh
McCue, Wendy M. Colella
McCulloch, Wayne B.
McCullough, Gary Leon
McCullough, Jon
McCullough, Chadwick
McCumbers, Alexander C
McCurdy, Melody
McCurrie, Stephen J.

Maxwell, Robert E.
Maxwell, Isaac K.
Maxwell, Jason S.
Maxwell, Miranda Shae
McDaniel, Amanda R. Stoner
McDaniel, D. Y.
McDaniel, V. Jean
McDaniels, Randall J.
McDaniels, Samuel Levi
McDermott, Kevin Waters
McDonald, Regina A. Steel
McDonald, Mary B.
McDonald, John Carl
McDonald, Marguerite E.
McDonald, Izetta J.
McDonald, Linda Louise
McDonald, Ian M.
McDonald, John Nathan
McDonald, James W.
McDonald-Ayodeji,
   Carolyn J.
McDonnell, Frank W.
McDonough, Patrick J.
McDowell, Stephanie L.
McDowell, Chelsea Lynn
   Long
McEldowney, William E.
McElhattan, Kent D.
McElhone, Harry S.
McElrath, Louella J.
McElroy, Bruce I.
McElroy, Mary Jane Metzger
McElroy, Alex Robert
McElroy, Alison Steele
McElroy, James T.
McElroy, Jonathan Zachary
McElveen '19, Jordan
McElwain, Reese
McEntee, Marcia Selwyn
McFadden, Rita H.
McFalls, Donna L.
McFarlan, Samantha
McFarland, Lyn J. Rossiter
McFarland, Lana S.
McFarlane, Todd E.
McFeeley, Sandra L. Cox
McFoy, Leigh Ann
McGaffin, Donald E.
McGallaird, H. W.
McGee, James A.
McGee, Elizabeth A.

McAvoy, Erin
McBee, Kevin N.
McBee, Karen S.
McBee, John W.
McGee, Lorrayne Marquette
McGee, Jesse Odell
McGee, Donna S.
McGee, Michael V.
McGee, Clark W.
McGee, David
McGee, Scott
McGehee, Wanda J.
McGhee, Sherri J.
McGhee, Stacy M. Goff
McGhee, Melanie R. Stalnaker
McGill, Haley Catherine Ware
McGill, Declan Thomas
McGlasson, Paul J.
McGlothlin, Joshua Shannon
McGlynn, Carletha D. Smith
McGoff, Diane M.
McGraw, Stewart Allen
McGraw, Richard W.
McGreevey, Timothy S.
McGuckin, Kathy
McGuire, Susan Bennett
McGurran, Shirley Y. Coontz
McGurrin, Colin J.
McHenry, Christine M. Ford
McHose, Edwina Buzzell
McHugh, Barbara Notoris
McIlroy, Gary A.
McIlvaine, Martha Marie
   Briegel
McIlvaine, Robert Morton
McInnes, Russell
McInroy, Natalie M. Torres
McInroy, Joseph
McIntyre, John F.
McKay, Owen E.
McKay, Faye Mitchell
McKeating, Jane M.
McKee, Gail Hagerman
McKee, Curtis Stanley
McKell, James F.
McKelvey, Thomas L.
McKenzie, Tish D. Davis
McKenzie, John J.
McKenzie, Carol R.
McKenzie, Scot York
McKenzie, Malroy

McCluskey, James
McCollam, Jessee C.
McCollam, Amanda Jane
McCollam, Maureen Miller
McKinney, Dana F.
McKinney, Randall H.
McKinney, Robert Keith
McKinney, Suzanne
McKinney, Carrie
McKinnie, Michelle L.
   Mullenax
McKown, Todd R.
McLain, John H.
McLaughlin, David E.
McLaughlin, Clarence G.
McLaughlin, George L.
McLaughlin, Elizabeth Price
McLaughlin, William R.
McLaughlin, Robert R.
McLaughlin, Kendra Taylor
McLaughlin, Margaret
   Trickett
McLaughlin, Frances Vance
McLaughlin, Richard
McLaughlin, Dermot
McLean, William D.
McLean, Robert E.
McLean, Scott K.
McLean, Robert P.
McLenithan, Michael John
McLennan, Ian Jacob
McLeod, Stephen D.
McLeskey, Matthew H.
McMahon, Donald C.
McMahon, Donna D.
   Decinque
McMahon, Melissa J.
   Calcaterra
McMahon, Susan M.
McMahon, Rebecca S. Leo
McMahon, Patricia
McManigle, Richard L.
McMann, Helen
McManus, Eleanor Channell
McMillen, Susan Jane
McMillen, Mark P.
McMillon, Ralph E.
McMillon, Susan M. Bunner
McMullen, Kelly A. Dubois
McMurray, Sandra Young
McMurray, Thomas

McCutcheon, Charles R.
McDade, Kaitlin Olivia
McDaniel, Ulta B.
McDaniel, Renea Michaela
McNally, Diane M.
McNamara, Patti
McNaughton, William R.
McNeal, Karen Strasburg
McNeel, John P.
McNeil, Paige Winchester
McNeish, Harry E.
McNemar, Jonathan Michael
McNinch, Kristin Lee
McNulty, Thomas Charles
McQuain, Johanna D.
McQuain, Michael Eric
McQuain, Sharon Laceil Jack
McQuary, Willard L.
McQuary, Mary Louise
   DuBose
McQuillen, Michael J.
McQuown, Susan Amme
McQuown, James E.
McRae, Crystal F. Barb
McSpadden, William V.
McSwain, Rita S.
McTaggart, Carmen Rose
   Lynne
McThomas, Michael P.
McVaney, Thomas
McVey, Anne C.
McVicker, Nell T.
McVicker, Elizabeth
   Woodford
McWilliams, Callie Anne
   Updike
McWilliams, Tina M.
   DiBacco
McWilliams, Cathy S.
   Cochran
McWilliams, Corey
Meabon, Jared Anton
Meabon, Jeromie
Mead, William B.
Mead, Karen Kassar
Meade, Shane C.
Meade, Jill M. Livingston
Meader, Roberta G.
Meader, David J.
Meadows, Roscoe B.
Meadows, Susan E.

McGee, Gerald B.
McGee, Oscar Basil
McGee, Robbin D. Klinger
McGee, Ava L.
Meadows, Melody J.
Meadows, Vickie L. Shomo
Meadows, Kasey Marie
Meadows, Linda
Meakem, Mary Carolyn
   Soliday
Meakem, Thomas J.
Mearns, Julie Ann Calef
Mears, David Richard
Mechas, Anthony M.
Meck, David Lynn
Meddings, Steven G
Mede, Alan S.
Mednick, Andrew S.
Meece, Barbara E. Phillips
Meehan, William J.
Meeker, Donald F.
Meeks, Sarah E.
Meeks, Stephanie Renea
Mehnaoui '20, Hedi
Meier, Jo Ann Simmons
Meierdiercks, Cecilia Martin
Meierdiercks, Donald R.
Meise, Amanda B.
Meise, Deborah S.
Meister, Jeffrey L.
Meitzler, Harry C.
Meizell, Steve
Melbert, Matthew David
Melbert, Erin Elizabeth
   Gamrod
Melchers, Philip
Mele, Phillip Anthony
Mele, Frank M.
Melese, Mahlet S
Mellace, Stephanie Lynn
Mellgren, Eric S.
Melling, Karen L. Herpich
Melson, Irene Rader
Melson, Allen W.
Melvin, Michael A.
Melvin, Patrick A.
Melvin, Christina L. Shields
Melzig, Douglas Eric
Mendez, Adriana P.
Mendonca, Jessica
Mendoza, Lisa J. Bonesteel

McKenzie, Shawn
McKeon, Alison Brooks
McKillop, William M.
McKinley, Charles H.
Mercer, Leslie A. Statzer
Merchant, Julie Wood
Merchant, Diane
Merecky, Edward
Meredith, Margaret H. Craven
Meredith, Robert W.
Meriau, Simon Oivier
Mero, Bruce C.
Mero, Thomas F.
Mero, Martha Sonner
Merriam, Craig W.
Merrill, Cierra Rose
Merrill, Benjamin S.
Merriman, Nicola Jay
Merriman, Denton L.
Merritt, Andrew Octave
Merritt, Betty Jean
Merryman, William H.
Mersfelder, James L.
Mersing, Mark
Mertz, Walter D.
Mertz, Craig
Merwin, Lawrence J.
Mesa, Elio J.
Meseguer Garcia, Alejandro
Meserve, Muriel A. Lewis
Meserve, David
Mesk, George P.
Messer, Robert J.
Messer, David Jack
Metheny, Brett Arlington
Metheny, Paula Jean
Metheny, Elise Nichole Cardot
Metten, Chad Edward
Metten, Curtis L.
Metz, Deborah A. Mason
Metz, William A.
Metz, James D.
Metz, Harry J.
Metz, Margaret L. Bell
Metz, Donna L. Caldwell
Metz, Matthew Michael
Metzner, Loren Michael
Mewborn, Ruth E. Robinson
Meyer, Rose A. Boserman
Meyer, Margaret G. Hankey
Meyers, Kathryn M. Bollinger

McNaboe, Allyson R.
   Armentrout
McNair, Eleanor Spangler
McNally, Karen J.
Micalizzi, Hilary Lutz
Micalizzi, Frank P.
Michael, Halima Hayley
Michael, Christopher J.
Michael, Sharon M. Koncsol
Michael, Kidus Menkir
Michael, Andrea Michelle
   Hedrick
Michael, Lanelle W.
Michael, James W.
Michael, Robert W.
Michaels, Lewis N.
Michalick-Draxton,
   Michelle L.
Michels, Rose
Michlovic, Thomas
Michos, Leon P.
Micic, Milos
Mick, Wilbert D.
Mick, Amanda J.
Mickis, Bob Lee
Mickunas, Wendy J.
   Buhrendorf
Middaugh, Robert L.
Middleton, George F.
Middleton-Hanshaw,
   Heather Dawn
Midkiff, Joe C.
Midkiff, Barbara Lynn Bird
Midkiff, John R.
Midthun, Kermit S.
Miehl, David G.
Miehl, Beverly Scharfenberg
Miers, William A.
Mihalyo, Stephen John
Mihyar, Wael G.
Mikesell, Lucinda A. Johnson
Mikolay, Dana Joyce Scott
Mikuski, Gail Summer
Milam, Diana H.
Milanovich, Nicholas G.
Milanovich, Joan Overstreet
Milantoni, Anna Marie Mathes
Milbourne-Friend,
   Brittany M.
Milbrada, Nicolena Coontz
Milbrada, Edward

Meadows, Paige Ellen
Meadows, Collin Haddad
Meadows, Margaret Isner
Meadows, Jason J.
Milhollan, Vivian E.
   Alexander
Millen, David B.
Miller, Miriam A.
Miller, Frank A.
Miller, Thomas A.
Miller, Margaret A.
Miller, William Adair
Miller, Ryan Allan
Miller, William Allen
Miller, Marjorie Allene
   Gibson
Miller, Molly Ann
Miller, Devin Antwan
Miller, David B.
Miller, Elizabeth Barnes
Miller, Richard Benjamin
Miller, Charles Brent
Miller, Jaime Brooke
Miller, Kathleen C. Buckley
Miller, Guy C.
Miller, Daniel C.
Miller, Andrew C.
Miller, Eileen Cody
Miller, Melanie D. Caynor
Miller, James D.
Miller, Justyn David
Miller, Charles E.
Miller, William E.
Miller, Clarence E.
Miller, Clarence E.
Miller, Linda G. Sullivan
Miller, Stella G.
Miller, Leigh Gardner
   Chadwick
Miller, Michael George
Miller, Joyce Helen Blacka
Miller, Elizabeth Howie
Miller, Krista I. Chenoweth
Miller, Roberta J. Fidler
Miller, Tammy J. Goldizen
Miller, Carol J. Montgomery
Miller, Patricia J. Morgan
Miller, Catherine J. Palavide
Miller, Courtney Jane
Miller, Rebecca Jo Haddox
Miller, Sandra K. McBee

Menjivar, Carlos Atilio
Mennig, Elizabeth Lee
    Jackson
Meola, Anthony J.
Miller, Margaret Loudin
Miller, Alma M.
Miller, Leonard M.
Miller, Lynn M.
Miller, Nicole Marie
Miller, Melanie N.
Miller, Erin N.
Miller, Timothy P.
Miller, James P.
Miller, Rosalea Poling
Miller, Mary R. Trimboli
Miller, Myron R.
Miller, Frederick R.
Miller, Janet R.
Miller, John R.
Miller, Rodnitta Renee
Miller, Jason Robert
Miller, Sharon Rose
Miller, Pamela S. Currence
Miller, Olive Shannon
Miller, Nora Sue
Miller, Robert Todd
Miller, Thomas
Miller, C. Douglass
Miller, Robin
Miller, Paul
Miller, J. Mark
Miller, Derek
Millett, Nicholas Miles
Millevoi, Amy L. Heilman
Millican, Mark Steven
Milliken, Susan Marie
Millner, Kelsie Nicole
Mills, Keith A.
Mills, Kyle Daniel
Mills, William E.
Mills, Jennifer H. Geary
Mills, Frederick H.
Mills, Roderica J.
Mills, Robert L.
Mills, Kimberly M.
Milne, Peter Barrett
Milosevic, Vladimir
Milstead, Dawn Amber
Miner, Kimberly Lynn
Miner, Jessica Renee
Minigh, Megan Jane

Meyers, James R.
Meyers, Daniel S.
Meyers, Melanie Shetter
Meyers, C. R.
Minnich, Annette
    Blankenship
Minnici, Dawn Marie
    Morrison
Minnick, Elizabeth Haylett
Minnick, Jennifer S.
    Tuholsky
Minor, Jeanne A.
Minor, Robyn Lohr
Minor, Whitney Marie
Mise, David H.
Mise, Lohrer Jones
Miserentino, Robert
Mish, John G.
Missildine, Mattie Kathryn
Mistry, Marilyn Stopp
Mitasev, Branko
Mitchell, Ashley A. Stark
Mitchell, Barbara E.
Mitchell, Debra E.
Mitchell, Walter F.
Mitchell, Charles Franklin
Mitchell, Gregory Frederick
Mitchell, Linda J. Mathews
Mitchell, Joseph J.
Mitchell, Calvin J.
Mitchell, Dakota James
Mitchell, Michael K.
Mitchell, Kimberly L.
Mitchell, James L.
Mitchell, Niquita Leigh Stone
Mitchell, Kenneth Leigh
Mitchell, Candace M. Smith
Mitchell, Andrea M.
Mitchell, Donna M.
Mitchell, Kathleen Marie
    Barndt
Mitchell, Sharon Renee
    McDowell
Mitchell, Charisse Renee
Mitchell, Ashley Renee
Mitchell, Helen Robinson
Mitchell, Michael Scott
Mitchell, Stephen T.
Mitchell, Malinda Wright
Mitchell, Jesse
Mitchell, Harbour

Miles, Cozette A. Doganieri
Miles, Morgan Emily Marie
Miles, Ta'Leaya Natima
Miles, Jessica Nikole
Miyamoto, Wakako V.
Miyatake, Yuko
Mlinarcik, John S.
Moats, Daniel F.
Moats, Peggy Lee Gatewood
Moats, Jacklin Sue
Mobaker, Clements N.
Moccia, Jeannie M.
Mockensturm, Martha L.
    Monroe
Modaber, Parvis H.
Moffat, John R.
Moffett, John C.
Moffett-Dziak, Alice A.
Mohney, Douglas L.
Moist, Aileen F. Teter
Moister, Matthew Robert
Moler, Calvin G.
Moler, Cornelia Wolverton
Molinillo-Corral, Silvia
Molloy, Arlaina L. Finck
Monahan, Jeannie L.
    McCauley
Monastersky, Eileen M.
    Eschbach
Monda, Carmen M.
Monday, Michael A.
Mondelli, Richard T.
Money, C. Elizabeth Barnsley
Moneypenny, Amy Jo
Mongold, Molly Danielle
    Vance
Mongold, Logan William
Monk, Sarah L. Grabe
Monroe, Amanda Beth
    Yeargan
Monroe, Betty Boyles
Monroe, Angela Dawn
Monroe, David E.
Monsour, Cicely N.
Montana, Julie J.
Monteith, William E.
Montemoino, Ty-Chon
Montgomery, Stephen B.
Montgomery, Richard B.
Montgomery, Joseph C.
Montgomery, Cheryl E.

Miller, Eleanor K.
Miller, Kirsten L.
Miller, Alexandra Leanne
Miller, Penny Lee
Montgomery, Barbara Gruden
Montgomery, Belinda Sue
Montgomery, Kimberley Sue
Montgomery, Michael W.
Montieth, Sherri L. Shepler
Monto, Matilda J. Campolio
Monto, Joseph R.
Montoney, Snyder J.
Montoney, Stephen Warren
Moon, Sandra Chidester
Moon, Ernest G.
Moore, Dorothy A.
Moore, Edward Aaron
Moore, Robert B.
Moore, Amy B.
Moore, Marguerite Channell
Moore, Sheryl D. Norris
Moore, Howard D.
Moore, Patricia D.
Moore, Matthew D.
Moore, Mark D.
Moore, Dorothy E. Johnston
Moore, Rachel Elizabeth
Moore, Sierra J. Blackburn
Moore, Rebecca J.
Moore, Christopher J.
Moore, Sharon J.
Moore, Edward J.
Moore, Anita Jane
Moore, Max Joseph
Moore, William K.
Moore, Faith K.
Moore, Stanley L.
Moore, Neil L.
Moore, John L.
Moore, Ellen L.
Moore, Karen L.
Moore, Robin L.
Moore, Marian L.
Moore, Julie L.
Moore, Tracey Lambert
Moore, Gayle LaVerne Paul
Moore, Karen Leonard
Moore, Sara Lucy
Moore, Catherine M. Dumire
Moore, Mary Margaret
    McQuain

Miningham, Robert D.
Minix, Stacy A.
Minix, Lisa Jane
Minners, Bruce
Moore, Regina R.
    Greathouse
Moore, Carla R.
    Pennington
Moore, Mary Virginia
Moore, Christopher W.
Moore, Richard W.
Moore, Lilly Wilmoth
Moore, Annette Y. Brothers
Moore, Carl
Moore, Elizabeth
Moore, Diamond
Moore, Delroy
Moore-Keish, Christopher E.
Moore-Withrow, Brenda L.
Moose, George R.
Moppert, Janet G.
Morales, Lisa Klinger
Morales, Van Michael
Moran, Lesley C.
Moran, Crystal Gail Gum
Moran, Carroll Gene
Moran, Ferd H.
Moran, Pauline Herrmann
Moran, Edward J.
Moran, Daniel J.
Moran, Peter J.
Moran, Aaron James
Moran, Dorothy M. Howell
Moran, Thomas Michael
Moran, Thomas N.
Moran, Siobain R.
Moran, Theodore S.
Moran, Suzanne Smith
Moran, Joseph W.
Moran, C. Carney
Morba, Nancy Ellen Potash
Morehead, Jeffrey P.
Moreno, Megan Rejohnna
Morgan, Suzan A. Lange
Morgan, Donald A.
Morgan, Leslie Ann
Morgan, Nicholas B.
Morgan, Thomas D.
Morgan, Eugene E.
Morgan, Jamie J. Mouse
Morgan, Barbara Jean

Mitchem, Cinnamon
Mitcherling, Michael J.
Mitlitsky, Amy Leigh Mayer
Miura, Tamiko
Morgan, Jessica Nicole Scott
Morgan, George P.
Morgan, Donna R. Wamsley
Morgan, Emily Rochelle
Morgan, Melinda S. Hornick
Morgan, Waller V.
Morgan, Calvin
Morgan, H. Maxwell
Morgan-Cutright, Betsy
    Lorraine
Morgenroth, Robert A.
Morgenroth, Ruth Ann Dahlin
Morgenroth, Donald G.
Mori, Ruka
Morice, William D.
Morici, Ashley S.
Morishita, Keiko
Morley, Leonard A.
Morley, Paul A.
Morley, Jessie Hegmann
Morrill, Norman S.
Morris, Susan DeAnn Morral
Morris, Karyn E.
Morris, Michael F.
Morris, Phyllis Franklin Glass
Morris, Kimberly G.
Morris, Marisa Lynn
Morris, Lucille Pritt
Morris, Andrew Ryan
Morris, Roy S.
Morris, Rebecca T.
Morris, Lynette Tamsin
Morris, Desmond Victor
Morrison, Teresa A. Werner
Morrison, Michael D.
Morrison, Jon D.
Morrison, Cynthia E. Shreve
Morrison, Ralph E.
Morrison, Robert F.
Morrison, Diana G. Miller
Morrison, Carrie H.
Morrison, William H.
Morrison, David Howard
Morrison, Wanda J. Cross
Morrison, Michael J.
Morrison, Elizabeth Jeanne
Morrison, Mary Margaret

Montgomery, Rachel
    Elizabeth Halperin
Montgomery, Margaret Fish
Montgomery, Ina L.
Morrissey, Eugene
Morrow, Ruthvan W.
Morse, Samantha LeeAnn
Morton, William E.
Morton, Mary Evelyn
Morton, Joseph H.
Morton, William J.
Morton, Taylor Jean
Morton, Deborah K.
Moscicki, Elizabeth Susan
Moser, John W.
Mosher, James C.
Moshier, Amanda Marie
Moshiri, Ali
Mosier, Edson
Mosketti, Diane Lynne
    Ippolito
Moss, James A.
Moss, Victoria Louise
Moudry, Lisa A. Weese
Mountain, F. Timothy
Mourier, Alexis Nicole
Mouse, Raymond L.
Mouse, Ella McDonald
Mouser, Tressa L. Holsberry
Mower, Richard Elwood
Mowton, Edward A.
Moyer, Stella F.
Moyer, David H.
Moyer, John S.
Moyers, Karla Ann
Mrakota, Emil R.
Mroz, Michael Matthew
Mroz, Marjorie
Mrozinsky, Jeffrey P.
Much, Nancy L. Davis
Mucha, Sydney B.
Mudge, Catherine R. Morral
Mueller, Lillie
Mugabe, Florence
Mugler, Charles P.
Mukherjee, Debolina
Mulder, Jennifer L.
Mulford, Terry W.
Mulhern, Daniel K.
Mullen, Mary R.
Mullenax, Michele A.

Moore, Bryan N.
Moore, Summer Nicole
    Chestnut
Moore, J. Steven
Mullenix, Shelby Gordon
Mullennex, Patricia A.
    Jakubuk
Mullennex, Victoria G.
    Thompson
Mullennex, Richard H.
Mullennex, Pamela I. Hedric
Mullennex, Jack L.
Mullennex, Donna M.
Mullennex, Harnus P.
Mullennex, L. Susan
Mullennex, Ryan Zachary
Mullens, Susan L. Jackson
Mullens, Catherine L. War
Muller, Missy A.
Muller, Ricky
Mullett, Arthur T.
Mulligan, Mary A. Leach
Mulligan, Nancy C. Hall
Mullins, Brinton A.
Mullins, James David
Mullins, Nida Dawn
Mullins, Larry E.
Mullins, Donald Earl
Mullins, Kelcie Patrice
Mullis, Troy D.
Mullis, Mary Long
Mullis, H. Thomas
Mulrain, Jeffry A.
Mulugeta, Samsone T.
Mulumba, Gina Ndaya
Mulvey, Tanya L.
Mumblow, Anthony G.
Muncy, Victor J.
Mundell, Julie Renee
Munn, Fred O.
Munns, Harold E.
Munns, George W.
Munoz, Marcelo R.
Munsey, Rosemary Somme
Muntz, John A.
Muntz, Edward A.
Murano, Robert
Murdock, Faith A.
Murdock, Robert McClell
Murphy, Susan A. Ellis
Murphy, Judith A. Howard

Skinner
Morgan, Adwina Jo Kisner
Morgan, Robert L.
Morgan, Cathleen M. Huet
Murphy, Mary K.
Murphy, Gary L.
Murphy, Kelly L.
Murphy, Jennifer Liveright
Murphy, Cheryl M. Gilchrist
Murphy, Timothy P.
Murphy, Melissa Rae
Murphy, Patrick Ryan
Murphy, Ann S. Kump
Murphy, Russell S.
Murphy, Caroline Sherbert
  Phipps
Murphy, Gregory Thomas
Murphy, Carol Zirbs
Murphy, Bill
Murray, Lisa A.
Murray, William F.
Murray, Keith F.
Murray, Jamie J.
Murray, Lee James
Murray, Nancy Jane
Murray, Barbara Jeanne
  Hogan
Murray, Haylee Madeline
Murray, Shaley
Murray, Brittany
Murry, Nancy
Murschell, Trey Daniel
Murschell, Jael Elizabeth
  Fedora
Muscarella, Richard C.
Muscat, Ashley Erin
Musgrove, I. Jean Morris
Mushtag, Shawgi M.
Musich, Richard J.
Musick, Phillip W.
Musta, Mark E.
Mustachio, Marci J.
Mustoe, Janna Lynn
Mutwalli, Leith S.
Muyumba, Francois N.
Myer, Dorothea O.
Myers, Cellene D. Zirkle
Myers, Regina E.
Myers, June Elizabeth Toth
Myers, Marcia Fortney
Myers, Mary H. Sterner

Carroll
Morrison, Jennifer Nicole
Morrison, Maxine Vanscoy
Morrissey, Kyle R.
Myers, Sheri Lynn
Myers, Jeff P.
Myers, Shawn R.
Myers, Joyce Robinson
Myers, Patrick Shane
Myers, Elizabeth Tullis Semet
Myers, Zachary
Myers, Amber
Myles, Wanda P.
Myrick, Karen Harger
Nabi, Candi
Naboka, Eileen M.
  Banschback
Naeny, Evelyn Trenholm
  Menzies
Naeny, T. Carter
Nafe, Stephen A.
Naffin, Paul G.
Nafzieger, Karen A. Forbes
Nagai, Tomoko
Nagel, Charles E.
Nagle, Jack A.
Nagui, Sherief Akef
Naguski, Eric A.
Naidu, Sheila Rowlands
Naill, Frances A. Stansel
Najarian, Mary A. Been
Nakajima, Mihoro
Nakamura, Koki
Nakasaki, Tomoyuki
Nalls, Emily A.
Nannen, Gerald W.
Napier, Robert S.
Naranjo, Juan Rafael B.
Narkevic, Chelsea Aleen
Narvaez, Daniel J.
Nash, Michael Thomas
Nasr, Mostafa
Nass, Marvin
Nasser, Donna E. Siebel
Nast, James M.
Natali, Joshua Jay
Natoli, Peter J.
Nau, Mark A.
Naudain, Raymond W.
Nauman, Charles H.
Neal, Edith Campolio

Mullenax, Mary Arnold
Mullenax, Linda D. Singleton
Mullenax, Candy L.
Mullenax, Laura Marie
Nearhoof, Jay G.
Nearman, Merrill K.
Needham, Susan E. Peirce
Neel, Marilyn Shook
Neeley, Kathryn Victoria
Neely, William L.
Neely, Jack L.
Neely, Thomas W.
Neese, Deborah Denise
  Gawthrop
Neese, Cliff J.
Neff, Susan E. VanGundy
Neff, Herbert
Neffke, Bruce B.
Nefflen, Louis H.
Nefflen, Louis Henry
Nefflen, Karl
Nefflen, Henry
Nefflen, Ken
Nehrebecki, John M.
Neill, Arthur F.
Neilson, Andrew S.
Neira, Louis F.
Neitzert, Carl F.
Nelan, Deric
Nell, James M.
Nelson, Ian Alexander
Nelson, Scott D.
Nelson, Gary Dale
Nelson, Anthony David
Nelson, Helen E.
Nelson, John E.
Nelson, Rachael Elizabeth
Nelson, Madeline Elizabeth
Nelson, John G.
Nelson, John G.
Nelson, Anita G.
Nelson, Jessica Gayle
Nelson, Diana L. Cassell
Nelson, Cheryl L.
Nelson, Jennifer L.
Nelson, Terry M.
Nelson, Theresa N. Heath
Nelson, Meredith N.
Nelson, Stephen R.
Nelson, Irvin S.
Nelson, David S.

Murphy, Roscoe E.
Murphy, William G.
Murphy, Tina J. Schlegel
Murphy, Robert J.
Nelson, Waitman W.
Nelson, Mary Ann
Nelson, Lee Ann
Nemchick, Rebecca J.
  Turnbell
Nerantzis, Perry P.
Nesbitt, Adam Brent
Nesbitt, Rebecca Lynn
Nesbitt, Christine Marie
  Hanna
Nesselrodt, Lawrence A.
Nesselrodt, Julian D.
Nestor, Cindy C. Snyder
Nestor, Randall Craig
Nestor, Robyn Denise
Nestor, Rocky E.
Nestor, Dale G.
Nestor, Robert G.
Nestor, Sierra Gabrielle
Nestor, Teresa L. Cooper
Nestor, Joyce M. Booth
Nestor, Rebecca M. Kalar
Nestor, Hugh M.
Nestor, Angela Nicole
Nestor, Linda S. Rhodes
Nestor, Austin Wayne
Nestor, Kevin
Nettles, Patrick H.
Neuburger, Chad M.
Neuenschwander, Shannon
  Nichole
New, Candace E.
New, Rowland I. C.
New, Rachel Irene
New, Lois Jean
New, Linda Lee Hurst
Newbold, Allyson J. Hicks
Newbraugh, Troy G.
Newbrough, Micalyn M
Newbrough, Theresa Weisz
Newcomer, Karen A. Brandt
Newell, Judith A.
Newhouse, Heather Nicole
Newing, Jinni L. Williams
Newlon, Jeanne Dawn
  Shipman
Newlon, Delmas G.

Myers, Thomas Jackson
Myers, Lisa L. Hebb
Myers, Marcia L. Robinson
Myers, Jason L.
Newman, Betty
  Cunningham
Newman, Jean Y.
Newpher, Trevyn
Newton, Margaret L. Zirk
Niblett, John R.
Nice, Terri Lynn
  Woodbridge
Nice, Christopher R.
Nice, Hattie R.
Nicely, Patricia Stemple
Nichol, Jacob Leland
Nicholas, David A.
Nichols, Mary Carolyn
  Shiflet
Nichols, Margaret E. Smith
Nichols, Robert G.
Nichols, Robert G.
Nichols, John H.
Nichols, Robert S.
Nicholson, Thomas D.
Nicholson, Effie J. Roy
Nicholson, Bridget L.
Nickels, Timothy C.
Nickens, Wesley Elmer
Nicodemus, Mary B. Kenney
Nicodemus, William R.
Nicoll, Robert D.
Nida, Ashley Ann
Nida, Steven E.
Nida, Paul G.
Nida, Megan Leigh
Nida, Jeffrey S.
Nidiffer, Sheri L.
Nied, Craig D.
Nieman, Mae Gladys Davis
Nieman, William J.
Nieves, Ruben J.
Nieves, Krista K. Rader
Nilsen, Laurie B. Stinchcomb
Nilsen, Susan E. Quick
Nilsen, Eric J.
Nilsen, Christine Marie
Nine, E. Grant
Nine, Grace
Niner, Kenneth P.
Ninesling, Frank A.

Neal, Mary M.
Neale, John H.
Neale, Valerie S. Corley
Neale, Elizabeth Shiflet
N'Jai, Adi E.
Nobakht, Sheridan L.
  Flanagan
Noble, Howard David
Noble, Barbara L. Perrotta
Noble, Matthew Thomas
Noble, Joyce Tuthill
Noble, Alison
Nobles, Susan M.
Nock, Daniel
Noel, Shelby G. Tacy
Noel, Diane L. Matlack
Nofsinger, William Ronald
Nohe, Charles A.
Nolle, Elizabeth Melita
Nolte, Gina Renee
Noonan, Valeria N. Tarantelli
Noonan, Reba Weiner
Nooney, Christina Cooper
Noor, Muhammad
Norcross, Christopher Lucas
Norcutt, David C.
Nordholm, Michael B.
Nordquist, Richard
Norford, Alice Murachanian
Norman, Douglas C.
Norman, Belva J. Shahan
Norman, Carolyn Masson
Norman, Margo Roseann
Normann, Ruthann Hallett
Norris, Wayne A.
Norris, Larry E.
Norris, Samuel J.
Norris, Ted
North, Charles E.
North, Sharon Hartley
North, Gary W.
Northrup, Tessie G. Phares
Norton, Taylor Ann
Norton, Nancy Huffman
Norton, Lisa M. Balogh-White
Norton, Danielle Marie
Norton, Katelyn Nicole
Norton, George W.
Norwood, Natalie Gayle
Norwood, Travis Robert
Norwood, Gena

Nelson, Brenda Sue
  Vandevender
Nelson, Maydell Turner
Nelson, Itis W. Lantz
Ntumba, Katenda Mimi
Nubel, Robert C.
Nubel, Christopher Robert
Nucilli, Amanda Marie
  Sponaugle
Nuckols, Ashlynn Ann
Nugent, Maynard Charles
Nugent, Michele L.
Null, Elizabeth A. Geary
Nulton, Roger M.
Nunn, Mary E. McCarrell
Nunn, James W.
Nurss, Amy L. Brunermer
Nuttall, Elizabeth Mitchell
Nuttall, William W.
Nutter, Anna D.
Nutter, Rocky G.
Nutter, Katherine I.
Nutting, Joan Correll
Nuzum, Ronna J.
Nye, Bradford V.
Nykun, Theodore Eugene
Obata, Hiroaki
Obermann, Carol L.
Oberton, Mark P.
O'Brian, Susan R.
O'Brien, William A.
O'Brien, Kevin C.
O'Brien, Patrick J.
O'Brien, Sheila J.
O'Brien, Bonnadette M. Bull
O'Brien, David P.
O'Bryan, Colin John
O'Callahan, Caigan Timothy
Ochap, Eugenia R. Gallucci
Ochiva, Dennis J.
Ochoa Urrea, Agustin
O'Connell, Ryan Curtis
O'Connor, Leslie A. Levy
O'Connor, Kimberly Ann
O'Connor, Robert E.
O'Connor, Mary E.
O'Connor, Kathleen
O'Connor Martin, Carrie Lynn
Oda, Masamune
O'Deen, Charles T.
O'Dell, James W.

Newlon, Jena Johnson
Newlon, G. Dale
Newman, JoAnna C.
Newman, John R.
O'Donnell, Matthew T.
O'Donnell, Dorothy
O'Dwyer, Aidan Mattias
O'Dwyer, Matthew
Oechsli, Bernard L.
O'Farrell, Timothy D.
Ogasawara, Ryoko
Ogawa, Makiko
Ogden, Amanda Dawn Ayers
Ogden-Bonner, Carrie L.
Oglebay, Jon C.
Ogrinz, Paul A.
Ohler, Oscar E.
Oigawa, Shiegeru
Ojanpera-Lynch, Elizabeth
  Josephine Glenna
Ojeda, Danny M.
Okawa, Satoru
O'Kernick, Delinda J.
O'Kernick, Della Marie
O'Kernick, Fred P.
O'Kernick, Pauline
O'Kernick, Joseph
Okkey, Aysegul Kucuk
Okoro, Emmanuel
Okoya, Peace Ideozu
Okun, Peter T.
Okun, Lisbet T.
Olaitan, Olaniyi Olumuyiwa
Oldaker, Courtney Nicole
Oldaker, William R.
Older, Jamie Stephanie
O'Leary, Greta L.
Oliver, Dan D.
Oliver, William Jackson
Oliver, Toni Lewis
Oliver, Jason M.
Oliver, Sameul R.
Oliverio, Andrea M.
Olivieri, Samuel G.
Olivieri, Denise N.
  Easterbrook
Olivo, John Joseph
Ollweiler, Frances L. Berman
Olowofoyeku, Mowunmi
  Olutunde
Olsen, Robert A.

Ninesling, Ruth R. DeJunis
Nishino, Ayano
Nitz, Joseph I.
Nitz, Barbara K. Long
Olson, Patricia Lee Wilson
Olwell, Matthew Josiah
O'Malley, Marlyne Irene Pugel
Omps, John Eugene
Omps, Millie Melynn
Omps, Matthew
Ondra, Margaret F. Allen
Ondra, Emil F.
O'Neal, Caitlyn Shirley
O'Neal, Carley
O'Neil, Brian C.
O'Neil, Gerard P.
O'Neill, David J.
Ono, Linda M.
Ono, Kaori
Oravec, Alan J.
Orders, Dorothy J. Hensil
Orebaugh, Jane M. Bookstaver
Orehosky, Jo-Anne Brink
Orehosky, Douglas John
Orehosky, Ann M. Kampf
Orehosky, Glenn S.
Ormesher, Thomas A.
Ormiston, Stephen S.
Orndorf, Kevin
Orosz, Lori A.
Orr, Frank J.
Orr, Deborah M. Boliner
Orr, Charles P.
Orr, Donna Roxann Nestor
Orr, Robert William
Orrantia, Diana
Orrison, Joe H.
Orrison, Jack L.
Orsburn, Debra L.
Orton, Clark E.
Orts, Veronica
O'Savio, Sherrie Holder
O'Savio, Roderick W.
Osberger, Marguerite Swiger
Osborn, Helen H.
Osborn, Leroy L.
Osborne, Richard C.
Osborne, Paul E.
Osborne, Linda Kees

Noss, Christina Carrie
Novellino, Anthony
Novitch, Edward H.
Noyes, Henry F.
Oseni, Denise Andrea Green
O'Shanahan, Antonio
Oshikiri, Manami
Ossorio, Nancy Piercy
Osterman, Susan E.
Ostrom, Roy S.
O'Sullivan, Patrick J.
Othman, Zayd Yousif
Otokawa, Ichiro
O'Toole, Timothy Brian
Ott, Jeffrey L.
Ottmann, Patricia A. Weale
Ottmann, David L.
Otto, Misty Diane
Ouellette, Meegan Anne Risner
Ouellette, Adam J.
Ouellette, Brian M.
Ouellette, Amy S.
Ougheltree, Audrey Mason
Ours, Kerri Beth
Ours, William Jordan
Ours, Karen P. Lackey
Ours, Brian
Out, Gregory C.
Outenpitak, Vitwat
Overholt, William A.
Overholt, Ethel B.
Owen, Sue Barrett
Owen, Robert E.
Owen, Marilyn Jamie
Owen, Patricia L. Bartlett
Owen, Jill M. Shoemaker
Owens, Marcia A. Taylor
Owens, Melissa Dawn Shahan
Owens, Mary E.
Owens, Terra K.
Owens, Winona Lee Cameron
Owens, Peggy McNeill
Owens, Bascom S.
Owens, Deatria Washington
Owens, Reginald
Owens, Rebecca
Oyewole, Abiodun S.
Ozee, Connie L. Wells
Pace, Nicholas A.
Pace, Anne Brigham

Odom, Melanie L. Stock
O'Donnell, Marita A.
O'Donnell, Ellen Clemens
O'Donnell, Thomas P.
Paden, Nicholas B.
Paden, Christopher Ryan
Paez, Carlos A.
Paez, Luis E.
Paez, Hilda M.
Pagano, Dom C
Page, Stuart Faulkner
Page, John H.
Page, R. L.
Page, Natalie
Paglia, Jennifer J. Ramirez
Paglia, Robert Leonard
Paige, Thomas M.
Painter, Earl C.
Painter, Luther E.
Painter, Richard J.
Painter, Virginia Kratzer
Painter, Tressa Nicole Keene
Paiz, Kenya Dominique
Pakk, George
Palavido, Cydell Lynn Carlson
Palavido, Frank
Palien, Beth Ann
Palko, Frank T.
Pall, Gwendolyn Irvine
Palm, Malcolm J.
Palm, Ann Manners
Palm, Jacob Robert
Palmer, Ronda D.
Palmer, Ronald Elwood
Palmer, Jennifer L. Touchette
Palmieri, Thomas E.
Panell, Lauren Patrice
Panella, Brent A.
Panzitta, Ralph A.
Panzitta, Dulcia Jean Lambert
Papaminas, Anastasios A.
Pappas, George
Parandeh, Gene
Paratore, Michael Paul
Parcher, Kenneth M.
Paretti, Andrew J.
Parg, Minnie
Park, Edward D.
Parken, John E.
Parken, Allison Forbes
Parker, Deborah Brooke

Olson, Juanita A. Straight
Olson, John Alexander
Olson, Bruce E.
Olson, Michele K. Johnson
Parker, Jessica R. Beattie
Parker, Gary R.
Parker, Alma
Parker, C. Joan
Parkes, John R.
Parkinson, Travis Aron
Parks, Cynthia Denise
Parks, Donna L
Parks-McIe, Kathleen Mary
Parlick, Ki-Sook
Parmesano, Anna J.
Parmesano, Mary
Parra, Gustavo E.
Parrack, Barbara E.
Parrack, Jodie J. Snyder
Parrack, Ryan L.
Parrack, Kara LeeAnne
Parrack, Rivanna Nicole Kyle
Parrack, Adrian R.
Parrack, Jon W.
Parrish, Noble C.
Parrish, David P.
Parry, Thomas
Parson, Leslie W.
Parsons, Owen A.
Parsons, Lucy Annetta
Parsons, Amy Bialek
Parsons, Katherine Campion
Parsons, Jocie D.
Parsons, Melody D.
Parsons, Jennifer Elaine
Parsons, Patricia Kavanagh
Parsons, James L.
Parsons, Sharon L.
Parsons, Melinda L.
Parsons, Melissa Nadine Heckler
Parsons, Elizabeth Reid
Parsons, Nicholas Sean
Parsons, Harold W.
Parsons, Carol
Parsons, Desiree
Parsons, John
Parthun, Linda E. Schaarschmidt
Partington, Kris A.
Partyka, Riley

Osborne, Tamara L. Carver
Osburn, Sicily Corley
Oseguera, Moises

Passero, Rebecca J.
 Heinzerling
Pastine, Jessica Erin Mallow
Pastuck, Ronald D.
Pastur, Benjamin Serge
Patchett, Roger L.
Paton, Thomas M.
Patrick, Cristine Anne
Patrick, Michelle L.
Patterson, Scott Allen
Patterson, Troy Dean
Patterson, Ruth Dietz
Patterson, Mary Kelly
Patterson, Sharon L.
Patterson, Elma M.
Patterson, Karen S.
Patterson, Francis
Patterson, Charles
Patterson, James
Patton, Robert A.
Patton, Linda L. Demastus
Patton, Eric N.
Pattrakulchai, Vorapong
Paturis, Mary M. Toompas
Paugh, Sarah Christina Scott
Paugh, Christian James
Paugh, Brian L.
Paugh, Julie Lynn
Paugh, Holly M.
Paugh, Hillary Neale
Paugh, Rhonda Novallis
Paul, John A.
Paul, Fraser Arthur
Paul, Michael Charles
Paul, Janelle L. Gainer
Paul, Robert Theodore
Paulmier, Cynthia S.
Pavese, Janine Y. Collins
Pavloska-Gjorgjieska,
 Dori V.
Pawelczyk, Christine N. Gum
Pawlak, Courtney Rose
Paxman, Gwen J. Rattenbury
Paxson, Richard D.
Payne, Virginia C.
Payne, Amanda Gari
 Mininger

Pace, Jeremy Edward-Patton
Pace, Eugenia Grace Triplett
Packard, Heather L. Urban
Pacl, Tamara A. Wallo
Payne, Williamson S.
Payne, Carl
Paynter, Rachel Gayle Barnes
Peach, David R.
Peacock, Gary E.
Peak, Dakota Carpenter
Peaker, Carla N. Linear
Pealer, Steven A.
Pearce, Suzie Held
Pearlstein, Rachel Morgan
Pearsall, Leigh Ann
Pearse, Marina Ann
Pearson, Carolyn E. Howell
Pearson, Sandra L.
Pearson, Alberta R. Weimer
Pearson, Jon T.
Peasak, Joshua P.
Peck, Caroline Carson
Peck, Marjorie Seip
Peck, Helen Stemple
Peck, Edward T.
Pecoraro, Christopher
Peek, Zoe A. Fausold
Peet, Owen MacKenzie
Peirce, Laurence B.
Peirce, Ella Hokman
Peirce, Dana L.
Pelchen, Betsy Jill Greenberg
Pelham, David Herbert
Pellegrin, Barbara Wade
Pemberton, Elliott Dan
Pemberton, Shelby Lynne
Pemberton, Gail Vera Jenkins
Penaloza, Jose L.
Pence, John S.
Pencek, Edward A.
Pendleton, Angela M.
Penisson, Janice Hodson
Penman, Stuart J.
Penman, Arthur L.
Penn, Gene E.
Penna, Richard H.
Pennington, Kevin Arthur
Pennington, Nan Bare
Pennington, Kristen Beth
Pennington, Emily D.
Pennington, Pamela D.

Bennett
Parker, Erin C. Malarkey
Parker, Edmund Emmanuel
Parker, Rashad Lamar
Pennington, Paula M.
Pennington, Kitty S. Woods
Pennington, Barbara
Pepe, Diana Lynn Williams
Peppard, Edward M.
Pepper, David Stephen
Pepple, Lynn R. Foor
Perdue, Shawna Irene
Pereira Carvalho, Everton
 Sales
Peretti, Norman B.
Perez, Michael
Perez-Barsh, Marisela
 Gutierrez
Perine, James
Perkins, Eugene B.
Perkins, Linda M.
Perkins, Jeffrey R.
Perkins, Clea
Perkins-Tomey, Brandi Renee
Perriello, Frank C.
Perrine, Jamey Donell
Perrotto, John N.
Perry, Rene' A.
Perry, Erma Gayle Arbogast
Perry, Elizabeth H. Lyon
Perry, Kimberly H.
Perry, Donald L.
Perry, Duncan M.
Perry, William P.
Perry, Florence R. Lytle
Perry, Frances Reves
Perry, Cathy Sue Whitesides
Perry, Phillip Wayne
Perry, Jeffrey
Perry, Gordon
Persinger, Rhetta Grace
Pessaro, Teresa L.
Peter, Friedrich Alexander
Peterka, Charles R.
Peters, Alfred Dale
Peters, Matthew David
Peters, Gregory E.
Peters, Stuart G.
Peters, Kenneth M.
Petersen, Joy Alice
Petersen, Adam Franklin

Pascuzzi, Frank B.
Pase, Deborah L.
Pase, Ray
Pass, Shawn Michael
Petersen, Patricia
Petersen, Tamara
Peterson, Mila Anderson
Peterson, Gertrude Auvil
Peterson, Julia Beauchamp
Peterson, Molly Fisher
Peterson, Nycole J. Soebbing
Peterson, Nancy R.
Peterson, Abbagayle
Pethtel, Hazel L.
Petrali, John P.
Petrella, Kayla Marie
Petrice, Vincent A.
Petrice, Melissa D. McNema
Petridis, Nick
Petrizzo, Angela C.
Petronio, Vicki S. Teter
Petry, Denise L. Sodaro
Pettis, Lawrence
Pettit, Elinor G.
Pettit, Betty June Windle
Pettit, Lawrence R.
Petz, Debra L.
Petzold, Dennis R.
Pevarnik, James F.
Peyton, Briscoe W.
Pezzi, Rosemary
Pezzuli, Virginia P.
Pezzulli, Frederick Anthon
Pezzulli, Frank
Pfau, Robert W.
Pfau, Iva
Pfeifer, Raymond
Pfeil, Karl Henry
Pfingst, Thomas P.
Pham, Martha
Phares, Myrtle A.
Phares, Danny Coleman
Phares, Isaac Creed
Phares, Nora E.
Phares, Debra Elaine
Phares, Bruce G.
Phares, Lorna J. Gibson
Phares, Patricia J. Gladwel
Phares, Lindsey J.
Phares, Michael J.
Phares, Betty Jean

Payne, Gloria Joan Marquette
Payne, V. Mae Overholt
Payne, Keith R.
Payne, Anita R.
Phares, Aileen Marteney
Phares, Dewey P.
Phares, Emerson P.
Phares, Rex R.
Phares, Lorraine Thompson
Phares, Stanley V.
Phares, Mabel Vanscoy
Phares, Eugene W
Phares, Charles Wilson
Phares, Strader
Phares, Beatrice
Phares, Kathleen
Phares, Verdie
Phares, Emerson
Phares, Okey
Phelps, Susan Barbara
  Niedhammer
Phelps, Lynne Bommer
Phelps, Richard G.
Phelps, Travis Keith
Phelps, Frederick W.
Philibin, Thomas M.
Phillips, Jarolyn A. Judy
Phillips, Kenneth A.
Phillips, Carol A.
Phillips, Jeffrey A.
Phillips, Deborah Albright
Phillips, Logan Allen
Phillips, Myra Ann
Phillips, Tina B. Jones
Phillips, Hayward C.
Phillips, Harry C.
Phillips, Thomas C.
Phillips, Randall C.
Phillips, Ricardo Cortez
Phillips, James D.
Phillips, James D.
Phillips, James D.
Phillips, James Dale
Phillips, William David
Phillips, Frank E
Phillips, Marie E.
Phillips, Gary E.
Phillips, George E.
Phillips, Freda F.
Phillips, Elizabeth G. Arnold
Phillips, Robert G.

Pennington, Marlana Kathryn
Pennington, Vicki L. Baer
Pennington, Chasity Lynn
  Barkley
Phillips, James K.
Phillips, Brenda K.
Phillips, Heather Katlyn
Phillips, Mary L. Jackson
Phillips, Sandra L. Silvester
Phillips, Beverly L.
Phillips, Hilda L.
Phillips, William L.
Phillips, Eric L.
Phillips, Casey Lee
Phillips, Jenny Lou Nelson
Phillips, Kimberly Lynn
  Tucker
Phillips, Alice M. Burky
Phillips, William M.
Phillips, Sally M.
Phillips, Sarah M.
Phillips, Diane Melanie
Phillips, Eric Michael
Phillips, Sara Moore
Phillips, Dawn Noel Powell
Phillips, H. R.
Phillips, Glenn R.
Phillips, Ronald R.
Phillips, Peggy S.
Phillips, Karen S.
Phillips, Allen Stuart
Phillips, Leonor T. Vivas
Phillips, Virginia Tyre
Phillips, Beth W. Rice
Phillips, Eric W.
Phillips, Neal W.
Phillips, Betty Yvonne Morris
Phillips, Chester
Phillips, Corder
Phillips, R. Bryan
Phillips, Heather
Phillips-Simmons, Lisa Carol
Phipps, Ruth Randolph
Phipps, Paul W.
Pickard, John Bleecker
Pickard, Karyn M.
Pickering, David
Pickett, Shannon
Piechocki, Scott A.
Piechocki, Evelyn Carr
Piechocki, Christopher Scott

Petersen, David L.
Petersen, Niel P.
Petersen, Peggy S. Corcoran
Petersen, John
Pierre, Nicola Frances
  Boucaud
Pierron, Dominique S.
Pierson, Timothy J.
Pierson, Joan L. Castles
Pierson, Cynthia Lee Horton
Pifer, Lindsey Leah
Pifer, Charles
Pifer '19, Shasta Nicole
Pigan, Donald
Pigott, Luther G.
Pike, Elena Joyce
Pike, Bruce K.
Pike, John Urban
Pike, John W.
Pilat, William G.
Pill, John T.
Pillado, Austin Joseph
Pillai, Sharon Marlene Dalton
Pilloni, Richard
Pimentel, Jessica Renae
  Coombs
Pinckney, Ian Quinton
Pingley, Rebecca A.
Pingley, Cynthia B. Weeks
Pingley, James E.
Pingley, Gretchen Gould Jester
Pingley, Gladys H.
Pingley, David H.
Pingley, Sondra J. Knicely
Pingley, Mary Jo Vollmer
Pingley, Sandra L. Pastine
Pingley, Michael L.
Pingley, Karma S. Ventress
Pingley, Norman
Pinkham, James F.
Pino, Nicolas S.
Pinto, Michael A.
Piotrowski, Adam T.
Piper, Susan G. Prutzman
Piper, Linda Hall
Piper, James W.
Piper, Thomas
Pipher, Belinda
Pisarcik, Jason P.
Pishtey, Joseph J.
Pishtey, Wallace

Phares, James K.
Phares, Barbara L. Georgeson
Phares, Roy L.
Phares, Susan Lynn Camara
Pitt, Elizabeth Jane Chambliss
Pittman, Stephen V.
Pitzer, Charles A.
Pitzer, Judy A.
Pitzer, Vickie Lynn
Pivarnik, Gregory R
Pizzoferrato, Anthony
Planakis, Sarah Jayne
Plant, Richard L.
Plantier, Thomas C.
Plantz, Jessica Lynn
Plasse, Arnold S.
Plassenthal, Megan
Plath, Stephen R.
Platz, Barry B.
Platz, Constance M.
  VonHagen
Plaza, Michael P.
Pledger, Tajee Antoinette
Pledger, Lance Roland
Plemons, Charles E.
Plescia, Patricia A. Ginter
Pletcher, Nicole Wratchford
Plitt, Karl E.
Plum, Barbara A.
Plum, Susan Hazel Carter
Plum, Clinton Joe
Plumley, Christine L.
Plummer, Brandon Lee
Plummer, Carol Sue Weese
Plush, Courtney B.
Poe, Beth A.
Poe, Ronald E.
Poe, Charles I.
Poe, Penny L. See
Poe, Beulah M. Bartlet
Poe, Linda R. Gedraitis
Poessl, Sabrina
Pogrebniak, Alexander
Pohl, Anna C. Oler
Poindexter, James T.
Point, Gayle L. Massi
Poland, Michelle L. Sullivan
Poland, Matthew P.
Polce, Tracy L.
Polcen, Jane Frances
Polhemus, John E.

Poscover, Max
Posey, Calli Beth
Posey, Marilyn E.
Posey, Adam Vincent
Putnam, Christopher A.
Putnam, David E.
Putzulu, Margaret H
Pyecha, David M.
Pyles, Howard E.
Pyles, Victor J.
Pyles, Lena L. Ayers
Pyles, Donna Lambert
Quarles, Paul B.
Quattro, Dana M.
Queen, Eliza Hall
Queen, Jeannine R. Fazio
Queener, James Daniel
Quick, Heather A.
Quick, Mary L. Fisher
Quick, Jean Morrison
Quick, Edwin Taylor
Quick, Ralph
Quinn, Shelia Christine
Quinn, Thomas E.
Quinn, Joseph G.
Quinn, Josephine McCall
Quinn, Patrick N.
Quinn, Evangeline Smith
Quirk, Clarence A.
Qulfat, Saleh M.
Rabibhadana, Rabibungse
Racine, Leslie A. Shaffer
Racine, Christopher R.
Rackey, Brianna Nicole
Racz, George
Rada, Patricia Drummond
Rada, Joseph W.
Radabaugh, Nicole A.
  Harrison
Radcliffe, Grace K. Abbitt
Rader, Samantha Brooke
Rader, Gerlene L.
Rader, Alec M.
Rader, Melodee R. Serrett
Raeder, Joshua Jerome
Raese, J. Curtis
Raezer, George Lorenz
Raezer, Suzanne M. Cox
Raffa, Jessica Susan
Rafferty, Brenda
Ragan, Jonathan Matthew

Pratt, Rebecca Dawn Martin
Pratt, Tyler James
Pratt, Seth Thomas
Praul, Edward J.
Raich, David H.
Raines, David Branson
Raines, Ruth P.
Raines, Albert R.
Raines, Pamela
Raino, John P.
Rairigh, Gregg H.
Rajca, John D.
Rajchel, Denise D'Annunzio
Rakestraw, Roberta A.
Ralston, John N.
Ramage, Sharon C.
Rambo, Edward W.
Ramey, Aaron M.
Ramirez, Mayra
Ramos, Gloria Vidal
Ramsay, Cynthia Sohn Reed
Ramsdell, Kathryn Hall
  Dunbar
Ramsey, Tommy J.
Ramsey, Matthew Scott
Ranalli, Walter J.
Randolph, Caroline B.
Randolph, Brian F.
Randolph, Warren G.
Randolph, Joel
Rankin, Joshua Aaron
Ransome, Jesse J.
Ranson, Genevieve Harriett
  Landrum
Rao, George A.
Rao, Christopher J.
Rapp, Alison Jo Hood
Rapp, Byron L.
Rappaport, Richard J.
Rappaport, Frances Wanda
  Klauber
Raschella, Dorie A.
Raschella, Geraldine E.
Raschella, Pamela Earle
Rasch-Hegelund, Niklas
Rasmussen, Yousuf
Rasulis, Mary K. Shoemaker
Rasulis, William
Raszka, John A.
Ratcliff, Olivia Hudson
Rathell, Mary Victoria

Pritt, Donald R.
Pritt, Donald S.
Pritt, Thaddeus
Pritt, T. McClellan
Ray, Ronald G.
Ray, Sylvia L. Peterson
Ray, Timothy Mark
Raye, Christopher C.
Rayfield, Kelly Chenoweth
Rayfield, Amrit
Raymond, Carol A.
Raymond, Susan M.
Razakhatskaya, Maryna
  Viktor
Razzano, Robert M.
Reabe, Patricia A. Smith
Reade, Sally Pettit
Reagan, Susan R. Simmons
Reall, Patricia L. Pennington
Reall, Kirsten L.
Rease, Cleon W.
Rebinski, Christine E.
Rebrook, Jacqueline Kay
Rechholtz, Rosalie A. Weill
Rechholtz, Richard R.
Rechucher, Medawual
Recinos, Diane E. Mullin
Recinos, Edwin R.
Reckart, Jo Anna McVey
Recknor, Wayne A.
Recknor, Deborah K. Miller
Rector, Timothy Brett
Rector, James C.
Rector, Robin Camp
Rector, John E.
Rector, Harriett Hays Nicely
Rector, John J.
Rector, Margaret L. Cox
Rector, James M.
Rector, Robert R.
Rector-Triplett, Norma Jean
  Townsend
Reda, Juanita Pritt
Reda-Wilson, Kimberly J.
Redman, Michael D.
Redman, Lillian R.
Redman, Ann S. Martino
Redmon, Justin Blake
Ree, Brenda S. Thomas
Reece, Jacqueline E. Jones
Reece, Christopher Ryan

Purvis, Matthew R.
Puryear, Bronson L.
Pusanik, Melissa Rae
Pushkin, Katherine A.
Reed, Jesse F.
Reed, Murray K.
Reed, Janice L.
Reed, Donna Maiorino
Reed, Julie Marie
Reed, James T.
Reed, Brett W.
Reed, John Wayne
Reed, H. Kenneth
Reed, Kevin
Reed-Chambers, Matthew
Reeder, Susan A.
Reel, Chass Brandon
Reel, Cynthia Dawn
Reel, Tara Dawn
Reese, Mark L.
Reeves, Donald A.
Reeves, Donald E.
Reeves, Ronald J.
Regan, Jessica Henderson
Regent, Mario C.
Reger, Carol Ashby
Reger, Tammy Lynn
Rehrer, Marsha B.
Reich, Judith McColly
Reich, Suzanne Ososki
Reich, Robert R.
Reich, Robert William
Reichart, Deborah Pavlovic
Reid, George A.
Reid, Alfred L.
Reid, Warren R.
Reid, John R.
Reid, Charles W.
Reiders, Warren R.
Reif, Tamara L. Pugh
Reif, Benjamin Thomas
Reinauer, Gertrude Carolan
Reinauer, Thomas H.
Reinhold-Kirby, Judith L.
Reinknecht, Patricia A.
Reitz, Michael John
Reitz, Nancy L. Cobb
Remsburg, Robert Y.
Rencich, Debra Lynn
  Marlinghaus
Rener, Anna Buchanan

Paris
Rager, Trista Aileen Odessa
Ragos, Anthony Robert
Ragsdale, Velma
Renner, Julius C.
Renner, Eugene H.
Renner, Adrienne K.
Rennix, Anna E.
Rennix, Charles R.
Reno, Joseph D.
Renz, Mackenzie Rae
    Dameron
Renzelli, Maria Dawn
Repaci, Charles M.
Repair, Romaine F.
Repair, Elizabeth K.
Repair, Harold N.
Repka, Joseph
Reppert, Ryan Richardson
Reshey, Marilyn A. Wine
Respess, Robert C.
Respess, Carolyn Collett
Restrepo, Carlos A.
Reto, Geraldine H.
Reustle, Harry G.
Revell, Mary Frances
    Scudder
Revell, Thomas Robert
Reverol, Osman E.
Revitt, Michael S.
Rexroad, Charlotte I.
    Wagoner
Rexrode, Roy E.
Rexrode, Trista Lee
Rexrode, Jordan Paige
Rexrode, Ann Poling
Reyburn-Steele, Miriam
Reyes, Sheila Antolini
Reynolds, John B.
Reynolds, Amy D. Moore
Reynolds, Adelbert J.
Reynolds, Barbara L. Trickett
Reynolds, David L.
Reynolds, Arden M.
Reynolds, Gabrielle Maren
Reynolds, John W.
Reynolds, Leigh Ann
Rhee, Syngman
Rhett, E. Dylan
Rhim, Seoung T.
Rhodes, John D.

Rathman, Kristin Danielle
Ratzman, Samuel S.
Raupach, Sharon Harris
Raven, William B.
Rhodes, Rachel R. Blackburn
Rhodes, Lydia Rachelle
Rhodes, Barbara
Rhymer-Plantier, Susan G.
Ricart, Thomas Eric
Riccio, Roberta A.
Rice, Charles A.
Rice, William B.
Rice, Lawrence E.
Rice, Deborah Faith
Rice, William H.
Rice, Kari L. Grize
Rice, Donald L.
Rice, David L.
Rice, Donna L.
Rice, Jennifer L.
Rice, Kathleen M.
Rice, James M.
Rice, Jonathan M.
Rice, Jeffrey P.
Rice, Kathryn P.
Rice, Kimberly S.
Rice, June Vanlue Viquesney
Rice, Catherine Wolfe
Rice, Taft
Rice-Misuraco, Eva M.
    Brosious
Rich, Joseph A.
Rich, Jennifer Dawn Thomas
Rich, Susan E. McWilliams
Rich, April Marie McKenzie
Rich, Edward R.
Rich, Sherry Russell
Richard, Timothy D.
Richard, Rachel Elizabeth
Richard, Virda Jones
Richards, Karen A. Gallagher
Richards, Beth A.
Richards, Guy B.
Richards, Daniel B.
Richards, Kelsey Faye
Richards, Leah Fitzwater
Richards, Tammy Louise
    Wilfong
Richards, Herbert M.
Richards, Steven P.
Richards, Robert R.

Reed, Harry A.
Reed, Karen Bozic
Reed, Shannon Danielle
Reed, Rachel Elizabeth
Richards, Robert W.
Richardson, Debra Ann Gill
Richardson, Daniel D.
Richardson, Charles D.
Richardson, Joel Jesse
Richardson, James R.
Richison, Abbie Jo Lowther
Richman, Jenna Leigh Burnett
Richmond, Jordan Ashby
Richmond, Alyssa Kathryn
Richter, Sheila I. Beitzel
Richter, DeeAnna Jayne
Richtmeyer, Andrew
Ricigliano, Lorraine M.
Rickard, Pamela W. Ridge
Riddle, Leticia Ann
Riddle, Timothy Douglas
Riddle, Jesse H.
Riddle, William Robert
Rideout, Henry
Rider, Ryan Joseph
Rider, Margaret Sites
Ridgely, Owenta M. Biller
Ridgeway, Jenniffer Lee
Ridgeway, H. Dale
Ridgway, H. D.
Ridgway, Erika L.
Ridgway, Marlene Mae
Ridgway Haugen, Janet L.
Ridpath, Frank M.
Riffey, Sarah Lynne
Riffle, Sheila D.
Riffle, Marsha Jean Wayts
Riffle, Donna Lynn Smith
Riffle, Marsha W.
Rifkin, Sidney C.
Riggleman, Robin A. Hartman
Riggleman, Gwen Alison
    Fitzgerald
Riggleman, Peggy Ann
Riggleman, Debra J. Shockey
Riggleman, Esker L.
Riggleman, Ciara Nicole
Riggleman, Bethany Rae
    Richards
Riggleman, K. Todd
Riggs, Cheryl Darling Dunn

Renfrew, Betsy
Rengel, Neil A.
Renna, Richard J.
Renner, Edith Buck
Rightmire, Margaret R.
    Taylor
Rightmire, Frank R.
Rightmire, Charles R.
Rightmire, Maxine Reed
Riley, Valerie Azizpour
Riley, Stacey B.
Riley, Allison Brooke
Riley, James Eric
Riley, Kathleen M. Cummin
Riley, Sharon M. Schneide
Riley, Michael P.
Riley, Curtis P.
Riley, David W.
Rimmer, James Philip
Rinaldi, JoAnn
Rindone, Chris M.
Rinehart, Leigh Ann
Rinehart, Elizabeth D.
Rinehart, Gerald J.
Rinehart, Lois M.
Rinehart, M. Neil
Ringe, Edward G.
Ringer, Brian L.
Ringer, M. Wayne
Ringh, William E.
Ringler, Baron J.
Ringler, Ray
Rininger, Robert A.
Rininger, Mary J. Graham
Rinker, Connie J.
Rinko, Breanna Jean
Riordan, Michael
Ripley, Brett B.
Rippey, James L.
Rise, George Dallas
Rise, Louisa Gibbons Dav
Ristau, Ricky J.
Ritchen, Bernard C.
Ritchie, Shane Charles
Ritchie, Catherine
    Cherokee-Rose
Ritenhouse, Ernest J.
Rittenhouse, Samuel W.
Ritter, Mary Frances Bake
Rivera, Miguel A
Rivers, Julia Christine

Rhodes, Bayli Dawn Helmick
Rhodes, Lindsey Jo
Rhodes, Mary L. Bliss
Roach, Phyllis M. Grogg
Roane, Scott H.
Robb, Sarah Jean
Robbins, Katherine A. Harris
Robbins, Thomas Joseph
Robbins, Sarah Lynn
Robbins, William S.
Robbins, Jennifer
Robenolt, Maribeth I. Headley
Roberts, Lisa A. Moody
Roberts, Sarah A. Smith
Roberts, Sally A. Thompson
Roberts, Dee Anna
Roberts, Frank Arthur
Roberts, Nicole C. Groves
Roberts, Judith E. Myers
Roberts, David Elwin
Roberts, Ruby L.
Roberts, David L.
Roberts, David M.
Roberts, Margaret R. Kump
Roberts, Christopher Raymond
Roberts, Irene S.
Roberts, Walter S.
Roberts, Garland Sewell
Roberts, John W.
Robertson, George A.
Robertson, Sheila D.
Robertson, Richard M.
Robinette, Joshua L.
Robinson, Carol A.
Robinson, Deidre A.
Robinson, Roger A.
Robinson, Elizabeth A.
Robinson, Mabel Brandenburg
Robinson, John D.
Robinson, Wilson E.
Robinson, Paul G.
Robinson, Jodi J.
Robinson, Wanda L. Barney
Robinson, Helen L. Cutright
Robinson, Deborah L.
Robinson, Shari L.
Robinson, Belinda May

Richards, Michele T. McCabe
Richards, Susanne Underwood
Richards, Leslie W.
Robinson, Melinda R.
Robinson, Sherman S.
Robinson, Debora S.
Robinson, David W.
Robinson, Ira
Robinson, Jasmine
Robison, John Robert
Robl, Robert T.
Roboski, William Charles
Robson, Kenneth R.
Robson, Susan Scott
Robson, Betsey Towler
Roby, Genevieve Elizabeth Warner
Roby, Kelsie Evonn
Roby, Fred Harman
Rochkovsky, George
Rochovansky, Nancy A. Voldstad
Rock, John-Carlo
Rocke, Jeffrey D.
Rocker, Paul
Rodden, Marcea Copeland
Rodeheaver, Paul E.
Rodeheaver, Ashley Elizabeth
Rodeheaver, Sarah K.
Rodeheaver, Terri L.
Rodeheaver, Earl N.
Rodeheaver, Leona
Roderiques, Abel J.
Rodger, Lawrence C.
Rodger, Kristen D. Constable
Rodgers, George C.
Rodgers, Peter H.
Rodgers, James Hurd
Rodgers, Carol J. Martin
Rodgers, Gregory James
Rodgers, Sara Showalter
Rodgers, Lanette
Rodish, James E.
Rodriguez, Rosendo F.
Rodriguez, Jorge G.
Rodriguez, Wendy Sue Fox
Rodriguez, Ernesto
Rodriquez, Miguel Angel
Roemmelt, Sarah Catherine Hasbrouck

Riggsby, Lori A.
Riggsby, Michael D.
Right, Craig M.
Right, Lee
Rogers, Nancy F. Chenoweth
Rogers, Blake L.
Rogers, Darin Patrick
Rogers, Carla R. Lantz
Rogers, Marc R.
Rogers, Lee R.
Rogers, David Scott
Rogers, Belle Spencer
Rogers, Frank W.
Rohl, Karen T.
Rohr, Shanna Louise
Rohr, Betty Smith
Rohrbough, Wallace G.
Rohrbough, Danielle N. Davis
Rohrer, Linda M.
Rojaks, Augusta
Rojas, Horacio R.
Rokich, Kimberly A. Smith
Roland, Marguerite Cicale
Roland, Catherine L. Blalock
Rolenson, Amberly D.
Rolle, Candy Johnson
Rollins, Ronald Allen
Rollins, David Arden
Rollins, Glenn M.
Roltsch, Albert L.
Roman, Riccarla A. Hayton
Roman, Luis A.
Roman, Samantha Elizabeth
Roman, Vincent
Romas, Suzanne E. Moore
Rome, Nancy M. Ropke
Romero, Lisbel C.
Romine, Rebecca Geis
Romine, Linda L.
Romine, Alan R.
Romine, Laurie
Ronan, Joi Huffman
Rondinella, Oreste R.
Rooney, Vincent A.
Rooney, Sandra M. Smith
Roop, Nellie I.
Roos, Robert Craig
Roos, Sally Wolffer
Roperto, Gregory J.
Rosales, Ellen Garbart
Rosario, Raymond

Rizer, Diana L. Smith
Rizzio, Jessica R.
Rizzio, Mark S.
Rizzo, Christopher V.
Rose, Tiffany Anne
Rose, Kenneth H.
Rose, Jamie Lee
Rose, Kevin M.
Rose, Arvella Mae
Rose, Ira O. Greathouse
Rose, Jerad Ovis
Roselle, William B.
Roselle, Paul
Rosen, Carol Jo Kindel
Rosenberg, Joshua B.
Rosenberg, Karl J.
Rosenberger, Stephen C.
Rosenberger, George E.
Rosenberger, Lillian Harris
Rosenberger, Caroline J.
Rosencrance, Barbara A. Kepley
Rosencrance, Kaylee Brooke
Rosencrance, Lillian Kelly
Rosencrance, Carlton
Rosencrance, John
Rosencrance, LaDonna
Rosengrant, John A.
Rosenman, Abraham W.
Rosier, Shelby D.
Rosier, Wendy Danielle
Rosier, Dennis
Ross, Richard A.
Ross, Darlene C.
Ross, Samantha Dawn
Ross, Jason E.
Ross, Samuel F.
Ross, Doan G.
Ross, Evelyn Goode
Ross, James H.
Ross, Judy J. Deivernois
Ross, Grace J. Harris
Ross, Robert J.
Ross, Donald J.
Ross, Robin J.
Ross, Lenore Kathryn Harman
Ross, Cecil L.
Ross, Catharine Lynn
Ross, Sheila Marie Barrickman
Ross, Shanda Marie

Hinkle
Robinson, Brandon Michael
Robinson, Bert P.
Robinson, Barbara Pollitz
Ross, Mason W.
Ross, Joseph
Ross, Jacob
Ross, Mike
Ross, Cameron
Ross, Cameron
Rosser, June A. Collett
Rosser, Jay
Rossi, Benjamin Brown
   Bosworth
Rossi, Amelia C. Bosworth
Rossin, Stacey Parrino
Rossiter, Eleanor May
Rossman, Todd G.
Roth, Josephine A. Tucci
Roth, Rezena A.
Roth, Jane Anne Purvis
Roth, William C.
Roth, Alicia Carrie
Roth, Betty Louise Urffer
Roth, Howard M.
Roth, William
Rothenburgh, William
Rotondo, Susan B. Cramer
Roughton, Jeanne
Rounds, Susan Thomas
Roupe, Caroline J.
Row, Winifred L.
   Montgomery
Rowan, Mary E.
Rowan, Richard E.
Rowan, Richard E.
Rowan, Kenneth L.
Rowe, Patrick J.
Rowe, Linda Kovacs
Rowe, Edward M.
Rowe, Sarah M.
Rowe, Kurt S.
Rowen, Vic
Rowley, Donald C.
Rowsey, Samantha
Roy, Darlene A. Smith
Roy, Jennifer A.
Roy, Allen Bruce
Roy, Shirley C.
Roy, Richelle Dean
Roy, Grace E.

Roger, Robert S.
Rogers, Dean Crawford
Rogers, Jack D.
Rogers, Bonnie Ellen Little
Roy, Sharon Henline
Roy, Craig L.
Roy, Stephanie Ours
Roy, Jaqueline T.
Roy, Hicel Teter
Roy, Kenneth W.
Roy, Ethan Wayne
Roy, Arthur
Royce, Virginia A. Daft
Royce, Jennifer Nicole
Royce, Benjamin Wayne
Roy-Jolly, Patricia Louise
Royster, Dick Moore
Royster, Kay Woodward
Rubenstein, Howard
Ruble, Barbara D.
Rubright, Robert G.
Ruby, William H.
Ruckiat, Phaichit
Ruckman, F. Wilmer
Ruddle, Carolyn C.
Ruddle, Troy Colin
Ruddle, Betty Ellen Fletcher
Ruddle, Lucy Hott
Ruddle, Tracey Michelle
Ruddle, Joe Reed
Ruddle, Mary Lee
Rude, Mildred A. Basham
Rudiger, Mary L. Hesketh
Rudnick, Sandra-Jo Moore
Rudnick, Leonard Walter
Ruff, Dawn C. Deaner
Rule, Misty Dawn
Rumbach, Natalie P.
Rundberg, Carl
Runner, Elaine M.
Runner, Cheryl R.
Runner, W. Miles
Runner, Robert
Rupp, Elizabeth Ann Harper
Rupp, Amber N. Spencer
Ruppert, Thomas O.
Rura, Michael S.
Rusak, Ryan
Ruscello, Mark Thomas
Rusch, Evelyn Hamlin
Rush, Marshall F.

Rosario, Karin
Rose, Judith A. Weese
Rose, Devon Alexander
Rose, Lee Ann Holfelder
Rusiewicz, Robert S.
Russ, Melissa L. Burnett
Russell, Katherine Anne
Russell, Holly B. Woolwine
Russell, Robert C.
Russell, Ruth Hammill
Russell, Mark L.
Russell, Virginia Roberts
Russell, Donald S.
Russell, Grace
Russetti, Susan R.
Russo, Lindsay Elizabeth
Ruth, Cynthia W. Monday
Rutherford, Henry A.
Rutherford, Marjorie Bennett
Rutherford, LuElla Everett
Rutherford, William F.
Rutherford, Dawes
Rutigliano, Antonio
Rutter, Beth A. Peoples
Ruyak, James D.
Ruzicka, David J.
Ryall, Charles R.
Ryan, Karina Ann
Ryan, Kay Elyse Stover
Ryan, Michael F.
Ryan, Terrence R.
Ryan, Jacqueline Ridolfi
Ryan, Robert
Rybczynski, Robin Jo White
Ryder, Katelyn Marie
Ryder, Elizabeth Row
Ryman, Kathleen E. Mellon
Rymer, Helen D.
Rymniak, Charles
Rynkievich, Stewart W.
Ryon, Henry S.
Sabeh, Raymond
Sable, Carly Joan
Sabo, Ann Louise Chikos
Sackett, Robert V.
Sacks, Amanda Ann Poling
Saddler, Deborah Lynne
Sadeghian, Khosrow
Sader, Julianna Chenoweth
Sadowitz, Jerome S.
Saeed, Showikar H.

Ross, Steven P.
Ross, Nan R.
Ross, Tammy Roberta Mulson
Ross, William V.
Sainato, John J.
Sainato, Betty S. White
Saito, Hirokazu
Saldana, Mary E. Henry
Salem, Humaid M.
Salerno, Rebecca Ann May
Salerno, Brian J.
Salerno, Timothy L.
Salisbury, Elizabeth Anne
Salisbury, Hazel Chapman
Salisbury, William D.
Salkeld, Nancy Harrah
Salmon, Kurt M.
Saltis, Sandra Kay
Salvador Lopez, Pablo
Salzman, Roger E.
Samara, Rebecca S. Baller
Samarzich, Alex Lazar
Samelian, A. K.
Samiy, Aly E.
Sammon, Cynthia L. Boyd
Samms, Charity Joy
Samples, Megan Renee
Sampson, Rebecca L. Black
Sampson, Dana L.
Sampson, Zoe Paige
Sampson, Icy Shahan
Sampson, Kathleen White
Samson, Erica Lynn
Samu, Bonnie L.
Sanchez, Josue Arquimedes
Sanchez, Debra R. Cole
Sanchez, Cesareo
Sanda, Paulette Forrest Payne
Sandercock, Steve F.
Sandercock, Tara J. McKenzie
Sanders, Nancy A. Rogers
Sanders, Catherine Amores
Sanders, Christina Butch
Sanders, Scott H.
Sanders, Roger Lowell
Sanders, Shirley M.
Sanders, Wesley
Sanders, A. Nancy
Sanders, Skylar
Sandford, Gordon R.
Sandle, Patricia A. Phillips

Roy, Kenneth E.
Roy, Arthur G.
Roy, James H.
Roy, Carrie Harman
Sands, Timothy Mark
Sanford, Emmy Juhnke
Sanford, Annette M. Phillips
Sanford, Broc
Sanson, Danielle Dawn
   Westfall
Santamaria, Donald Frank
Santamaria, Maria Gertrude
   Erhard
Santello, Teresa L. Paugh
Santiago, Robert F.
Santmyer, Laura A. Billups
Santmyer, Faye Elbon
Santoro, Matthew
Santulli, Annmarie Theresa
Santurro, Sergio
Sanzari, John R.
Sapp, Teresa A.
Sapp, Mark O.
Sarber, Leona T. Price
Sarcona, John J.
Sarfino, Brian Gregory
Sargent, Barbara D.
Sargent, David L.
Sargo, Kimberly A. Holcomb
Sari, Andrew Michael
   Morata
Sarles, Steven W.
Sarmiento, Luis
Sarno, Ronald Jame
Sato, Mitsutoshi
Satterfield, Danielle
Satterwhite, Sarah Kathleen
Sattler, Richard W.
Sauchuk, William Joseph
Saucy, Devin Marie
Saul, Bradford Biddle
Saul, Barry I.
Saulais, Christophe Gerard
Sauls, Nancy A. Basile
Saunders, Kirk D.
Saunders, Stephen Daniel
Saunders, Frances I.
   Farrington
Saunders, Ken I.
Saunders, Lisa Miller
Saunders, Donna Shipman

Rush, Marshall F.
Rush, Barclay J.
Rush, David K.
Rush, Erma L. Grimes
Savage, Catherine S. Haines
Savage, Amanda
Saville, Sarah A.
Savory, Daniel James
Savoye, Stanley R.
Sawtell, Edward G.
Sawyer, Robert A.
Sawyer, Camille Esposito
Sawyer, George W.
Saxton, Harold Arthur
Sayre, Brian E.
Sayre, Vaughn V.
Sayre-Bahnsen, Constance
Scahill, Joyce
Scanlan, Angela Jean
   Musolino
Scannell, Karen E.
Scarberry, Whitney Ellen
   Grove
Scarberry, Serena Lynn
   Williams
Scarella, Robert J.
Scarfo, Rosie M.
Scarfo, Frank
Scavuzzo, Elizabeth Ann
   Krasemann
Scavuzzo, Christopher D.
Schaarschmidt, Emanuel L.
Schaber, Peter C.
Schabow, John W.
Schadewald, Charles A.
Schadewald, Natasha Anne
Schaefer, Steven C.
Schaefer, Kristen L. Zullinger
Schaefer, Ottie L.
Schaefermeyer, Lynne M.
   Snyder
Schaeffer, Lillian Elizabeth
   Wilcock
Schafer, Ruth Barbette
   Clement
Schafer, John Douglas
Schafer, Donald J.
Schafer, Tana R.
Schalm, Paul J.
Schattin, Robert
Scheck, Bradley J.

Saffle, Brittany A.
Saffle, Hannah Marie
Saia, Robert A.
Sain, Gary C.
Scheller, Walter J.
Schemering, Kristen Jane
Schempp, Dorothy Jean Smith
Scherer, Hubert L.
Scherich, Rebecca J.
Scherich, Eugene W.
Scherling, Karen D. Kauffman
Schick, Grayson Clark
Schilansky, Lilia
Schimpf, Karl D.
Schindel, Susan Dowds
Schindler, William
Schlechte, Anna R. Schott
Schleipman, Peter F.
Schlomer, Melinda J. Moll
Schlossareck, Laurie E.
Schmader, Barbara Barbour
Schmertzler, Henry R.
Schmidlen, Virginia Knutti
Schmidt, Arthur F.
Schmidt, Ronald H.
Schmidt, George J.
Schmidt, Michele L.
   Schranghamer
Schmidt, Laura M.
Schmidt, Dixie R.
   Bowser-Perando
Schmitt, John A.
Schmitzer, Douglas K.
Schmucker, Zachary Joseph
Schnabel, Bruce P.
Schnaufer, John M.
Schnebly, Sharon
Schneck, Patrick Carrigan
Schneider, Peggy Phillips
Schneider, Frank
Schoch, Kathleen
   Formanowski
Schoch, John J.
Schoen, Stephen G.
Schoettinger, Mary G. Patrick
Schoettinger, David G.
Schollenberger, David K.
Schollenberger, Daniel O.
Schollhammer, David J.
Scholz, Christopher Jude
Schoolcraft, Sue A.

Sandridge, Teresa Lynette
   Gainer
Sandridge, Leslie Olinda
Sands, Joni Marie Winans
Schoonover, Donna J.
   Lambert
Schoonover, George Kiess
Schoonover, Emma L.
   Crawford
Schoonover, Elizabeth Lacy
Schoonover, Mason Lea
Schoonover, Florence Marie
   Sayger
Schoonover, Susan R.
Schoonover, Bernice Seitz
Schoonover, Carl W.
Schoonover, Irl
Schramm, Rachel Nicole
Schreiber, Thomas E.
Schreiber, Sara Kade
Schreiner, Carissa Lauren
Schreurs, Blake A.
Schreurs, Barbara Christine
   Thelen
Schroeder, James A.
Schroeder, Michael S.
Schubert, Mary E. Posluszny
Schubert, Joseph G.
Schuck, Judy Lynn Mohler
Schuckert, Craig C.
Schueler, Ann M.
Schuesselin, Ken Leigh
Schulman, Michael
Schultheis, Marquel
Schultz, Susan M. Lapriore
Schulz, Carol Ann
Schumacher, Tom C.
Schumacher, Walter L.
Schumacher, Dona Virginia
   Collis
Schumann, Marie K.
Schumann, Edgar
Schupak, Jody W.
Schurg, Eugene
Schurman, Mary M.
Schutz, Virginia Wolfe
Schwab, Hannah Leigh
Schwartz, Sandra Adair Miller
Schwartz, Nancy J. Nolte
Schwartz, Lauren K.
Schwartz, Susan Marie

Sautter, L. James
Sauzer, Stacie M. Kirchner
Savage, Lorna Alan Dale
Savage, Steven S.
Schweikowsky, John
Schweinler, Kurt J.
Schwerdtfeger, Jacquelyn
  Sue Stubblefield
Sciara, Charles
Sclopis, Carmen M.
Scoggins, Robert B.
Scoggins '19, Jonathan
Scott, Virginia A. Long
Scott, Sarah A. Nethery
Scott, Brian Andrew
Scott, Stacy Ann
Scott, Robert B.
Scott, Elvie Beamer
Scott, Courtney Beth
Scott, Willis C.
Scott, Roger F.
Scott, Haley Faith
Scott, Maurice G.
Scott, Christian Garrett
Scott, Charlotte Gum
Scott, Robert H.
Scott, Robert I.
Scott, Linda J. Kane
Scott, Katherine K. Barkley
Scott, Jesse L.
Scott, Dorothy L.
Scott, Millie L.
Scott, Barry Lee
Scott, Marie Long
Scott, Ruth P. Cunningham
Scott, William R.
Scott, Harry R.
Scott, George R.
Scott, Gary R.
Scott, Cynthia Reilly
Scott, Christiana Renee
Scott, Allyson Rizzio
Scott, George W.
Scott, Glenn
Scott, Wayne
Scott, Amber
Scott-Calor, Mary Beth
Scowcroft, Carl
Scully, Daniel W.
Seabolt, Tina Marie
Seago, Kyle Preston

Scheffler, Gerald F.
Scheifly, Luke C.
Schell, Beverly D.
Schell, Vicki J.
Sears, Jennifer Leigh Pell
Sears, Tiffany Marie
Seat, Marie Kisner
Seate, Blanche L. Ferguson
Seaton, Howard B.
Seaton, Anthony Michael
Seaver, Katherine R.
Sebolt, Scott A.
Sechler, Hunter Gordon
Sechrengost, David
Secor, Scott Harold
See, Deborah A. Baer
See, Jeffrey A.
See, Chad E.
See, Cheryl Jo Swecker
See, Samantha Jo
See, Ernest L.
See, Raymond W.
See, E. Lorentz
Seel, Emily K.
Seelinger, Dorothy Campolio
Seem, Robert P.
Seetoo, Thomas B.
Seger, Dennis E.
Seibert, Machelle L. Moore
Seidhoff, John A.
Seigfried, Colby Allan
Sekiguchi, Hirono Ishikawa
Selders, Tiffany Rivers Taylor
Seldomridge, Gary A.
Selert, Jessica J. Polak
Self, Kelsey Ann
Self, Judy Lynn Turnage
Selger, Donald E.
Selleck, Ethan Arthur
Selleck, Lindsey
Sellers, William H.
Sellers, Brandon Terry
Sellick, John L.
Semendinger, David H.
Semendinger, Della Mae Pope
Semendinger, Paul R.
Semler, James W.
Semones, Veda L.
Sendling, Casey Nichole
  Marsh
Sendling, Charles

Schoonover, Todd A.
Schoonover, Jacob Allen
Schoonover, Jerry D.
Schoonover, Heidi Janeen
Sening, Erich Stefan
Senne, Arthur M.
Senseney, Martha E.
Serafini, Amanda G.
Serback, Alexis
Sermo, Mary Jo
Serna-Cortes, Alfredo
Servies, John W.
Sessoms, Lincoln
Setar, Charles
Setler, Glenda M. Witek
Setterstrom, Tork R.
Severino, Rebecca Hastings
Sevik, Paul C.
Seville, Pamela E. Berg
Seward, Ella Mae Strader
  Bryant
Sexton, Jessica Caroline Moats
Seybolt, Richard C.
Shackelford, Juliann Noel
Shackleford, Glenn
Shaffer, Mary A. Cutright
Shaffer, Michael A.
Shaffer, Stacey Brook Lewis
Shaffer, Mary Elizabeth
Shaffer, Mary Frances
Shaffer, Melanie I.
Shaffer, Earl J.
Shaffer, Robert J.
Shaffer, Kenneth J.
Shaffer, Robert Lee
Shaffer, Samantha Lin
  Bundock
Shaffer, Effie M. Humphrey
Shaffer, Linda M.
Shaffer, Nicole M.
Shaffer, Kelley Marie
Shaffer, Ashley Renae
  Cunningham
Shaffer, Howard W.
Shaffer, Thomas
Shaffer, Jennifer
Shaffer, Stephanie
Shafman-Shreve, Amiee
Shahan, Vernon A.
Shahan, James B.
Shahan, Donald B.

  Heidler
Schwartz, Jordan S.
Schwartz, Doug
Schwartzman, Michael J.
Shahan, Barbara
Shallcross, William
Shalloo, Matthew G.
Shamansky, Paul R.
Shamble, Elizabeth
  Alessandro
Shamble, David Michael
Shampine, Leah
Shanabarger, Eileen Arboga
Shanabarger, Mike D.
Shanahan, Paul H.
Shanahan, John V.
Shand, Terry P.
Shank, Nancy C. Bowen
Shank, Autumn Dawn
Shank, Thomas
Shantz, Leslie Ann
Shapiro, Sarah S. Kunzle
Shapiro, Robert T.
Sharitz, Raymond Thomas
Sharp, George Addison
Sharp, Mabel Belle
Sharp, Mary E. Guire
Sharp, Thomas E.
Sharp, Ricky Icen
Sharp, Tonyia J. Hicks
Sharp, Chasity Lynn Simmo
Sharp, Lisa Marie
Sharp, Kathleen McNeal
Sharp, Whitney Nicole
Sharp, Jane Price
Sharp, Aaron Thomas
Sharp, Brenda
Sharpes, Lila Sue
Sharpless, Louise Brownin
Shastri, Lalitha P.
Shastri, Prem
Shattuck, Ella V. Hockenber
Shaver, Mark A.
Shaver, Tara Renea Thorpe
Shaw, Cynthia A. Wargo
Shaw, Peggy L. Sherman
Shaw, Robert L.
Shaw, Harriet Martin
Shaw, Ronda Ruth Mastor
  (Dornon)
Shaw, Richard

Seal, Jason C.
Seal, Martha L.
Seals, Danielle Vacca
Seaman, Barbara Cox
Shea, Robert P.
Sheakley, Edward A.
Shean, Laura K.
Shear, Heather R.
Shearer, Carmel Lynn
Shears, Patty L.
Shears, Christy
Sheedy, Michael J.
Sheeler, Risa Ruth
Sheenan, Marie B. Polyak
Sheets, Leslie Ann Rexrode
Sheets, Richard C.
Sheets, Forrest D.
Sheets, Paul D.
Sheets, Johnny L.
Shelden, Meagan Hope
Sheldon, Thomas K.
Shelton, Laura Jo Corley
Shelton, Sharon K.
Shelton, Harry L.
Shelton, Sharon Lynn
    Kalbaugh
Shelton, Judith Lynn
Shelton, Sarah Nicole
Shelton, Roger V.
Shelton, Kathryn Watring
Shennard, Lori Jean Nem
Shepard, Norman E.
Shepard, Haley Nicole
Shepard, Rebecca R.
Shepherd, Mary A. Powell
Shepherd, Scott R.
Shepler, Fred C.
Shepler, Bryan Sterling
Sheppard, Thomas F.
Sheppard, Michael L.
Sheppo, Michael G.
Sheppo, Karen Sue Groves
Sheridan, Jennifer Grassman
Sherline, Lee B.
Sherman, Paul D.
Sherman, Melinda Leigh
Sheron, David William
    Puckett
Sherrard, Kalee Laign
Sherrill, Nelson B.
Sherrill, Adrienne M.

Senefe, Nurgul
Senic, April Lynn George
Senic, Lisa M. Hedrick
Senic, Shane
Shesler, Albert T.
Shestak, Joan C.
Shibuya, Hiromi
Shields, David Cameron
Shields, David E.
Shields, Mary Lou Sechrist
Shields, James Nelson
Shields, Hamilton R.
Shields '21, Sadie Rose
Shifflett, Susan E. Meckley
Shifflett, Jennie L. Bennett
Shifflett, Kristy Leah
Shiflet, Justin Allen
Shiflet, Casandra Anne
    Wallace
Shiflet, Shirley Joy Fox
Shiflet, Donald
Shiflett, Ritchie D.
Shiflett, Nathan D.
Shiflett, Linda Jean
Shiflett, Matthew Keith
Shiflett, Eric L.
Shiflett, Nicole Lyn
Shiflett, Katelyn Marie Harris
Shiflett, Hannah Rose
Shiflett, Edward
Shigeta, Hiroki
Shillingburg, Linda Louann
Shimbo, Nicola M.
Shimizu, Miki
Shimp, Cheryl A. Miller
Shimp, Randall L.
Shinaberry, April L.
Shinaberry, Rebecca Mewha
Shine, Misti Dawn Sherman
Shinkowski, Jennifer Lynne
    Patterson
Shinn, Jerry
Shipley, Ronald A.
Shipley, Roger Francis
Shipman, Jennifer Ann
    Fortney
Shipman, Cathryn J. Sutton
Shipman, John P.
Shipp, Naola Hart
Shipp, Joseph L.
Shirao, Yoshie

Shahan, Michael E.
Shahan, Courtney L.
Shahan, Robert Leon
Shahan, Shawn P.
Shockey, Sierra Brooke
    Thorne
Shockey, Dale E.
Shoemaker, Paul B.
Shoemaker, Chad E.
Shoemaker, Herman Glenn
Shohov, Panteleymon
Shoji, Chie
Shollenberger, Brian S.
Shomo, Stark A.
Shomo, Robert Jospeh
Shomo, Eldon
Shore, Robin K.
Shorr, D. Terry
Short, Rebekah Etter
Short, Jennifer J.
Short, Steven M.
Shott, Alexandra Holbrook
Shough, Kimberly Ann
Showalter, William D.
Showalter, Kimberly Lynn
    Simmons
Showen, Charles R.
Shrader, Bonnie R.
Shrader, Courtney
Shreve, Oid Davis
Shreve, Clarissa Dawn
Shreve, Richard E.
Shreve, Tyler Joseph
Shreve, Emily Mae
Shreve, Autumn Marie
Shreve, Jaime Marie
Shreve, Laco R.
Shreve, Tammy Sue Sheets
Shreve, J. W.
Shreve, Miranda
Shreve, Brett
Shreve, Chantel
Shriver, Catherine F
Shriver, Danielle Leah Oates
Shriver, Laura Massi
Shropshire, Bonnie Lee Cain
Shryock, Hillary P. Cederberg
Shryock, Richard W.
Shue, Michael E.
Shue, Ethan
Shugarts, Wendy S.

Shawareb, Tony M.
Shawver, Darlene Shortridge
Shay, Thaddeus D.
Shay, Andrew D.
Shumate, Patricia Elizabeth
    Canelon
Shumway, Christine Kesling
Shumway, Douglas
Shupp, Brenda L. Schoonover
Shupp, Carrie Lynn
Shurling, Emma F. Harsh
Shurow, Ashley N.
Sibley, Eric Vincent
Sibley, Scott
Sicca, Derek Edward
Sidwell, E. C.
Sidwell, Christian
Siedhoff, John A.
Siedhoff, C. H.
Siehler, Richard T.
Siertl, Nancy C. Keiss
Siertl, Hans C.
Sigety, Sharon E. Duggan
Sigety, Elmer J.
Sigley, Mariam D.
Sigley, Carmen Georgeta
Sigley, Johna L.
Sigley, Michelle Lynn Stump
Sigley, Rick
Sigurdsson, Laura L. Weinert
Sigurdsson, Stefan O.
Silberman, Benno
Silbert, Dorothy Ann
Silcosky, Donald N.
Silcox, James J.
Siler, Wanda M.
Siler, Sue Ellen
Silva, Milagro Azucena
Silva, Christopher Kirk
Silverman, Carol Bateman
Silverman, Stanley G.
Silverman, Jay Jeffrey
Silverthorn, David R.
Silvester, Bridget A.
    Chenoweth
Silvester, Kimberly A.
Silvester, Tony
Simcoe, Alison L.
Simcoe, June Marion
Simione, David A.
Simkins, Robin Rowe

Spencer
Sherwood, Ronald A.
Sherwood, Robert J.
Sherwood, Anthony
Simmons, Virginia C. Rast
Simmons, James C.
Simmons, Wallace D.
Simmons, Kayla Dawn
Simmons, Jennifer E.
    Swanson
Simmons, Clarence E.
Simmons, William E.
Simmons, Robert H.
Simmons, Cynthia L. Price
Simmons, Richard L.
Simmons, Delores L.
Simmons, Anita Lee
Simmons, Lynn Marie
    Thomas
Simmons, Ginny Marie
Simmons, Sandra McQuain
Simmons, Deidre N. Painter
Simmons, Eugene N.
Simmons, Richard P.
Simmons, Thomas P.
Simmons, Charles R.
Simmons, Ian Scott
Simmons, James Thomas
Simmons, Brenda
Simmons, Karen
Simms, Richard A.
Simms, David A.
Simms, Oliver J.
Simon, Elise Clara Marie
Simon, Gail H. Sneddon
Simon, Jonathan M.
Simon, Michelle R.
Simon, Jewell Ware
Simoncic, John S.
Simone, Samantha L.
Simonin, Jerry
Simons, Betsy Dianne
Simons, Crystal Jean
Simons, Ariel Shannon White
Simpkins, Bradford L.
Simpson, John B.
Simpson, Norma B.
Simpson, Edward H.
Simpson, Harper Jay
Simpson, Willa Jean Coberly
Simpson, Andrew M.

Shirey, Burton B.
Shirk, Jeffrey D.
Shirk, Sheila McGrath
Shirley, Christine M.
Simpson, Lisa
Simpson '19, Kevin Alfonso
Sims, Michael A.
Sims, Teresa L.
Sinclair, Rebecca Ruth
Sindicich, Jeffrey D.
Sindy, Bethany E.
Sine, Terry S.
Sines, Earl B.
Sines, Stephen G.
Sines, Tiffanie L.
Sines, Donna M.
Sines, Jon Russell
Singleton, Thomas A.
Sinisgalli, Anton A.
Sinkule, Ronald
Sions, Michael Bradley
Sions, Bridget Danielle Ours
Sipe, Natosha L.
Sisco, Gerald A.
Sisk, Dakota Shae
Sisler, Jennifer D.
Sisler, Kristy Lynn
Sisley, Alisa D. Rohrbough
Sisman, Warren R.
Sisson, Jon E.
Sisson, Danielle L Varner
Sisson, Ronda Lea
Sites, Harlan B.
Sites, Ryan Beth Cooper
Sites, Rubie C. Mallow
Sites, Jerrena D. Thompson
Sites, Gene H.
Sites, Linda J.
Sites, Elwood N.
Sites, Christopher P.
Sites, Sandra S.
Sites, Holly W.
Sittler, Richard E.
Sitton, Jontasia Dawn
Siva, Nicole Jane Armstrong
Sizemore, Stephanie Jayne
    Hammons
Sizemore, Edward S.
Sjoman, Ashley Lisa
Skaff, Amy L. Silvers
Skala, Lois Bennett

Shull, Peter L.
Shumaker, Frank M.
Shuman, Victoria Dawn
Shuman, Betty L.
Skidmore, Jonnie Ann Lane
Skidmore, Ernest C.
Skidmore, James C.
Skidmore, Charles Gerald
Skidmore, Eleanor J. Roy
Skidmore, Carol J.
Skidmore, Keith L.
Skidmore, Ronald L.
Skidmore, Sara Paige
Skidmore, Karen Porterfield
Skidmore, Pauline White
Skimore, Lenny D.
Skinner, Joyce Click
Skinner, William J.
Skinner, Jennings R.
Skinner, Sonja Sahar
Skipper, Renee Marie Grove
Sklan, Dorothea E. Crecraft
Skon, Kathleen McDonald
Skon, James S.
Skrastad, Norman
Skuder, William B.
Skuhrovec, Todd A.
Skvarka, Paul A.
Sladecek, Kelly J.
Slagle, Glenda C. Sharp
Slater, Tracy A.
Slater, Raymond E.
Slater, Margaret K.
Slater, Andrew P.
Slatton, Sarah Elizabeth
Slaubaugh, Jolena Michelle
Slaubaugh, Ethan Wayne
Slaughter, Julia Ann Reed
Slaughter, Bethany Rose
Slavin, Esther D. Dobbins
Slayton, James R.
Sleeman, James A.
Sleeman, William T.
Slifer, Gerald
Slifko, Daniel Phillip
Slipakoff, Jay H.
Sloan, Mary G. Ward
Slockbower, Robert C.
Slocum, Donald H.
Slocum, John R.
Slorah, John B.

Simkins, Wayne
Simmons, Steven A.
Simmons, Marc A.
Simmons, Susan Ann House
Sluijmer-Woodworth, Nancy
    Woodworth
Slupe, Frank L.
Slusser, Mary H. Duckworth
Sluyter, Mark C.
Smail, Julia L. White
Small, Jessica Caitlyn
Small, Brandi
Smallwood, James D.
Smarr, Janet L. Gould
Smarra, Alexa Nicole
Smart, David M.
Smart, Leigh M.
Smatana, Richard P.
Smetanick, Ann J. Ross
Smetanick, Patrick J.
Smidinger, Max E.
Smiecinski, Ralph F.
Smiley, Robert S.
Smiley, John William
Smith, Lauren A. Barger
Smith, Gerald A.
Smith, Brendan A.
Smith, George A.
Smith, Judith A.
Smith, Hillis A.
Smith, Caitlyn Amy
Smith, Megan Armstrong
Smith, Louise B.
Smith, Matthew B.
Smith, Philip B.
Smith, Taleah Belford
Smith, Carolyn Beth
    Cunningham
Smith, Rita C. Peoples
Smith, Grace C.
Smith, Sidney C.
Smith, Walter C.
Smith, Elaine Caplinger
Smith, Valerie Carty
Smith, Dorothy Chenoweth
Smith, Alice D. Degler
Smith, Newton D.
Smith, Stephen D.
Smith, Ryan D.
Smith, Douglas D. C.
Smith, Rebecca Danielle

Simpson, Barbara Reid
Simpson, Robert W.
Simpson, Joyce Ziman
Simpson, Robert
Smith, Martha E. Godwin
Smith, Lynda E. Wright
Smith, Alfred E.
Smith, Larry E.
Smith, Michael E.
Smith, Norma E.
Smith, Mary E.
Smith, Vincent E.
Smith, Amee Elisabeth
Smith, Stacey Elizabeth
Smith, Holly Elizabeth
Smith, Jerry Eugene
Smith, Mariwyn Faith
  McClain
Smith, Sherwood Finley
Smith, Dorsey G.
Smith, Robert G.
Smith, Jeffery G.
Smith, Larry Gail
Smith, Dena Giompalo
Smith, Joe H.
Smith, Timothy H.
Smith, Charles H.
Smith, Margaret Hedgecock
Smith, Andrew Holt
Smith, Adam Hunter
Smith, Charles I
Smith, Hardinge Inloes
Smith, Carolyn J.
Smith, Richard J.
Smith, Kelly J.
Smith, Anita K. Jones
Smith, Alan K.
Smith, Sandra Kay Wilfong
Smith, Richard Kimball
Smith, Marjorie Knight
Smith, Bessie L. Ammons
Smith, Janet L. Johnson
Smith, Phyllis L. Shirkey
Smith, Nancy L. Thomas
Smith, Robert L.
Smith, Robert L.
Smith, Wilton L.
Smith, Terry L.
Smith, James L.
Smith, Terri L.
Smith, Teresa L.

Skala, Donald J.
Skeeter, Darrell E.
Skerbetz, David A.
Skidmore, Kristie A. Bennett
Smith, Nicholas Lee
Smith, Samantha Lee
Smith, Luceba Long
Smith, Christine Lynn
Smith, Loretta Lynn
Smith, Linda M. Burky
Smith, Mary M. Sellers
Smith, Charles M.
Smith, Elizabeth M.
Smith, Inez M.
Smith, John M.
Smith, Stacy M.
Smith, Kevin M.
Smith, Jeana M.
Smith, Teresa Marie Webster
Smith, Betsie Marie
Smith, Marion Marston
Smith, Linda Massey
Smith, Samantha Metheny
Smith, Valerie Michele
Smith, Jill Michelle Gidel
Smith, Ashleigh Michelle
Smith, Ellen Mills
Smith, Alexis Morgan
Smith, Daniel Nathan
Smith, Kelly Nicole
Smith, Briana Nicole
Smith, Heidi P. Wehr
Smith, Alecia R. Stout
Smith, James R.
Smith, Robert R.
Smith, Terry R.
Smith, Paul R.
Smith, Alan R.
Smith, Jan R.
Smith, Robert R.
Smith, Diana R.
Smith, Theodore R.
Smith, Jacqueline Ramona
Smith, Linda S. Lambert
Smith, Richard S.
Smith, George S.
Smith, William S.
Smith, Catherine Snyder
Smith, Colin T.
Smith, Mariah Taylor Marie
Smith, Jakob Tyler

Slorah, Patricia Perkins
Slota, Eugene S.
Slotnick, Ruth C.

Smith, Edgar
Smith, Elijah
Smith, Marner
Smith, Rilla
Smith, Carlton
Smith, James
Smith, Peggy
Smith, Robin
Smith, D. Mark
Smith, Anne
Smith, Lora
Smith, Lyle
Smith, Kayla
Smith, Tim
Smith, Rodanne
Smith, Jared
Smith, Donna
Smith, Breanna
Smith, Erica
Smith-Cordingly, Sandra J.
Smithers, Krystal K. Warden
Smithson, Crystal Lewis
Smithson, Joshua Robert
Smits, Edward John
Smoes, Carolyn Roberts
Smoley, Jonathan William
Smolski, Elizabeth Anne
Smoot, Haley Anne
Smoot, Ryan C.
Smouse, Betty M.
Smucker, Benjamin E.
Smyth, Anita Norton
Smyth, William
Snead, Heather Michelle
Sneberger, Mark A.
Sneberger, John J.
Snedegar, Nunley B.
Snedegar, Martha Bogue
Snedegar, Paul
Snedeker, Amy J.
Snell, James W.
Snelson, Reta J.
Snelson, Obed J.
Snelson, Andrew L.
Snelson, Helen Wamsley
Snelson, Marilyn Winn
Snelson, Eva Wood

Smith, Miranda Dawn
Smith, MacKinzie Diane
Smith, Elizabeth E. Boniface
Smith, Carole E. Crider
Snider, Jessica Rayne
Snider, Marsha
Snoderly, Allison Louise
Snodgrass, Richard D.
Snodgrass, June Hines
Snodgrass, Charlene Tyre
Snorr, David T.
Snow, Bennett E.
Snyder, Elizabeth A. Buckius
Snyder, Ray A.
Snyder, Arlene B. Campbell
Snyder, William B.
Snyder, Sara Beth McCoy
Snyder, Irene Burky
Snyder, Erma C.
Snyder, Richard Davis
Snyder, Lisa Dawn
Snyder, Mary E. Cox
Snyder, Harry E.
Snyder, Dottie G.
Snyder, Connie H. Warner
Snyder, David H.
Snyder, Carol J. Swecker
Snyder, Benny J.
Snyder, Hannah Jordan
Snyder, Karen L. Petersen
Snyder, Amy L.
Snyder, Jennifer L.
Snyder, Kirk L.
Snyder, Denise M.
Snyder, Haley Marcia-Ann
Snyder, Alisa Marie
Snyder, Hannah Palmer
Snyder, Bryan Patrick
Snyder, Zachary Scott
Snyder, Ann Stanley
Snyder, Norma V.
Snyder, Craig W.
Snyder, Verl
Sobolewski, Susan O'Donnell
Sodergreen, Margery
  Edwards
Sokolinsky, Mark R.
Solari, Brandon J.
Soler, Ricardo
Soliday, Theodore D.
Soliday, Junius T.

Smith, Renee L.
Smith, Gina L.
Smith, Robert L.
Smith, Sherri Lea
Soltis, Alina Michelle
Soly, Peter E.
Soly, Kristine L.
Sombongse, Akechart
Somers, Donna E. Forinash
Somerville, Thomas W.
Sommer, Robert P.
Sommer, Robert Philip
Sommer, Charlotte
Son, Jae Jin
Songer, Iris J.
Soper, Ruth Landrum
Soriano, Kathern M. Hill
Soriano, Robert
Sostre, Richard
Souders, Tobias
Souren, Lee T.
Sours, Mari Cathern
Soussan, Andre Max
South, Walter M.
Souvannaphan, Kimberly
  Richardson
Sow, Shayna La Jane Dodd
Sow, Aliou
Sowards, Abigail Cameron
Sowers, David A.
Spade, Christopher Eugene
Spagnoletti, Brian T.
Spahr, Donald E.
Spangler, Brittany Amber
Spann, Michael F.
Spark, Diane L. Kassai
Sparks, Hillary Louise
Sparks, Derek Paul
Spaulding, Judith L.
Spaur, Evelyn G. Frame
Speaker, Juanita Kitay
Spear, Carla Louise
Spears, Julie A. Hillyard
Spears, Kathryn Renee
  Kitzmiller
Specht, Carol J. Anderson
Specht, David
Spector, Donna Raasch
Speh, William H.
Speicher, Harper H.
Speilman, Burge L.

Smith, Howard W.
Smith, Richard W.
Smith, Malcolm W.
Smith, Calette W.
Spencer, Beth Palausky
Spencer, Cynthia R.
Spencer, James S.
Spencer, Carolyn S.
Spering, Jennifer G. Ambrose
Spering, James
Spicer, Donald E.
Spicer, Arlen G.
Spies, Clifford Jack
Spiggle, Isabel C. Eshelman
Spine, Janet S. Galeota
Spino, William Anthony
Spitalsky, Sandra
Spitsnaugle, Tristram Ryan
Spivey, Kim R.
Spivey, C. B.
Spoerl, Richard T.
Sponaugle, Danielle Bible
Sponaugle, Steven D.
Sponaugle, Lela L.
Sponaugle, Kandice Lee
Sponaugle, Steven P.
Sporn, Max
Sprague, Hanora Nichols
Sprenkle, Jack
Spring, Richard L.
Springer, Debora Lynne
Sprinkle, Wesley James
Sproles, Jane Lee
Sprouse, Joanne C. Perkins
Sprouse, Connie M.
Squires, Joshua Matthew
Squires, Thomas
Squyres, Ellen Jenkins
Squyres, Madeline Robinson
Srisupa, Brenda M. Hornick
St. Clair, Dorsey Diane
St. Hilaire, Stephanie M
St. Lawrence, Alice Wolf
Staab, Rosemary A.
Staack, David R.
Stack, Richard J.
Stack, Joseph James
Stacy, Dorothy Steele
Staerz, Tim
Stafford, Margaret C.
Stager, Megen Edack

Snelson, Alonzo
Snider, Mary Josephine Poe
Snider, Nancy K. Coberly
Snider, Mary P.
Stakey, Kathleen A.
Stala, Thomas
Staley, Donald Ray
Stallard, Margaret D.
  Davidson
Stalnaker, Harold B.
Stalnaker, John B.
Stalnaker, Kathryn D. Kiess
Stalnaker, Vilas D.
Stalnaker, George D.
Stalnaker, Kimberly D.
Stalnaker, Gleda D.
Stalnaker, Shelby Danielle
Stalnaker, Jacqueline Dawn
Stalnaker, Austin E.
Stalnaker, Kenn E.
Stalnaker, Hannah Elizabeth
Stalnaker, Barbara G.
Stalnaker, Jenna Gilmore
Stalnaker, Ricky I.
Stalnaker, Ana Isabel Moreno
Stalnaker, Matthew Jack
Stalnaker, Alexander L.
Stalnaker, Katie Marie
Stalnaker, Charles N.
Stalnaker, Fonso Overton
Stalnaker, Norma P.
  Daetwyler
Stalnaker, Gertrude Parsons
Stalnaker, James W.
Stalnaker, Cameron
Stalnaker, Icie
Stalnaker, Harold
Stalnaker, Ariana
Stalnaker, Hilary
Standel, Charles
Stanfield, Patricia Baker
Stanford, Savannah Ann
Stanley, Jonathan David
Stanley, Margaret L. MacVean
Stanley, Kenneth M.
Stanley, Paul W.
Stansberry, Dylan Howard
Stanton, Rosalie J.
Stanton, Donna M.
Starcher, Catherine Adams
Starcher, Steven Allen

Solomon, Therese Bonasso
Solomon, Rachel C. Belch
Solon, Leona H.
Solter, Diana N.
Stark, Anthony J.
Stark, Stephanie L.
Stark, Louis William
Starkey, Peggy Ann Knigh
Starr, Robert L.
Starr, Jessica
Startt, Wayne E.
Startzel, David A.
Stasse, Edwin F.
Staten, Kathleen E.
Stathers, Ruby Marie
Stathopulos, William
Staton, Theresa Lehman
Stauffer, Robin L.
Steakley, Betty F. Polhemu
Stedman, Susan L.
Steel, James C.
Steele, Harney A.
Steele, Robert C.
Steele, Donna D. Mustach
Steele, Jill R. Mazzei
Steele, Brandon Sean
Steele, Hazel Tracy
Steelman, Peggy Hamilton
Steelman, James N.
Steen, James T.
Steen, James
Steensland, Blaine E.
Steensland, Wendy Mills
Steerman, Travis
Steerman-Brake, Edie L.
Steever, Anna L.
Steffens, Richard George
Steffens, Kenneth W.
Steffick, Betty Coffman
Stehle, Meaghan Elaine Eyl
Steiger, Laura Ann Kahn
Stein, Carlos Armando
Stein, John H.
Stein, John O.
Stein, Connie Sue Nofsing
Stein, Robert W.
Steinberg, William D.
Steinbrecher, Henry W.
Steindler, Robert M.
Steindler, Jean Phares
Steindler, Mary Wanless

Spence, Catherine Ann Meyers
Spence, Ian M.
Spence, Gregg S.
Stem, Anna Marie
Stemple, James C.
Stemple, Twyla D.
Stemple, Alan D.
Stemple, Kelly I. Smith
Stemple, Dorothy Jean Mollohan
Stemple, Dorothy M. Phares
Stemple, Danny R.
Stemple Hinchman, Sharon Lee
Stepaniak, Raymond
Stephens, Paula Fromhart
Stephens, Joyce Helene Houser
Stephens, Margaret Meredith
Stephenson, Lucius H.
Stephenson, Todd L.
Stephenson, Taylor
Sterling, Wallace L.
Stern, Joan Raye Montgomery
Steuer, Camilo
Stevens, Peter Bartlett
Stevens, Lois Bogardus
Stevens, Andrea D.
Stevens, W. I.
Stevens, Marcella Jane McDonnell
Stevens, Ronald W.
Stevens, Adam
Stevenson, Kiara Taj'ala
Stevenson, Helen
Stewart, Kara B. Anderson
Stewart, Judith Brown
Stewart, Allen D.
Stewart, Jesse J.
Stewart, Joan L. Harris
Stewart, David L.
Stewart, Anna M. Roth
Stewart, Ross Matthew Thomas
Stewart, Robert Murphy
Stewart, Tessa Rae
Stewart, Robert Scot
Steyer, Erika Marie
Stibravy, John A.

Stahl, Paula J. Nelson
Stahl, Gregory R.
Stahle, Julie Ann Noble
Stahle, Dale C.
Stillwater, Robin Coriander
Stillwell, Mary Pettrey
Stiltner, Marjorie Matney
Stimeling, Amy L. Atkinson
Stineman-Horvath, Patricia A.
Stinger, Cynthia E.
Stinn, Matthew J.
Stinson, Jack O.
Stinus, Kathy
Stirling, Barbara B. Habel
Stirling, Robert B.
Stirrup, Paul S.
Stitely, Ashley Gayle
Stockton, Lydia Ana Pagan
Stoeltzing, Richard H.
Stoeltzing, Judy Miller
Stofko, Phyllis Jane Snell
Stokely, John A.
Stokes, Jane E. Morrison
Stokes, Alicia
Stolfi, Jeremy J.
Stoll, Frederick J.
Stoller, Robert
Stollsteimer, Kathy D. Goff
Stone, Katie Ann Smith
Stone, Edward J.
Stone, James M.
Stone-Kroska, Catherine A.
Stoner, Kimberly Gloria Stanley
Stoner, Craig J.
Stoner, Richard L.
Stoner, Abigail M.
Stoner, Tobi Neal
Stoner, M. Lynn Viereck
Stonesifer, Scott R.
Stoop, Grace E. Lindsay
Stoop, Douglas M.
Storm, Janelle Lori Adams
Storm, Travis W.
Storm Vanleeuwen, Daniel J.
Stote, Joseph W.
Stottlemeyer, Cynthia A.
Stottlemyer, James M.
Stottlemyer, Robert V.
Stouffer, Susan M. Byers
Stout, Richard C.

Starcher, Emily Edith
Starcher, Angela
Starford, Marguerite P. Goodwin
Stover, Thomas M.
Stover, Chelsie Marie
Stover, Eric
Strader, John F.
Strader, Maude
Straight, Roy L.
Strait, Sara Anne
Strait, Melinda L. Marsh
Strait, David W.
Strait, Chelsea
Straley, Sharon Burdick
Straley, Howard
Strauss, Jeffrey M.
Straw, Charles A.
Straw, Thomas W.
Street, Patrick Alan
Street, Amanda K.
Streets, Courtney Brooke
Streets, Cathy J.
Strniste, Barbara A. Fridley
Strobbe, Connie L.
Strock, Judith Littlefield
Strohecker, Sally
Strohm, Robert Frank
Strohm, Samuel G.
Strom, Lita L. Bowe
Strong, John F.
Strong, Ronald J.
Strong, Stuart P.
Strosnider, Donald R.
Strothers, Juwan Andre
Stroud, Teresa A.
Stroud, Stacey L. Pingley
Stroud, Caley
Struntz, Anton T.
Strynar, Aaron Robert
Stuart, Glynnis A. Jones
Stuart, Kimberly A. Lyons
Stuart, Robert H.
Stubblefield, Allene L. Carlson
Stubblefield, Frank M.
Stubblefield, Pamela McConnell
Stuiber, Herman G.
Stull, Kelly E.
Stull, Nola Marie Lucas
Stump, Geraldine Christian

Steinitz, William
Steinmiller, Brian
Stell, Harold T.
Stellato, Mabel L.
Sturdivant, Angela Mari Young
Sturgill, Daniel A.
Sturgis, Marion Horton
Sturgis, Wesley S.
Sturm, Patricia B.
Sturm, Sophia Catherine Bonner
Sturm, Ryan Charles
Sturm, Cynthia L. Markley
Sturm, Dorothy M.
Sturm, Paige Nicole
Sturtevant, Edwin C.
Stutler, Aubrey D.
Stutler, Scott R.
Stutler, Courtney Savannah McKinney
Stutzman, Bruce A.
Stutzman, Linda G. Leaf
Styer, Kimberly A.
Suba, John F.
Sudbrink, William H.
Suder, Justin Lee
Suder, Emil R.
Sudick, Gerald
Suesli, April R. Nestor
Suess, Terry J.
Suess, Lisbeth Spluga
Sugarman, Jason Francis
Sugarman, M. Colleen Stevens
Suits, Michael W.
Sulley, John W.
Sullins, Mary A. Hamelman
Sullivan, Cynthia B. Kittle
Sullivan, Amanda Dawn Helms
Sullivan, Eugenia E. Rolland
Sullivan, Robert E.
Sullivan, Donald J.
Sullivan, Patrick J.
Sullivan, Molly K.
Sullivan, Elizabeth Lane
Sullivan, Tara Rae
Sullivan, Sean Richard
Sullivan, Mark S.
Sullivan, Vincent T.

Stier, Geraldine Nocera
Stiffel, Richard C.
Stiles, Michelle L.
Stiles, Jerry N.
Summerfield, Sandra K.
Summerfield, Connie L.
Summerfield, Jessie Marie
    Sutton
Summerfield, Jack Russell
Summers, Matthew A.
Summers, Martha E.
Summers, Rebecca L.
    Murray
Summers, George L.
Summers, Ada M.
Supak, Mary Elizabeth
    Bryant
Supak, Velma Jean Sturm
Supak, Jean Sturms
Supak, Edward
Suter, David J.
Sutherland, James Andrew
Sutherland, Colin Donald
Suthramchai, Amphol
Sutphen, Susan Renee
Sutphin, Brian C.
Sutter, Carl J.
Sutter, Chelsie Margaret
Sutton, Susan A.
Sutton, David H.
Sutton, John L.
Sutton, Helen Schneider
Sutton, Christopher T.
Suzuki, Kaori
Svedman, John M.
Svedman, Marjorie Pelizoto
Svoboda, Calvin S.
Swan, Jennifer G. Kendell
Swan, Grainne Knowles
Swan, John L.
Swan, Bediako Prescott
Swan, Santana Sue
Swan, Leslie
Swancott, Nikolaus Allen
Swaney, David P.
Swank, Christopher James
Swank, Debra L.
Swarts, Jane L. Evans
Swartz, Larisa Draeger
Swartz, Paul H.
Swartz, W. Edward

Stout, Erin Elizabeth
Stover, Caitlin A.
Stover, Megan L. Meherg
Stover, Robert L.
Swecker, Jessica B.
Swecker, Stephanie D.
    Rosencrance
Swecker, Leonard D.
Swecker, Edwin E.
Swecker, Russell G.
Swecker, Brooke Nicole
Swecker, Troy R.
Swecker, Arden R.
Swecker, John W.
Sweeney, Lance C.
Sweeney, Dawn M.
Sweeney, James P.
Swegel, Nicole M.
Sweitzer, Jeannette Lois
Swick, Betsy A. Whetzel
Swick, Iowana D.
Swick, Melvin R.
Swick, Michael Troy
Swift, Gary T.
Swiger, Patricia A.
Swiger, Deborah L. Ward
Swiger, Arden L.
Swiger, Alan L.
Swiger, Katelynn Marie
    Hanek
Swiger, Chauncey Sabastian
Swiger, Mary Wegman
Swisher, Brooke N.
Swisher, Joshua O'Neil
Swisher, Zachary
Swope, Pamela W. Mays
Sydnor, Joshua W.
Sye, Brian D.
Sylva, Michelle Lee
Symons, Charles David
Symons, Elisa Hunter
Sypolt, Lisa D. Lewis
Sypolt, Charity Louise
Sypolt, Megan Nicole
    Shoemaker
Sypult, Sharron E. Cline
Sytch, John
Szeker, Donna J.
Tabler, Patricia Little
Tabscott, Ernest E.
Tacina, Jeff C.

Stump, Taylor Renee
Stump, Pauline
Sturdivant, Charles Brent
Sturdivant, Lisa M.
Tacy, Carl R.
Tacy, Mary See
Tacy, Mary W.
Tacy, Joseph Wilson
Tacy, Gail
Tadler, John F.
Tadler, Mary Harvey
Tafuni, Donald G.
Tagliabue, Robert W.
Taillon, Kathleen A.
    Wratchford
Tait, Christian G.
Takei, Shoko
Takizawa, Takashi
Talbert, Arch
Talbot, Kelly Marie
Talbot, Amanda Marie
Talbott, Hoy A.
Talbott, Dorothy Allee
Talbott, Irvin D.
Talbott, Anita F. Kendell
Talbott, R. H.
Talbott, Suzanne K. Combs
Talbott, Allen K.
Talbott, Jean Kittle
Talbott, Darroll L.
Talbott, Cynthia S. Ward
Talbott, Lewis W.
Talbott, Kenneth
Talbott, Mary
Talkington, Sabrina S.
    Morrison
Talla, Donna M.
Tallman, Kimberly A.
    Chenoweth
Tallman, Elizabeth A.
Tallman, Lucille
Talman, Rachel Brown
Talton, Dustin Wayne
Tambascio, Adam
Tan, Peter L.
Tanaka, Naoko
Tanaka, Chieko
Tannehill, Mark G.
Tanner, Justin Gene
Tanner, Frankie Woods
Tantillo, Frank A.

Summer, Ada Mae
Summerfield, Allen David
Summerfield, Stephanie
    Dawn Bennett
Tarantelli, Ernest J.
Taraschi, Theresa M. Knoll
Targonsky, Macarius
Tarone, John
Tarplee, Margaret
Tarr-Whelan, Scott Davis
Tase, Brenda Lea
Tasker, Janice Lee
Tasker, Randall
Tatarka, Diane
Tate, Janise A.
Tatosian, Ralph
Tatterson, Thomas Joe
Tatterson, Janet Leigh Banger
Taweel, Jeffrey Garland
Taxacher, Dennis L.
Tayler, Samuel Gregory Alan
Taylor, Rebecca A. Kimble
Taylor, Judith A. Malcolm
Taylor, Rodney A.
Taylor, John A.
Taylor, Jeremy A.
Taylor, David A.
Taylor, Constance Altfather
Taylor, Ashley Ann Dove
Taylor, Kimberly Ann
Taylor, William B.
Taylor, Nancy B.
Taylor, Mataya Brooklyn
Taylor, Howard C.
Taylor, Kathleen Cain
Taylor, Neil Christopher
Taylor, Lula Fisher
Taylor, Wesley Franklin
Taylor, Frank G.
Taylor, Holly Gordon
Taylor, Marcel Harris
Taylor, Brittany Heather
Taylor, Christine J. Thompson
Taylor, William John
Taylor, Andrew Justin
Taylor, Vincent K.
Taylor, William Kenneth
Taylor, Dawn Kimberly
Taylor, April L. Hood
Taylor, Mary L. Richards
Taylor, Boyd L.

Tenney, Debbie Jo
Tenney, Christina K.
Tenney, Lenora L. Gross
Tenney, Christopher L.
Thulander, O. Alan
Thurmond, Joshua C.
Thursby, Barbara A. Jenkins
Tiano, Virginia Bell
Tibbs, Jennifer K. Allison
Tibuk, Kerem
Tice, David A.
Tice, Sandra Lurae Barkley
Tidaback, Edward Christopher
Tidwell, Erica
Tiedeman, Katrina Lynn
Tieste, Ronald B.
Tighe, Michael J.
Tighe, Glen
Tillman, Brenna Kathleen
Tillman, Terry L. White
Tillotson, Karen Gordon
Tilly, Robert H.
Timbrook, AnnMarie Grace
Timbrook, Whitney Hope
Timpert-Semple, Nancy J.
Tincher, Kelly Elizabeth
Tingler, Ida A.
Tingler, Stephanie D.
Tingler, Jessica Eleanor Wilfong
Tingler, Jennifer L. Raines
Tingler, Angela M. Bennett
Tingler, Christopher W.
Tinney, William A.
Tinney, Homer A.
Tinney, Elizabeth W. Snyder
Tinney, Charles W.
Tinsley, Dwane Lamont
Tinsley, Simon Peter
Tinsley, Malik S.
Tinsley, James W.
Tippie, Penny Mobley
Tipton, Brianna Renae
Titcher, Carolyn Ann Darnall
Tobias, Anna Kramer
Tobin, Sara Elizabeth
Toennies, John M.U.
Tognoli, Breanna Le
Tokarski, Cass
Tolar, Paul K.

Thomas, Paul A.
Thomas, Joan A.
Thomas, Howard B.
Thomas, Daniel Brown
Tomaro, Kimberly J.
Tomazin, Courtney S. Fisher
Tomblyn, Mark A.
Tomblyn, Nancy B. Hunsaker
Tomblyn, Philip C.
Tomblyn, Stephen G.
Tombs, R. Bradley
Tomlin, Sally Donaldson
Tomson, Theodora Ashby
Toner, James C.
Toole, Charles H.
Toole, Nancy M.
Toothman, Whitney A.
Tooze, Robert Leland
Topal, Samuel
Topolosky, Tracy L. Smith
Toranto, Anton J.
Torbert, Kimberly K.
Torlish, Candace C. Gagliardi
Torok, Coley L. Grimstead
Torrence, Katelynn Marie
Torres, Ruben D.
Torres, Alexander Jonathan
Torres, Sandy
Tortorici, Steven
Toth, Cory A.
Toth, Janet M. Slaugenhaupt
Totin, David Robert
Totlis, Kenneth C.
Totsuka, Naoko
Touchet, Michaela Ann
Toumayan, Mario H.
Touvell, Charles R.
Towe, A. Tina Cortellesi
Towell, John Matthew
Towery, Mary F. Ashcraft
Townley, Elizabeth Anne Salsbury
Townsend, Lorn G.
Townsend, Norma J.
Townsend, John G.
Townsend, Connie S.
Tracey, Jonathan Edward
Tracy, Vere Bly
Tracy, Steven D.
Tracy, Mark E.
Tracy, Glenn P.

Thompson, Patrick Andrew
Thompson, Patricia Ann Huffman
Thompson, Robert D.
Traver, Sara B. Poole
Travers, David K.
Travis, Sabrina F. Swecker
Traynor, Valerie E. Walsh
Treadgold, Anthony G.
Treadway, William
Trettel, Gail Marie Park
Trevey, John Andrew
Trewick, Keith E.
Triant, Monica Dahn
Trice, Carol Schmick
Trickett, Gary F.
Trickett, Forrest V.
Trigg, Peter Woodside
Triggs, Emily
Trimble, Vanessa Nichole
Tripkovic, Zlatko
Triplett, Randall A.
Triplett, Silvia Boyero
Triplett, James D.
Triplett, Charlie E.
Triplett, Robert C.
Triplett, Victoria J.
Triplett, George A.
Triplett, Georgia L. Bowersox
Triplett, George Raphael
Triplett, William W.
Triplett, Alexandra L.
Tripoli, Paul J.
Tritt, Elizabeth E. Pritt
Trivett, Brenda K. Anderson
Troastle, David S.
Troetschel, Jacob Neil
Trojan, Joan Lazo
Trouwborst, John C.
Trouwborst, Sue Tomlinson
Trowbridge, Cassandra Clarridge
Troxal, Roberta Jo
Troxal, Stormie Jo
Troxell, Keith Chase
Troy, Renee Anne Lancaster
Troyer, Elizabeth Joanne Glaser
Troyer, Jeremy Robert
Trudgeon, Adalia La-Ree
True, April Dawn Teter

Thorsen, Pearl Porter
Thorsen, Reinhart
Thrasher, Edward R.
Thrasher, Charles T.
Trump, Jeffrey S.
Trunich, Deborah A.
Trusgnich, Steven
Tsaparas, Glen E.
Tubbs, William J.
Tubbs, Gail Thayer Lewis
Tucci, Frank C.
Tuccinardi, Michael F.
Tucker, Arriahn Alahni
Tuckwiller, Emogene Bowe
Tuesing, W. Thomas
Tufan, Yalin
Tuholsky, Mark J.
Tuley, Megan Amber
Tull, Lillie Mae Parks
Tull, Robert W.
Tully, Sarah E.
Tumino, Michael F.
Tuning, Phyllis G.
Tuning, Preston
Turansky, Shirley A. Hull
Turbyne, Jeffrey D.
Turley, Rebecca Ann Wolf
Turley, Joel D.
Turley, Glen E.
Turley, William K.
Turner, Charlotte A. Wiseman
Turner, Timothy A.
Turner, Kathryn Aaren
Turner, Amy Catherine
Turner, Thomas D.
Turner, John H.
Turner, William J.
Turner, Sharon K. Wolfe
Turner, Alford Lee
Turner, William Lewis
Turner, Robert Mitchell
Turner, Sydney Renee
Turner, Sherilyn Sue Van Bockern
Turner, Timothy Wayne
Turney, Rose A. Davis
Turpin, Stephanie M. Geil
Turschmann, Kristin Nico
Turske, Philip James
Tusing, Ingeborg L.
Tustin, Stephen Robert

Tolin, Janet
Tolley, James Kenneth
Tolley, Leslie W.
Tomanek, William
Tweedy, Robert S.
Twigg, Ashley Brook Goff
Twing, Russell L.
Twyman, Tyler Heath
Tydings, Lauren Elizabeth
Tyler, Diana S.
Tyre, Sean Cole
Tyre, Hayley J.
Tyree, Willa B.
Tyson, Jason C.
Tyson, James W.
Tysor, Deborah
Uchiyama, Chiyo
Udofia, Michael John
Ueda, Hiroyuki
Ukiwo, Elizabeth Ann Chaar
Ullman, Peter J.
Ullman, Margaret Rice
Ullom, Kurt D.
Ulrich, Brandon
Umpenhour, Betty Barkley
Umpenhour, Charles M.
Umstead, Mary Elizabeth
Underwood, Lee Andrew
Underwood, Nathaniel B.
Underwood, Forest F.
Underwood, Traci L.
Underwood, Jennifer
   Nicole McDaniels
Underwood, Samantha
   Ranee
Underwood, Mariah S.
Underwood, Ginny
Unger, Jane C.
Updike, Dale
Upson, Demetrius Jeremy
Urban, Ryan E.
Urban, Tammy L. Hileman
Urban, Kathlynn L.
Urban, Kim
Urbati, Michael R.
Uribe, Enrique
Urso, Thomas Emmanuel
Urstadt, Brenda L.
Urweider, Keith Herbert
Usui, Ryo
Utz, Keith A.

Trainer, Kimberly P.
Tran, Phuong Minh
Traore, Stephanie Ann Sproul
Trapp, Ann M.
Valencia, Brandi L. Nichols
Valentine, Jane Harriet Pester
Valentine, Bonnie J. Wiles
Valentine, Mary Lowther
Valentine, Gene O.
Valentine, T. Robert
Valentine, Dorian
Valero, Erick Valerio
Valiente, David
Vallieres, Samuel
Van Brunt, William Clifton
van der Voort, Willemijn
Van Dyke, Trudi McCall
Van Gundy, Melissa A.
   Thomas
Van Gundy, Douglas A.
Van Horn, Teresa Ann
Van Horne, Allen R.
Van Metre, Sarah J. Spinks
Van Metre, David R.
Van Reenan, Jacqueline M.
   Thompson
Van Reenan, James W.
Van Wagner, Harry D.
VanArsdale, Raymond
VanBrunt, Deborah Chilgren
VanBrunt, Jennifer L.
VanBuskirk, Philip D.
VanBuskirk, Linda L.
Vance, Sherry D.
Vance, Rhonda F. Bonner
Vance, Terri J. Waybright
Vance, Douglas J.
Vance, Rebecca Jane
   Chenoweth
Vance, Cindy L.
Vance, Snowden Lester
Vance, Linda Lou
Vance, Ann Margaret Tinney
Vance, C. Michelle Judy
Vance, Helen R.
Vance, B. Shasta
Vance, Rebecca W.
Vance, Adrienne
Vandenbergh, G. David
Vanderbilt, Taylor
VanderEls, Elizabeth Purdum

Trujillo, Felipe J.
Truman, Lois Y.
Trumbo, Josie D.
Trumbull, Tod R.
Vandevander, George R.
Vandevander, Michelle Renea
Vandevander, Kelly Renee
   Wilfong
Vandevender, Angela D.
Vandevender, Alexis Dawn
VanDevender, Gary J.
Vandevender, Charles J.
VanDevender, Jennifer Lyn
Vandevender, Jessy Nicole
   Pifer
Vandevender, Kenneth
Vangulick, Charles S.
VanHook, Karl A.
VanMarter, Melissa A.
   Midkiff
VanMeter, David P.
VanNatta, Emma Mae
   Stalnaker
VanNewkirk, Kimberly A.
VanNewkirk, Jessica Lynn
VanNoy, Lance Conrad
VanNoy, Lucinda E.
VanNoy, Diana Lynn Conrad
Vanpelt, Alma P. Stalnaker
Vanscoy, Leo D.
Vanscoy, Buddy D.
Vanscoy, Medora E.
Vanscoy, Dorothy Glenn
   Coberly
Vanscoy, Cecil Glenn
Vanscoy, Clarence H.
Vanscoy, Kelli L. Freeman
Vanscoy, Richard Neil
Vanscoy, Betty Newlon
Vanscoy, William R.
Vanscoy, Travis Tyler
Vanscoy, Fred
Vanture, C. Roger
VanWagner, Mary Godby
VanWinkle, Richard D.
VanWinkle, Albert W.
Vanyushkin, Dmitry
Varchetto, Katrina Allyssa
Varchetto, Lucy D.
   Del Signore
Varchetto, Monica Ilene Guye

Tuttle, Steven Boothe
Tuttle, Robert J.
Tuttle, Donna Jane Lee
Tuttle, John L.
Varchetto, Patrick
Varela, Debra L. Dunbrack
Vargas, Colleen Ann Souder
Vargas, Laura Maria
Vargo, Michael D.
Vargo, Rodney H.
Vargo, Louis N.
Varner, Julia Ann Lytle
Varner, Harold Bardwell
Varner, Howard D.
Varner, Joan Hammonds
Varner, Susan K. Mallow
Varney, Linda J. Muench
Varney, Charles J.
Vartelas, Jerry
Vasiljevic, Aleksandar
Vasquez, Constance K. Smith
Vasquez, Susan L. Wheeler
Vasquez, Rafael
Vaughan, Joanne Carol
   Dougherty
Vaughan, Jeffrey O.
Vawter, Megan J. Kesslar
Vazquez, Carlos A.
Vazquez, Eduardo A.
Vedral, Stephanie Nichol
Veiga, Mary del C.
Veirs, John G.
Vellenoweth, James R.
Velott, Stephen M.
Veltre, Rebecca L. Hollowood
Venevongsoth, Douangneth
Vensel, Douglas R.
Vera, Diana R.
Veramessa, Jodi S. Manholt
Verbonitz, Rebecca Dawn
Vermette, Mark Edward
Vermillion, Dorothy
   Pennybacker
Vernon, Donald F.
Vernon, Rachel Marie
Vesic, Petar
Veskimae, Toomas
Vest, Louise Buzzerd
Vest, Donald C.
Vest, Annetta J.
Vest, Marvin L.

Vacchio, Erin Carroll
Vacco, Michael C.
Vadakin, Charles E.
Valach, James Michael
Vidone, Romeo A.
Vidone, Lena Bioletti
Vidt, Pamela Ann Kelley
Vidt, Louis George
Viernstein, Dale D. Ditmars
Viernstein, Karl R.
Vieyra, Darragh James
Vigilanti, Benny P.
Viglianco, Eva M.
Vigon, Adam S.
Vild, Danielle Nichole
Villa, Anne E.
Villasmil, Luis A.
Vilseck, Betty A.
Vilseck, August K.
Vineyard, John C.
Vineyard, Amber Dawn
Vineyard, Daniella Marie
Vinson, Matthew D.
Vinson, Bobbi J. Green
Visnich, Evelyn Taylor
Visnich, Peter
Visnich, Sam
Visniski, Darcie A.
Vitari, Patti A. Fleming
Vitiello, John Derrick
Vitullo, Camilla Morgan
  Boucek
Vivian, David J.
Vocke, Thomas P.
Vodde, Judith Dianne
  Johnson
Voelker, Robert L.
Voisey, Nancy G. Morrison
Vollert, Warren M.
Vollmer, Dorothy J. Smith
Vollmer, Kenneth L.
Voloshin, Lynn P.
Voloski, Adam T.
Volper, Raymond C.
Volper, Pamela P. Begg
Volz, William F.
Von Bruton, Connie D.
von Doemming,
  Maximillian F.
von Schilling, Frances E.
  Warner

VanderEls, John R.
Vandevander, Gloria G.
Vandevander, Deborah
  Kristina Ware
Voorheis, Mindy M. Poole
Votaw, Justine L. Booth
Vreeland, Charles W.
Vrielynck, Ann Y.
Vris, Thomas
Vrolijk, Stefan
Vroom, Peter
Wacker, Craig A.
Wad, Horace O.
Wada, Sachiko
Waddell, Jordon
Waddill, Roger G.
Wade, Eleanor King
Wade, Brittany Morgan
Wade, Diane R.
Wade, Marie Webster
Wade, W. Quintus
Wadler, Dennis M.
Wadley, Scot C.
Wadsworth, Jennifer Lynn
Waggoner, George W.
Wagler, Alice Elizabeth
Wagner, Teresa A. Moore
Wagner, Leigh Anne Rogers
Wagner, Frances Baker
Wagner, Robert C.
Wagner, Peggy Christina
  Talbot
Wagner, Joseph G.
Wagner, Alvin H.
Wagner, William J.
Wagner, Deanna Jackson
Wagner, Marsha Jean Kesling
Wagner, Charles R.
Wagner, Cory R.
Wagner, Melissa R.
Wagner, Mark S.
Wagner, Sara Talbott
Wagner, Rosemary
Wagner, George
Wagoner, Craig Alan
Wagstaff, Anna Tyre
Waid, Alexis L. Kowalecki
Waid, Aaron S.
Wainer, Arthur D.
Waite, Sarah Leonard
Waites, Stephanie Leigh

Varchetto, Richard Matthew
Varchetto, Augustine P.
Varchetto, Guy R.
Varchetto, Luke
Waldo, Jessica Lynn
  Scowcroft
Waldron, Edna M.
Waldron, Charlotte Pittman
Waliky, Donna
Walk, Edward J.
Walk, Bruce M.
Walker, Donald B.
Walker, Kent Cogar
Walker, Susannah D. Watring
Walker, Bradley Daniel
Walker, Wallace G.
Walker, John G.
Walker, Geoffrey H.
Walker, Bonnie J. Beatty
Walker, Edward J.
Walker, Lisa J.
Walker, Melinda Jane
  Tarr-Whelan
Walker, Jeanne L Swet
Walker, Sherri Lemmermann
Walker, Amy M. Yurkiewicz
Walker, Clemence Margaret
  Perry
Walker, Lewis Midgley
Walker, Mary Rebecca
Walker, James S.
Walker, Brian S.
Walker, Bonita Weaver
Walker, Frederick
Walkes, Sylvia H.
  Vandersluijs
Walkes, Kendall
Walkut, Virginia Myers
Wall, James K.
Wallace, Suellen B.
Wallace, Teena C.
Wallace, Kathy Coldren
Wallace, James E.
Wallace, Nancy J. Unger
Wallace, Bryant Matthew
Wallace, Herbert N.
Wallace, Rebecca Rockwell
Wallace, James W.
Wallace, Jonathan W.
Wallace, Jabez
Walle, Sean E.

Vest, G. Ellis
Vetrone, Cosmo J.
Vickers, Heather A. Hawkins
Vickers, Douglas B.
Walls, Kimberly Dawn
  Barnhart
Walls, Zane L.
Walsdorf, Richard M.
Walsh, Amber Donice Tice
Walter, Jane Elizabeth
  Schackner
Walter, Jonathan H.
Walter, Geneva Hamrick
Walter, William
Walters, Vicki A. Whytsell
Walters, William Bradley
Walters, Megan Isabella
Walters, Barbara Kay Fullmer
Walters, David
Walthall, Margaret L.
  McMeans
Walton, Janal Louise
  Burrowbridge
Walton, Theodore R.
Walwik, William N.
Walworth, Gary D.
Wamsley, Thomas A.
Wamsley, Abbie C. Holler
Wamsley, Tamara D.
Wamsley, Natasha Dawn
  Tallman
Wamsley, Stephen E.
Wamsley, Susan G.
Wamsley, Dorothy Herring
Wamsley, Rita L. White
Wamsley, Joshua Lowry
Wamsley, Lisa M. Tennant
Wamsley, Erin Marie
Wamsley, Camilla Paige
Wamsley, Charles W.
Wamsley, Sue
Wamsley, Augustine
Wamsley-Taylor, Amy
  DeVore
Wangensteen, John N.
Wango, Hans
Waniga, Howard A.
Wanless, Jeremy S.
Wanless, John V.
Wantuch, David B.
Ward, Kristina A.

VonBruton, Joanna Rennix
vonHaven, Ellis J.
Voorhees, Neil R.
Voorheis, Jonathan G.
Ward, Kristina Dyan Price
Ward, Lucille Friel
Ward, William G.
Ward, Mittie H. Rice
Ward, Robert J.
Ward, Austin J.
Ward, Thomas J.
Ward, Martha K.
Ward, Brian L.
Ward, Janice Louise
Ward, Brandie Lynn
Ward, James M.
Ward, Jacquette M.
Ward, Kayla Maria
Ward, Krista Marie
    Cunningham
Ward, Kathleen
    Mavourneen Martin
Ward, Georgia Pearl Carter
Ward, Bradley T.
Ward, William W.
Ward, Teresa
Warden, Drema D. Loveless
Warden, George H.
Warden, Debra Slater
Warder, Phyllis L. Chipley
Ware, Frederick D.
Ware, Christopher D.
Ware, LaTosha Danielle
Ware, Karen Didriksen
Ware, Don Eric
Ware, Drew G.
Ware, Tricia J. Reger
Ware, Dorothy J.
Ware, Vickie L. Shifflett
Ware, Judith L. Whetsell
Ware, Ethel M. Collett
Ware, Tessa Marie Yokum
Ware, Mildred Moore
Ware, Ashley Nicole Cassidy
Ware, Reta Phares
Ware, Elaine Pizzoferrato
Ware, Bryan S.
Ware, Reco
Ware, Harold
Warehime, Troy A.
Warehime, Vickie R.

Walden, Richard B.
Walden, Lois E. Harrell
Walden, Thomas E.
Walden, Helen M.
Warner, Scarlett Amber
Warner, Jennifer C. Tingler
Warner, Kristina Dawn Tacy
Warner, Lucille F. Creegan
Warner, Deborah G.
Warner, Charles J.
Warner, Jenny L.
Warner, Timothy L.
Warner, Megan Maria
Warner, Leah Marie
Warner, Crystal Michele
    Huffman
Warner, Gloria S.
Warner, Veryl
Warner, Michael
Warner, Andrew
Warner '21, Ashley
Warnock, David A.
Warren, John A.
Warren, Katherine Ann
    McGlothlin
Warren, Claude D.
Warren, William G.
Warren, Barbara Louise Frank
Warren, Leesl R. McCoy
Warren, Sharon Scharfenberg
Warren, Matthew T.
Warren, Robert W.
Wartenburg, Otto Carl
Warth, Mary M. Gras
Washburn, Thomas O.
Washington, Marjorie Harrell
Washington, Naila Kai
Washington, Tonisha Makeba
Washington, Patricia Stevens
Watanabe, Yuko
Waterfall, Bradley C.
Waterman, David W.
Waters, Mary E.
Waters, Stuart R.
Watkins, Samantha Marie
    Howell
Watkins, Steven
Watraes, Leigh A.
Watring, John Adams
Watring, Wade N.
Watring, JoEllen Simpson

Wallin, Naomi W. Thorne
Walling, Pamela K.
Wallingford, Jonell
Walls, Jessie Diane Canada
Watson, Howard K.
Watson, Carl R.
Watson, Angela R.
Watson, Skylee Rakel
Watson, Brock Ward
Watson, Calvin
Watts, Richard C.
Watts, Leslie M. Sylvain
Watychowicz, Patrick S.
Waugh, Micheal A.
Waugh, Loetta Harris
Waybright, Marie A.
Waybright, Harvey D.
Waybright, Michelle D.
Waybright, Chandra Deigh
Waybright, Miriam E. Forney
Waybright, Timothy J.
Waybright, Tracy L.
Waybright, Andrew
    Zephaniah
Waybright, Troy
Wayne, Brandy Ellen
Wayt, Joni Broeren
Weagley, Daulton Michael
Weaner, Barbara B.
Weaner, Robert W.
Weaver, Amy Beth Brown
Weaver, Raleighanne Grace
Weaver, Frank H.
Weaver, Misty Lynn
Weaver, Brandee Michelle
    Schwarting
Weaver, Jennifer N.
Weaver, Michael S.
Weaver, Garrick
Weaving, Sandra K. Douglas
Weaving, William Stark
Webb, Elizabeth J. Dillon
Webb, Craig M.
Webb, Brian Matthew
Webb, James R.
Webb, Wendy S.
Webb, Michael Scott
Webber, Larry S.
Weber, Frances Barbara
Weber, Wendel E.
Weber, Joseph E.

Ward, Frank A.
Ward, B. Alecia
Ward, Robert B.
Ward, Angela D. Pritt
Webster, W.D.
Webster, Charles
Weeden, Jane P. Vicellio
Weekley, Betty M.
Weeks, Jennifer
Weese, Judith A. Coberly
Weese, Lisa A.
Weese, Cynthia A.
Weese, Marcus Adam
Weese, Rebecca Butcher
Weese, Keith Conrad
Weese, Scott E.
Weese, Brooke Elizabeth
Weese, Freda Elma Grimes
Weese, Elma F. Grimes
Weese, Arnold F.
Weese, Lana Jill Johns
Weese, Douglas K.
Weese, Victor L.
Weese, Heather M.
Weese, Donna Montoney
Weese, Frances Nelson
Weese, Perle Poling
Weese, Patrick S.
Weese, James W.
Weese, Sue
Weese, Amanda
Weese, Peter
Wegman, Margaret I. Hofer
Wegman, Douglas P.
Wegman, Werner
Wegweiser, Herbert F.
Wehri, Samantha Ann
Wehrle, William A.
Wehrle, Mary M. Spivey
Wehrle, Leroy R.
Wehrle, Charles
Weidenbacker, Ruth B.
    Morrison
Weidman, John C.
Weidner, Dennis M.
Weiford, Sara Anne
Weiford, Vicki R.
Weiford, Teresa S. Knick
Weigle, Harold A.
Weil, Henry A.
Weil, John Larry

Ware-Tingler, Melody Marie
Warlick, Kathryn A. Miller
Warmbein, Kurt J.
Warner, Marcus Alan
Weinreb, Michael P.
Weinrich, Richard J.
Weinstein, Pearl Linksman
Weintraub, Matthew Gabriel
Weintraub, Clay Thomas
Weintraub, Samantha
Weires, David Kris
Weiser, Daniel
Weiss, Joel M.
Weiss, Joseph M.
Weissenberger, Gary H.
Weissenborn, Donald A.
Welch, Nicole Candace
Welch, Roann Dawne
Welch, Roslynn Knaggs
Welch, Leslie Marie
Welch, Douglas P.
Welch, Naomi Pauline Minor
Welke, Melissa L.
Welker, James E.
Wellings, Chelsea Rose
Wellman, John C.
Wellman, Edward Joseph
Wellman, Joseph
    Paul-Patrick
Wellman, Carl R.
Wells, James Donald
Wells, Charles E.
Wells, Vicki L.
Wells, April Lyn
Welsh, William E.
Welsh, Kenneth Jack
Welty, Patricia A. Hennessy
Wendell, Patricia Phillips
Wendling, Irving P.
Wendt, James E.
Wendt, Becky Shetron
Wendt, William W.
Wengryn, Daniel
Wentz, Nichole L.
Wentzel, David Alfred
Wenzel, John Ross
Wenzel, Jeffrey William
Werner, Stuart A.
Werner, Kenneth J.
Werner, Ashley
Werner, David

Watson, Kenneth C.
Watson, Raymond C.
Watson, Euraline G.
Watson, Thomas H.
West, Lynn Mitchell
West, George
Westbye, Robert J.
Westby-Gibson, Douglas
    Thompson
Westerfield, Jaye
Westervelt, David J.
Westfall, James Donald
Westfall, Christina L.
Westfall, Alison N.
Weston, Debbie E. Dugan
Westridge, Deborah Jenkins
Wetherill, Samuel P.
Wetrogan, Howard G.
Wetzel, Sharon S.
Whalen, George E.
Whanger, Willa Nottingham
Wharton, Timothy M.
Wheale, Kerstin Marie
Wheatley, Arthur E.
Wheeland, Edward L.
Wheeland, Roberta Peters
Wheeler, Carl A.
Wheeler, Linda Anne Charlton
Wheeler, Thomas E.
Wheeler, Wednesday G.
    Brown
Wheeler, John H.
Wheeler, Karmin K. Flagle
Whelan, Amy L. Holland
Whelan, Brian Paul
Whelan, Michael
Whetsell, Richard A.
Whetsell, Robert C.
Whetsell, Patricia Currence
Whetsell, Susan D. Potenzano
Whetsell, Harry E.
Whetsell, David E.
Whetsell, Floyd G.
Whims, Kimberly Anne
Whipkey, Neil H.
Whipple, Helena Gilbert
Whipple, Barbara S.
    McClellan
Whitacre, Brooke Logan
Whitacre, Lee S.
Whitaker, Stephen Philip

Weber, William R.
Weber, William
Webley, Kimberly S. Bennett
Webster, Kelsea Nicole Lane
White, Don A.
White, William A.
White, Steven Andrew
White, Rebecca Ann
White, Gordon B.
White, Timothy Brian
White, Raymond C.
White, Morris D.
White, Christopher D.
White, Lisa D.
White, Deborah D.
White, Stephanie Dawn Price
White, Lisa Dawn
White, Rachel Eva-Marie
White, Jeffrey F.
White, Ellen Graham
White, Christopher H.
White, Sandy I.
White, Roy J.
White, Bonnie June
    McDonald
White, Deborah K. Higdon
White, Jennifer K. Shaw
White, Donald K.
White, Diane K.
White, Sharon K.
White, Janet L. Franke
White, Connie L. Kisamore
White, Helen L. Smith
White, Regina L. Wirth
White, Edward L.
White, Marty L.
White, Michael L.
White, Gay L.
White, Joshua L.
White, Victor L.
White, Shari L.
White, Mary Lou Laing
White, Teresia Louise
White, Julie Louise
White, Cassandra Lynn
White, Dottie M.
White, Clarence M.
White, Jeana M.
White, Michael M.
White, Julianne Marie
White, Pauline McCusker

Weimer, Mark Aaron
Weimer, Theresa L.
    Shinaberry
Weimer, Alma
White, Kora Mikeal
White, Erica N.
White, Kenneth O.
White, Chester R.
White, Chester R.
White, Daniel Raymond
White, Robert Richard
White, Nancy Rising
White, F. Robert
White, Hobart S.
White, Mark S.
White, William T.
White, Kristin Tonie
White, Andrew V.
White, Walter W.
White, Judson W.
White, Ethan Wesley
White, Megan Yvonne Card
White '19, Jonathan Trista
White '19, Courtney
Whited, Traci Mininger
Whitehair, Anita Dawn
Whitehill, Roberta R. She
Whiteman, Rebecca J. Bak
Whiteman, Gary
Whiteside, Theresa Edmund
Whiting, Leonard B.
Whiting, Betty Callison
Whitlach, Robert E.
Whitley, Richard J.
Whitman, John E.
Whitman, Louise Thomas
Whitman, J. Robert
Whitmoyer, Phyllis Dukz
    Kauffman
Whitmoyer, R. David
Whitney, Eric B.
Whitten, Paige Robin
Whittle, Alfred E.
Whoolery, Kayla Brooke
Whorlow, Robert T.
Wiborg, Cheryl C. Andrew
Wickard, Kimberly A.
Wickline, John R.
Wicks, James T.
Wida, Paul J.
Widdoes, H. Brandt

Winston, Stephanie L. Teter
Winter, Kimberly A. Cervera
Winter, Jackson Blair

Wright, George Christian
Wright, Mark Edward
Wright, Giles Ernest
Wright, Lillian H.
Wright, Sandra Hanna
Wright, Marjorie Jane Poling
Wright, Deborah Jean
   Feather
Wright, Billie Jo Fortney
Wright, Rachael Kathryn
   Felton
Wright, Chester Kilby
Wright, Jodi L. Chick
Wright, Robert L.
Wright, Babs Lyn
Wright, Rachel Mc Clain
Wright, Sydney Rae
Wright, Jaclyn Ranae Crane
Wright, David William
Wright, R. Gerald
Wright, W. A. Stewart
Wrobleski, Robert P.
Wroten, Laura M. Vermilye
Wulin, Tina Marie
Wunderlich, Autumn
   Victoria
Wuslich, Joseph M.
Wuslich, Samuel R.
Wyand, Donna W. Burris
Wyant, Meghan Elizabeth
Wyant, Angela R.
Wyatt, Dunton A.
Wyatt, Ruth A.
Wyatt, Ellis Christopher
Wyatt, Robin D.
Wyatt, Margaret E.
Wyatt, Timothy E.
Wyatt, Stella L.
Wyatt, Nicole Lynn
Wyatt, Valerie S.
Wyatt, Terry W.
Wyckoff, Matthew T.
Wyland, Glen A.
Wylie, Thomas C.
Wyman, Anthony S.
Wyne, Harry F.
Wysocki, William J.

Wolf, Debra
Wolfe, Christopher A.
Wolfe, Lori E.
Wolfe, Howard H.
Yake, David John
Yamada, Masakazu
Yamamoto, Yoshinori
Yamamura, Koji
Yamanaka, Miki
Yamauchi, Madoka
Yamokoski, Jonah John
Yang, Shu-Chi
Yanushkevich, Dmitry
Yarbrough, Grace C. Stalnaker
Yarbrough, Ann Page Turner
Yaroch, Benjamin J.
Yassemi, Yass
Yates, Donald Cameron
Yeager, Norman A.
Yeager, James A.
Yeager, Carl F.
Yeager, Herman G.
Yeager, Barbara H.
Yeager, Patrick Henry
Yeager, Deborah L. Wildman
Yeager, Pamela Lynn George
Yeager, Shane Trevor
Yeager, Mary
Yee, Clyde E.
Yergeau, Kaylee Ann
Yerkes, James B.
Yeuell, Louisa Sager
Yildirim, Emre
Yingling, Barbara A. Barlow
Yingling, Darren A.
Yip, Peter Y.
Yoak, Andrea
Yoakum, Robert G.
Yob, Cheryl L. Moran
Yocum, Erin N. Price
Yoder, Wendi
Yokai, Ayako
Yokum, Kevin Allan
Yokum, Nora G. Harper
Yokum, Donna M. Everett
Yokum, Ankara Nicole
Yokum, Kristina Renee
   Weiford
Yokum, Connie Sue
Yokum, Clarence W.
Yokum, Hazel

Wooddell, Frances Kump
Wooddell, Robert M.
Wooddell, Josephine Rice

Yorty, Diane Blinco
Yoshida, Naoko
Yoshii, Yuki
Yoshimoto, Kazuhiko
Yoshimura, Mika
Yost, Shirley S.
Young, Kelsey Ann Hall
Young, Linda Anne
Young, Todd C.
Young, Karen D. Arnold
Young, Troy Daniel
Young, Daniel E.
Young, Barry G.
Young, Amanda J.
Young, Christopher John
Young, Sestilia K.
Young, Erin Karla
Young, Virginia L.
Young, Robert L.
Young, Jan Lee DeFoe
Young, James M.
Young, Ko Cha'Ta Seth
Young, George
Young, Buddy
Young, Paul
Youngberg, Karen L. Carey
Yount, William D.
Yount, Monna Fae Harman
Yount, James O.
Youtsey, Thomas O.
Yow, Kimberley K.
Yowell, Charles Hamilton
Yozie, Charlene Phyllis
Yris, Jill C. Schoof
Yris, Craig E.
Ystueta, William F.
Yulo, Frank R.
Yutz, Ann Mary Gilbert
Yutz, Robert R.
Yutzy, Garrett D.
Zabajai, Thorton Maui
Zabohonski, Katya
Zabriskie, May
Zacavish, Trevor Marshal
Zadeh, Timor E.
Zader, Gustave C.
Zader, Margaret Parsons

Wright, James Arthur
Wright, Harley Barbara
   Sandford
Wright, Michael C.
Zahler, Thomas Michael
Zahn, Catherine A. Wilkinson
Zahn, Gary M.
Zaki, Jessie
Zambelli, Joseph M.
Zambelli, Christopher P.
Zanardelli, John Joseph
Zandee, Kristin B. Haskett
Zanella, Elena Marie
Zanganeh, Shapur A.
Zapf, Heather Anne
Zarnegar, Hassan
Zator, Russell E.
Zeart, Janice K. Carlson
Zeart, John S.
Zebuhr, Michael A.
Zeek-Quirk, Elaine E.
Zeese, Marc C.
Zeiger, Dale L.
Zelenko, Susan
Zelinko, Theodore
Zelov, Peter E.
Zentgraf, Diane Durnal
Zervos, Barbara Georgetson
Zevola, Daniel J.
Ziai, Mohsen
Zick, Robert T.
Zickefoose, Thelma Kiess
Zickefoose, Sanya
Ziegler, Pence A.
Ziegler, Elizabeth A.
Ziegler, Penny Hanley
Ziegler, Edward N.
Ziemba, Mary F. Lucas
Ziesemer, Florence A.
Zifferblatt, Jacqueline L.
   Faulkner
Zilich, Mary Francis Groghan
Zilich, Joseph N.
Zimmer, Joseph C.
Zimmer, Peter D.
Zimmer, John Lawrence
Zimmerer, James Andrew
Zimmerman, Jenneth Ann
   Hammer
Zimmerman, Todd E.
Zimmerman, Jennifer Honish

Yackulics, Margaret E.
Yager, Barbara Hutchinson
Yahagi, Sayo
Yahres, Toni James
Zimmermann, Meghan P.
	Johnson
Zinicola, Michele George
Zinn, Lucille G. Smith
Zinzi, Marie Feoranz
Ziobron, Edward
Zirbs, Steven Anders
Zirbs, Linda S.
Zirk, Jonna Renea Burnside
Zirkle, Rebecca Lynn
Zirkle, Natasha Paige
Zirkle-Yokum, Tiffany
	Nichole
Zito, Charles L.
Ziviello, Lee Marquette
Zizzi, Elinor Pingley
Zoccolillo, James Louis
Zoller, Frank T.
Zorn, Matthew Douglas
Zorn, Benjamin John
Zrake, James N.
Zsombik, Diane C. Tauber
Zuboy, Jacob
Zuelsdorf, Floy Yokum
Zulparova, Dilafruz
Zumba, Joseph G.
Zumbach, Virginia Malcomb
Zuniga, Ivan Fernando
Zurbuch, Jeanine R. Stivers
Zurbuch, Emily Rose
Zwickel, Larry

Yomura, Yuki
Yoo, Jung A.
Yordon, Jorge
York, Mary D.

Zafari, Yadoliah
Zagar, Lano Audas
Zagar, Frank L.
Zahairy, Abdullah Ahmed

Zimmerman, Sandra L. Moo
Zimmerman, James L.
Zimmerman, Andrew P.
Zimmerman, Paul Vaugha

"Rally the people of West Augusta! You don't know who you are until you know where you came from. By God's grace, shall West Augusta people soar like Eagles. United We Stand! Every crisis changes…Thank God, and count your blessings. In God We Trust."

-   George Triplett

"IN GOD WE TRUST"

"UNITED WE STAND"

www.ingramcontent.com/pod-product-compliance
Lightning Source LLC
Chambersburg PA
CBHW080443030726

47592CB00011B/2954